Choice Experiments Informing Environmental Policy

NEW HORIZONS IN ENVIRONMENTAL ECONOMICS

Series Editors: Wallace E. Oates, *Professor of Economics, University of Maryland, College Park and University Fellow, Resources for the Future, USA and* Henk Folmer, *Professor of Research Methodology, Groningen University and Professor of General Economics, Wageningen University, The Netherlands.*

This important series is designed to make a significant contribution to the development of the principles and practices of environmental economics. It includes both theoretical and empirical work. International in scope, it addresses issues of current and future concern in both East and West and in developed and developing countries.

The main purpose of the series is to create a forum for the publication of high quality work and to show how economic analysis can make a contribution to understanding and resolving the environmental problems confronting the world in the twenty-first century.

Recent titles in the series include:

The Impact of Climate Change on Regional Systems
A Comprehensive Analysis of California
Edited by Joel Smith and Robert Mendelsohn

Explorations in Environmental and Natural Resource Economics
Essays in Honor of Gardner M. Brown, Jr.
Edited by Robert Halvorsen and David Layton

Using Experimental Methods in Environmental and Resource Economics
Edited by John A. List

Economic Modelling of Climate Change and Energy Policies
Carlos de Miguel, Xavier Labandeira and Baltasar Manzano

The Economics of Global Environmental Change
International Cooperation for Sustainability
Edited by Mario Cogoy and Karl W. Steininger

Redesigning Environmental Valuation
Mixing Methods within Stated Preference Techniques
Neil A. Powe

Economic Valuation of River Systems
Edited by Fred J. Hitzhusen

Scarcity, Entitlements and the Economics of Water in Developing Countries
P.B. Anand

Technological Change and Environmental Policy
A Study of Depletion in the Oil and Gas Industry
Shunsuke Managi

Environmental Governance and Decentralisation
Edited by Albert Breton, Giorgio Brosio, Silvana Dalmazzone and Giovanna Garrone

Choice Experiments Informing Environmental Policy
A European Perspective
Edited by Ekin Birol and Phoebe Koundouri

Choice Experiments Informing Environmental Policy

A European Perspective

Edited by

Ekin Birol

Research Fellow, International Food Policy Research Institute, Washington DC, USA and Research Associate, Department of Land Economy, University of Cambridge, UK

Phoebe Koundouri

Assistant Professor in Economics, DIEES, Athens University of Economics and Business, Greece

NEW HORIZONS IN ENVIRONMENTAL ECONOMICS

Edward Elgar

Cheltenham, UK • Northampton, MA, USA

Published by
Edward Elgar Publishing Limited
Glensanda House
Montpellier Parade
Cheltenham
Glos GL50 1UA
UK

Edward Elgar Publishing, Inc.
William Pratt House
9 Dewey Court
Northampton
Massachusetts 01060
USA

A catalogue record for this book
is available from the British Library

Library of Congress Control Number: 2008924972

ISBN 978 1 84542 725 2

Printed and bound in Great Britain by MPG Books Ltd, Bodmin, Cornwall

Dedication

This book is dedicated to Prof. David W. Pearce, our teacher, colleague and friend.

The front cover displays the photo of Cheimaditida Wetland in Greece. Chapter 11 in this book presents the results of a choice experiment study undertaken to investigate the efficient and sustainable management of this wetland. The photo was taken by Ekin Birol in 2004.

Contents

Contributors

Jeff Bennett is Professor of Environmental Management in the Crawford School of Economics and Government at the Australian National University. He has 30 years experience as a teacher, researcher and consultant in the fields of environmental economics, natural resource economics, agricultural economics and applied micro-economics. He is a member of the Academic Advisory Board of the Centre for Independent Studies, a co-editor of the *Australian Journal of Agricultural and Resource Economics* and a member of the editorial boards of the *Australasian Journal of Environmental Management* and *Economic Analysis and Policy*. He was President of the Australian Agricultural and Resource Economics Society in 2004 and a pro-bono Director of Wetland Care Australia, 2000–04. Jeff is also Principal of the consulting group Environmental and Resource Economics.

Ekin Birol is a Research Fellow at the Markets, Trade, and Institutions Division of the International Food Policy Research Institute (IFPRI), Washington DC, USA and a Research Associate of the Department of Land Economy, University of Cambridge, UK. Her current research focuses on food and water safety in developing countries. From 2004 to 2007 Ekin was a Research Fellow of Homerton College, University of Cambridge, where she conducted research on the development and application of economic methodology for informing efficient and equitable policies for sustainable management of genetic and water resources in several countries at different stages of economic development. She worked as an economic consultant for IFPRI from 2004 to 2005 and for Bioversity International (formerly International Plant Genetic Resources Institute), Rome, Italy from 2001 to 2004. She also worked as a Research Fellow at the Centre for Social and Economic Research on the Global Environment, University College London, UK, from 2000 to 2004, and as an affiliated lecturer at the Department of Economics, University of Reading, UK, from 2004 to 2005. Ekin obtained a PhD in economics, concentrating on agricultural, environmental and natural resource economics, an MPhil in economics, concentrating on econometrics and development economics, and an MSc in environmental and resource economics, all from University College London, UK.

Danny Campbell is a Post-Doctoral Research Fellow at the Gibson Institute for Land, Food and Environment, Queen's University Belfast, Northern Ireland. He has obtained a PhD in environmental economics, an MSc in rural development and a BSc in agricultural economics, all from Queen's University Belfast. Danny's main area of research concerns the economic valuation of environmental and natural resources with a particular emphasis on the methodological and econometric issues associated with discrete choice models. Other research interests include spatial econometrics, rural development and agricultural economics. Current and recent research projects include the economic valuation of rare and endangered fish species, agri-environmental schemes, rural landscapes, water quality and cleanup of unauthorised landfill and contaminated land.

Michael Christie is a Lecturer in Environmental Economics at the Institute of Rural Sciences, University of Wales Aberystwyth. He holds an honours degree in agriculture and a PhD in environmental economics, both from the University of Aberdeen. He has over 12 years experience in undertaking environmental valuation research. Recent studies have included economic evaluations of countryside recreation and amenity, biodiversity, agri-environmental schemes, geological heritage, coastal defence and water quality. These studies have utilised a range of valuation methods including travel cost models, contingent valuation, choice experiments and contingent behaviour models.

Sergio Colombo is a researcher at the Agricultural Economics Department of the Institute of Agrarian Research (IFAPA) of the Andalusia Government. His main research deals with environmental economics and policy design, the econometrics of externalities control and the economics of rural development. Colombo's research is focused on the use of stated preference methods for environmental valuation; on evaluating the efficiency of different policy instruments to achieve environmental targets; on the accuracy and reliability of the methods for environmental benefits transfer; and on modelling ecological–economic inter-linkages in the British uplands. In the last few years, he has published several articles on the economic valuation of environmental externalities for environmental policy design. He has a PhD in Environmental Science and Technology from the University of Granada, Spain.

Jeanne Dachary-Bernard is a researcher at CEMAGREF. Her PhD in economics is entitled *A multi-approach for landscape economic valuation*, and is from the University of Bordeaux IV. Dr Dachary-Bernard has contributed to a research programme of the French Ministry of Ecology and

Sustainable Development (S3E-2002) in which the choice experiments method was applied to landscape valuation. Her professional interest lies in relationships between agriculture and the environment, and their implications in the spatial localisation of agricultural activities. She is also involved in the transfer of results from the individual scale to a larger scale in order to supply aggregated indicators to public decision makers. Dr Dachary-Bernard has been lecturing on quantitative, methodological and basic economics at the University of Bordeaux since 2000.

Nick Hanley is Professor of Environmental Economics at the University of Stirling and author of several textbooks on environmental economics and cost-benefit analysis. He is an expert on environmental valuation and environmental cost-benefit analysis, and has worked extensively on landscape and biodiversity valuation and on the use of economic analysis in the design of agri-environmental policy. He has published many articles on economic valuation and environmental policy design and acts on the editorial boards of three academic journals as well as supervising PhD and other research projects. He has previously worked with eftec on a choice experiment survey to value the landscape benefits of hill farming. He has a PhD from the Department of Agricultural Economics, University of Newcastle-on-Tyne.

Paula Horne works as a Senior Research Scientist at the Finnish Forest Research Institute. She is a leader of the research programme 'Safeguarding forest biodiversity – policy instruments and socio-economic impacts'. Her recent research has focused on non-market forest goods and services and their governance, such as game management, forest management in recreation areas and biodiversity conservation. In recent years, she has been leading the evaluation of the socio-economic impacts of the forest biodiversity programme METSO in Finland.

W. George Hutchinson is Professor of Environmental Economics and Director of the Gibson Institute of Land, Food and Environment at Queen's University Belfast, Northern Ireland. He has degrees in economics and business administration and a PhD in environmental valuation economics. His main research interest are in experimental economics, contingent valuation and discrete choice modelling applied to environmental, health and safety economics. He has worked full time in these research area since 1991 and has been principal supervisor of 10 PhDs in non-market valuation. He has published more than 40 topic-related papers in international peer-reviewed journals including *The Journal of Environmental Economics and Management*. *Land Economics* and *Ecological Economics*, and presented papers at major international conferences such as those of the American Economic Association, the Royal Economic Society and the Economic Science Association. He has led work packages under the EU Framework's CAMAR Programme (contract 8001-CT90-0008), the EU 6th Framework, Global Change and Ecosystems and EU LEADER II and INTER REG IIIA Programmes. With a US University he is co-applicant in two US National Science Foundation Grants (2000) and (2004) researching management, decision making and risk. He has also led research projects for the Department of the Environment (Northern Ireland) and for the Republic of Ireland's Research Stimulus Fund. He has acted as Consultant to the OECD and to the UK Department of the Environment, Food and Rural Affairs (Defra). Professor Hutchinson's work is cited in the UK Treasury Green Book on the Economics of Public Sector Project Appraisal.

Helen Johns has worked as an environmental economist at eftec since October 2004, after gaining her MSc in environmental and resource economics from University College London, UK. Her main interests are the informational problems surrounding the valuation of complex environmental goods (such as ecosystem services) and the economics of climate change, with particular experience in greenhouse gas emissions trading. Her current and recent projects include a major research project for the European Commission in preparation for the implementation of the Environmental Liability Directive, an assessment of the economic benefits of groundwater resources for the Environment Agency, a review of the potential for a tradeable permit system in flood management, and an overview of how valuation evidence is used by Defra and related agencies.

Katia Karousakis is an environmental economist and policy analyst at the Environment Directorate of the Organisation for Economic Co-operation and Development (OECD). She holds a BSc from the University of York (UK), a Master's from Duke University (USA) and a PhD from University College London (UK). She has worked on a number of areas in the field of environmental and resource economics and policy, including climate change, waste management, water resources and transport.

Andreas Kontoleon is a lecturer (Assistant Professor) in Environmental Economics at the Department of Land Economy at the University of Cambridge. He is also the Director of the MPhil Degree in Environmental Policy at Cambridge University, a Senior Research Fellow at the Department of Economics UCL, co-founder of the Cambridge based C-LEED research centre and co-director of the BIEOCON network. He holds a PhD in Economics from UCL and an MPhil in Economics from the University of Cambridge. He had published numerous peered review articles and books in the areas of micro-econometrics, welfare economics, environmental regulation, biodiversity economics and development economics. His latest book, published by Cambridge University Press, is a state of the art *Handbook* on the economics of biodiversity conservation. Further, he has worked on numerous research projects for several policy organisations (including the OECD, China Council, UK DETR, European Commission). Recently he has been undertaking collaborative research with the University of Beijing on assessing the environmental and welfare impacts of forest and land use policies in rural China.

Phoebe Koundouri has been an Assistant Professor in Economics at the Department of International and European Economic Studies (DIEES), Athens University of Economics and Business (Greece) since 2005. She holds a BA from the University of Leicester, UK (1994) and an MPhil (1995), MSc (1996) and PhD (2000) in Economics from the University of Cambridge, UK. During 1997–2005, she held academic positions (as Lecturer A and B) at the Economics Departments of the University of Cambridge, London Business School, University College London and University of Reading. She has published eight books and more than a hundred articles in edited volumes and academic journals (including leading journals such as: *The American Journal of Agricultural Economics, Journal of Applied Econometrics, Journal of Environmental Economics and Management, Land Economics, Environmental and Resource Economics, Economic Policy and Water Resources Research*), mainly in the field of environmental, resource and agricultural economics, as well as in the field of applied econometrics, economic development and policy. She is currently an associate editor of the academic journals *Environment and Development Economics*, *Economics* the *Open Agriculture Journal* and *Open Agricultural Reviews*, while she has acted as a referee for many academic journals, book publishers and research funding foundations. She has coordinated a number of research projects and has been a consultant to the European Commission, the World Bank, the OECD, the European Bank of Reconstruction and Development, the UN and NATO, as well as many other international and national organizations and governments of developed and developing countries. She has organised a number of international conferences, mainly in the field of water resource economics and management. She has given public and academic lectures all over the world, and received scholarships and prizes for academic excellence from various institutions and foundations. Her CV has been included in many biographical publications, such as *Who's Who in the World, Who's Who in Science and Engineering* and *The Cambridge Blue Book* (International Biographical Centre).

Yiannis Kountouris has been a PhD candidate at DIEES, Athens University of Economics and Business, Greece, since 2006. He holds a BSc from the Department of Economics of the University of Cyprus and an MSc from the Department of Economics, Queen Mary College, University of London, UK. His research interests include environmental economics, agricultural economics, applied econometrics and applied welfare economics.

Edelmiro López is Associate Professor with the Department of Applied Economics at Universidade de Santiago de Compostela (USC), Spain. His research area is agricultural and land economics. He has published several books and many articles dealing with topics related to land markets, agrarian structures and the Galician economy. Since August 2005, he has been the Director General of the Galician Rural Development Agency (AGADER) in the Autonomous Government of Galicia.

Maria L. Loureiro is a researcher with IDEGA and a faculty member of the Department of Economic Analysis of the Universidade de Santiago de Compostela (USC), Spain. Her research interests are related to agricultural and environmental economics. She obtained a Masters and a PhD in agricultural economics at Washington State University, USA (2000). Prior to USC, her academic experience included faculty positions at Colorado State University, USA and the Universidad Carlos III de Madrid, Spain, and a post as researcher at the Norwegian Agricultural Economics Research Institute (Oslo). She has published her work in international journals, including *Land Economics*, *Environmental and Resource Economics* and *The American Journal of Agricultural Economics.*

Joan Mogas is a Professor at the University Rovira i Virgili, in Catalonia, Spain. His principal research is in the field of environmental economics.

Paulo A.L.D. Nunes is Professor of Environmental Valuation at the School for Advanced Studies in Venice International University, Italy. He is also Senior Economist at the Fondazione Eni Enrico Mattei. Paulo Nunes holds an MA and a PhD in economics from the Katholieke Universiteit Leuven, Belgium. His main areas of expertise include economic valuation of environmental goods; cost-benefit analysis; econometrics of non-market valuation; economics of biodiversity; economics of impure altruism; welfare analysis; and policy guidance. Past academic positions include post-doctoral research fellow at the Vrije Universiteit Amsterdam (the Netherlands), professorial lecturer at the Johns Hopkins University School of Advanced International Studies, Bologna

Center (Italy), researcher at the Centre of Excellence for Sustainable Development, University Ca' Foscari of Venice (Italy), and visiting researcher at the Department of Economics, University of California San Diego (USA).

Ece Özdemiroğlu is the founding director of eftec, the UK's leading specialist environmental economics consultancy. Her main interests are methods of gathering quantitative evidence that environmental and other non-market resources have economic values, and ways of incorporating this evidence into decision making both in terms of policy and project design and appraisal. Since 1992, Ece has worked on over 150 projects, the majority of which she has managed. Her clients have included most UK government departments, the European Commission, the European Investment Bank, the World Bank, the Global Environment Facility and the governments of Turkey, the Netherlands, South Africa, the People's Republic of China and Mongolia among others. She has co-edited or co-authored 11 books and contributed to several articles and conference papers. She is currently working on cost-benefit analyses for two multi-billion pound water quality and supply projects in the UK. She is also advising two UK government departments: Defra on the estimation of benefits from water quality improvements as part of the research programme to implement the Water Framework Directive; and the Department for Transport on the economic cost of the landscape impacts of transport schemes.

Pere Riera is a Lecturer in Environmental Economics at the Autonomous University of Barcelona, Spain. He is also the coordinator of COST Action E45 on best practice protocols in forest valuation and the scientific director of MEDFOREX, a network of research institutions interested in Mediterranean Forest Externalities.

Riccardo Scarpa is a Professor in Environmental Economics at the Management School of the University of Waikato, New Zealand, where he teaches econometrics, and resource and environmental economics. His main research interest is in the econometrics of non-market valuation and he likes to operate in an interdisciplinary context. After his Laurea in Agricultural Sciences in Italy, he completed an MSc in Environmental Sciences at the University of Wales, and gained his PhD from the University of Wisconsin-Madison, USA, in Forest Economics. He has recently published economics papers relating to forest externalities, agriculture, livestock, food choice, outdoor recreation, benefit transfer, experimental design, water services, traffic calming, conservation and methods of estimation via simulation. He has acted as a reviewer for over thirty economics journals, and published in over twenty. He has supervised the doctoral work in economics of seven PhD students and over twenty Masters students.

Chiara Maria Travisi graduated in Environmental Sciences at the Università Milano-Bicocca in March 2000 and in December 2003 she received her PhD degree in ecology from the Università di Milano, Italy. In November 2002 she started to work on her PhD in environmental economics at the Department of Spatial Economics of the Vrije Universiteit Amsterdam, the Netherlands, which was completed in March 2007. Since September 2003 she has collaborated with the Regional and Urban Economics Group at the Politecnico di Milano, and with the Fondazione Eni Enrico Mattei (FEEM), Italy. She is currently a researcher at FEEM in the programme 'Sustainability Indicators and Environmental Valuation', and contract Professor of Urban Economics and Policy at the Politecnico di Milano.

Mitsuyasu Yabe is an Associate Professor at the Department of Agricultural and Resource Economics at Kyushu University in Japan. His areas of expertise are agricultural economics and environmental economics. He has been involved in a variety of research activities in the evaluation of externality in agricultural production, water resource conservation, food safety bio-fuel policy and the economics of genetically modified foods.

Contact details of contributors

Jeff Bennett
Professor, Environmental Management and Development Programme
Crawford School of Economics and Government
J G Crawford Building
The Australian National University
Canberra ACT 0200 Australia
Tel: + 61 2 6125 0154
Fax: + 61 2 6125 8448
Email: jeff.bennett@anu.edu.au
Website: http://www.crawford.anu.edu.au/staff/jbennett.php

Ekin Birol
Research Fellow
Markets, Trade, and Institutions Division
International Food Policy Research Institute
2033 K Street, NW
Washington DC, 20006-1002, USA
Tel: +1 202 862 5617
Fax: +1 202 467 4439
Email: e.birol@cgiar.org

Danny Campbell
Gibson Institute for Land, Food and Environment
Queen's University Belfast, Northern Ireland.
Tel: +44 (0) 28 9097 4155
Fax: +44 (0) 28 9097 6513
Email: d.campbell@qub.ac.uk

Michael Christie
Institute of Rural Sciences
University of Wales Aberystwyth
Aberystwyth, Ceredigion, Wales, SY23 3AL, UK
Tel: + 44 (0) 1970 622217
Fax: + 44 (0) 1970 611264
Email: mec@aber.ac.uk

Sergio Colombo
Department of Agricultural Economics (IFAPA)
Centro de Granada
Apdo 2027
18080 Granada
Spain
Email: scolombo@ugr.es

Jeanne Dachary-Bernard
Research Fellow in Spatial Economics
CEMAGREF - 'Amenities and dynamics of rural areas' research unit
50, Avenue de Verdun – Gazinet.
33612 Cestas Cedex, France
Tel: +33 5 57 89 26 99
Email: Jeanne.Dachary-Bernard@cemagref.fr

Nick Hanley
Department of Economics
University of Stirling
Stirling FK9 4LA, UK
Email: n.d.hanley@stir.ac.uk

Paula Horne
Finnish Forest Research Institute
Unioninkatu 40 A, 00170 Helsinki, Finland
Tel: +358-10-211 2220
Fax: +358-10 211 2104
Email address: paula.horne@metla.fi

W. George Hutchinson
Gibson Institute for Land, Food and Environment
Queen's University Belfast, Northern Ireland.
Tel: +44 (0) 28 9097 6545
Fax: +44 (0) 28 9097 6513
Email: g.hutchinson@qub.ac.uk

Helen Johns
eftec
Economics for the Environment Consultancy Ltd
73–75 Mortimer Street, London W1W 7SQ
Tel: +44 (0) 207 5805383
Fax: +44 (0) 207 5805385

Email: helen@eftec.co.uk
Website: www.eftec.co.uk

Katia Karousakis
Environment Directorate, OECD
2, rue Andre-Pascal
75775 Paris Cedex 15, France
Tel: +33 (0) 1 45 24 98 83
Fax: +33 (0) 1 44 30 61 84
Email: katia.karousakis@oecd.org

Andreas Kontoleon
Lecturer in Economics, Department of Land Economy
University of Cambridge
19 Silver Street, Cambridge, CB3 9EP, UK
Tel: +44 (0) 1223 339773
Fax: +44 (0) 1223 337130
E-mail: ak219@cam.ac.uk
Website: www.landecon.cam.ac.uk/staff/profiles/akontoleon.htm

Phoebe Koundouri
Assistant Professor in Economics
Department of International and European Economic Studies (DIEES)
Athens University of Economics and Business
76, Patission Street, Athens 104 34, Greece
Tel: +30 210 8203455
Fax: +30 210 8214122
Email: pkoundouri@aueb.gr
Website: www.aueb.gr/deos/gr/kountouri.html

Yiannis Kountouris
Department of International and European Economic Studies
Athens University of Economics and Business
76, Patission Street, Athens 104 34, Greece
Fax: +30 210 8214122
Email: ykountouris@aueb.gr

Edelmiro López
IDEGA-Avda das Ciencias s/n.
Campus Sur. 15782
Santiago de Compostela, Spain
Tel: +34-981563100(14339)

Fax: +34-981599935
Email: eaedel@usc.es

Maria L. Lourerio
IDEGA-Avda das Ciencias s/n.
Campus Sur. 15782
Santiago de Compostela, Spain
Tel: +34-981563100 (ext. 14337)
Fax: +34-981599935
Email: maria.loureiro@usc.es

Joan Mogas
Departament d'Economia
Universitat Rovira i Virgili
Avda. Universitat,1
43204, Reus, Spain
Tel:+ 34 977 759851
Fax:+ 34 977 300661
Email: joan.mogas@urv.cat

Paulo A.L.D. Nunes
Professor of Environmental Valuation
School for Advanced Studies in Venice Foundation,
Venice International University
Island of San Servolo, 30100 Venice, Italy
Tel: +39 041 271 95 65
Email: pnunes@unive.it

Also:

Lead Economist
Fondazione ENI Enrico Mattei
Sustainability Indicators and Environmental Valuation Programme
Palazzo Querini Stampalia, 30122 Venice, Italy
Tel: + 39 041 271 14 00 (Secr. 453)
Fax: + 39 041 271 14 61
Email: paulo.nunes@feem.it

Ece Özdemiroğlu
eftec
Economics for the Environment Consultancy Ltd
73–75 Mortimer Street, London W1W 7SQ
Tel: +44 (0) 207 5805383

Fax: +44 (0) 207 5805385
Email: ece@eftec.co.uk
Website: www.eftec.co.uk

Pere Riera
Departament d'Economia Aplicada
Universitat Autonòma de Barcelona
Edifici B
08193, Bellaterra, Spain
Tel: 34 93 5812993
Fax: 34 93 5812292
Email: Pere.Riera@uab.es
Website: http://selene.uab.es/prieram/

Riccardo Scarpa
Economics Department, Waikato Management School
University of Waikato
Hamilton, New Zealand
Tel: +64 (0) 7838 4848
Fax: + 64(0)78384331
Email: rscarpa@mngt.waikato.ac.nz

Chiara M. Travisi
Fondazione Eni Enrico Mattei
C.so Magenta 63, 20123 Milano, Italy
Tel: +39 02 520 36945
Fax: +39 02 520 36946
Email: chiara.travisi@feem.it

Also:

Politecnico of Milano, Group of Regional Economics,
Department of Management Economics and Industrial Engineering
Email: chiara.travisi@polimi.it

Mitsuyasu Yabe
Associate Professor, Department of Agricultural and Resource Economics
Kyushu University
6-10-1 Hakozaki, Higashiku, Fukuokashi 812-8581 Japan
Tel: +81 (0) 92 642 2959
Fax: +81 (0) 92 642 2959
Email: yabe@agr.kyushu-u.ac.jp

Foreword

W.L. (Vic) Adamowicz*

Understanding preferences for environmental quality is an important component of environmental economics and is increasingly important for policy makers. Credible assessment of peoples' values for environmental quality is required to address some of the key issues affecting our time. Understanding the impacts of climate change, for example, requires accurate assessments of how people respond to changes in climate and how they value such changes. Policy responses to climate change also require information on preferences and demand. The Millennium Ecosystem Assessment highlighted the importance of ecosystem goods and services to the global economic system. Understanding the value of ecosystem goods and services and integrating this information into policy development continues to be an important global challenge. This volume contributes significantly to these issues of environmental valuation and policy development within Europe.

The title of this book suggests that the volume is focused on a preference elicitation method, choice experiments, as a mechanism for informing environmental policy. While the book does provide a large number of examples of choice experiments and illustrates how the information from these cases is used in policy development, the book is much broader than this. It provides an assessment of the literature on environmental valuation in Europe. It outlines some of the key environmental policy issues facing European countries and provides information on preferences and values associated with policy options. It also provides a set of state of the art examples of preference elicitation and analysis. This volume will be of interest to a variety of audiences. The book provides insights that will be useful to policy makers interested in understanding the public's preferences for environmental quality and it will be useful to academics and graduate students interested in cutting edge applications of stated preference methods.

While each chapter provides an interesting case study, what is notable is the diversity and range of the presentations in the book. There is variation in the types of environmental goods examined: in the econometric methods

* Department of Rural Economy, University of Alberta, Canada.

employed; in the choice sets presented to respondents; and in the way the results are integrated into policy analysis. The book has its cornerstone in an outstanding review of valuation studies in Europe. This chapter provides a basis for the field in Europe and will be excellent reading for students and practitioners in the field. All of the studies collect primary data. This is very laudable given the lack of primary data in the area of environmental valuation. These data will undoubtedly be rich sources of information for time to come. Finally the chapters often provide more detail than one would find in a journal paper. This additional detail will be useful to readers and to individuals designing future studies.

Choice experiments as a mechanism for evaluating preferences for environmental quality began to appear in the environmental economics literature in the 1990s (earlier in the geography literature – but these placed little emphasis on the valuation aspects). The early applications used relatively simple experimental designs and econometric methods. This volume reflects the advances that have been made in the field since then. There is considerable sophistication in experimental design, in presentation, and notably in econometric analysis. Of particular note is the emphasis on heterogeneity of preferences, something that our early studies in the 1990s ignored (or simply could not incorporate because of the limitations of econometric tools). An understanding of heterogeneity is important for policy analysis. An assessment of who will benefit or lose, or the distribution of benefits, is often at least as important as how much the benefit or loss will be. The importance of heterogeneity is clearly identified in the studies in this volume.

While the chapters in this book reflect technical advances in the literature, what is probably most important is the creativity that is reflected in the papers. Readers of this volume will notice how researchers have taken innovative approaches in framing the issues, presenting tradeoffs or analyzing data. It is this creativity that is a key contribution to the literature. The choice experiments of the 1990s were simple tables and the analysis was relatively standard evaluation of main attribute effects. These experiments include visual aids, the welfare measures include analysis of scenarios and incorporate heterogeneity, and at times multiple methods are used to identify different components of value. In many cases psychometric or other preference information is used to triangulate with the choice experiment data. The range of issues examined also reflects considerable creativity – topics include flood control, forest conservation, noise reduction, land use and recreation.

In conclusion, this volume provides a creative set of studies of preferences for environmental quality in Europe. The range of methods and applications is very impressive, as is the background and context provided.

What remains to be seen, for these studies and for many analyses of environmental values, is how they will be used in policy development. Casual observation suggests that there is increasing use of environmental valuation research in policy analysis and development. A goal of this volume and other works in this area is to move to improved integration of environmental valuation into policy. The chapters in this volume will certainly help illustrate the role that choice experiments and environmental valuation can play in informing policy.

1. Introduction

Ekin Birol and Phoebe Koundouri

BACKGROUND

The Choice Experiment Method (CEM) is a Stated Preference Method (SPM) of environmental valuation, adopted from marketing and transport economics literature (see for example, Louviere and Hensher, 1982; Louviere and Woodworth, 1983; Louviere 1988; Louviere 1992). Similarly to the other SPM, the Contingent Valuation Method (CVM), CEM can elicit the total economic value (that is, both use and non-use values) of non-market environmental goods, which can in turn be used to inform the design of efficient and effective policies for their sustainable management and conservation.

The CEM has a theoretical grounding in Lancaster's characteristics theory of value (Lancaster, 1966), and an econometric basis in models of random utility (Thurstone 1927; Manski, 1977). Consequently, this method is based on the notion that any environmental good can be described in terms of its characteristics, or attributes, and the levels that these attributes take (with or without a policy change). Once attributes and their levels are identified, experimental design theory is used to generate different profiles of the environmental good in terms of its attributes and the levels these attributes take. These profiles are then assembled in choice sets which are presented to the respondents, who are asked to state their preferences on multiple occasions. Hanley *et al.* (1998) define the CEM as a highly 'structured method of data generation'.

One of the attributes which is typically included in a choice experiment study is a monetary cost or benefit attribute. The monetary attribute and the random utility framework on which the CEM is based allow for the estimation of welfare estimates, that is, willingness to pay (WTP) or willingness to accept (WTA) compensation, for changes in the levels of environmental attributes (Hanemann, 1984). Specifically, the CEM can provide four types of information about the values of environmental goods: (i) which attributes are significant determinants of the values that stakeholders (for example, local or national public, farmers, visitors to a recreational site) place on environmental goods; (ii) the implied ranking of these attributes amongst the relevant stakeholders; (iii) the value of changing more than one of the attributes at once; and (iv) the total economic value of an environmental good (Bateman *et al.*, 2003).

Since the first application of the CEM to environmental management problems by Adamowicz *et al.* (1994), there has been increasing interest in the use and development of this method both by academics and practitioners. A vast majority of the earlier choice experiment applications to environmental issues were implemented in North America and Australia (see for example Boxall *et al.*, 1996; Adamowicz *et al.*, 1997; Morrison *et al.*, 1999; Rolfe *et al.*, 2000), as is evident from the four published books on theory and practice of the CEM by North American and Australian academics (Louviere *et al.*, 2000; Bennett and Blamey, 2001; Hensher *et al.*, 2005; Kanninen, 2007). In recent years, however, there has been an increasing number of applications of this method in European countries, as presented in this volume, and most recently several noteworthy choice experiment studies have been carried out in developing countries (see for example, Scarpa *et al.*, 2003a, 2003b; Othman *et al.*, 2004; Naidoo and Adamowicz, 2005; Bienabe and Hearne, 2006).

The popularity of the CEM is increasing rapidly as a result of the various advantages this method possesses over the CVM, as well as over the Revealed Preference Methods (RPM), such as the Hedonic Pricing Method and the Travel Cost Method. Advantages as well as disadvantages of the CEM are discussed in great detail in Hanley *et al.* (1998), Louviere *et al.* (2000), Bennett and Blamey (2001) and Bateman *et al.* (2003). We present below a summary of the main advantages of CEM over CVM and RPM.

The main advantage of CEM over CVM lies in its ability to measure the value of the attributes that make up the environmental good. Since environmental policies are generally concerned with changing the levels of attribute quantity or quality, rather than losing or gaining the environmental good as a whole, this advantage of the CEM makes it preferable over the CVM for informing environmental policies. Moreover, the ability of CEM to decompose the value of the environmental good into the value of its attributes makes this method more applicable to benefits transfer compared to the CVM (Hanley *et al.*, 1998; Bateman *et al.*, 2003).

The CEM also avoids several of the biases prevalent in CVM. Response difficulties in CVM (for example, 'yea-saying' bias in dichotomous choice contingent valuation studies and the difficulty of stating a value in an open-ended contingent valuation) can be avoided in CEM. This is because respondents are more familiar with the choice approach; the levels of the monetary attributes are already specified in the choice sets and respondents get repeated sets of choices in which they can reveal their preferences. The strategic bias is also minimised as the monetary values are already defined in the choice sets and hence the respondents cannot over- or understate their true valuation. In addition, insensitivity to scope is eliminated; particularly if the choice sets presented to the respondents are complete and carefully designed, respondents should not misinterpret the scale of the good or its attributes. Finally, since levels of the monetary attribute are already predetermined and contained in choice experiments, the large discrepancies between WTA and WTP values found in CVM (Kahneman *et al.*, 1990) can be avoided in CEM.

The CEM also has several advantages over the RPM. Most importantly, unlike RPM, the CEM can elicit the values of non-market environmental goods that have no related or surrogate markets. A major drawback of using RPM is that because the attributes and attribute levels of the environmental good do not vary over time in a single cross-section, the value of changes in the quality or quantity of the environmental good provided are difficult to estimate. Coefficients on attributes in models estimated from choices in actual settings provide only limited predictions of the impact of changing policies (Louviere *et al.*, 2000). In other words, the new situation (after the change in the quality or the quantity of the environmental good) may be outside the current set of experiences. Thus, simulation of the new situation generally involves extrapolation outside the data range used to estimate the model (Adamowicz *et al.*, 1994). CEM can be designed to cover a wider range of attribute levels in cases where revealed data do not encompass the range of proposed quality or quantity changes in the attributes of an environmental good. In other words, the CEM can be used to consider an array of policy options and states of the world that are fundamentally different from the existing ones.

Another common problem with RPM is multi-collinearity among multiple attributes, generating coefficients with the wrong signs or implausible magnitudes, and making it difficult to separate attribute effects (Greene, 2000; Louviere *et al.*, 2000; Freeman, 2003; Hensher *et al.*, 2005). Separation of these attributes may be necessary, however, in order to represent benefits and costs accurately in policy analysis (Adamowicz *et al.*, 1994). The CEM eliminates multi-collinearity among the attributes since in experimental designs attribute levels are designed as orthogonal (Bateman *et al.*, 2003).

The aim of this book is to draw attention to the wealth and diversity of several recent state-of-the-art choice experiment studies that have been undertaken in Europe in the last few years. The main emphasis of the book is to highlight how this method can be employed to inform environmental, agricultural, natural resource management and food policies at the European Union (EU) level. Case studies presented in this volume are from eight countries across the EU, including Finland, France, Greece, Ireland,

Italy, Poland, Spain and the UK, and cover a wide array of issues ranging from landscapes, biodiversity, cultural heritage, noise pollution, forests and water resources to food labelling. The findings reported in this book reveal that the monetary cost and benefit values captured through the CEM for various stakeholders can be used to inform the efficient, effective and equitable design and implementation of various EU-level policies and directives, such as the Common Agricultural Policy, the Water Framework Directive, the Forestry Strategy, the Habitats Directive and food labelling systems to name a few. Finally, the book also presents some of the most recent developments in choice experiment theory and analysis, as well as several interesting and cutting edge applications of these developments.

STRUCTURE OF THIS BOOK

This book aims to cover comprehensively several environmental, agricultural and natural resource management issues that can be tackled with the CEM, as well as the EU-level environmental, agricultural and natural resource management and food policies that can be informed using this method. The following chapters of this volume are summarised below.

In Chapter 2, Birol, Koundouri and Kountouris, provide an extensive, but by no means exhaustive, review of choice experiment studies undertaken in EU countries to date. The aim of the review is to present the current status of choice experiment applications in the EU, with details of the environmental goods and their attributes valued; monetary values obtained; implications for the design of EU directives and regulations; and the econometric models and survey modes employed in each study. To this end, choice experiment applications are reviewed covering a wide array of environmental, natural resource, agricultural, food and energy issues implemented in various EU countries. Moreover, the EU-level environmental, natural resource, agricultural, food and energy policies, directives and regulations which these choice experiment studies aim to inform are introduced.

The following four chapters present choice experiment studies which aim to inform those EU-level regulations and directives pertaining to rural landscape management. In Chapter 3, Campbell, Hutchinson and Scarpa estimate the benefits the Irish public derive from the Rural Environment Protection (REP) Schemes. REP Schemes were developed following Agri-environmental Regulation EC No. 2078/92, which states that all EU countries should 'support agricultural production methods that are environmentally friendly and conserve rural areas'. Public WTP was captured for the improvement of eight important landscape attributes under the

REP Schemes: wildlife habitats; rivers and lakes; hedgerows; pastures; mountain land; stonewalls; farmyard tidiness; and cultural heritage. This study concludes that there is a considerable range in the values that the public derive from landscape improvement measures under the REP Scheme, and overall the attribute most valued is rivers and lakes, and the attribute least valued is hedgerows. When the individual-specific WTP estimates are contrasted with the average cost of the REP Scheme across the Irish adult population, the results indicate that the Scheme contributes substantial benefits to rural landscapes. The results of this chapter can also be used to inform decisions concerning the allocation of resources for each of the landscape attributes.

In Chapter 4, Johns, Hanley, Colombo and Őzdemiroğlu investigate the public's valuation of various landscape attributes of Severely Disadvantaged Areas (SDAs) in England. SDAs are classified under 'Less Favoured Areas', where following the EU Council Directive 75/268/EEC on mountain and hill farming, farmers receive Hill Farm Allowance (HFA) payments. These payments aim to compensate farmers for adverse geographical conditions and encourage conservation of landscape attributes. The aim of this chapter is to inform the revision of these payments in England. Consequently, local and regional residents' and visitors' valuations of five landscape attributes were estimated in seven regions, six of which hold SDAs. The attributes included in this choice experiment were heather moorland and bog; rough grassland; broadleaf and mixed woodland; field boundaries; and cultural heritage. This chapter indicates that overall the public is WTP for improvements in the upland attributes, and the attribute that generates the highest benefits is cultural heritage. There are, however, significant variations in valuations across the regions, which should be taken into consideration when revising the HFA payments to farmers in these SDAs.

In Chapter 5, Dachary-Bernard examines tourists' and main home and second home residents' preferences for various landscape attributes to inform agri-environmental schemes in Brittany, France. Landscape attributes including moorland, hedged farmlands and farm buildings are valued. The findings reveal that values derived from these landscape attributes differ across the three stakeholder groups: tourists have the highest WTP for modern farm buildings to be well concealed; main home residents prefer moorland with trees the most; and second home residents have a high WTP for dense hedged farmlands. When the valuations of these attributes are aggregated over the relevant stakeholders for various landscape conservation programmes, the programme which promotes densely hedged farmland, well-concealed farm buildings and moorland with a lot of trees generates the highest total benefits. These results have important implications for landscape management policy in Brittany, which currently promotes clean and trimmed moorlands.

The final case study on landscape management (Chapter 6) is by Loureiro and López, who investigate tourists' preferences for various landscape attributes in Galicia, Spain. Tourists' WTP was estimated for four landscape and cultural attributes, namely historical-cultural heritage; traditional customs, food products, and rural settlements; local environment; and agro-forest landscape. The results show that tourists derive the highest benefits from protection of the local environment (maintaining clean rivers, cleaning open spaces and collecting and recycling waste), followed by protection of the traditional agro-forestry landscape (including wine terraces, autochthonous forests and autochthonous livestock). These findings are informative in the formulation of agri-environmental policies which aim to sustain rural settlements and conserve rural landscapes in the area.

The choice experiment method is applied to inform food policy in Chapter 7, by Kontoleon and Yabe. Consumer preferences for attributes of a food product, namely eggs, are investigated for several production attributes, such as health quality certification labels, living conditions for hens and pesticide use in feed production. Specifically, this chapter elicits the preferences of UK consumers for eggs that may have been derived from chickens fed with animal feed that contained varied percentages of genetically modified (GM) organism content. Motivational and attitudinal drivers of food consumer behaviour were also introduced into the analysis. The findings of this study reveal that there is considerable heterogeneity with respect to preferences for GM foods. Three distinct and coherent consumer segments are identified with varying levels of consumer aversion towards GM foods. The authors conclude that there are strong welfare-enhancing arguments for extending the EU labelling regime to include food products derived from animals fed with GM feed, as well as for the establishment of viable separate production tracks. These results, however, also imply that there isn't sufficient market segmentation to support a policy change of reducing the percentage of allowable traces of GM foods in non-GM certified foods substantially below the current minimum threshold of adventitious contamination level of 1 per cent.

The following three chapters present choice experiment case studies on various aspects of forestry resources management. In Chapter 8, Horne assesses the role and acceptability of various policy instruments in forest biodiversity conservation on privately owned forest lands in Southern Finland. This study estimates the public's valuation of forest biodiversity conservation and the trade-offs they make between different elements of it, such as the percentage of forest protected, employment impacts and policy instruments. Specifically, three kinds of policy instruments were studied:

acquisition of private land by the state; conservation contracts with private land owners; and advising and planning. Similarly to Chapter 7, the public are segmented on the basis of their attitudes, this time towards nature conservation, and the impact of their attitudes on their preferences and welfare distribution are examined. Even though the results demonstrate considerable heterogeneity between the different attitude segments' preferences for forest biodiversity conservation, overall there was consensus in the choice of the conservation policy instruments. Those policy instruments based on voluntariness of forest owners, that is, advising and planning and conservation contracts, were preferred to a more authoritarian approach of land acquisition.

In Chapter 9, Riera, Mogas and Bennett estimate the value of several attributes of forests in Catalonia, Spain, to help inform afforestation programmes. Values of recreational attributes, such as picnicking, driving through and mushroom picking in the forest, as well as environmental attributes of CO_2 sequestration and erosion decrease were estimated in this choice experiment. The results of the choice experiment analysis reveal that the public derives benefits from afforestation programmes, especially those which allow picnicking and picking mushrooms, sequester higher levels of CO_2, do not allow the use of cars in forest ways and decrease the risk of erosion. These findings have important implications for the evaluation of afforestation programmes, as forest planners can use the information presented in this chapter to include the public good values of forests in their optimisation scenarios for forest management in Catalonia.

In Chapter 10, Christie and Hanley study the recreational aspects of forests in the UK. The main forest user groups' valuations of various forest recreation attributes are investigated; these user groups include general forest users, cyclists, horse riders and nature watchers. For each of these four recreation groups, eight attributes were specified: four attributes were activity-specific (for example, for cycling, these were type of trail, optional obstacles, bike wash facilities, changing and shower facilities), while the remaining four attributes were identical for all groups and included general facilities, information, surroundings and distance. The preferences of each of the groups for recreational forest management attributes were investigated. The results provide valuable information which is expected to inform the development of forest policy in terms of the management of forests to maximise social benefits, and in particular to provide evidence in support of some of the key objectives of the EU Forest Action Plan (Commission, of the European Communities, 2006). As the authors state, the study presented in this chapter (and the study in Chapter 9) provide evidence of the welfare benefits associated with recreational use of forests. Christie and Hanley conclude that these benefits highlight the contribution that forests make towards enhancing people's 'quality of life' – a key goal of the EU Forest Action Plan.

Chapters 11 and 12 employ the choice experiment method to inform water resources management policies in Greece and Poland respectively. The results presented in these chapters have implications for the efficient and effective implementation of the Water Framework Directive (WFD, 2000/60/EC), as well as for other EU-level directives, including the EU Birds Directive (1979/409/EC) and the EU Habitats Directive (1992/43/EC). Birol, Karousakis and Koundouri investigate non-use and use values of water resources in Chapter 11 through evaluating the benefits the Greek public derives from several functions and services generated by the sustainable management of the Cheimaditida Wetland. Wetland management attributes valued in this choice experiment are biodiversity, open water surface area, facilities for research and educational activities and retraining of local farmers in environmentally friendly techniques. The analysis of the data identified two different segments in the Greek population: over half of the sample derive significant and positive values from all four of the wetland management attributes, whereas the rest only value open water surface area and retraining of local farmers significantly. When these benefit estimates are aggregated over the population for different wetland management programmes and weighted against the costs of these programmes, it is found that the programme which generates high levels of biodiversity, open water surface area and research and educational opportunities, and retrains 150 local farmers, generates the highest total net benefits.

In Chapter 12 Birol, Koundouri and Kountouris apply this method to study local residents' trade-offs between flood risk reduction and biodiversity-rich habitat conservation in the Bobrek catchment, located in the Upper Silesia Region of Poland. Specifically, local residents' preferences for reduction in flood risk, access to the river for recreational activities and conservation of biodiversity in the river catchment are investigated. The findings reveal that the residents of the catchment area derive the highest benefits from reduction of flood risk to a low level, followed by recreational activities and biodiversity conservation in the area. Moreover, residents whose houses have been flooded in the past are WTP the highest for reduction in flood risk, whereas those residents who are wealthier are WTP the most for conservation of high levels of biodiversity. These results have important repercussions for the design of efficient and effective river management projects and policies in the area which comply with the requirements of the WFD and other EU-level directives.

The final case study presented in this volume is by Nunes and Travisi in Chapter 13, where the authors estimate the value of noise abatement of the Brennero railway to the residents of Trento, located in the North-East of

Italy. Specifically, residents' WTP for reduction in rail noise level, height of trackside barriers and investment in trains and track technology are estimated. The findings of Nunes and Travisi reveal that the residents strongly prefer a noise policy that relies on investments in improving trains and track technology rather than one that increases the height of the trackside barriers. The latter policy in fact generates significant disutility, resulting in unacceptable levels of aesthetic and microclimatic costs to the residents. This finding suggest that the railway noise abatement policy should focus on 'at the source' noise measures (based on technological investments) or at least, that investments in new technologies on train vehicles and tracks should be combined with more standard trackside barriers that are not excessively high. These findings are informative for adoption of EU noise pollution regulations, such as Directive 2002/49/EC on assessment and management of environmental noise.

The final chapter, Chapter 14 by the editors, concludes the book by summarising the main findings and policy implications of the case studies presented. This chapter also points out the methodological developments achieved in the studies, and highlights the importance and value of choice experiment studies for informing European-level policies pertaining to environmental, agricultural, food and natural resource management issues.

REFERENCES

Adamowicz, W.L., P.A. Kupris and M.M. Veeman (1999), 'Consumers Responses to the Potential Use of Bovine Somatotrophin in Canadian Dairy Production', *Canadian Journal of Agricultural Economics*, Vol. 47, pp. 151–163.

Adamowicz, W.L., J. Louviere and M. Williams (1994), 'Combining Stated and Revealed Preference Methods for Valuing Environmental Amenities', *Journal of Environmental Economics and Management*, Vol. 26, pp. 271–292.

Adamowicz W.L., J. Swait, P. Boxall, J. Louviere and M. Williams (1997), 'Perceptions versus Objective Measures of Environmental Quality in Combined Revealed and Stated Preference Models of Environmental Valuation', *Journal of Environmental Economics and Management*, Vol. 32, No. 1, pp. 65–84.

Bateman, I.J., R.T. Carson, B. Day, W.M. Hanemann, N. Hanley, T. Hett, M. Jones-Lee, G. Loomes, S. Mourato, E. Özdemiroğlu, D.W. Pearce, R. Sugden and S. Swanson (2003), *Guidelines for the Use of Stated Preference Techniques for the Valuation of Preferences for Non-market Goods*, Edward Elgar, Cheltenham, UK, and Northampton, MA, USA.

Bennett, J.J. and R.K. Blamey (2001), *The Choice of Modelling Approach to Environmental Valuation*, Edward Elgar, Cheltenham, UK, and Northampton, MA, USA.

Bienabe, E. and R.R. Hearne (2006), 'Public Preferences for Biodiversity Conservation and Scenic Beauty within a Framework of Environmental Services Payments', *Forest Policy and Economic*, Vol. 9, pp. 335–348.

Boxall, P.C., W.L. Adamowicz, J. Swait, M. Williams and J. Louviere (1996), 'A Comparison of Stated Preference Methods for Environmental Valuation', *Ecological Economics*, Vol. 18, pp. 243–253.

Freeman, A.M. (2003), *The Measurement of Environmental and Resource Values: Theory and Methods* (Second ed.), Resources for the Future, Washington, D.C.

Greene, W.H. (2000), *Econometric Analysis* (Fifth ed.), Prentice Hall International, New York.

Hanemann, W.M. (1984), 'Welfare Evaluations in Contingent Valuation Experiments with Discrete Responses', *American Journal of Agricultural Economics*, Vol. 66, pp. 332–341.

Hanley, N., R.E. Wright and W.L. Adamowicz (1998), 'Using Choice Experiments to Value the Environment', *Environmental and Resource Economics*, Vol. 11, No. 3–4, pp. 413–428.

Hensher, D., J. Rose, W. Greene (2005), *Applied Choice Analysis: A Primer*, Cambridge University Press, Cambridge.

Kahneman, D., J. Knetsch and R. Thaler (1990), 'Experimental Tests of the Endowment Effect and the Coase Theorem', *Journal of Political Economy*, Vol. 98, No. 6, pp. 1325–1348.

Kanninen, B.J. (ed.) (2007), *Valuing Environmental Amenities Using Stated Choice Studies*, Springer, Berlin.

Lancaster, K. (1966), 'A New Approach to Consumer Theory', *Journal of Political Economics*, Vol. 74, pp. 217–231.

Louviere, J.J. and D.A. Hensher (1982), 'On the Design and Analysis of Simulated Choice or Allocation Experiments in Travel Choice Modelling', *Transportation Research Record*, Vol. 890, pp. 11–17.

Louviere, J.J. (1988), *Analyzing Decision Making: Metric Conjoint Analysis*, Sage Publications, Inc, Newbury Park, CA.

Louviere, J.J. (1992), 'Experimental Choice Analysis: Introduction and Overview', *Journal of Business Research*, Vol. 24, pp. 89–96.

Louviere, J.J., D.A. Hensher, J.D. Swait and W.L. Adamowicz (2000), *Stated Choice Methods: Analysis and Applications*, Cambridge University Press, Cambridge.

Louviere, J.J. and G. Woodworth (1983), 'Design and Analysis of Simulated Consumer Choice Experiments or Allocation Experiments: An Approach Based on Aggregate Data', *Journal of Marketing Research*, Vol. 20, pp. 350–367.

Manski, J. (1977), 'The Structure of Random Utility Models', *Theory and Decision*, Vol. 8, pp. 229–254.

Morrison, M., J. Bennett and R. Blamey (1999), 'Valuing Improved Wetlands Quality using Choice Modelling', *Water and Resource Research*, Vol. 35, pp. 2805–2814.

Naidoo, R. and W.L. Adamowicz (2005), 'Biodiversity and Nature-Based Tourism at Forest Reserves in Uganda', *Environment and Development Economics*, Vol. 10, No. 2, pp. 159–178.

Othman, J., J. Bennett and R. Blamey (2004), 'Environmental Values and Resource Management Options: A Choice Modelling Experience in Malaysia', *Environment and Development Economics*, Vol. 9, pp. 803–824.

Rolfe, J., J.J. Bennett and J. Louviere (2000), 'Choice Modelling and its Potential Application to Tropical Rainforest Preservation', *Ecological Economics*, Vol. 35, No. 2, pp. 289–302.

Scarpa, R., A. Drucker, S. Anderson, N. Ferraes-Ehuan, V. Gomez, C.R. Risopatron and O. Rubio-Leonel (2003a), 'Valuing Animal Genetic Resources in Peasant Economies: The Case of the Box Keken Creole Pig in Yucatan', *Ecological Economics*, Vol. 45, No.3, pp. 427–443.

Scarpa, R., E.S.K. Ruto, P. Kristjanson, M. Radeny, A.G. Drucker and J.E.O. Rege. (2003b), 'Valuing Indigenous Cattle Breeds in Kenya: An Empirical Comparison of Stated and Revealed Preference Value Estimates', *Ecological Economics*, Vol. 45, No. 3, pp. 409–426.

Thurstone, L. (1927), 'A Law of Comparative Judgement', *Psychological Review*, Vol. 4, pp. 273–286.

2. Applications of the choice experiment method in Europe: a review

Ekin Birol, Phoebe Koundouri and Yiannis Kountouris

INTRODUCTION

This chapter reviews several noteworthy applications of the choice experiment method undertaken in European Union (EU) countries to date. The review summarises choice experiment studies implemented in various EU countries covering a wide geographical area, including those located in the West (France, Germany and the UK), South (Greece, Italy, Spain and Portugal) and North of the EU (Denmark, Finland and Sweden), as well as those countries located in Eastern and Central Europe which have recently joined the EU (Hungary and Romania).

The choice experiment studies presented in this chapter cover a wide array of environmental, natural resource, agricultural, food and energy issues, ranging from conservation of wetlands and biodiversity to efficient management of water resources, and from labelling of foodstuffs to alternative energy sources. These studies are aimed at informing the design and implementation of various EU-level environmental, natural resource, agricultural, food and energy policies and directives, such as the Agri-environmental Regulation (EC No. 2078/92), food labelling systems (EC No. 2081/92 and 2082/92), the Water Framework Directive (EC No. 2000/60), the Birds Directive (79/409/EEC), the Habitats Directive (92/43/EEC) and the Landfill Directive (1999/31/EC), to name a few.

The review presented in this chapter is by no means exhaustive, but it aims to present the status of the choice experiment application in the EU to date, with details of the attributes valued in each study; the monetary values estimated; implications for the design and implementation of various EU-level policies, directives and regulations; and the econometric models and survey modes employed. The next section presents choice experiment studies on biodiversity, agri-environmental schemes and agriculture. Choice experiment studies that inform food policy are reviewed in the following section. This is followed by the review of choice experiment studies that value water resources and forest resources. The final review section summarises various choice experiment studies on renewable energy and noise and air pollution, as well as waste management. The Appendix to this chapter provides a table summarising the choice experiment studies reviewed; it reports the authors, year of study, environmental good valued, country, attributes, sample size, survey mode, econometric specification and value estimates of each study.

AGRI-ENVIRONMENTAL, WILDLIFE AND NATURE CONSERVATION SCHEMES

The EU reformed Common Agricultural Policy (CAP) advocates conservation of several attributes of agricultural landscapes (for example cultural, environmental, assimilative and historical). The EU therefore embraces the concept of multifunctional agriculture, as explicitly spelled out in its EC No. 2078/92 Agri-environmental Regulation, which states that all EU countries should 'support agricultural production methods that are environmentally friendly and conserve rural areas'.

Agri-environmental schemes stemming from this regulation aim to encourage production of environmental, social and cultural goods in the countryside, by providing the farmers with the necessary monetary incentives for provision of these goods. Public spending on agri-environmental schemes is an increasingly important component of agricultural policy, hence policy makers in EU countries are in need of information on how agri-environmental schemes can be best designed to maximise the economic benefits provided.

In addition to the agri-environmental schemes, there is also Council Directive 92/43/EEC on the conservation of natural habitats and of wild fauna and flora. An ecological network of special protected areas, known as 'Natura 2000', was specifically set up to co-ordinate nature conservation policy within the Member States. Furthermore, there are other EU-level regulations, such as the EU Birds Directive (79/409/EEC) and the EU Habitats Directive (92/43/EEC), which aim to conserve several important ecological functions, services and species in the Member States.

The choice experiment method can inform efficient and effective design of these schemes and implementation of these regulations by providing policy makers with information on the public's preferences for various social, environmental and cultural features of the landscapes, natural habitats and species. These preferences are expressed in terms of their willingness to pay (WTP). The choice experiment method also provides information on farmers' and other stakeholders' preferences (or valuation of, in terms of their willingness to accept (WTA) compensation) for various agricultural production, landscape and natural resource management methods which provide these features.

Hanley *et al.* (1998a; 2003), Li *et al.* (2004), Christie *et al.* (2006) and Bennett and Willis (2007) are examples of choice experiments that aim to investigate the public's preferences to inform the design of efficient agri-environmental and wildlife schemes and nature conservation programmes. Hanley *et al.* (1998a) report the results of a choice experiment study on Environmentally Sensitive Areas (ESA) in Scotland, where such agri-environmental schemes are being implemented. For the Breadalbane ESA, Hanley *et al.* identify farm woodlands, archaeological features, heather moors, wet grasslands and drystone walls as important landscape features which could be affected by the agri-environmental schemes. Their findings reveal that the public values agri-environmental schemes to improve farm woodlands the highest, followed by heather moors and wet grasslands, whereas their valuation of schemes that improve archaeological features are the lowest. Agri-environmental schemes in this ESA should therefore prioritise provision of woodlands on farms.

Christie *et al.* (2006) estimate the benefits the public derive from conservation of biodiversity and enhancement of farmland to inform the design of efficient agri-environment and wildlife management schemes in Cambridgeshire and Northumberland, England. They estimate the public's valuation of various biodiversity attributes including protection of familiar, rare and unfamiliar species of wildlife; restoration and recreation of habitats; and restoration of ecosystem services. Their results reveal that the majority of the respondents are WTP for biodiversity enhancements, that is, they do value biodiversity, although they are indifferent to how biodiversity protection is achieved. The public supports those biodiversity conservation policies which target rare familiar species of wildlife; recover populations of rare unfamiliar species; protect and enhance habitats; and restore ecosystem services that affect humans. These results provide support for policies such as Biodiversity Action Plans which target rare, unfamiliar species, as well as for inclusion of biodiversity conservation, habitat protection and enhancement and ecosystem restoration in agri-environment and wildlife management schemes.

Another choice experiment study that focuses on nature conservation is that of Li *et al.* (2004). They investigate the preferences of the Finnish public for increasing the area under preservation to evaluate the welfare effects of the Natura 2000 Nature Conservation Programme. Analysis of the choice experiment data reveal that there is considerable heterogeneity within the public, but overall, the Finnish public is more sensitive to a decrease in nature conservation compared to an increase, as the mean WTA for a decrease is four times higher than the mean WTP for an increase. Moreover, the marginal value of nature preservation becomes zero after a certain level (which is specified to be a 3 per cent increase in the size of the current preserved area). These results are expected to aid policy makers in their cost-benefit analysis of alternative nature preservation programmes in Finland.

The choice experiment method can also be employed to generate information on the benefits of conservation of a single species. Hanley *et al.* (2003), for example, investigate public preferences over the design of wild goose conservation policy in Islay, Scotland. Investigations of the preferences of various stakeholders, including the general Scottish public, local residents and visitors to the wildlife area, reveal that on the whole, respondents are WTP for the conservation of wild geese in Scotland. These stakeholders, however, exhibit very different preferences for how geese are conserved: the general public and visitors are WTP significant amounts for a policy which stops the shooting of geese; both visitors and local residents prefer a strategy that targets endangered species rather than all goose species, whereas the public did not differentiate between the two; and visitors prefer geese to be conserved throughout Scotland rather than at special sites. Moreover, there is evidence of utility losses for a population increase of 50 per cent; utility gains from maintaining the current population levels; and the locals are WTP for a 25 per cent increase in goose numbers. These findings have implications for the design of conservation policy for wild geese in Islay, Scotland.

Recently, Bennett and Willis (2007) carried out a choice experiment in England and Wales to investigate the public's trade-off between conservation of badgers and cattle production. They estimated the economic values that the public place on the changes in the size of the badger population; various means of managing the badger population; and controlling bovine tuberculosis (bTB) in cattle caused by badgers. They found that the public are concerned about bTB in cattle and they are WTP considerable amounts through higher taxes in order to control this disease. Even though the estimated value for the changes in the size of the badger population is relatively low, the results reveal that the public place a very high value on not having a policy that intentionally kills a large number of badgers. These results have useful policy implications for the management of badger population to control bTB in cattle in England and Wales.

A few choice experiments also study preferences for the design of agri-environmental, rural and nature conservation policies from the farmers' and other landowners' points of view. Horne and Petajisto (2003) estimated the landowners' preferences for the management of moose, which used to be an endangered species in Finland. Under a strict control of usufruct rights, moose populations have been restored, but there are large fluctuations in population levels. Preferences for moose population level are investigated for four types of landowners, divided according to their participation in moose hunting and if they had noticed considerable browsing damage in the forest. The findings reveal that even though there is considerable heterogeneity across the types of users, the majority of users, including those who benefit from hunting, would prefer a lower level of moose population, especially in the regions adjacent to the landowners' property.

Toma and Mathijs (2004) undertook a choice experiment study in the agricultural region of Cazanesti in Romania to investigate farmers' trade-offs between environmental quality, that is, water pollution from agricultural sources (mainly from farm animals), and environmental efforts. The results reveal that although farmers' preferences are heterogeneous, overall they prefer the status quo, that is, low environmental quality in the form of polluted water and no investment in environmental efforts. The agri-environmental schemes in Romania would therefore need to be designed to provide these farmers with the necessary monetary incentives to encourage them to undertake those agricultural practices that maximise environmental quality, that is, water quality in this case.

Another choice experiment study, which studies the preferences of farm families for those agricultural production methods that generate multi-functional agriculture, is by Birol *et al.* (2006a). This study investigates Hungarian farmers' preferences for using traditional farming methods on their small family farms, termed home gardens. The study investigates farmers' valuation of those agricultural practices which generate several agrobiodiversity components, including crop variety diversity, landraces, agro-diversity and organic production, which generates soil micro-organism diversity. Choice experiment data were collected from farmers located across 22 communities in three regions of Hungary. The results reveal that farmers in the most isolated communities derive the highest values from crop variety diversity, and among those, the elderly derive the highest values from landraces. Moreover, across the regions farm families that are wealthier and more educated value organic production methods most highly, followed by those who are poorer, older and located in the most isolated communities. Agro-diversity is valued highly across the country, but most highly by those farm households who manage large fields alongside home gardens, due to the complementarity between feed production in the field and livestock production in the home gardens. Overall, these results reveal that with the environmental, cultural and historical benefits they generate, home gardens should be included in the Hungarian agri-environmental schemes, and those households that value the benefits they generate the most would be the least-cost options to target for these schemes.

Chapters 3, 4, 5 and 6 in this volume present further examples of how the choice experiment method can be applied to value various attributes of the countryside and landscape, in order to inform agri-environmental policies in Ireland, England, France and Spain, respectively.

GENETICALLY MODIFIED FOOD AND FOOD LABELLING

The safety, security and origin of food are important issues in the EU, and the choice experiment method can help inform the implementation, adaptation and formation of food policy. EU regulations on genetically modified organisms (GMOs) aim to protect human health and the environment whilst ensuring the free movement of safe genetically modified (GM) products in the EU. Only GMOs and GM food or feed products that have been assessed as safe for health and the environment are authorised for use in the EU. The EU legislative framework on GMOs is considered to be one of the strictest in the world, and includes various directives and regulations, such as Directive 2001/18/EC on the deliberate release into the environment of GMOs, applying to the intentional introduction of GMOs; Regulation EC No. 1829/2003 on GM food and feed; Regulation EC No. 1946/2003 on transboundary movements of GMOs; Directive 98/81/EC on the contained use of genetically modified micro-organisms, and Regulation EC No. 1830/2003 concerning the traceability and labelling of GMOs and the traceability of food and feed products produced from GMOs.

In addition, through Council Regulations EC No. 2081/92 and 2082/92, the EU created labels known as PDO (Protected Designation of Origin), PGI (Protected Geographical Indication) and TSG (Traditional Speciality Guaranteed) to promote and protect agricultural products. These labels are expected to encourage diverse agricultural production in a rural development context, protect product names from misuse and imitation, and help provide product information to consumers.

Burton *et al.* (2001) studied British consumer attitudes towards GMOs in food and the extent to which these attitudes translate into WTP to avoid these products. The choice experiment method is suitable for investigation of this issue, since it allows for GMOs to be presented alongside a number of other potential consumer concerns (for example, on farm chemical use, food health risk and locally versus globally produced food), allowing for investigation of the trade-offs that food consumers make in real decision making. They found that GM food is an important food concern. Consumers are

WTP significant increases in their food bills to avoid GM food, and their attitudes towards organic food are useful indicators of their attitudes towards GM food. There are, however, significant differences in consumer preferences between GM technologies in which plants are modified by the introduction of genes from other plants and those GM technologies in which plants are modified by the introduction of genes from animals and plants. Their results also indicate that consumers are WTP higher food bills for a reduction in chemical use, for safer food and for locally produced food, where consumers' WTP for these attributes increases with the frequency of their purchase of organic food. A follow-up study by Rigby and Burton (2005) investigated the heterogeneity in consumer preferences further and revealed that even though the average WTP measures are not significantly different in the two studies, there is considerable heterogeneity in WTP for all but one of the attributes, which was not captured by Burton *et al.* (2001). Inclusion of the status quo in the analysis reveals that the consumers in the UK are WTP to preserve the current system, that is, a non-GM food market.

EU regulations on foodstuff, such as restrictions on GM food and hormone-treated meat, also have implications for its trade with other countries. Lusk *et al.* (2003) employed a choice experiment to compare EU (French, German and British) and US consumers' preferences for beef from hormone-treated and/or GM-fed cattle, and analysed the implications of various trade policies given the differences in consumer preferences across these countries. Their results indicate that compared to the US consumers, French consumers derive higher values from beef from cattle that have not been administered added growth hormones. There are, however, no statistically significant differences across the US, German and British consumers' WTP for non-hormone-treated beef. Overall, EU consumers derive significantly higher values from beef from cattle that have not been fed GM feed compared to their US counterparts. There is considerable heterogeneity for steak attributes among US and British consumers, whereas French and German consumers are relatively more homogenous in their preferences. These results have implications for trade policies between the US and the EU: first, the lack of differences in consumer preferences for hormone-treated beef does not justify the EU ban on its import from the US; and second, EU consumers' high WTP for non-GM-fed beef suggests that US exporters of GM foodstuff will encounter strong resistance in the EU markets.

Carlsson *et al.* (2007) conducted a choice experiment to estimate Swedish consumers' WTP for two GM-free meat products, namely chicken and beef, under a labelling regime and under a ban. They conclude that, similarly to Lusk *et al.* (2003), consumers are WTP a high price premium for livestock fed with GM-free fodder. Hence they conclude that a mandatory labelling scheme can be welfare enhancing. Moreover Carlsson *et al.* find that the difference between consumer WTP for a ban and WTP for a labelling scheme is not statistically significant. Consequently, they argue that a ban cannot be welfare enhancing if a labelling scheme is in place. These results have implications for whether or not to ban GM food or to have a labelling scheme in place.

The choice experiment method has also been employed to investigate animal welfare versus biotechnology (GM food) issues. Lagerkvist *et al.* (2006) estimate Swedish consumers' trade-offs for several pork production attributes related to animal welfare, including type of housing system, tail docking and castration, the last including the three levels: surgical castration, no castration and immunocastration. These attributes imply trade-offs between animal welfare concerns and food safety risks due to the use of biotechnology, as well as food quality (for example, taste). The findings reveal that when taste quality is controlled for, consumers accept potential food safety risks associated with biotechnology to alleviate animal welfare problems related to surgical castration. However, consumers prefer pork from surgically castrated boars over pork from non-castrated boars, suggesting that taste quality dominates animal welfare concerns. Lagerkvist *et al.* conclude that immunocastration is a socially viable alternative, and abolition of the surgical castration of pigs should be supported since immunocastration provides several potential public and agribusiness advantages, including potential cost savings in procedures, gains from higher growth rates for pigs as well as animal welfare improvements.

Several choice experiment studies explore consumers' WTP for various labelling and certification systems which signal the origin, safety or method of production of the foodstuff. Scarpa and Del Giudice (2004) investigated urban consumers' preferences for various attributes of extra-virgin olive oil in three Italian cities, namely Naples, Rome and Milan. Certification (whether PDO/PGI, organic or no certification) and geographic origin (North-Centre or South of Italy, or unknown origin) were among the attributes studied. The results indicate that consumers prefer olive oil from their own region, revealing a home bias. Moreover, there is considerable heterogeneity in consumer preferences for various certification programmes in the olive oil market. Consumer preferences for olive oil with organic certification decrease from North to South. Even though consumers' valuation of PDO/PGI dominates the organic certification in each of the three cities, the degree of dominance increases from North to South.

Another certificate of quality indication and EU recognition of regionally specific food products is the Region of Origin (ROO). Scarpa *et al.* (2005) investigate the importance of regional (both national and territorial) identity in consumer perceptions of specific food product categories.

Employing data from Italian consumers, the significance of the ROO attribute is explored for grapes, oil and oranges. The results indicate that similarly to Scarpa and Del Giudice (2004) there is home bias for all three food products, although in varying degrees. For olive oil, the domestic origin attribute is an important determinant of choice. For oranges and grapes, ROO is influential on consumer choice, however not quite as dominant, compared to organic growing techniques for oranges and ripeness for grapes. Moreover, there is significant preference heterogeneity for grapes and oil but not for oranges, providing agribusinesses with information on both the strength of market demand and taste variation. Overall, the results of this study provide valuable information for labelling food (for example, PDO food marking, organic certification) and product marketing strategies for the agribusiness industry.

Enneking (2004) studied German consumers' WTP for quality assurance schemes which aim to improve food safety in the meat sector. Consumers were presented with six different sausage brands, including a national premium brand, with and without the 'quality and safety' (Q&S) label; a national brand which exhibited a low degree of brand awareness, with and without the Q&S label; two organically produced brands; and a reduced fat brand and a low price brand, both without the Q&S label. The findings reveal that quality labelling significantly influences consumer choice, that is, consumers are WTP higher prices for food safety improvements. Sausage suppliers that indicate food safety with a Q&S label can charge up to 20 per cent more than those suppliers that do not. This result supports the recent literature indicating that certificates that aim to reduce information asymmetries in the food market are influential in product choice. Enneking concludes that the results of this study provide a case for public support of third party certification and hence for the Q&S system.

Another study that investigated food product quality attributes is that of Carlsson *et al.* (2005). In this study, consumer WTP for existing, as well as currently non-existent private and public attributes of Swedish agriculture were estimated. Six agricultural products were studied in a combination of two products per survey: chicken and ground beef; pork chops and eggs; and milk and grain. The attributes included in the choice experiment varied depending on the food product, but issues explored included, among others, labelling of farm origin and choice of husbandry; a ban on GM fodder; labelling if GM fodder is used; nutritional information (for example, omega 3 enriched eggs); free range production; and transport of animals. The findings reveal that consumers do not value animal welfare attributes similarly across livestock types studied. Moreover, the results indicate that consumers' WTP to ensure a total ban on the use of GM fodder is higher than their WTP for labelled GM food, indicating that there might be a market failure even if GM food is labelled. Surprisingly, for egg production, consumer WTP for the use of battery cages is not significantly different from their WTP for free-range eggs. In addition, consumers are WTP high premiums for some animal welfare attributes, including slower growth chickens, outdoor production of pigs and free-range barns in milk production. Consumers also prefer no or restrictive use of spraying and analysis of soil and grain for cadmium content in grain production. Overall, the data exhibit significant heterogeneity in consumer preferences, revealing important information for agribusinesses, such as the identification of market shares and niche markets. The results are also informative for food policy formulation on an array of agricultural and food issues.

Chapter 7 reports the results of a state-of-the art choice experiment on consumers' preferences for GM food and other production methods (for example, organic and free range) in the UK, and presents a thorough discussion of the policy implications of the results for GM food regulations in the EU.

WATER RESOURCES MANAGEMENT

The importance of efficient, effective, equitable and sustainable allocation of water resources in the EU, and the need for an integrated management approach to solve water quantity and quality related problems have been recognized by the EU policy makers, and are reflected in the EU's recent Water Framework Directive (WFD, 2000/60/EC). The WFD aims to protect and achieve a 'good status' for all water resources by 2015, where water resources include surface water, groundwater, inland water, rivers, lakes, transitional waters, coastal waters, wetlands and aquifers. This 'good status' is set to be achieved with a combined approach of emission limit values, quality standards and the introduction of more efficient water prices. Choice experiment studies can provide valuable information for efficient and effective establishment and implementation of several of these measures. Several noteworthy choice experiment studies have been undertaken throughout the EU to value various aspects of water resources, including their quality and quantity and ecological and recreational functions, as well as commercial uses.

A number of choice experiment studies have focused on wetland management. Willis *et al.* (2002) investigated water company consumers' trade-offs between increased security of water supply and potential environmental impacts on local wetland sites and the flows of Amberley and Pulborough brooks in south-east England. The results of this study suggest that environmental services from natural river flows (that is, river levels and bird and plant numbers and diversity in wetlands) generate substantial benefits, given that the water supply to customers was reasonably secure at the time of this study. Customers were WTP increased water charges to secure the preservation of wetland habitats. These findings highlight that the relevant authorities should recognise environmental impacts when reviewing water company prices and service standards.

Carlsson *et al.* (2003) applied a choice experiment in southern Sweden to generate information on how best to design wetlands to maximise social benefits. Investigating the public's valuation of several wetland attributes, they found that the public derives the highest benefits from higher levels of biodiversity and improved walking facilities, whereas they derive losses from improvements to surrounding vegetation, crayfish and fenced waterline attributes.

Similarly, Birol *et al.* (2006a) investigated the public's preferences for attributes of the Cheimaditida Wetland in Greece, in order to recommend sustainable management options. The results of the econometric analyses indicated that there is considerable heterogeneity in the preferences of Greek public for wetland attributes. Overall they derive significant and high values for both use and non-use values generated by the wetland, including biodiversity, open water surface area, research and education activities in the wetland and retraining of farmers to environmentally friendly farming practices. A cost-benefit analysis of alternative management options revealed that the highest total net economic benefits are reached when all attributes are managed at high levels and 150 local farmers are re-trained.

More recently, Birol and Cox (2007) estimated the local public's WTP for conservation of the Severn Estuary wetland in England. The values of various wetland management attributes were elicited, including wetland area, creation of habitats for otters, which are a threatened mammal species, number of protected bird species and number of locals employed in agriculture from irrigation water supplied by the wetland. The results reveal that there is considerable heterogeneity in the sample, though both environmental, social and economic wetland attributes generate positive and significant values. The public, however, derive significantly lower values from irrigation-related employment compared to environmental attributes. This information could help policy makers and managers of the wetland in formulating water allocation decisions that maximise social welfare.

Nunes *et al.* (2004) investigated fishermen's preferences for commercial activities, namely clam fishing, in a natural wetland, Venice lagoon in Italy. The attributes considered in this choice experiment were fishing area, fishing system employed and price of the annual permit. All these attributes are found to be significant determinants of fishermen's wetland management choices. The study also found that adopting the most environmentally friendly and traditional fishing system would result in significant welfare losses for the respondents and the population they are drawn from.

Willis *et al.* (2005) employed the choice experiment method to estimate water company customers' WTP for improvements in several services they provide in Yorkshire, England. Specifically they estimated customers' (both residential and business) WTP for improvements in the levels of 14 services, including security of supply; interruption to supply; drinking water (biological and chemical discoloration); sewage escape into property or land; odour and flies; pollution incidents; ecological quality of rivers; use of inland waters for recreation; and the water quality of bathing beaches, among others. Their analysis reveals that customers place the highest value on maintaining a good water supply, in terms of ensuring that temporary interruptions to water supply to properties are minimised. Moreover, customers also place considerable value on drinking water quality, improving the ecological quality of river water, reducing the number of properties affected by odour and flies from sewage treatment works, and finally, increase in the number of areas for recreation. Improvements to bathing water above the existing EU standard, however, have a very low value, since bathing activities are not common in the area. The findings of this study are directly relevant to water industry regulation policy in the UK, among other relevant EU-level policies.

Several choice experiment studies estimate the value of surface water quality and quantity. Hanley *et al.* (2005; 2006a) examined the public's WTP for improvements in the quality of water resources in the River Wear and River Clyde in Scotland. Their results reveal that the public derives the highest benefits from a good level of riverbank condition followed very closely by good levels of the ecology attribute, where the definition of a good level was compatible with the conditions set by the WFD for a good ecological quality status of rivers. Similarly, Hanley *et al.* (2006b) valued improvements in river ecology in the Motray and Brothock catchments in Scotland. They investigated the public's WTP for ecological improvements, flow rate and employment. The highest WTP is estimated to be for improvement in the ecology of the rivers, whereas WTP for improvements in river flow conditions and employment in local farms are found to be lower, but significant.

Alvarez-Farizo *et al.* (2007) evaluated the public's valuation of attaining good ecological status for the River Cidacos in Spain, according to the requirements of the WFD. Various river management attributes, including aesthetic and environmental aspects of the river's ecology as well as the quantity and quality of urban water supplies, were valued in this choice experiment. The results of the analysis reveal that all of these attributes are significant factors in affecting individual choice. Furthermore the members of the public interviewed did not reveal a difference in behaviour when acting in their own interest, compared to their behaviour when acting in the collective interest.

Hasler *et al.* (2005) employed the choice experiment method to value groundwater protection in Denmark. Specifically, the values of two qualitative attributes related to drinking water quality and aquatic environment quality were investigated. The findings reveal that both of these attributes significantly affect public utility. The Danish public therefore reveal strong preferences for naturally clean groundwater as well as good ecological conditions and purified water. Statistical tests disclosed that there is no dominant attribute and respondents are willing to trade among the levels of the attributes.

The choice experiment method was also applied in the context of angling, a recreational activity dependent on water resources. Paulrud and Laitila (2004) valued management policies for recreational angling in the Kaitum River in Sweden using catches of different species at different sizes as attributes. Their analysis points to the conclusion that although the size and number of the catch is an important determinant in individual decision making, there is no significant difference in the valuations of different species of fish. Furthermore, the impacts on individual welfare from alternative policies vary from negative to positive depending on the size of the permitted catch number.

Several choice experiment studies included characteristics of water resources as attributes in the context of valuation exercises of wider environmental goods. Colombo *et al.* (2005; 2006; 2007), for example, estimated the value of reducing soil erosion in Spain. Among the attributes used in this study, surface and ground water quality were included alongside other attributes such as landscape change and flora and fauna quality. Their results indicate that water quality is a significant factor affecting the public's choice of policy alternatives for soil conservation. Furthermore, the public is WTP the most for high levels of water quality, followed by improvements in landscape desertification.

Travisi and Nijkamp (2004) included groundwater contamination from fertilizers and pesticides as an attribute in a choice experiment which investigated Milanese residents' WTP for agricultural environmental safety. The results indicate that the impact of the groundwater contamination attribute on utility is highly significant, where reducing groundwater contamination by 50 per cent raises the probability of choosing the agricultural scenario by 2 per cent. Milanese residents are also found to value improvements in biodiversity levels and reductions in impacts on human health significantly and highly.

Applications of the choice experiment method to water resources management issues are also included in this volume. Chapter 11 estimates the

Greek public's valuation of the sustainable management of the Cheimaditida Wetland in Greece, and Chapter 12 investigates the residents' trade-offs between flood risk reduction and recreational and biodiversity attributes of rivers in the Upper Silesia Region in Poland. These chapters also discuss the implications of their results for informing EU WFD.

FOREST MANAGEMENT

The Forestry Strategy of the EU establishes a framework for forest-related actions in support of sustainable forest management based on the co-ordination of the forest policies of the Member States and Community policies, and initiatives relevant to forests and forestry. The Strategy emphasises the importance of the multifunctional role of forests and sustainable forest management for the development of society. The EU Habitats Directive and Natura 2000 are also relevant to the management of European forests.

Hanley *et al.* (1998b) investigated the UK public's preferences for various forest attributes to inform forest management policies that maximise the social value of forestry. The forest landscape management attributes valued in this choice experiment included species diversity, how the forest was felled and the shape of plantations when seen at a distance. Their results indicate that the public prefers improvements in all of these attributes, where the modification of forests to an organic shape was most highly valued, followed by a small-scale felling regime and high species diversity.

Lehtonen *et al.* (2003) employed the choice experiment method to estimate the non-market benefits of forest conservation in Finland. Among the attributes they used were information and education, number of endangered species, conservation contracts and conservation areas. All of these attributes, except information and education, are found to affect individual utility. Regarding the policy implications, the authors state that the estimated benefits of the conservation plans are in excess of their costs of implementation, even if the forest in question is at an age close to commercial maturity.

Horne *et al.* (2005) estimated visitors' valuation of five forest municipal recreation sites around Helsinki. Alternative models specific to each recreational site were estimated. The findings of this study indicate that the public values species richness significantly across all the sites studied. In another study on forestry in Finland, Horne (2006) investigated private forest owners' preferences for various characteristics of voluntary contracts for forest biodiversity conversation. Forest owners were asked to state their WTA compensation for applying conservation measures that would impose restrictions on forest use for given time horizons. The results show the sensitivity of welfare to changes in the contractual characteristics of forest management.

Chapters 8, 9 and 10 in this volume estimate various stakeholders' valuations of use (recreational) and non-use (biodiversity) attributes of forests in Finland, Spain and the UK respectively, and discuss implications for the EU Forest Action Plan as well as for those EU regulations and directives related to biodiversity conservation.

GREEN ENERGY, ENVIRONMENTAL POLLUTION AND WASTE MANAGEMENT

The EU is at the forefront of international efforts to combat climate change and played a key role in the development of the Kyoto Protocol. As a signatory to the Kyoto Protocol, the EU has agreed to cut its greenhouse gas emissions to 8 per cent below 1990 levels by 2008–2012. As one of the initiatives to reach this target, the EU aims to increase the fraction of electricity consumption from renewable sources to 12 per cent by 2010 according to Directive 2001/77/EC. All Member States have adopted national targets for the share of electricity production from renewable energy sources. Information on various social and environmental costs and benefits of alternative renewable energy sources are needed, and a few noteworthy choice experiment studies have been conducted to evaluate the costs and benefits of various renewable energy sources.

Utilisation of wind power by means of wind farm construction has received considerable attention, mainly due to these farms' highly visible effects on local landscapes. Álvarez-Farizo and Hanley (2002) examined the social costs of constructing wind farms in La Plana of Zaragoza, Spain. The impacts of wind farm construction on the protection of cliffs, fauna and flora and landscape were investigated. The main findings reveal that adverse environmental impacts associated with the construction of wind farms generate significant social costs, and the public values impacts on flora and fauna more highly than impacts on cliffs and landscape.

In two papers, Sundqvist (2002a, 2002b) examined residential and non-residential users' valuation of the environmental impacts of hydropower in Sweden. In both surveys, a measure of water quantity, namely the downstream water level, was included. Neither group is found to derive significant benefits from water quantity, implying that the downstream water level does not affect individuals' or businesses' choice of hydropower production arrangements.

Bergmann *et al.* (2006) investigated the environmental and social costs and benefits of renewable energy investments in Scotland. Renewable technologies considered in this study included hydro, on-shore and off-shore wind power and biomass. The magnitude and significance of several external costs and benefits of renewable energy investments were estimated, including those pertaining to landscape quality, and wildlife and air quality, as well as creation of long-term employment. The findings indicate that the public derives considerable benefits from those renewable energy investments that avoid impacts on landscapes and wildlife, as well as those that do not create additional air pollution. Even though these preferences do not vary by income level, there is considerable heterogeneity between urban and rural households, the latter deriving higher values from wildlife benefits, reductions in air pollution and employment creation. The value estimates of this choice experiment are employed to calculate and compare the benefits generated by alternative renewable energy investments. The findings suggest that the Scottish public derive the highest benefits from off-shore wind farms, followed by biomass power plants, whereas they derive large costs from on-shore wind farms.

The EC Landfill Directive (1999/31/EC) aims to improve standards of landfilling across Europe, and sets out successive targets for reducing biodegradable municipal waste to 75 per cent of the 1995 baseline by 2010, 50 per cent by 2013 and 35 per cent by 2020. Choice experiment studies were also employed to inform the management of municipal solid waste (MSW) in EU countries.

Garrod and Willis (1998) estimated the impact on local residents of a well-established landfill waste disposal facility in England. Residents' WTP to reduce the levels of several types of disamenities (for example, dust, litter, noise, smell) arising from the site were estimated. The results indicate that the cost of the landfill in terms of lost amenity value to local residents is relatively low. Disamenity caused by dust and litter is higher than that caused by odour, although there is no significant difference. Disamenity caused by noise, however, was not statistically significant. The authors conclude that the residents are not WTP higher taxes to reduce the disamenity levels because they have become used to them and learnt to accept them. The relatively small impact of externalities from the landfill site is not surprising because in the UK planning permission is only given to those landfills whose adverse effect on the environment and amenity is less than any environmental gains arising from the landfill site. Garrod and Willis suggest that an *ex post* choice experiment shortly after the opening of a landfill site would give a more realistic measure of the cost of its disamenities.

The UK has one of the poorest records in the EU with regard to the proportion of MSW that is sent to landfills. Failure to meet the targets of the Landfill Directive would mean that the UK could face a very high non-compliance fine to be paid by the local authorities, which are deemed responsible for the UK's failure to meet its targets. Local authorities therefore need information on how to prioritise the recycling services and facilities they offer to their residents. Karousakis and Birol (forthcoming) employed a choice experiment in several London boroughs to examine the determinants of household recycling behaviour and to estimate the recycling service attributes that are valued most highly by the public. Their results show that households across London are WTP significantly higher monthly council taxes for an increase in the number of dry materials collected. Moreover, they are also WTP higher taxes for compost collection, a service that was not available in most of the London boroughs when the study was implemented.

There are also several choice experiment studies from transport literature which have direct implications for improving local environmental quality (for example, noise pollution, regulated by Directive 2002/49/EC on the assessment and management of environmental noise, and air pollution, regulated by Directive 96/62/EC on ambient air quality assessment and management) as well as indirect implications for wider environmental problems, such as climate change. Some of the most notable studies carried out in EU countries include Wardman *et al.* (1997), Carlsson *et al.* (2004), Wardman and Bristow (2004), Hiselius (2005) and Arsenio *et al.* (2006)

Wardman *et al.* (1997) evaluated the impacts and benefits of improved cycling facilities in Leeds, England. Value estimates of the benefits of unsegregated cycle lanes and segregated cycle paths reveal that it is important to improve the safety of cycling and distance cyclists from the noise and pollution of urban traffic. The authors conclude that investment in cycling facilities could lead to significant increases in cycling, such that even costly investments may prove to be worthwhile in an economic evaluation of user benefits. The results, however, do not suggest that such investments could on their own achieve target levels of increased cycle use. Wardman *et al.* argue that other traffic management and restraint measures are needed in order to achieve target levels of increased cycle use. The results of this study are expected to inform UK policy makers in devising policies and projects to meet the National Cycling Strategy targets, which are put in place to alleviate traffic congestion and environmental pollution.

Wardman and Bristow (2004) estimated households' valuation of traffic-related noise levels and air quality in Edinburgh, Scotland. Their findings show that variations in air quality are valued more highly than variations in noise, where households' valuations vary according to their size, income level and whether or not they have children. Overall, it was found that relatively large proportions of residents experience a noisy environment and poor air quality where improvements in noise and air quality are quality of life priorities.

Carlsson *et al.* (2004) estimated the value of noise disturbance from air traffic in Stockholm, Sweden. They employed two surveys to estimate the value of an increase and decrease in the number of flights per day. In particular, they investigated the time of day and day of the week of the air traffic movements. The results show that a significant proportion of respondents prefer the current situation. Moreover, a larger number of non-traders and lower WTP levels were found in the 'decrease' version of the survey. This finding indicates the existence of endowment effects according to which individuals are reluctant to pay for improvements compared to the status quo.

Hiselius (2005) investigated the public's preferences for transportation of hazardous materials by railway in two Swedish cities. The public's valuations of the quantity of hazardous material transferred, the timing of the transport and the classification of the hazardous material were estimated. The results show that all attributes are significant factors affecting individual scenario choice.

Arsenio *et al.* (2006) examined the preferences for inner city road traffic noise reductions in Portugal. Their results reveal self-selectivity, where those with higher marginal values for noise tend to live in quieter apartments. The authors conclude that this finding suggests that the common use of a cut-off level of noise below which no annoyance or cost is deemed to occur may be inappropriate as it will undervalue the preferences of those in quiet areas who are WTP relatively large amounts to preserve that quiet.

In this book, residents' preferences for local environmental quality, namely their valuation of rail noise abatement, are investigated in Chapter 13. That chapter reports the results of a case study from Italy and discusses the implications of the results for EU- and national-level noise pollution management regulations.

CONCLUSIONS

This chapter has reviewed some of the most noteworthy examples of choice experiment applications carried out in the EU countries to date. This review is by no means exhaustive, but merely serves to highlight how this method can be applied to tackle various environmental, agricultural, food labelling and natural resource management issues. Furthermore, the chapter draws attention to how this method can inform the implementation, adaptation and development of various EU policies, regulations and directives. A summary of all the studies reviewed above can be found in Table A2.1.

The next chapters of this book present state-of-the-art applications of the choice experiment method to various environmental, agricultural, food and natural resource management issues, and discusses in detail how their results could inform EU policies, regulations and directives.

APPENDIX

Table A2.1 Summary of choice experiment studies carried out in the EU to inform environmental, agricultural, food and natural resources management policies

Authors (year)	Environmental Good Valued	Site, Country	Attributes	Sample Size and Survey Mode	Econometric Specification	WTP/WTA Estimates
Choice Experiment Studies of Agri-Environmental Schemes, Wildlife and Nature Conservation						
Hanley, MacMillan, Wright, Bullock, Simpson, Parsisson and Crabtree (1998)	Environmentally Sensitive Areas	Scotland	Farm woodlands; archaeological features; heather moors; wet grasslands; drystone walls; annual tax	Face to face interviews with 256 members of the public	Conditional Logit	WTP in £/household/year: 50.46 for farm woodlands; 6.65 for archaeological features; 22.95 for heather moors; 20.85 for wet grasslands; 11.30 for drystone walls.
Hanley, MacMillan, Patterson and Wright (2003)	Wild goose conservation	Islay, Scotland	Species; means of control; location; population change; tax	Face to face interviews with 426 members of the public, 205 local residents and 212 visitors	Conditional Logit	WTP in £/household/year: Scottish public (visitors): 9.23 (6.74) to stop shooting; visitors (residents)

						16.5 (12.26) for conserving endangered species only; visitors 6.73 for conservation in all sites of Scotland and 6.73 for 25% rise in population; residents – 29.67 if goose population rose by 50%; 24.98 to avoid 10% fall in population.
Horne and Petäjistö (2003)	Moose management	Finland	Moose population in Finland; moose population in the area adjacent to the farm; rent from the hunting club; deductibles covered by the landowner; % of compensation	Mail survey of 765 landowners	Conditional Logit	WTA in € for 40% reduction in the moose population level in Finland and 40% reduction in moose population in the region adjacent to the property: 204 for those who noticed browsing damage and did not hunt; 137 for those who did not notice

Table A2.1 (continued)

Authors (year)	Environmental Good Valued	Site, Country	Attributes	Sample Size and Survey Mode	Econometric Specification	WTP/WTA Estimates
						browsing damage and did not hunt: 84 for those who noticed browsing damage and hunted.
Li, Kuuluvainen, Pouta, Rekola, Tahvonen (2004)	Nature conservation	Finland	Nature conservation area; types of nature conserved (swamps, shores, wetlands, forests); income tax	Mail survey of 562 members of the public	Nested Logit with interactions	WTP in FIM/household/ year: 782 for 3% increase in nature preservation and –3422 for 3% reduction.
Toma and Mathijs (2004)	Water pollution from agriculture	Romania	Environmental (water) quality; environmental effort	Face to face interviews with 99 farm households	Binary Logit with interactions	57% chose option with polluted environmental (water) quality and no environmental effort.
Birol, Smale, Gyovai (2006)	Agro-biodiversity conservation	Devevanya, Orseg-Vend and Szatmar Bereg Environmentally	Crop variety diversity; landrace cultivation; agro-diversity;	Face to face interviews with 104 farmers in Devevanya,	Conditional Logit with interactions	WTA in €/household/ year: Devevanya ESA: 404 for agro-diversity; 235 for organic production;

		Sensitive Areas (ESAs), Hungary	organic production; % of household food consumption obtained from the home garden	109 farmers in Orseg-Vend and 110 farmers in Szatmar Bereg		Orseg-Vend ESA: 111 per crop variety; 95 for landrace cultivation; 100 for agro-diversity; Szatmar Bereg ESA: 141 per crop variety; 83 for landrace cultivation; 198 for agro-diversity; 76 for organic production.
Christie, Hanley, Warren, Murphy, Wright and Hyde (2006)	Biodiversity conservation	Cambridgeshire and Northumberland, England	Familiar species of wildlife; rare, unfamiliar species of wildlife; habitat quality; ecosystem process; annual tax	Face to face interviews with 343 members of the public in Cambridgeshire and 391 members of the public in Northumberland	Conditional Logit	WTP in £/household/year: Cambridgeshire (Northumberland): 35.65 (90.59) for protecting rare familiar species; 93.49 (97.71) for protecting both rare and common species; 34.4 (71.15) for habitat restoration and 61.36 (74) for habitat recreation; 53.62 (105.22) for recovery of ecosystem

Table A2.1 (continued)

Authors (year)	Environmental Good Valued	Site, Country	Attributes	Sample Size and Survey Mode	Econometric Specification	WTP/WTA Estimates
						services relevant for humans; 42.21 for recovery of all ecosystems; 115.15 (189.05) for ensuring recovery of, and −46.68 for slowing down decline of rare unfamiliar species.
Bennett and Willis (2007)	Badger conservation vs control of bovine tuberculosis (bTB) in cattle	England and Wales	Badger populations; management strategy; cattle with bTB slaughtered per year; increase in tax	Telephone interviews with 402 members of the public	Conditional Logit	WTP in £/household/year: 0.10 for every additional 100 000 badgers; 1.52 for every 10 000 reduction in cattle slaughtered; 68.31 not to have badger culling; 13.58 to have badger contraception

						and 22.40 to have badger tunnels. Aggregating over the populations of England and Wales in £: 22/badger; 3298/animal for reduction in cattle slaughtered due to bTB; 1480 m total to avoid badger culling.
Choice Experiment Studies of Genetically Modified Food and Food Labelling						
Burton, Rigby, Young and James (2001)	Food production systems	Manchester, England	Weekly food bill; production technology; on-farm chemical use; food miles; food health risk	Drop-off and collect surveys with 228 members of the public	Conditional Logit with interactions	WTP in % change in food bill: 26.25–471.95 for GM free diet, depending on gender; 13–103.2 for a 10% reduction in chemical use; 5.2–27.10 for a 10% reduction in food miles; 21.35–41.6 for a reduction in food risk from 1/10 000 to1/15 000. All estimates vary depending on whether

Table A2.1 (continued)

Authors (year)	Environmental Good Valued	Site, Country	Attributes	Sample Size and Survey Mode	Econometric Specification	WTP/WTA Estimates
						infrequent, occasional or committed purchasers of organic food.
Lusk, Roosen and Fox (2003)	Beef production	France, Germany, UK and USA	Marbling; tenderness; animal administered growth hormones; animal fed GM corn; price	Mail survey of 93 members of the public in France, 45 in Germany, 109 in UK and 566 in USA	Conditional Logit and Random Parameter Logit	WTP in $ per pound of beef from cattle not administered growth hormones: France: 9.94; Germany: 7.29; UK: 7.39; USA: 8.12. WTP in $ per pound of beef from cattle not fed GM: France: 9.32; Germany: 7.67; UK: 6.31; USA: 3.31.
Enneking (2004)	Labelling of packaged liver sausages	Four cities in Northern Germany	Six different brands of sausage with organic, low fat and low degree of brand	Computer-assisted face to face interviews with 321 consumers	Conditional Logit	WTP €0.34 for Q&S label attached to a national premium brand, and WTP $0.11 for Q&S label attached to a

			awareness attributes; Q&S label price	of packaged liver sausages		national brand with low degree of brand awareness.
Scarpa and Del Giudice (2004)	Extra-virgin olive oil	Milan, Rome and Naples, Italy	Appearance; geographic origin; certification; price	Face to face interviews with 300 consumers of olive oil	Random Parameter Logit	Predicted % of consumers with negative preferences: Milan: 21.36 for oil from South; 0 for oil from North/Centre; 18.68 for organic oil; 18.1 for PDO/PGI label; Rome: 15.23 for oil from South; 7.09 for oil from North/Centre; 18.25 for organic oil; 11.63 for PDO/PGI label; Naples: 12.81 for oil from South; 5.68 for oil from North/Centre; 34.56 for organic oil; 22.95 for PDO/PGI label.
Carlsson, Frykblom and Lagerkvist (2005)	Production of six agricultural products: chicken	Sweden	Label; fodder; outdoor production; transport; growth; cages;	Mail survey of 710 members of the public	Random Parameter Logit	WTP in SEK/kg for chicken: 7.92 for label if GM fodder used; 15.73 for ban of GM fodder; 6.74 for herd

Table A2.1 (continued)

Authors (year)	Environmental Good Valued	Site, Country	Attributes	Sample Size and Survey Mode	Econometric Specification	WTP/WTA Estimates
	and ground beef; pork chops and eggs; and milk and grain		omega 3; barn system; cow–calf together; spraying; cadmium; cost			kept outdoors; −3.31 for mobile slaughter house; 11.28 for slower growth chickens. WTP in SEK/kg for beef: 7.31 for labelling of farm origin and choice of husbandry; 6.17 for label if GM fodder used; 18.74 for ban of GM fodder; 1.82 for herd kept outdoors; 3.77 for mobile slaughter house. WTP in SEK/kg for pigs: 3.54 for labelling of farm origin and choice of husbandry; 3.45 for label if GM fodder used; 21.69 for ban of GM fodder;

27.5 for herd kept outdoors; 3.17 for mobile slaughter house. WTP in SEK/dozen for eggs: 4.94 for label if GM fodder used; 13.39 battery cages and free-range coexist; 21.11 battery cages banned; 2.12 omega 3 enriched. WTP in SEK/litres for milk: 3.46 for label if GM fodder used; 6.52 for ban of GM fodder; 2.67 for free range indoor; 1.43 for cow–calf together 8–12 weeks. WTP in SEK/2kg for grain: 4.16 for labelling of farm origin and choice of husbandry; 6.8 for restrictive use of spraying; 5.5 for soil and grain analysed for cadmium.

Table A2.1 (continued)

Authors (year)	Environmental Good Valued	Site, Country	Attributes	Sample Size and Survey Mode	Econometric Specification	WTP/WTA Estimates
Rigby and Burton (2005)	Food production system	Manchester, England	Weekly food bill; production technology; on-farm chemical use; food miles; food health risk	Drop-off and collect surveys with 228 members of the public	Random Parameter Logit with interactions	WTP in % change in food bill: 41.7–462.3 for GM free diet, depending on gender; 11.7–60.2 for a 10% reduction in chemical use; 4.6–22.4 for a 10% reduction in food miles; 21.9–36.3 for a reduction in food risk from 1/10 000 to 1/15 000. All estimates vary depending on whether infrequent, occasional or committed purchasers of organic food.
Scarpa, Philippidis and	Production and labelling	Italy	Packaging attributes; production	Computer-administered surveys	Conditional Logit, Random	66.33% of households prefer domestic table grapes,

Spalatro (2005)	of grapes, oil, oranges		attributes (integrated pest management; organic production; national product; regional origin; quality certified); price	with 2000 members of the public	Parameter Logit and Random Parameter Logit with interactions	and 77.56% of households prefer territorial certification of origin for olive oil, supporting the notion of home bias.
Lagerkvist, Carlsson and Viske (2006)	Pork production	Sweden	Type of housing system; tail docking; fixation; castration; price	Mail survey of 286 members of the public	Binary Heteroske-dastic Logit	WTP in SEK/kg: for indoors (plenty of straw): 34.4; outdoors: 47.9; no castration: −15.9; immunocastration: 15.7; no tail docking (tail biting can occur): –10.6; no tail docking (tail biting prevented): 7.9; fixation at delivery: 48.6; fixation banned: 54.3.
Carlsson, Frykblom and Lagerkvist (2007)	Chicken and beef production	Sweden	Label; fodder; outdoor; transport; growth; price	Mail survey of 395 members of the public with an	Random Parameter Logit	WTP in SEK/kg for chicken (beef): without opt-out: GM fodder not used but allowed: 30.13 (32.54); use of

Table A2.1 (continued)

Authors (year)	Environmental Good Valued	Site, Country	Attributes	Sample Size and Survey Mode	Econometric Specification	WTP/WTA Estimates
				opt-out option and 362 without opt-out option		GM fodder banned: 30.59 (30.12); with opt-out: GM fodder not used but allowed: 26.75 (38.95); use of GM fodder banned: 24.31 (34.69).
Choice Experiment Studies on Water Resources Management						
Sundqvist (2002a)	Alternative hydroproduction effects	Sweden	Downstream water level; erosion and vegetation; fish; electricity price/kWh	Mail survey of 479 residential users	Random Effects Probit	WTP in SEK/kWh: water level increase by 25%: 0.54; water level increase by 50%: −0.56.
Sundqvist (2002b)	Alternative hydroproduction effects	Sweden	Downstream water level; erosion and vegetation; fish; electricity price/kWh	Mail survey of 479 non-residential users	Random Effects Probit	WTP in SEK/kWh: water level increase by 25%: 0.77; water level increase by 50%: 0.71.
Willis, McMahon,	Water services vs	Amberley and	Frequency of hosepipe	Face to face	Conditional Logit	WTP in £: 1.42 for 1% change in

Garrod and Powe (2002)	environment	Pulborough brooks, England	bans; risk of water supply interruptions; bird and plant diversity; river levels	interviews with 412 members of the public		number of birds and plant diversity; 4.27 for change in river flows.
Carlsson, Frykblom and Liljenstolpe (2003)	Wetland management	Staffanstorp wetland, Sweden	Surrounding vegetation; fish; biodiversity; fenced waterline; crayfish; walking facilities; cost	Mail survey of 468 members of the public	Random Parameter Logit	WTP in SEK: high biodiversity: 719.75; medium biodiversity: 493.76; fish: 292.49; fenced waterline: −183.55; crayfish: −56.30; walking facilities: 601.41.
Nunes, Rossetto and de Blaeij (2004)	Clam fishing management	Venice Lagoon, Italy	Fishing area; fishing system; annual permit	Face to face interviews with 114 members of the public	Conditional Logit with Interactions	WTP €/year model without interactions (with interactions): Fishing area: 568 (811); fishing system: 1005 (2546).
Paulrud and Laitila (2004)	Sport fishing management	Kaitum River, Sweden	Catch/day of grayling; catch/day of brown	Mail survey with 569 completed responses over	Conditional Logit	In SEK/day: 16.81 for grayling and brown trout <30cm; 109.39 for grayling and brown

Table A2.1 (continued)

Authors (year)	Environmental Good Valued	Site, Country	Attributes	Sample Size and Survey Mode	Econometric Specification	WTP/WTA Estimates
			trout; bag limit/day of grayling; Bag limit/day of brown trout; fee/day	three years		trout 30–40cm; 333.36 for grayling and brown trout >40cm; 43.50 for bag limit grayling and brown trout.
Travisi and Nijkamp (2004)	Agricultural environmental safety	Milan, Italy	Biodiversity; human health; groundwater contamination; food expenditure household/month	Drop-off and collect surveys of 302 members of the public	Conditional Logit	WTP in €/household/month: biodiversity: 23.01–24.57; human health: 2.5–3.14; groundwater contamination: 12.28–16.21.
Colombo, Hanley and Calatrava-Requena (2005)	Soil conservation	Andalusia, Spain	Landscape change; water quality; flora and fauna quality; jobs created; area; tax	Face to face interviews with 310 members of the public	Conditional Logit and Random Parameter Logit	WTP in €: 21.865 for improvement of water quality to medium level; 29.352 for improvement of water quality to high level; 17.428 for small improvement in landscape

						desertification; 22.88 for moderate improvement in landscape desertification; 14.922 for medium flora and fauna quality; 17.765 for high flora and fauna quality.
Hanley, Adamowicz and Wright (2005)	Water quality improvements	River Wear, England	Ecology; aesthetics; riverbank condition; water rates	Face to face interviews with 340 members of the public	Random Parameter Logit	WTP in £ for improvements: 11.12 for ecology; 11.10 for aesthetics; 11.94 for riverbank condition.
Hasler, Lundhede, Martinsen, Neye and Schoi (2005)	Groundwater protection	Denmark	Drinking water quality; aquatic environment quality; cost	Mail survey with 584 members of the public	Conditional Logit	WTP in DKK for model with (without) ASC: 1899 (2855) for naturally clean groundwater; 912 (1777) for purified groundwater; 1204 (1818) for very good condition; −1759 (−1627) for bad conditions.
Willis, Scarpa	Water company	Yorkshire, England	Security of supply;	1000 residential	Conditional Logit	WTP in £/household for the Conditional

Table A2.1 (continued)

Authors (year)	Environmental Good Valued	Site, Country	Attributes	Sample Size and Survey Mode	Econometric Specification	WTP/WTA Estimates
and Acutt (2005)	service improvements		interruption to supply; drinking water (biological and chemical); drinking water (discoloration); leakage; inadequate pressure; lead; sewage escape into property; sewage escape to land; odour and flies; pollution incidents; ecological quality of rivers; use of inland waters	customers and 500 businesses	(quadratic), Nested Logit (quadratic); Random Parameter Logit	Logit Model: 0.317 for security of supply; 2.275 for interruption to supply; 0.025 for drinking water (biological and chemical); 0.783 for drinking water (discoloration); 0.697 for leakage; 1.536 for inadequate pressure; 0.148 for lead; 0.025 for sewage escape into property; 0.106 sewage escape to land; 0.935 for odour and flies; 0.03 for pollution incidents; 0.637 for ecological quality of rivers; 0.415 for use of inland waters for recreation;

			for recreation; bathing beaches water quality; cost			0.081 for bathing beaches water quality.
Birol, Karousakis and Koundouri (2006)	Wetland management	Cheimaditida Wetland, Greece	Biodiversity; open water surface area; research and education; retraining of farmers, one-off tax	Face to face interviews with 407 members of the public	Conditional Logit, Random Parameter Logit, Random Parameter Logit with interactions and Latent Class	WTP €/respondent: biodiversity: 7.7; open water surface area: 8.45; research and education: 3.93; retraining of farmers: 0.127/farmer.
Hanley, Wright and Alvarez-Farizo (2006)	Water quality improvements	River Clyde and River Wear, Scotland	Ecology; aesthetics; riverbank condition; water rates	Face to face interviews with 210 members of the public	Random Parameter Logit	WTP in £ for improvements: for River Clyde (Wear) 38.70 (12.19) for ecology; 28.57 (12.07) for aesthetics; 42.99 (12.67) for riverbank condition. Pooled sample: 18.19 for ecology; 15.68 for aesthetics; 19.57 for riverbank condition.

Table A2.1 (continued)

Authors (year)	Environmental Good Valued	Site, Country	Attributes	Sample Size and Survey Mode	Econometric Specification	WTP/WTA Estimates
Hanley, Colombo, Tinch, Black, and Aftab (2006)	Water quality improvements	Motray and Brothock catchments, Scotland	Ecological improvement; flow rate; employment; water rates	Mail survey of 348 residents of Motray catchment and 344 residents of Brothock catchment	Random Parameter Logit	WTP in £: 10.11 for slight ecological improvement; 25.65 for big ecological improvement; 3.40 for employment; 3.50 for flow rate.
Alvarez-Farizo, Hanley, Barberán and Lázaro (2007)	Water quality improvements	Cidacos River, Spain	Habitat; river surroundings; water supplies for urban and agricultural services; monthly shopping bill	Face to face interviews with 24 experts	Conditional Logit with interactions	WTP in €/households/month: 4.6–7.8 for habitat; 3.7–5.2 for river surroundings; 3.2–6.1 for water supplies for urban and agricultural services.
Birol and Cox (2007)	Wetland management	Severn Estuary, England	Wetland area; otter holt creation; no. of protected bird species; irrigation-related	Face to face interviews with 100 members of the public	Conditional Logit with interaction	WTP in £/person on average: 13.8 for wetland area/ha; 31.6 for otter holt creation; 1.2 for one more protected bird species; 0.06 per

			employment; water rates			person in irrigation-related employment.
Choice Experiment Studies on Forest Resources Management						
Hanley, Wright and Adamowicz (1998)	Forest landscape management	UK	Felling regime; shape; species diversity; tax	Face to face interviews with 181 members of the public	Conditional Logit	WTP for improvements in £/household/year: 12.89 for felling regime; 13.90 for shape; 11.36 for species diversity.
Lehtonen, Kuuluvainen, Pouta, Rekola and Li (2003)	Forest conservation	Southern Finland	Information and education; conservation contracts; conservation areas; biotopes at favourable levels of conservation; no. of endangered species; annual income tax	Mail survey of 1500 members of the public	Nested Logit	WTP in €/year: information and education: 0.3; conservation contracts: 5.5; conservation areas: 4.15; no. of endangered species: −0.3.
Horne, Boxall, and Adamowicz (2005)	Forest management	Helsinki, Finland	Species richness in site; average species richness; variance of species richness;	Face to face interviews with 431 visitors	Conditional Logit	Welfare impact of new management scenario with changes in scenery and species richness is a loss of −€10.36, however this value varies from €34.27

Table A2.1 (continued)

Authors (year)	Environmental Good Valued	Site, Country	Attributes	Sample Size and Survey Mode	Econometric Specification	WTP/WTA Estimates
			scenery at each site; change in municipal taxes			to −€50.11 depending on the sub-group and their preferences for different scenery.
Horne (2006)	Forest biodiversity conservation	Southern Finland	Initiator of the contract; restrictions on forest use; duration of the contract; cancellation policy; compensation ha/year	Mail survey with 1181 usable responses	Conditional Logit	Average compensation for forest conservation estimated at €224/ha/year.
Choice Experiment Studies of Green Energy, Environmental Pollution and Waste Management						
Wardman, Hatfield and Page (1997)	Transport mode and cycling facilities	Leeds, England	Car/bus time; car/bus cost; cycle time;	Face to face interviews and drop-off	Conditional Logit	Estimated values of time for cycling pence/min: 9.58–21.28 for no facilities; 7.53–19.24 for unsegregated

			cycle facilities en route; weather; facilities at destination	and collect surveys with 221 members of the public		facilities; 2.85–14.58 for segregated facilities, depending on the weather conditions. Estimated value of time for car/bus pence/min: 1.54.
Garrod and Willis (1998)	Landfill waste disposal	Crawcrook Quarry and Landfill Site, England	Reduction in number of days per year with noise disturbance; smell; dust and litter; council tax/household/year	Face to face surveys with 73 local residents	Conditional Logit	WTP £/household/day: 0.11–0.18 (depending on the model specification) to reduce number of days when respondent suffers from dust and windblown litter from the site; 0.09–0.14 (depending on the model specification) to reduce number of days when respondent can smell the site from his/her home.
Alvarez-Farizo and Hanley (2002)	Environmental impacts from wind farm construction	La Plana of Zaragoza, Spain	Protection of cliffs; protection of flora and fauna; protection of landscape; increase in taxes	Face to face interviews with 488 members of the public	Conditional Logit	WTP Pta/year: 3580 for cliff protection; 6290 for fauna and flora protection; 6161 for landscape protection.

Table A2.1 (continued)

Authors (year)	Environmental Good Valued	Site, Country	Attributes	Sample Size and Survey Mode	Econometric Specification	WTP/WTA Estimates
Carlsson, Lampi and Martinsson (2004)	Air traffic noise reduction	Stockholm, Sweden	Decreases in: early morning flights; morning flights; afternoon flights; evening flights; during weekdays and weekends	Mail survey of 717 residents	Mixed Logit	WTP SEK/month for increase (decrease): weekdays: early morning: 2.21–4.48 (4.62–1.18); morning: 7.85–28.60 (−11.11to −4.44); afternoon: −15.12–0.20 (−13.65–2.64); evening: 3.15–8.86 (8.48–19.96). weekends: morning: 0.52–7.81 (10.27–29.93); afternoon: −2.08–8.33 (–5.32–16.18); evening: 3.82–8.68 (14.81–35.66).
Wardman and Bristow (2004)	Traffic-related noise and air quality	Edinburgh, Scotland	Air quality; noise; car times; bus times; cost	Face to face interviews with 398 members of the public	Conditional Logit with interactions	WTP/household/pence/week: 6.9–42.4 for 1% increase in air quality; 0–24.2 for 1% improvement in noise level, depending

						on the household income level, size and composition.
Hiselius (2005)	Transportation of hazardous materials by railway	Lund and Borlänge, Sweden	Number of wagons with hazardous material; time of transport; classification of hazardous material; altered housing cost per month	Mail survey of 319 residents in Lund and 180 residents in Borlänge	Random Parameter Logit	SEK/month for low income (medium-high income) households: number of wagons: twice: WTA 246 (278); half: WTP 75 (85); none: WTP: 167 (190). Classification: Class 1: WTP: 61 (70); Class 3: WTA: 383 (434); Time of transport: WTP: 46 (53); Night time: WTP: 12 (13).
Arsenio, Bristow and Wardman (2006)	Noise reduction	Portugal	Various definitions of inner city noise	Face to face in-house interviews with 412 local residents	Random Parameter Logit	WTP in € (income group): for a house on the lower floor 0.80 (10th percentile), 1.42 (50th percentile), 3.04 (90th percentile); for a house on the upper floor 1.21 (10th percentile), 2.16 (50th percentile), 4.61 (90th percentile).

Table A2.1 (continued)

Authors (year)	Environmental Good Valued	Site, Country	Attributes	Sample Size and Survey Mode	Econometric Specification	WTP/WTA Estimates
Bergmann, Hanley and Wright (2006)	Renewable energy investments	Scotland	Landscape quality; wildlife; air quality; jobs; electricity price	Mail survey of 211 members of the public	Conditional Logit with interactions	WTP in £/household/ year: 8.1 for no landscape impact; 11.98 for improvement in wildlife; 14.13 for no increase in air pollution.
Karousakis and Birol (forth-coming)	Kerbside recycling services	London, England	Materials collected (paper, glass, aluminium); collection of compost; collection of textiles; frequency of collection; monthly council tax	Face to face interviews with 188 members of the public	Conditional Logit with interactions	WTP in £/household/ month: sample average: 2.678 for one more material; 1.19 for compost; Kensington and Chelsea: 2.763 for one more material; 1.228 for compost; Richmond-upon-Thames: 2.864 for one more material; 1.272 for compost; Westminster: 2.604 for one more material; 1.158 for compost.

REFERENCES

Alvarez-Farizo, B., Hanley, N. (2002), 'Using conjoint analysis to quantify public preferences over the environmental impacts of windfarms: an example from Spain', *Energy Policy*, 30: 107–116.

Alvarez-Farizo, B., Hanley, N., Barberán, R., Lázaro, A. (2007), 'Choice modeling at the "market stall": individual versus collective interest in environmental valuation', *Ecological Economics*, 60(4): 743–751.

Arsenio, E., Bristow, A.L., Wardman, M. (2006), 'Stated choice valuations of traffic related noise', *Transportation Research Part D: Transport and Environment*, 11(1): 15–31.

Bennett, R., Willis, K. (2007), 'The value of badger populations and control of tuberculosis in cattle in England and Wales: a note', *Journal of Agricultural Economics*, 58(1): 152–156.

Bergmann, A., Hanley, N., Wright, R. (2006), 'Valuing the attributes of renewable energy investments', *Energy Policy*, 34: 1004–1014.

Birol, E., Cox, V. (2007), 'Using choice experiments to design wetland management programmes: the case of Severn Estuary Wetland, UK', *Journal of Environmental Planning and Management*, 50(3): 363–380.

Birol, E., Karousakis, K., Koundouri, P. (2006), 'Using a choice experiment to account for preference heterogeneity in wetland attributes: the case of Cheimaditida wetland in Greece', *Ecological Economics*, 60: 145–156.

Birol, E., Smale, M., Gyovai, A. (2006), 'Using a choice experiment to estimate farmers' valuation of agrobiodiversity on Hungarian small farms', *Environmental and Resource Economics*, 34(4): 439–469.

Burton, M., Rigby, M., Young, T., James, S. (2001), 'Consumer attitudes to genetically modified organisms in the UK', *European Review of Agricultural Economics*, 28(4): 479–498.

Carlsson, F., Frykblom, P., Lagerkvist, C.-J. (2005), 'Consumer preferences for food product quality attributes from Swedish agriculture', *Ambio*, 34(4–5): 366–370.

Carlsson, F., Frykblom, P., Lagerkvist, C.J. (2007), 'Consumer benefits of labels and bans on GM foods: choice experiments with Swedish consumers', *American Journal of Agricultural Economics*, 89 (1): 152–161.

Carlsson, F., Frykblom, P., Liljenstolpe, C. (2003), 'Valuing wetland attributes: an application of choice experiments', *Ecological Economics*, 47: 95–103.

Carlsson, F., Lampi, E., Martinsson, P. (2004), 'The marginal values of noise disturbance from air traffic: does the time of the day matter?', *Transportation Research Part D: Transport and Environment*, 9 (5): 373–385.

Christie, M., Hanley, N., Warren, J., Murphy, K., Wright, R., Hyde, T. (2006), 'Valuing the diversity of biodiversity', *Ecological Economics*, 58(2): 304–317.

Colombo, S., Calatrava-Requena, J., Hanley, N. (2006), 'Analysing the social benefits of soil conservation measures using stated preference methods', *Ecological Economics*, 58: 850–861.

Colombo, S., Calatrava-Requena, J., Hanley, N. (2007), 'Testing choice experiment for benefit transfer with preference heterogeneity', *American Journal of Agricultural Economics*, 89(1): 135–151.

Colombo, S., Hanley, N., Calatrava-Requena, J. (2005), 'Designing policy for reducing the off-farm effects of soil erosion using choice experiments', *Journal of Agricultural Economics*, 56(1): 81–95.

Enneking, U. (2004), 'Willingness-to-pay for safety improvements in the German meat sector: the case of the Q&S label', *European Review of Agricultural Economics*, 31(2): 205–223.

Garrod, G., Willis, K. (1998), 'Estimating lost amenity due to landfill waste disposal', *Resources, Conservation and Recycling*, 22: 83–95.

Hanley, N., Adamowicz, W., Wright, R.E. (2005), 'Price vector effects in choice experiments: an empirical test', *Resource and Energy Economics*, 27: 227–234.

Hanley, N., Colombo, S., Tinch, D., Black, A., Aftab, A. (2006), 'Estimating the benefits of water quality improvements under the Water Framework Directive: are benefits transferable?', *European Review of Agricultural Economics*, 33(3): 391–413.

Hanley, N., MacMillan, D., Patterson, I., Wright, R. (2003), 'Economics and design of nature conservation policy: a case study of wild goose conservation in Scotland using choice experiments', *Animal Conservation*, 6: 123–129.

Hanley, N., MacMillan, D., Wright, R.E., Bullock, C., Simpson, I., Parsisson, D., Crabtree, B. (1998), 'Contingent valuation versus choice experiments: estimating the benefits of environmentally sensitive areas in Scotland', *Journal of Agricultural Economics*, 49(1): 1–15.

Hanley, N., Wright, R.E., Adamowicz, V. (1998), 'Using choice experiments to value the environment: design issues, current experience and future prospects', *Environmental and Resource Economics*, 11(3–4): 413–428.

Hanley, N., Wright, R.E., Alvarez-Farizo, B. (2006), 'Estimating the economic value of improvements in river ecology using choice experiments: an application to the water framework directive', *Journal of Environmental Management*, 78: 183–193.

Hasler, B., Lundhede, T., Martinsen, L., Neye, S., Schoi, J.S. (2005), *Valuation of groundwater protection versus water treatment in Denmark by choice experiments and contingent valuation*, NERI Technical Report No. 543, National Environmental Research Institute, Aarhus, Denmark.

Hiselius, L.W. (2005), 'Using choice experiments to assess people's preferences for railway transports of hazardous materials', *Risk Analysis*, 25(5): 1199–1214.

Horne, P. (2006), 'Forest owners' acceptance of incentive based policy instruments in forest biodiversity conservation: a choice experiment based approach', *Silva Fennica*, 40: 169–178.

Horne, P., Boxall, P.C., Adamowicz, W.L. (2005), 'Multiple-use management of forest recreation sites: a spatially explicit choice experiment', *Forest Ecology and Management*, 207: 189–199.

Horne, P., Petäjistö, L. (2003), 'Preferences for alternative moose management regimes among Finnish landowners: a choice experiment approach', *Land Economics*, 79(4): 472–482.

Karousakis, K., Birol, E. (forthcoming), 'Investigating household preferences for kerbside recycling services in London: a choice experiment approach', *Journal of Environmental Management*.

Lagerkvist, C.J., Carlsson, F., Viske, D. (2006), 'Swedish consumer preferences for animal welfare and biotech: a choice experiment', *AgBioForum*, 9(1): 51–58.

Lehtonen, E., Kuuluvainen, J., Pouta, E., Rekola, M., Li, C.-Z. (2003), 'Non-market benefits of forest conservation in southern Finland', *Environmental Science and Policy*, 6(3): 195–204.

Li, C-Z., Kuuluvainen, J., Pouta, E., Rekola, M., Tahvonen, O. (2004), 'Using choice experiments to value the Natura 2000 nature conservation programs in Finland', *Environmental and Resource Economics*, 29: 361–374.

Lusk, J.L., Roosen, J., Fox, J.A. (2003), 'Demand for beef from cattle administered growth hormones or fed genetically modified corn: a comparison of consumers in France, Germany, the United Kingdom, and the United States', *American Journal of Agricultural Economics*, 84(6): 16–29.

Nunes, P.A.L.D., Rossetto, L., de Blaeij, A. (2004), 'Measuring the economic value of alternative clam fishing management practices in the Venice Lagoon: results from a conjoint valuation application', *Journal of Marine Systems*, 51: 309–320.

Paulrud, A., Laitila, T. (2004), 'Valuation of management policies for sport-fishing on Sweden's Kaitum River', *Journal of Environmental Planning and Management*, 47(6): 863–879.

Rigby, D., Burton, M. (2005), 'Preference heterogeneity and GM food in the UK', *European Review of Agricultural Economics*, 32(2): 269–288.

Scarpa, R., Del Giudice, T.D. (2004), 'Market segmentation via mixed logit: extra-virgin olive oil in urban Italy', *Journal of Agricultural and Food Industrial Organization*, 2(1): 141–160.

Scarpa, R., Philippidis, G., Spalatro, F. (2005), 'Product-country images and preference heterogeneity for Mediterranean food products: a discrete choice framework', *Agribusiness*, 21(3): 329–349.

Sundqvist, T. (2002a), 'Quantifying non-residential preferences over the environmental impacts of hydropower in Sweden: a choice experiment approach', in *Power generation choice in the presence of environmental externalities*, Doctoral Thesis, Lulea University of Technology, Sweden.

Sundqvist, T. (2002b), 'Quantifying household preferences over the environmental impacts of hydropower in Sweden: a choice experiment approach', in *Power generation choice in the presence of environmental externalities*, Doctoral Thesis, Lulea University of Technology, Sweden.

Toma, L., Mathijs, E. (2004), 'Stated environmental preferences in a Romanian rural community', *Post-Communist Economies*, 16(2): 215–227.

Travisi, C., Nijkamp, P. (2004), *Willingness to pay for agricultural environmental safety: evidence from a survey of Milan, Italy, residents*, Tinbergen Institute Discussion paper TI, 04-070/3, Tinbergen Institute, Amsterdam and Rotterdam the Netherlands.

Wardman, M., Bristow, A.L. (2004), 'Traffic related noise and air quality valuations: evidence from stated preference residential choice models', *Transportation Research Part D: Transport and Environment*, 9(1): 1–27.

Wardman, M., Hatfield, R., Page, M. (1997), 'The UK national cycling strategy: can improved facilities meet the targets?', *Transport Policy*, 4(2): 123–133.

Willis, K.G., McMahon, P.L., Garrod, G.D., Powe, N.A. (2002), 'Water companies service performance and environmental trade-offs', *Journal of Environmental Planning and Management*, 45(3): 363–379.

Willis, K.G., Scarpa, R., Acutt, M. (2005), 'Assessing water company customer preferences and willingness to pay for service improvements: a stated choice analysis', *Water Resources Research*, 41: 1–11.

3. Using mixed logit models to derive individual-specific WTP estimates for landscape improvements under agri-environmental schemes: evidence from the Rural Environment Protection Scheme in Ireland

Danny Campbell, W. George Hutchinson and Riccardo Scarpa

INTRODUCTION

After more than fifty years of European Union (EU) agricultural policies designed to support farm incomes through farm commodity prices, there has been a significant shift in emphasis. With an increased focus on area-based payments and payments for the supply of environmental goods, agri-environmental schemes have become an important component within the Common Agricultural Policy (CAP), as also discussed in Chapters 4, 5 and 6 of this volume. Within this context, the Rural Environment Protection (REP) Scheme was introduced in the Republic of Ireland in 1994. Designed to pay farmers for carrying out their farming activities in an environmentally friendly manner, the Scheme is aimed at creating incentives for farmers to maintain and improve the broadly defined rural environment and the rural landscape.

By the end of 2004, over €1.5 billion had been paid to Irish farmers under the REP Scheme. Assessing whether the Scheme has offered value for money requires an examination of both its costs and benefits. While the financial costs are readily available, calculating the benefits is more problematic. Aside from the financial benefits farmers derive from participation, the REP Scheme offers a range of benefits to society (Gorman *et al.*, 2001; Mannion *et al.*, 2001). Some of these are the enhanced value of rural landscape aesthetics, recreation amenities, improved water quality, wildlife preservation and the maintenance of historical and archaeological features. Moreover, since no studies have sought to estimate these benefits, very little is known about their extent and magnitude (DAF, 1999). A monetary valuation of an Environmentally Sensitive Area Scheme in Northern Ireland was conducted by Moss and Chilton (1997) and a number of studies in other countries have examined the non-market benefits of agri-environmental schemes (for a review see Stewart *et al.*, 1997). Differences in the schemes and population characteristics, however, mean these estimates can only provide an approximation of the non-market benefits of the REP Scheme. Agri-environmental policy in Ireland is also of interest in that it is unique in the EU in the combination of its comprehensiveness and its being available to all farmers throughout the country (Emerson and Gillmor, 1999). With this in mind, a key objective of this study was to quantify some of the non-market benefits arising from such a comprehensive and universal policy.

Landscape conservation and improvement is currently one of the priorities of the revised CAP and the vision of a multifunctional agriculture it intends to promote (Randall, 2002). The policy measures of the REP Scheme contribute to various rural landscape attributes, and hence a multi-attribute valuation approach is warranted. At the same time the public good and non-market nature of rural landscapes favour the use of a stated preference methodology. Reported in this chapter are the results from two discrete choice experiments that were carried out to address the public's willingness to pay (WTP) for the major farm landscape improvement measures within the REP Scheme in Ireland.

Using a mixed logit specification which accounts for unobserved taste heterogeneity, this chapter derives WTP distributions for each of the main landscape attributes improved by the scheme based on parameter estimates obtained from the individual conditional distributions. Since benefits estimates for strict improvements impose conceptual lower bounds on values which may be estimated in different ways, the occurrence of negative values in inference must therefore be excluded by making adequate assumptions in model specification and estimation (Train and Weeks, 2005). In this chapter, estimates are bound such that they are strictly positive while allowing for preference variation within the sample, using an approach proposed by Hensher and Greene (2003). Individual-specific estimates from all attributes are subsequently adjusted and combined to account for baselines and levels of improvement resulting from the implementation of the REP Scheme. Individual-specific WTP estimates are thus obtained for the contribution of the Scheme to rural landscapes. This result is subsequently contrasted with the average cost of the Scheme across the Irish adult population. Results indicate that the REP Scheme contributes substantial benefits to rural landscapes.

The remainder of the chapter is organised as follows. The next two sections provide a brief background on the REP Scheme and an outline of the design of the experiment, including the attributes, experimental design and consistency tests respectively. The subsequent section specifies and explains the mixed logit model used to obtain individual-specific WTP estimates for each of the landscape attributes. The fifth section reports and discusses the relevant results from the analysis and details the approach used to calibrate the individual-specific WTP estimates derived from the mixed logit model. The final section draws some conclusions and policy implications.

THE REP SCHEME

The reform of the CAP has addressed environmental concerns by promoting environmentally friendly farming since 1992. Council Regulation 2078/92 promoted farmers to the roles of managers, stewards and custodians of the rural environment alongside that of food commodity producers. For the first time Member States were required to establish region-specific agri-environmental schemes. Against this backdrop, in 1994 Ireland developed the REP Scheme with the stated objectives (DAF, 2004c) of:

- establishing farming practices and production methods which reflect the increasing concern for conservation, landscape protection and wider environmental problems.
- protecting wildlife habitats and endangered species of flora and fauna.
- producing quality food in an extensive and environmentally friendly manner.

The overall intention of the REP Scheme is to make support payments to farmers conditional on their implementing good and/or environment-friendly farming practice. The Scheme is about paying farmers to provide public goods in the form of environmental services (Hamell, 2001), on the assumption that opportunity costs are being incurred in order to farm in an environment friendly manner.

By the end of 2004, about a third of all farms and agricultural land in Ireland was involved in the Scheme, which is voluntary and available universally, rather than being restricted to specific areas of the country. However, to qualify farmers must be farming at least three hectares of land and undertake to implement the Scheme on all of the holding and to farm it according to an individual comprehensive agri-environmental plan for five years. Farmers in the Scheme must undertake eleven basic measures, which are directed towards controlling nitrogen use and stocking rates, controlling waste and effluent around the farmyard and protecting water quality, hedgerows, stonewalls and features of archaeological or historical importance on their farm. They must also choose two biodiversity undertakings. In addition to the basic premium, extra payments are available to farmers who undertake supplementary measures.

SURVEY DESIGN

Attributes Used in the Choice Experiments

The discrete choice experiment exercises reported here involved several rounds of design and testing. This process began with a qualitative review of opinions from the policy administrators. Having identified the policy-relevant attributes, further qualitative research was carried out to refine the definitions of these attributes so they could be used in the survey. This was achieved through a series of focus group discussions, with members of the public. To ensure a geographical spread and to enable the identification of potentially different perspectives, four focus groups were conducted around Ireland. Following the focus group discussions, pilot testing of the survey instrument was conducted in the field. This allowed the collection of additional information, which along with expert judgement and observations from the focus group discussions, was used to identify and refine the landscape attributes and their levels. In the final version of the survey a total of eight important landscape attributes were identified: Wildlife Habitats, Rivers and Lakes, Hedgerows, Pastures, Mountain Land, Stonewalls, Farmyard Tidiness and Cultural Heritage.

Three levels were used to depict each landscape attribute according to the level of action made to conserve or enhance it. To minimise respondent confusion the levels for each landscape attribute were denoted using the same labels: A Lot Of Action, Some Action and No Action. While the A Lot Of Action and Some Action levels represented a high level and an intermediate level of improvement achievable within the REP Scheme respectively, the No Action level represented the unimproved or status quo condition. Image manipulation software was used to prepare photo-realistic simulations representing the landscape attributes under different management practices and levels of agricultural intensity. This involved the manipulation of a 'control' photograph to depict either more of or less of the attribute in question. This method was used so that on the one hand the changes in the attribute levels could be easily identified while holding other features of the landscape constant. On the other hand the respondent would not perceive as ostensibly unrealistic the computer-generated landscape illustrations. The Wildlife Habitats attribute depicted a field with different degrees of biodiversity. A range of levels of green cover on lake water reflecting eutrophication levels were used to represent the Rivers and Lakes attribute. The Hedgerows attribute was shown under different management practices. Different stocking densities in lowland and upland areas were used to depict the Pastures and Mountain Land attributes respectively. The Stonewalls attribute illustrated the consequence that their condition and absence has on the appearance of the countryside. Similarly, the Farmyard Tidiness attribute portrayed a farmyard at different levels of tidiness and the Cultural Heritage attribute showed the impact that different management practices have on old farm buildings and historical features. All images and accompanying text were tested in the focus group discussions and pilot study to ensure a satisfactory understanding and scenario acceptance by respondents.

The cost attribute was described as the Expected Annual Cost of implementing the alternatives represented in the choice questions. This attribute was specified as the value that the respondent would personally have to pay per year, through their Income Tax and Value Added Tax contributions, to implement the alternative. These are realistic payment vehicles for EU-funded and government-funded agricultural policies. As discussed later in more detail, the experimental design was sequential to allow for Bayesian learning (Ferrini and Scarpa, 2007) and the survey was administered in three phases, plus a pilot. This enabled the levels of the monetary attribute to be adjusted in response to the preliminary findings following each phase of the survey. Altogether seven price levels, ranging from €15 to €80, were used to represent the Expected Annual Cost attribute. The price levels that were used in each phase of the survey are shown in Table 3.1.

Table 3.1 Expected Annual Cost attribute price levels used during each phase of the survey

	€15	**€20**	**€35**	**€40**	**€50**	**€65**	**€80**
Phase 1		✓	✓		✓	✓	✓
Phase 2		✓					✓
Phase 3	✓	✓		✓	✓		

Sampling Method

In order to achieve a spatially representative sample, the sampling approach for the survey was firstly stratified according to 15 broad regions and five different community types (county boroughs; towns 10 000+; towns 5000 – 10 000; towns 1500 – 5000; and rural less than 1500) within the four standard areas of Dublin, Rest of Leinster, Munster and Connaught/Ulster. This approach was to ensure that all data generated could be analysed by the Nomenclature of Territorial Units for Statistics (NUTS) II and III regions, in addition to a range of urban and rural classifications. Within each of these broad regions, the appropriate number of primary sampling units, that is Electoral Divisions (EDs), was chosen. In total 100 EDs were selected.

The second stage of the sampling procedure involved the systematic sampling of six individuals within each of the pre-selected EDs. At each ED, the interviewer adhered to a quota control matrix based upon the known profile of Irish adults in the NUTS II regions in terms of age within sex, and socio-economic status. Within each ED, the nucleus of each cluster of interviews was an address selected on a probability basis from the 2003 Register of Electors. In order to limit interviewer bias the interviewers followed a random route procedure (for example first left, next right and so on) calling at every fifth house to complete an interview, until their controls were fulfilled.

The Discrete Choice Experiments

The central objective of the public survey was to elicit WTP estimates for the eight landscape attributes. Evidence from the focus group discussions revealed that respondents had difficultly evaluating choice tasks with more than five attributes. To circumvent this, the survey contained two separate choice experiments, each comprised of four randomly assigned landscape attributes and a cost attribute. Crucially, this enabled WTP estimates to be obtained for the eight rural landscape attributes for all respondents. The attributes used in each choice experiment are listed in Table 3.2. To avoid any biases that might exist due to the ordering of the two choice experiments, two versions of each questionnaire were developed, each version with a different sequence of presentation to the respondent of the two sets of choice tasks.

In each choice experiment respondents were asked to indicate their preferred alternative in a panel of repeated choice sets. Each choice set consisted of two experimentally designed alternatives, labelled Option A and Option B, and a status quo alternative, labelled No Action, which portrayed all the landscape attributes at the No Action level with zero cost to

Table 3.2 Landscape attributes used in each choice experiment

Choice experiment A	Choice experiment B
Wildlife Habitats	Mountain Land
Rivers and Lakes	Stonewalls
Hedgerows	Farmyard Tidiness
Pastures	Cultural Heritage

the respondent. Before both choice experiments, respondents were initially acquainted with the four landscape attributes used during the succeeding choice experiment. This was achieved by providing a show card for each of these attributes and allowing respondents time to examine them. When respondents had fully familiarised themselves with these attributes they were shown a sample 'rehearsal' choice set with three alternatives and were told that it represented rural environmental policy options open to the Government. An example of the choice sets used in choice experiments A and B are presented in Figures 3.1 and 3.2 respectively.

Respondents were made aware that achieving environmental standards and keeping management practices in place would require financial support and that each policy had an associated cost. Respondents were informed that the Expected Annual Cost attribute represented the value that they personally would have to pay per year, obtained through their Income Tax and Value Added Tax contributions, for the rural environmental policy. All of the options were explained to the respondents. They were then asked to consider all three alternatives and to indicate their most preferred option. When making their choice, respondents were asked to consider that rural environmental policy options were restricted only to these three alternatives. Respondents were reminded to take into account whether they thought the rural environmental policies were worth it to them. Following the rehearsal choice set, respondents were faced with a series of at least six choice sets.

Experimental Design

Since different experimental designs can significantly influence the accuracy of WTP estimates (Lusk and Norwood, 2005), it is important to use an experimental design that minimises an efficiency criterion. Given the national scope of this study, and the cost of surveys of this kind, sample size was also an issue. To increase sampling efficiency a sequential experimental design with a Bayesian information structure was employed (Sándor and Wedel, 2001).

A review of recent studies on experimental design (see Ferrini and Scarpa, 2007) reveals that the values in the matrix of attribute levels should

	Option A	Option B	No Action
Wildlife Habitats	 A Lot of Action	 No Action	 No Action
Rivers and Lakes	 A Lot of Action	 Some Action	 No Action
Hedgerows	 A Lot of Action	 Some Action	 No Action
Pastures	 A Lot of Action	 Some Action	 No Action
Expected Annual Cost	€ 80	€ 20	€ 0

Figure 3.1 Example of a choice set used in choice experiment A

be chosen so as to minimise some expected measure of variance, such as the D_p-optimality criterion:

$$D_p\text{-criterion} = \det\{I(\beta)^{-1}\}^{1/p}, \tag{3.1}$$

where $I(\cdot)$ is the information matrix of the multinomial logit model and p is the number of attributes. A more informative Bayesian measure,

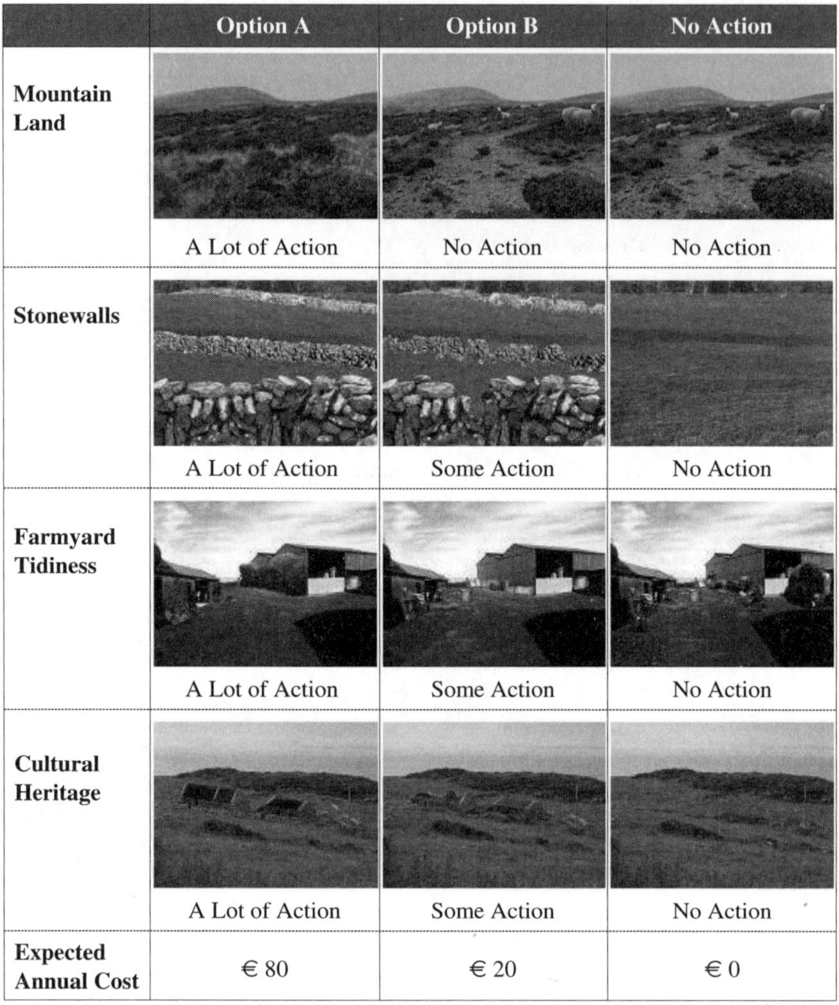

Figure 3.2 Example of a choice set used in choice experiment B

the D_b- optimal criterion, suggested in Sándor and Wedel (2001), which is the expected value of the D_p-criterion with respect to its assumed distribution over β or π(β) was adopted with the arrangement of values in the matrix of attribute levels such that:

$$D_b\text{-criterion} = E_\beta[\{\det I(\beta)^{-1}\}^{1/p}] = \int_{\mathbb{R}^p} \{\det I(\beta)^{-1}\}^{1/p} \pi(\beta) d\beta. \quad (3.2)$$

As a prior an informative multivariate normal distribution centred on β was used with a variance-covariance matrix, both of which were derived initially from the first phase of the survey, and subsequently updated at each phase by the pooled dataset from previous phases of sampling using Gauss. This is achieved in practice by simulating the value of this criterion by drawing from the assumed distribution of βs, computing the value of the criterion for each draw, and then averaging it out. The best allocation of values is found by using heuristic algorithms, such as swapping and relabelling (Huber and Zwerina, 1996) and cycling (Sándor and Wedel, 2001):

$$\tilde{D}_b = \frac{1}{R}\sum_{r=1}^{R}\left\{\det I(\beta)^{-1}\right\}^{1/p}, \tag{3.3}$$

where R is the number of draws.

Starting from a conventional main effects fractional factorial in the first phase, a Bayesian design was employed in the second wave of sampling. The design for the final phase incorporated information from the first and second phases. However, not all values of the attributes were allocated in the design by the above approach. The numerical values of cost were assigned on the basis of realism and so as to balance the probabilities of choices across alternatives in the choice set (see Kanninen, 2002). For further information and an evaluation of the efficiency of the sequential experimental design approach used in this study see Campbell (2006), Scarpa *et al.* (2007) and Ferrini and Scarpa (2007).

MIXED LOGIT MODEL SPECIFICATION

Mixed logit models provide a flexible and computationally practical econometric method for any discrete choice model derived from random utility maximisation (McFadden and Train, 2000). The mixed logit model obviates the three limitations of standard logit by allowing for random taste variation, unrestricted substitution patterns and correlation in unobserved factors (Train, 2003). Mixed logit does not exhibit the strong assumptions of independent and identically distributed (*iid*) error terms and its equivalent behavioural association with the independence of irrelevant alternatives (IIA) property.

In mixed logit the stochastic component of utility is portioned additively into two parts (Hensher and Greene, 2003). One part is perhaps correlated over alternatives and heteroskedastic over individuals and alternatives, and another is *iid* over alternatives and individuals:

$$U_{ni} = \beta_n' x_{ni} + [\eta_{ni} + \varepsilon_{ni}], \tag{3.4}$$

where x_{ni} is a vector of observed explanatory variables that relate to alternative i and to individual n; β_n is a vector of parameters of these variables for person n representing the individual's tastes; η_{ni} is a random term with zero mean whose distribution over individuals and alternatives depends in general on underlying parameters and observed data relating to alternative i; and ε_{ni} is a random term with zero mean that is *iid* over alternatives, does not depend on underlying parameters or data, and is normalised to set the scale of utility (Brownstone and Train, 1999). The mixed logit class of models assumes a general distribution for η_{ni}, which can take on a number of distributional forms such as normal, lognormal, or triangular (McFadden and Train, 2000). Denote the density of η_{ni} by $f(\eta_{ni}|\Omega)$ where Ω are the fixed parameters of the distribution. For a given η_{ni}, the conditional probability for alternative i is logit, since the remaining error term is *iid* extreme value:

$$L_{ni}(\beta_n|\eta_{ni}) = \frac{\exp(\beta_n' x_{ni} + \eta_{ni})}{\sum_j \exp(\beta_n' x_{nj} + \eta_{nj})}, \tag{3.5}$$

where L_{ni} is the logit probability. Since η_{ni} is not given, the unconditional choice probability becomes the integral of L_{ni} over all values of η_{ni} weighted by the density of η_{ni}:

$$P_{ni}(\beta_n|\Omega) = \int_{\eta_{ni}} L_{ni}(\beta_n|\eta_{ni})\, f(\eta_{ni}|\Omega)\eta_{ni}. \tag{3.6}$$

Models of this form are called mixed logit since the choice probability is a mixture of logits with $f(\cdot)$ as the mixing distribution (Brownstone and Train, 1999). The probabilities do not exhibit the IIA property and different substitution patterns may be attained by appropriate specification of $f(\cdot)$. While in most applications the mixing distribution $f(\cdot)$ is specified to be continuous, it can also be specified to be discrete, with η_{ni} taking a finite set of distinct values. In this case the mixed logit model becomes the latent class model.

Different types of mixed logit models have been used in empirical work, which differ in the type of structure that is placed on the model, or, more precisely, in the specification of $f(\cdot)$. One approach, as used by Brownstone and Train (1999), is to specify an error components structure that creates correlations among the utilities for different alternatives. The specification employed in this chapter is the random-parameters, or random-coefficients, approach. Random parameters specification of the mixed logit model is also employed in Chapters 4 and 12 of this volume. For further details refer to Revelt and Train (1998), Layton and Brown (2000) and references cited therein.

Individual-Specific Conditional Estimates of Landscape Values

The mixed logit model accommodates the estimation of individual-specific preferences by deriving individuals' conditional distribution based (within sample) on their known choices (that is prior knowledge) (Hensher and Greene, 2003; Scarpa *et al.*, 2005). These conditional parameter estimates are strictly same-choice-specific parameters, or the mean of the parameters of the sub-population of individuals who, when faced with the same choice set made the same choices. This is an important distinction since it is not possible to establish, for each individual, his or her unique set of estimates, but rather to identify a mean and standard deviation estimate for the sub-population who made the same choice (Hensher *et al.*, 2005). Using Bayes' Rule, the conditional choice probability is:

$$H_{ni}(\beta_n|\Omega) = \frac{L_{ni}(\beta_n)g(\beta_n|\Omega)}{P_{ni}(\beta_n|\Omega)}, \tag{3.7}$$

where $L_{ni}(\beta_n)$ is the likelihood of an individual's choice if he or she had this specific β_n, Ω is the set of parameters in the underlying distribution of β_n, $g(\beta_n|\Omega)$ is the distribution in the population of β_ns, and $P_{ni}(\Omega)$ is the choice probability function defined in open-form as:

$$H_{ni}(\Omega) = \int_{\beta_n} L_{ni}(\beta_n)g(\beta_n|\Omega)\, d\beta_n. \tag{3.8}$$

Bounding of Taste Intensities

A key element of the mixed logit model is the assumption regarding the distribution of each of the random parameters. These can take a number of predefined functional forms, the most popular being normal, lognormal, uniform and triangular (Hensher *et al.*, 2005). In most applications, such as Layton and Brown (2000), Revelt and Train (1998) and Train (1998), the random parameters are specified as normal or lognormal. Greene *et al.* (2005) and Greene *et al.* (2006) have used uniform and triangular distributions. However it is well known that choices of some commonly employed mixing distributions imply behaviourally inconsistent WTP values, due to the range of taste values over which the distribution spans. Normal and lognormal distributions are particularly problematic (Train and Weeks, 2005). This is due to the presence of a share of respondents with the 'wrong' sign in the former, and the presence of fat tails in the latter. This is of particular importance in a study concerned with improvements from the status quo, on which taste intensities are expected to be positive. For a general discussion on bounding the range of variation in random utility models see Train and Sonnier (2005), who propose a Bayesian estimation approach; for an application of bounding directly to the expenditure function see Train and Weeks (2005). Following Hensher and Greene (2003), a bounded triangular distribution is used in this chapter, in which the location parameter is constrained to be equal to its scale. Such a constraint forces the distribution to be bounded over a given orthant, the sign of which is the same as the sign of the location parameter (see Hensher *et al.* (2005) for a description of the triangular distribution in this context). In practice, for all random parameters associated with the various categories of rural landscape improvements, it is assumed that $\beta \sim \tau(\theta)$, where θ is both the location and scale parameter of the triangular distribution $\tau(\cdot)$. This includes cost, which is bounded to the negative orthant.

Estimation Procedure

Computation of mixed logit choice probabilities using classical estimation procedures typically requires Monte Carlo integration. The basis of this computation is the generation of pseudo-random sequences that are intended to mimic independent draws from the underlying distribution of the random variable of integration. An alternative approach proposed by Bhat (2001) and Train (1999) replaces these pseudo-random sequences with sequences based on a deterministic Halton sequence. One-dimensional Halton sequences are created using any prime number $p(\geq 2)$. The unit interval [0,1] is divided into p equally-sized segments, and the endpoints or breaks of these segments form the first p numbers in the Halton sequence. Successive numbers in the sequence are generated by further subdividing each segment into p equally-sized segments and adding the breaks in a particular order. The resulting Halton draws thus achieve greater precision and coverage for a given number of draws than pseudo-random draws, since successive Halton draws are negatively correlated and therefore tend to be self-correcting (Train, 2003). Accordingly, many fewer draws are needed to assure reasonably low simulation error in the estimated parameters. In fact both Bhat (2001) and Train (1999) demonstrate that for a mixed logit model, 100 Halton draws provide results that are more accurate than 1000 pseudo-random draws. Overall the application of Halton draws allows a decrease in computation time without sacrificing precision. However while multi-dimensional Halton sequences generally provide better coverage than the corresponding pseudo-random number sequences, problems with high correlation can occur between sequences constructed from higher primes, and thus sequences used in higher dimensions. To ameliorate this, modified procedures such as scrambled and shuffled Halton draws have been used (for example Bhat, 2003; Hess and Polak, 2003). Both these sequences have been found to outperform the standard Halton sequence. As a result, shuffled Halton sequences with 100 draws are used in this chapter to estimate the mixed logit models.

RESULTS AND DISCUSSION

In total, the survey was administered by experienced interviewers to a representative sample of 600 respondents drawn from the Irish adult population in 2003/4. With a further 166 potential respondents refusing to complete the interview, the overall response rate was 78 per cent. During the interview, each respondent completed two choice experiments. For each choice experiment respondents indicated their preferred alternative in a panel of repeated choice contexts, each choice consisting of two experimentally designed alternatives and a status quo (No Action) alternative.

Mixed Logit Models Results

Since this chapter focuses on the distribution of part-worths (WTP values) for individuals in the sample, the results from the multinomial logit models are omitted. Instead, readers are referred to Campbell (2006) for these results. The model of choice for the derivation of individual-specific welfare measures is the mixed logit model. Table 3.3 reports the parameter estimates obtained from choice experiment A. The parameter estimates obtained from choice experiment B are reported in Table 3.4. Both models were produced using NLOGIT (see Greene, 2002). Parameter estimates in both models were generated using 100 shuffled Halton draws. In both models, all the attributes were specified as random, thereby enabling unobserved sources of heterogeneous preferences among respondents to be captured. This was constrained using triangular distributions to ensure non-negative WTP for landscape improvements over the entire range of the distribution. Contrary to Revelt and Train (1998), the mixed logit models were not found to be unstable when all attributes were allowed to vary over the population. The mixed logit model specifications used in this chapter do not include any alternative specific constants effects and do not

Table 3.3 Mixed logit model results for choice experiment A

Attributes	Mean		Standard deviation	
	Beta	Std error	Beta	Std error
Wildlife Habitats: A Lot Of Action	0.842	0.064***	0.842	0.064***
Wildlife Habitats: Some Action	0.610	0.065***	0.610	0.065***
Rivers and Lakes: A Lot Of Action	1.803	0.074***	1.803	0.074***
Rivers and Lakes: Some Action	1.046	0.061***	1.046	0.061***
Hedgerows: A Lot Of Action	0.387	0.059***	0.387	0.059***
Hedgerows: Some Action	0.157	0.059**	0.157	0.059**
Pastures: A Lot Of Action	0.684	0.059***	0.684	0.059***
Pastures: Some Action	0.643	0.063***	0.643	0.063***
Expected Annual Cost	−0.010	0.001***	0.010	0.001***
Log-likelihood	−3373.480			
χ^2	2679.133***			
Pseudo-R^2	0.284			
Bayesian information criterion	6832.124			

Notes:
** Significance at 5 per cent.
*** Significance at 1 per cent.

incorporate any socio-demographic or attitudinal characteristics of the respondents. Instead the mixed logit models reported explain choice between the policy alternatives solely as a function of their attributes. This approach was adopted because the focus of this chapter was to explore the trade-offs between the attributes and, hence, WTP estimates. As noted by Louviere *et al.* (2003), this approach has merits in that it also enables the trade-offs between the attributes to be investigated without complex relationships.

The log-likelihood function at convergence is –3373.480 for choice experiment A and –3775.392 for choice experiment B. Both models are found to be statistically significant, with a χ^2 statistic of 2679.133 and 1901.676 for choice experiments A and B respectively against a χ^2 critical value of 16.919 (with 9 degrees of freedom at alpha equal to 0.05).

Across both models, all estimated coefficients are found to be statistically significant at the 1 per cent level, except for the coefficient associated with Hedgerows at the Some Action level of improvement, which was found to be significant at the 5 per cent level. Importantly, coefficients are also found to have the expected sign. Notice also that the mean and standard deviation coefficients are identical. This is because they were constrained to be

Table 3.4 Mixed logit model results for choice experiment B

Attributes	**Mean**		**Standard deviation**	
	Beta	**Std error**	**Beta**	**Std error**
Mountain Land: A Lot Of Action	1.041	0.064***	1.041	0.064***
Mountain Land: Some Action	0.598	0.059***	0.598	0.059***
Stonewalls: A Lot Of Action	0.870	0.058***	0.870	0.058***
Stonewalls: Some Action	0.531	0.056***	0.531	0.056***
Farmyard Tidiness: A Lot Of Action	0.794	0.057***	0.794	0.057***
Farmyard Tidiness: Some Action	0.502	0.055***	0.502	0.055***
Cultural Heritage: A Lot Of Action	0.587	0.057***	0.587	0.057***
Cultural Heritage: Some Action	0.577	0.058***	0.577	0.058***
Expected Annual Cost	−0.012	0.001***	0.012	0.001***
Log-likelihood	−3775.392			
χ^2	1901.676***			
Pseudo-R^2	0.201			
Bayesian information criterion	7635.974			

Note: *** Significance at 1 per cent.

equal under a triangular distribution. With the possible exception of the Pastures and Cultural Heritage attributes, the relative dimensions of the estimated coefficients for the landscape attributes at A Lot Of Action vis-à-vis Some Action conform with theoretical expectations of decreasing marginal utility. To illustrate this, the kernel-smoothed distributions of the individual-specific WTP estimates conditional on observed choices (Hensher and Greene, 2003) for each of the landscape attributes are presented in Figure 3.3. From the distributions, it is apparent that for all landscape attributes except for Pastures and Cultural Heritage, the implied monotonicity of the two levels of action is adequately reflected in the magnitude of individual-specific WTP estimates. It is also clear that the attribute most valued is Rivers and Lakes and the attribute least valued is Hedgerows.

Calibration of Landscape Benefits Arising from the REP Scheme

In the choice experiments, respondents were asked to indicate their preferred option on the basis that it would be implemented on all farms throughout Ireland. While this provides WTP estimates for the landscape attributes, it does not reflect WTP for the landscape improvements arising from the REP Scheme. Using 2003 as a reference year – the year in which

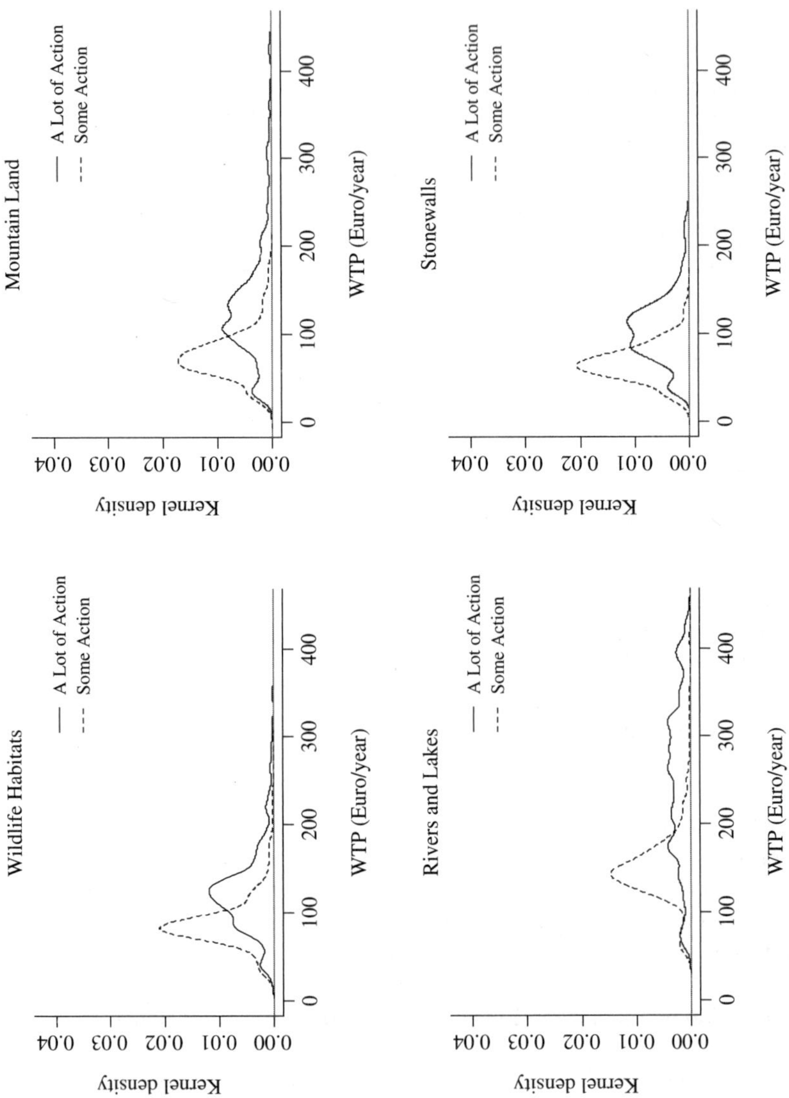
Wildlife Habitats
Mountain Land
Rivers and Lakes
Stonewalls
A Lot of Action
Some Action
Kernel density
WTP (Euro/year)
0.00
0.01
0.02
0.03
0.04
0
100
200
300
400

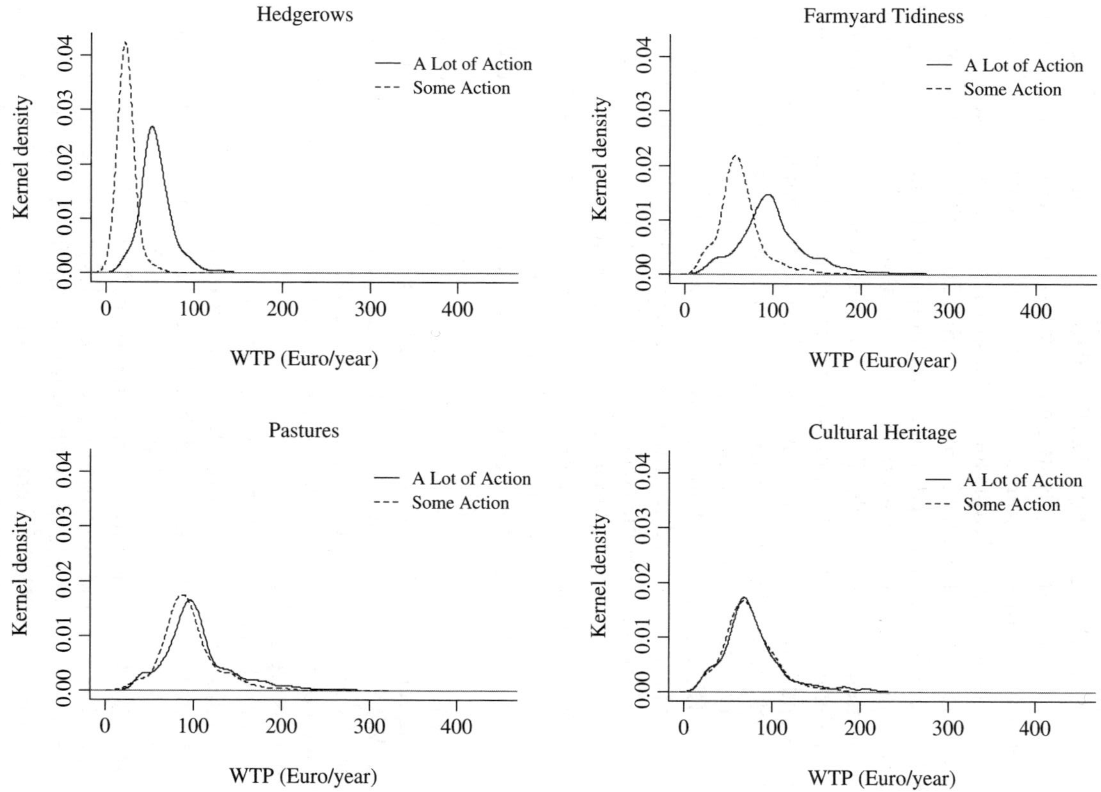

Figure 3.3 WTP distributions for the REP Scheme landscape attributes

the survey fielding began – the individual-specific WTP estimates are thus adjusted to provide realistic estimates for the landscape improvements arising from the REP Scheme. They are first adjusted to take account of the proportion of farms in the REP Scheme – only 27 per cent of all farms were paid under the Scheme in 2003 (DAF, 2004b). Furthermore, because the Mountain Land and Stonewalls attributes are less prevalent on some farms in comparison to attributes found on all farms such as Farmyard Tidiness and water courses (that is Rivers and Lakes) their values were scaled down in accordance with agricultural statistics (CSO, 2000; DAF, 2004a). WTP estimates were further adjusted to take account of baselines and the level of improvement resulting from the implementation of the REP Scheme. Both the baseline and the levels of improvement are defined in terms of the three attribute levels: No Action, Some Action and A Lot of Action. Baselines and levels of improvement resulting from the implementation of the REP Scheme are based on a semi-quantitative assessment of the landscape quality of farms within the Scheme and farms not in the Scheme conducted by O'Leary *et al.* (2004; 2005). As a result, for each landscape attribute WTP is calculated for the improvement under the REP Scheme from: (1) No Action to Some Action, (2) No Action to A Lot Of Action, and (3) Some Action to A Lot Of Action. They are then added to provide an overall WTP estimate for the improvements under the REP Scheme for each of the farm landscape attributes. Boxplots for these are presented in Figure 3.4. From Figure 3.4, it is clear that highest individual-specific WTP estimates for landscape improvement under the REP Scheme are for improvements concerning Rivers and Lakes. Non-overlapping notches also indicate rejection of the null of equal medians. Finally, the individual-specific WTP estimates from each of the landscape attributes are added together to provide an overall individual-specific WTP estimate for the landscape benefits provided under the REP Scheme in 2003. Results from this analysis are depicted in Figure 3.5.

Assessing whether the REP Scheme offers value for money also requires an examination of the costs associated with it. In 2003 the total cost of the REP Scheme was approximately €195 million, combining payments made under the REP Schemes 1 and 2 and administration and inspection costs (see DAF, 2004b). Averaging this cost across the total Irish adult population (aged 15 years and over) (CSO, 2003), enables it to be compared with the overall individual-specific WTP estimates for the landscape benefits provided under the REP Scheme. The average cost of the REP Scheme across the Irish adult population in 2003 was estimated at €63; this is indicated by a vertical line in Figure 3.5.

From Figure 3.5, it is clear that there is a considerable range in the values that the public are WTP for the landscape benefits provided under the REP

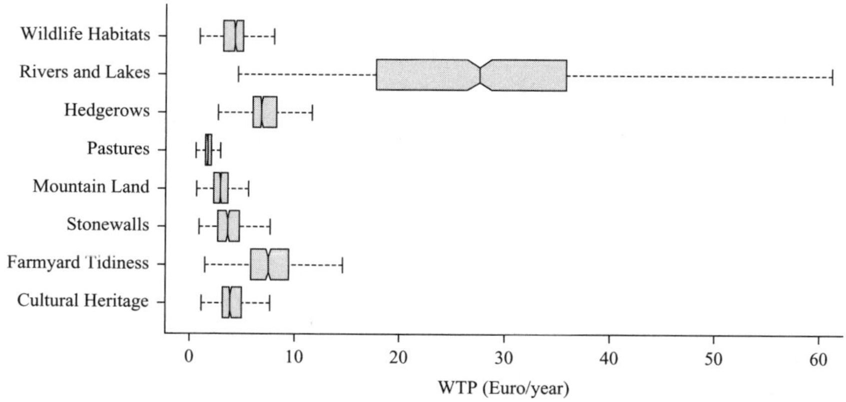

Note: Boxplots – sometimes referred to as box and whisker plots – are a non-parametric method and are graphical devices which can be used to capture a large amount of information. The plot shows the median, 'hinges' corresponding with the first and third quartile of a distribution (that is, the 25th and 75th percentile points in the cumulative distribution) as well as outliers. An observation is classified as an outlier when it is located outside a given multiple of the inter quartile range (that is, the difference in value between the first and third quartile), below or above respectively the value for the first quartile and third quartile. The standard multiple, which is used in the boxplots presented here, is 1.5 times the interquartile range. Notches are also drawn to show the 95 per cent confidence interval of the median.

Figure 3.4 Boxplots of WTP for improvements to the landscape attributes under the REP Scheme

Scheme. It is also apparent that for a sizeable proportion of respondents, WTP for the landscape benefits of the Scheme alone exceeded the average cost of the Scheme across the Irish adult population. Further investigations identified that 256 respondents (41 per cent) had a WTP above the average cost of the Scheme across the Irish adult population and that the individual-specific WTP ranged from 23 per cent to 191 per cent of the average cost of the Scheme.

CONCLUSIONS AND POLICY IMPLICATIONS

Reported in this chapter are the findings from two choice experiments that were carried out to address the value of a number of farm landscape improvement measures within the Rural Environment Protection (REP) Scheme in the Republic of Ireland. The attributes in question were improvement of: Wildlife Habitats, Rivers and Lakes, Hedgerows, Pastures, Mountain Land, Stonewalls, Farmyard Tidiness and Cultural Heritage.

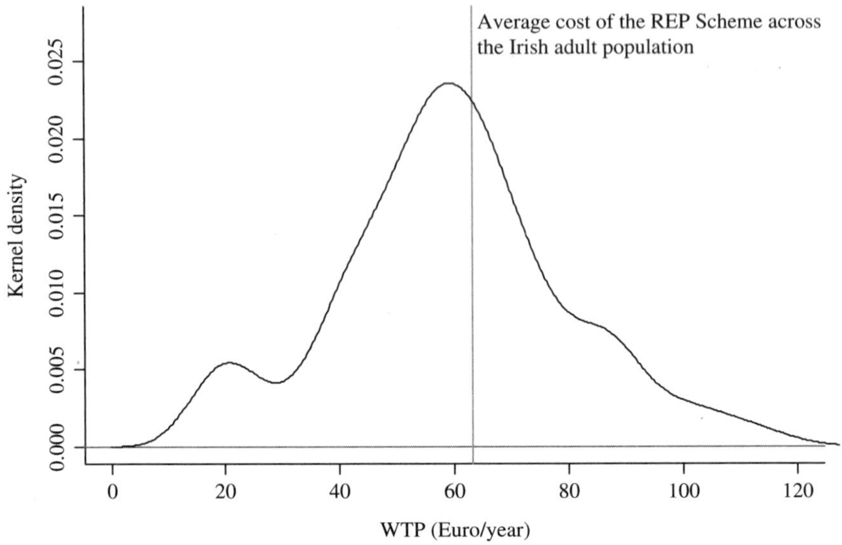

Figure 3.5 Distribution of WTP for landscape improvements under the REP Scheme

Each of these attributes was represented under three different management practices according to the level of action made to conserve and/or enhance it: No Action, Some Action and A Lot Of Action. Since valuation of landscapes are very subjective, and verbal description can be interpreted differently on the basis of individual experience, each level of improvement was qualified and presented to respondents by means of digitally manipulated images of landscapes to represent accurately what is achievable within the policy under valuation.

This study also attempted to take stock of some of the main advances in the areas of multi-attribute stated preference techniques. In particular, following recent results in market research, a sequential experimental design with an informative Bayesian update to improve the efficiency of estimates was implemented. The heterogeneity of the structural parameters of the random utility model was addressed using distributions that bounded the implied WTP estimates. The methodological approach applied in this chapter also enabled the calibrated individual-specific WTP estimates to be directly compared with the average cost of the REP Scheme across the Irish adult population.

There are clear policy uses of the value estimates reported in this study, as they provide a means to evaluate the level of investment in ongoing activities that conserve and/or enhance rural environmental landscapes within the CAP. The results can also be used to inform decisions concerning the allocation of resources for each of the landscape attributes. Based on the results reported in this chapter, the landscape feature to which the public attach the highest value is Rivers and Lakes. Results also revealed that there is a considerable range in the values that the public attach to the landscape improvement measures under the REP Scheme in Ireland, and in many cases they were found to exceed the average cost of the Scheme across the Irish adult population. Aside from the landscape benefits, other important benefits arising from the REP Scheme would include improvements to drinking water, biodiversity, enhanced recreational opportunities, rural development and contributions to farmer's incomes and the broader rural economy. While further research would be necessary to quantify these additional benefits, it is reasonable to assume that, when added to the landscape benefits estimated in this study, the total benefits provided by the REP Scheme are likely to exceed the costs associated with it. On this basis the REP Scheme would seem to be justified.

ACKNOWLEDGEMENTS

This work was supported by funding from the Irish Department of Agriculture and Food under the Research Stimulus Fund and Teagasc under the Walsh Fellowship Scheme. The opinions expressed are those of the authors and need not reflect the Funders' positions.

REFERENCES

Bhat, C.R. (2001), 'Quasi-random maximum simulated likelihood estimation of the mixed multinomial logit model', *Transportation Research Part B*, 35, 677–693.

Bhat, C.R. (2003), 'Simulation estimation of mixed discrete choice models using randomized scrambled Halton sequences', *Transportation Research Part B*, 37, 837–855.

Brownstone, D. and K. Train (1999), 'Forecasting new product penetration with flexible substitution patterns', *Journal of Econometrics*, 89, 109–129.

Campbell, D. (2006), *Discrete Choice Experiments Applied to the Valuation of Rural Environmental Landscape Improvements*, unpublished PhD thesis, Belfast: Queen's University Belfast.

CSO (2000), *Census of Agriculture Main Results*, Cork: Central Statistics Office.

CSO (2003), *Census 2002: Principal Demographic Results*, Cork: Central Statistics Office.

DAF (1999), *Evaluation of the Rural Environment Protection Scheme*, Dublin: Department of Agriculture and Food.

DAF (2004a), *Compendium of Irish Agricultural Statistics*, Dublin: Department of Agriculture and Food.

DAF (2004b), *Rural Environment Protection Scheme: Facts and Figures 1994–2003*, Dublin: Department of Agriculture and Food.

DAF (2004c), *Terms and Conditions of the Rural Environment Protection Scheme*, Dublin: Department of Agriculture and Food.

Emerson, H.J. and D.A. Gillmor (1999), 'The Rural Environment Scheme of the Republic of Ireland', *Land Use Policy*, 16, 235–245.

Ferrini S. and R. Scarpa (2007), 'Designs with a priori information for nonmarket valuation with choice experiments: a Monte Carlo study', *Journal of Environmental Economics and Management*, 53(3), 342–363.

Gorman, M., J. Mannion, J. Kinsella and P. Bogue (2001), 'Connecting environmental management and farm household livelihoods: the Rural Environment Protection Scheme in Ireland', *Journal of Environmental Policy and Planning*, 3, 137–147.

Greene, W.H. (2002), *NLOGIT Version 3.0: Reference Guide*, New York: Econometric Software.

Greene, W.H., D.A. Hensher and J.M. Rose (2005), 'Using classical simulation-based estimators to estimate individual WTP values', in R. Scarpa and A. Alberini (eds), *Applications of Simulation Methods in Environmental and Resource Economics*, Dordrecht: Springer Publisher, pp. 17–34.

Greene, W.H., D.A. Hensher and J.M. Rose (2006), 'Accounting for heterogeneity in the variance of unobserved effects in mixed logit models', *Transportation Research Part B*, 40, 75–92.

Hamell, M. (2001), 'Policy aspects of the agriculture-environment relationship', *Tearmann: The Irish Journal of Agri-Environmental Research*, 1(1), 1–10.

Hensher, D.A. and W.H. Greene (2003), 'The mixed logit model: the state of practice', *Transportation*, 30, 133–176.

Hensher, D.A., J.M. Rose and W.H. Greene (2005), *Applied Choice Analysis: A Primer*, Cambridge: Cambridge University Press.

Hess, S. and J. Polak (2003), 'An alternative method to the scrambled Halton sequence for removing correlation between standard Halton sequences in high dimensions', paper presented at the *European Regional Science Conference*, Jyväskylä, August.

Huber, J. and K. Zwerina (1996), 'The importance of utility balance in efficient choice designs', *Journal of Marketing Research*, 33, 307–317.

Kanninen, B.J. (2002), 'Optimal designs for multinomial choice experiment', *Journal of Marketing Research*, 39, 214–227.

Layton, D.F. and G. Brown (2000), 'Heterogeneous preferences regarding global climate change', *The Review of Economics and Statistics*, 82(4), 616–624.

Louviere, J.J., D.A. Hensher and J. Swait (2003), *Stated Choice Methods: Analysis and Application*, Cambridge: Cambridge University Press.

Lusk, J.L. and F.B. Norwood (2005), 'Effect of experimental design on choice-based conjoint valuation estimates', *American Journal of Agricultural Economics*, 87(3), 771–785.

Mannion, J., M. Gorman and J. Kinsella (2001), 'Connecting farming and society: a living countryside perspective', *Tearmann: The Irish Journal of Agri-Environmental Research*, 1(1), 11–17.

McFadden, D. and K. Train (2000), 'Mixed MNL models for discrete response', *Journal of Applied Econometrics*, 15, 447–470.

Moss, J. and S. Chilton (1997), *A Socio-Economic Evaluation of the Mourne Mountains and Slieve Croob Environmentally Sensitive Areas Scheme*, Belfast: Queen's University Belfast.

O'Leary, T., A. McCormack, W.G. Hutchinson, D. Campbell, R. Scarpa and B. Riordan (2004), 'Putting a value on the farm landscape', paper presented at the *National REPS Conference*, Tullamore, 3 November.
O'Leary, T., A. McCormack, A. Dhubháin, W.G. Hutchinson, D. Campbell, R. Scarpa and B. Riordan (2005), *Landscape Impacts of REPS: A Quantitative Assessment*, Report to the Department of Agriculture and Food, Dublin.
Randall, A. (2002), 'Valuing the outputs of multifunctional agriculture', *European Review of Agricultural Economics*, 29(3), 289–307.
Revelt, D. and K. Train (1998), 'Mixed logit with repeated choices: households' choices of appliance efficiency level', *The Review of Economics and Statistics*, 80(4), 647–657.
Sándor, Z. and M. Wedel (2001), 'Designing conjoint choice experiments using managers' prior beliefs', *Journal of Marketing Research*, 38, 430–444.
Scarpa, R., D. Campbell and W.G. Hutchinson (2007), 'Benefit estimates for landscape improvements: sequential Bayesian design and respondents' rationality in a choice experiment study', *Land Economics* (November), 83(4), 617–634.
Scarpa, R., K.G. Willis and M. Acutt (2005), 'Individual-specific welfare measures for public goods: a latent class approach to residential customers of Yorkshire Water', in P. Koundouri (ed.), *Econometrics Informing Natural Resource Management*, Cheltenham, UK and Nottingham, MA, USA: Edward Elgar.
Stewart, L., N. Hanley and I. Simpson (1997), *Economic Valuation Studies of the Agri-Environment Schemes in the United Kingdom*, Stirling: University of Stirling.
Train, K. (1998), 'Recreation demand models with taste differences over people', *Land Economics*, 74(2), 230–239.
Train, K. (1999), *Halton Sequences for Mixed Logit*, Berkeley: University of California.
Train, K. (2003), *Discrete Choice Methods with Simulation*, Cambridge: Cambridge University Press.
Train, K. and G. Sonnier (2005), 'Mixed logit with bounded distributions of correlated partworths', in R. Scarpa and A. Alberini (eds), *Applications of Simulation Methods in Environmental and Resource Economics*, Dordrecht: Springer Publisher, pp. 117–134.
Train, K. and M. Weeks (2005), 'Discrete choice models in preference space and willing-to-pay space', in R. Scarpa and A. Alberini (eds), *Applications of Simulation Methods in Environmental and Resource Economics*, Dordrecht: Springer Publisher, pp. 1–16.

4. Economic valuation of environmental impacts in the Severely Disadvantaged Areas in England

Helen Johns, Nick Hanley, Sergio Colombo and Ece Özdemiroğlu

INTRODUCTION

'Less Favoured Areas' (LFAs) are areas where farmers receive compensatory allowances to make up for geographical factors resulting in higher agricultural production and transportation costs. The classification was instigated at the EU level in 1975 (Council Directive 75/268/EEC), and usually applies to hilly or mountainous areas, as well as some islands. Payments are also intended to acknowledge the role farmers play in maintaining the landscape and rural communities. In England there are two grades of LFAs, comprising mostly of uplands: Disadvantaged Areas (DAs) and Severely Disadvantaged Areas (SDAs). LFA designation is primarily intended to support farming in these less accessible places, rather than being an environmental designation.

SDAs are often remote hill-farming areas which would face particular difficulty in maintaining economic competitiveness without subsidy. In England they include the Pennines, Lake District, Yorkshire Dales, North York Moors, Peak District, parts of the English–Welsh border, Exmoor and Dartmoor.[1] Disadvantaged Areas tend to be slightly less hilly areas on the fringes of SDAs. LFAs in England receive different rates of payment under the Single Payment Scheme, and can also apply for Hill Farm Allowance (HFA) payments, worth in total about £27 million per annum, which have associated environmental conditions. This study was undertaken to feed into a revision of the HFA in 2005. The ultimate policy objective of the HFA revision is to reward sustainable land management and the provision of public benefits associated with hill farming.

The objective of the study is to estimate the changes in external environmental values in the SDAs associated with land use changes expected to follow from potential revisions of the HFA. It is assumed that each one of the several upland attributes could potentially be changed – for better or worse – by any changes in support to upland farming, represented by different scenarios of policy change.

The populations affected by policy revision are: (i) local/regional residents; (ii) visitors to upland areas; and (iii) a 'non-user' or rather 'non-resident' population living further away from the areas of concern. In order to estimate the economic value held by the first two groups, surveys took place in the six Government Office Regions (GORs) in England containing SDAs (North West, North East, Yorkshire and Humber, East Midlands, West Midlands and South West). SDAs in other parts of the UK were explicitly excluded. This was done in order to estimate the economic value of SDAs *within each region* as expressed by the population of that region. In addition, the economic value of the attributes of the SDAs as held by the population living in GORs which do not contain SDAs was also investigated. In order to save time and budget, instead of undertaking a stated preference survey in each of the three GORs without SDAs, we implemented a survey in one of those, namely, the South East GOR. Importantly, however, we did not seek to measure values held by respondents in one SDA region for landscape features in another SDA region. This feature of our design, undertaken in order to keep the survey instrument of manageable size, means we are unable to quantify any spillover in value between GOR regions. For example, we do not know how people living in the North West region value landscape features of uplands in the South West region. This is a shortcoming of the present study and would influence the relative and absolute compensating surplus estimates for the policy options studied.

This chapter presents the valuation methodology used in the study, reports the results of the study and validity testing and suggests a number of conclusions of relevance to policy revision.

REVIEW OF UK LANDSCAPE VALUATION STUDIES

The literature review undertaken in preparation for the study covered previous valuation studies which examined upland landscape in the UK. Typical landscape attributes examined by the studies reviewed include the physical extent of broad habitat categories (moorland, wetland, broadleaved woodland, heather moorland, scrub) and diversity of habitat components (either the species diversity of habitats, or of some other consideration, for example, age diversity of woodlands).

Willis and Garrod (1993) used contingent valuation to assess preferences for a range of different landscapes in the Yorkshire Dales which could result from future subsidy changes. These were described in the survey as: intensive and semi-intensive agricultural, planned, conserved, sporting, wild and abandoned. The respondents consisted equally of residents of Craven local authority district in North Yorkshire and visitors to the area. Changes were illustrated to respondents pictorially. The outcome of such questions revealed fairly predictable preferences: most people would prefer more wild flowers and broadleaved woodland, fewer modern sheds and less wire fencing. Overall, the status quo landscape was the most popular, with nearly 50 per cent of respondents choosing it, with the conserved landscape also popular. The survey revealed strong preferences against intensive and semi-intensive landscapes. Willingness to pay (WTP) for the preferred landscape ranged from £18–35 per household per annum.

A study by Hanley *et al.* (1998) assessed the economic value of the conservation benefits of the Breadalbane Environmentally Sensitive Area (ESA) in Highland Perthshire. This was achieved by using both the contingent valuation and choice experiment (CE) methods for comparison purposes. The relevant populations were considered to be the UK general public, local residents and visitors. In the choice experiment, the attributes were broadleaved woodland, moorland, wetland, dry stone dykes and archaeological sites, which are all features which farmers receiving ESA payments are obliged to conserve. The policy scenarios pursued were simply 'policy on' and 'policy off', that is, a world with ESA payments and one without. Respondents expressed positive WTP for all the attributes at the 'policy on' levels, showing distinct preferences for greater levels of broadleaved woodland, heather moors and wet grasslands. Dry stone walls and archaeology commanded lower WTP.

Bullock and Kay (1997) also performed a contingent valuation study on upland attributes in Scotland, but in the Central Southern Uplands south of Edinburgh and Glasgow. They were testing for WTP for agricultural policies that produced landscapes associated with extensive grazing. Three policy options were presented: business-as-usual, extensive and very extensive. The landscapes were illustrated pictorially (using symbols indicating the abundance of wildlife), and no attempt was made to elicit values for individual landscape attributes. Local residents, birdwatchers and visitors to local beauty spots were surveyed. The results showed a clear preference for landscapes with more extensive grazing and with more tree cover than at present.

White and Lovett (1999) performed a contingent valuation study on a particular estate (Levisham) in the North York Moors to measure WTP to maintain or enhance the estate. WTP for different landscape features was not sought, although qualitative preferences for habitat types associated with or reduced by sheep farming, such as heather moorland, semi-natural woodlands and unimproved pasture were sought. Many more respondents preferred either heather moorland or semi-natural woodlands compared to unimproved pasture, and indicated different motivations for these choices (heather moorland for landscape, woodland for biodiversity and scarcity value). Fewer than half the participants indicated a positive WTP to maintain or enhance the estate, with half of the zero WTP bids being protest bids stating that National Parks should pay for themselves.

Overall, the studies indicate that the landscapes of upland areas and other agricultural areas are generally valued by the public. The studies reviewed do not agree on whether respondents tend to prefer a particular landscape because it has always been familiar to them, that is, attachment to the status quo. Willis and Garrod (1993) report a clear preference for the status quo. By contrast, Bullock and Kay (1997) tested specifically for this bias by actually asking respondents which landscape they found more typical. They found that respondents did not necessarily prefer this landscape, and that overall respondents preferred a more extensified landscape. These different findings could reflect regional differences, or they could reflect a more conservative attitude by residents in a designated National Park.

METHODOLOGY

Most of the upland attributes included in this study are examples of non-market goods – goods which, while contributing towards individuals' welfare, are not traded in markets and therefore if they are to be valued, must be valued by methods other than those using market data. A choice experiment approach was chosen in preference to contingent valuation for the key reasons outlined in Chapter 1.

Selection of Attributes and their Levels

In terms of environmental impacts, a long list of fourteen environmental attributes which could be affected by the policy changes associated with upland areas was initially suggested by the project steering group: heather moorland and bog; improved grassland; rough grassland; hay meadows; bracken; gorse; arable and set-aside land; broadleaf and mixed woodland; coniferous woodland; field boundaries; cultural heritage; water quantity; water quality; and greenhouse gas emissions.

However, it was considered that a maximum of five upland attributes – with the addition of a sixth cost attribute – was feasible for the choice experiment (in order not to overload respondents with information; see for example Louviere *et al.*, 2000). The following attributes were chosen on the basis that (i) they are among the most likely to be affected by changes in LFA policy; and (ii) they were shown to be important in the study focus groups.

- **Heather moorland and bog:** *Calluna vulgaris* (heather) dominates heather moorland, although the extent of that domination varies from very high in dry heath (typically on well-drained nutrient-poor acid soils) to lower in wet heath (found on wetter, peaty soils). In areas of high rainfall, over flatter areas and in hollows, bog habitat may be found. This high conservation value habitat is often characterised by a high cover of *Sphagnum* mosses. These habitats are all typically used as extensive grazing, particularly for sheep. All of these habitats can be found over peat or peaty podsol soils, and peat erosion is often a problem when the habitat is overgrazed or subject to nutrient enrichment.
- **Rough grassland:** This definition applies to areas typically used for extensive grazing, usually by sheep, and in this study is taken to include acid grasslands (including grass-dominated moorland) and calcareous grasslands. In areas of poor soil quality (acidic, nutrient poor), acid grasslands may often contain some heather, or may be intermixed with heather moorland.
- **Broadleaf and mixed woodland:** In upland areas this habitat may consist of a mix of native species, or be dominated by one. In different parts of the country different species may dominate or be of higher conservation importance. The spread of established woodland can be assisted by reduced grazing and ground preparation (for example, scarification). The most common species found naturally establishing in upland areas is birch. Note that this habitat category is taken to include woodland habitats that may contain native conifers such as yew and juniper.
- **Field boundaries:** Included in this attribute are hedges, stone walls, ditches, banks and lines of trees, but not modern fences. Field boundaries prevent the passage of animals and demarcate fields, as well as being part of the visual landscape. In many upland areas, field boundaries are made up of traditional dry-stone walls. However, hedges can also be common and these can be a valuable habitat for many species.
- **Cultural heritage:** This attribute may be taken to include the visual presence in the landscape of traditional farm buildings. Less visual aspects may be the presence of animals on hill sides, traditional breeds, or traditional farming practices such as shepherding with sheep dogs.

The cost attribute was defined as an 'increase in tax payments by your household each year' with an indefinite payment period. A more specific 'payment vehicle' such as council tax or a new national tax was not used, as focus group results indicated that these would be likely to lead to higher protest votes; some respondents expressed the view that it was either unfair for the whole country to pay for a local benefit, or unfair for local people to pay for a national asset such as a National Park.

Table 4.1 shows the attribute levels used in the choice experiment. The appropriate range of values to use was decided on the basis of consultation with policy makers and experts.

Table 4.1 The levels of each attribute used in the choice experiment

Attribute	Definition	Attribute levels
Heather moorland/ bog	*Calluna vulgaris* (heather) dominated moorland, often found over peaty soils. Bog habitat in wetter areas.	−12% **−2%** +5%
Rough grassland	Areas typically used for extensive sheep grazing, including acid and calcareous grasslands. May be intermixed with heather moorland.	**−10%** +5% +10%
Broadleaf and mixed woodland	May consist of a mix of native species, or be dominated by one. May contain native conifers such as yew and juniper.	**+3%** +10% +20%
Field boundaries (for every 1km, *x*m is restored)	Hedges, stone walls, ditches, banks and lines of trees, but not modern fences.	$x=50$ $\boldsymbol{x=100}$ $x=200$
Cultural heritage	Traditional farm buildings and farming practices.	**Rapid decline** No change Much better conservation
Cost	Amount paid per household per year through higher tax payments.	£2, £5, £10, £17, £40, £70 (the baseline of £0 was not given as an option in other scenarios)

Note: Attribute levels in bold indicate those levels which were used for the choice card baseline.

Experimental Design

Each choice card shown in the choice experiment part of the questionnaire presented three scenarios with different levels of attribute changes. The first scenario represented the nominal choice card baseline, which is identical on all the choice cards. The other two scenarios presented different levels of change over the baseline, described by different levels of the upland attributes.

These two other scenarios showed the attribute levels in different combinations, chosen from one of the three levels for each upland attribute (or six levels for cost) presented in Table 4.1. A full set of combinations of the six attributes at their various levels would create a total of 1458 possible scenario combinations.[2] In order to narrow this down into a reasonable number of scenarios which could be tested, a fractional factorial design was used to reduce the number of scenarios, while still maintaining the possibility of estimating 'main effects', that is, the effects of the attributes on respondents' choices (Louviere *et al.*, 2000). The fractional factorial design selected 36 'alternative policy' scenarios, which were then grouped into

	Policy Option	Choice Card Baseline	Policy Option A	Policy Option B
	Change in area of heather moorland and bog	A loss of 2% (–2%)	A gain of 5% (+5%)	A loss of 2% (–2%)
	Change in area of rough grassland	A loss of 10% (–10%)	A gain of 10% (+10%)	A loss of 10% (–10%)
	Change in area of mixed and broadleaf woodlands	A gain of 3% (+3%)	A gain of 20% (+20%)	A gain of 10% (+10%)
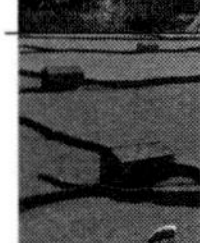	Condition of field boundaries	For every 1km, 100 m is restored	For every 1km, 200 m is restored	For every 1km, 50 m is restored
	Change in farm building and traditional farm practices	Rapid decline	Much better conservation	No change
	Increase in tax payments by your household each year	£0	£70	£10

Figure 4.1 Example of a choice card used in the survey

choice sets to be presented to respondents following the procedure proposed by Street *et al.* (2005).

This process resulted in 18 choice cards with two 'alternative policy' scenarios per card (each pair compared with the choice card baseline). Given that it would not be practical for an individual to make that many choices, each respondent was shown six out of the total set of 18 cards.[3] Therefore, the sample was divided into thirds: one third of respondents presented with cards 1–6, one third presented with cards 7–12, and one third with cards 13–18. The sequence of cards was rotated between respondents (for example, respondent 1 saw cards 1–6 in order, respondent 2 saw cards 2, 3, 4, 5, 6, 1 and so on), in order to avoid any 'ordering effect'.

Questionnaire Design and Implementation

The questionnaire consisted of three sections: (A) attitudes, opinions and uses; (B) choice experiment valuation section; and (C) follow-up and socio-economic questions. The attitude and use section included questions on how often respondents visited the countryside and SDAs in their region; how important they thought environmental policy was in relation to other policy areas; which areas of environmental policy they considered to be important; and whether they or anyone else in their household belonged to an environmental, heritage, outdoor recreation or farming organisation, such as the National Trust or Ramblers' Association.

After an initial pilot survey sample of 50 respondents, the stated preference study was implemented separately in seven out of the nine English Government Office Regions (GORs): the six containing SDAs and the South East region. Conducting the survey in only one GOR that does not contain SDAs was a decision made due to time and budget limitations and on the assumption that the results from the South East could be transferred to the two other regions without SDAs (London and the East).

All the regional questionnaires used the same attributes and the same percentage changes, which allowed comparison of WTP results across regions. However, the percentage changes obviously translate into different absolute amounts in different regions.

Three hundred respondents in each of the six GORs which contain SDAs, as well as 300 respondents in the South East GOR, were interviewed. The survey mode was face-to-face, door-to-door personal interviews. Each sample was chosen according to quotas for age, gender, socio-economic group and also whether respondents resided in an urban or rural area. Table 4.2 summarises for each region the proportions of survey respondents for each sampling quota along with (in brackets) comparative proportions according to the 2001 Census or equivalent data. Other socio-economic

Table 4.2 Principal socio-economic characteristics of survey samples

	North West	North East	Yorks. and the Humber	West Midlands	East Midlands	South West	South East
Total no. respondents	335	300	312	318	314	301	345
Gender (%)							
Males	48(48)	49(49)	50(49)	49(49)	46(50)	46(50)	48(50)
Females	52(52)	51(51)	50(51)	51(51)	54(50)	54(50)	52(50)
Age brackets (%)							
18–34	42(33)	34(32)	33(32)	33(33)	39(32)	30(30)	35(32)
35–54	32(42)	42(43)	43(42)	38(42)	36(42)	41(42)	40(43)
55–70	26(25)	24(36)	24(25)	29(25)	26(25)	29(28)	25(26)
Socio-economic group[1] (%)							
ABC1	35(48)	43(37)	40(38)	48(46)	46(43)	47(48)	57(53)
C2DE	65(52)	56(63)	59(62)	52(54)	54(57)	52(52)	42(47)
Distribution of sample (and population) between rural and urban areas							
Rural	11(12)	12(19)	23(20)	15(16)	39(30)	32(34)	20(22)
Urban	89(88)	88(81)	77(80)	85(84)	61(70)	68(66)	80(78)
Employment status (%)							
Full-time	52	43	40	32	37	35	33
Part-time	11	12	12	19	14	18	12
Other[2]	24	39	40	36	42	37	44

Education (%)							
School only	83	80	80	66	80	72	79
University	16	11	9	34	7	15	21

Notes:

1. Market Research Society definitions: A: professionals, very senior managers, etc.; B: middle management in large organisations, top management or owners of small businesses, educational and service establishments; C1: Supervisory, clerical, junior managerial / administrative / professional; C2: Skilled manual workers; D: Semi-skilled and unskilled manual workers; E: On state benefit, unemployed, lowest grade workers.
2. Retired, unemployed, students, etc.

Figures in brackets represent the figures according to official statistics.

Employment status and education percentages may not add up to 100 per cent due to refused answers.

characteristics of the final survey respondents which are important but which were not specified in the form of sample quotas are also presented in Table 4.2. Apart from some relatively minor deviations from the quotas in particular age or socio-economic groups in particular regions, the survey sample is representative. It was originally planned also to have survey quotas based on location in urban, rural (but not SDA) and SDA areas. However, the proportion of the population actually living in SDAs in each region was too small for this to be feasible or necessary: overall only 37 out of 1800 (2 per cent) respondents in SDA GORs would have been interviewed.

RESULTS AND DISCUSSION

Experiences, Perceptions, Attitudes

It was clear that most respondents were environmentally aware and concerned, the vast majority (88 per cent) replying that they considered environmental policy to be very or quite important related to other policy areas. However, protecting the countryside did not rank highly as an environmental concern compared to controlling air pollution or tackling climate change. Overall, 24 per cent of respondents (or members of their household) belonged to some kind of environmental, heritage, outdoor recreation or farming organisation.

A very high proportion (84 per cent) of respondents visited the countryside and a similarly high proportion (79 per cent) visited SDAs for recreational purposes. Respondents in most regions said that they visited the countryside more than they visited SDAs, as would be expected. Unsurprisingly, this was especially true in the South East, which does not have any SDAs. Oddly, in the North West region more respondents said that they visited SDAs for recreational purposes than the countryside. It is possible that in a region like the North West, where SDAs dominate the landscape, the initial term 'countryside' conjured up flatter, less wild countryside to respondents.

With regard to stated preference studies, there are three types of validity which should be considered: content, construct and convergent validity. The validity tests involve the analysis of responses about attitudes towards the survey, econometric analysis of the WTP function, and comparison of the findings against prior expectations and other studies.

Content Validity

Content validity assesses whether the stated preference study asked the right questions in a clear, understandable and appropriate manner with which to obtain a valid estimate of the WTP measure under investigation. This can include examining the reasons behind respondents having positive and zero WTP responses, as well as general attitudes towards the survey.

Those respondents who chose at least one policy option in the choice experiment other than the choice card baseline indicated that they had non-zero WTP for improvements to the upland attributes. The proportion of respondents who were willing to pay for improvements in the upland attributes, the proportion identified as genuinely having zero WTP (for example, because they can't afford to pay or because the changes aren't important to them) and the proportion deemed to have expressed zero WTP for protest reasons (for example, objecting to the payment vehicle) are summarised in Table 4.3.

The number of protest bids varies widely across regions, with a very high level in the North East and a relatively low number in the West Midlands. The level of protest bids are at the high end or slightly in excess of the range (6–25 per cent) found in comparable studies detailed in the literature review section above. The proportion of protest bids in the North East is particularly high. This could be because other studies have focused on valuing much more specific areas, such as a particular Environmentally Sensitive Area or even a particular estate.

The most frequently cited reasons for having positive WTP were personal enjoyment of the countryside, environmental concern and preserving cultural heritage. The most frequently cited reasons for having zero WTP were inability to afford (a genuine reason) or that the government should pay (a protest reason).

Table 4.3 Percentage of respondents willing to pay for improvements to upland attributes

Section B (CE for own region)	North West	North East	Yorks. and the Humber	West Midlands	East Midlands	South West	South East	Overall
Positive WTP (%)	56	48	60	81	65	75	65	64
Genuine Zero WTP (%)	18	9	9	5	12	8	8	10
Protest Zero WTP (%)	26	44	31	14	23	17	26	26

Construct Validity

The purpose of construct validity is to gauge whether respondents' choices are internally consistent, and whether the expected relationships between WTP and explanatory variables based on economic theory hold. This is achieved by examining whether coefficients on certain attitudinal and socio-economic variables have the expected signs. One of the variables most commonly used in this test is income. Due to the high income non-response rate, it had to be excluded from regression models in most regions. However, the cost attribute, which is another variable commonly used for this test, had a significant and negative coefficient in all regions, in line with prior expectations.

The probability of respondents making particular choices was initially analysed using a conditional logit (CL) model, firstly using only the levels of attributes as explanatory variables, and then introducing socio-economic and attitudinal variables to the model to test the effect of relevant individual characteristics on choice. Typically, a nested logit model would also be tested, that is, a model which attempts to explain the factors behind a respondent having either zero or non-zero WTP, and is then used to model respondents' choices given that they have non-zero WTP. However in some regions, the survey dataset did not contain enough zero WTP observations that were not protest results to run a nested logit model.

An important implication of the model specification used in analysing the CE responses is that selections from the choice set must obey the 'independence from irrelevant alternatives' (IIA) property. This property states that the relative probabilities of two options being selected are unaffected by the introduction or removal of other alternatives. If a violation of the IIA hypothesis is observed, then more complex statistical models are necessary that relax some of the assumptions used. There are numerous formal statistical tests than can be used to test for violations of the IIA assumption. In this study we employed the test developed by Hausman and McFadden (1984), being the most widely used.

If the data of a specific region did not pass the IIA test, even after including in the model specification the respondents' socio-economic, demographic and attitudinal variables, a random parameter logit (RPL) approach was chosen for the analysis. This approach is also employed in other chapters of this volume, including Chapters 3 and 11. Using this model specification it is also possible to circumvent the limitation of the conditional logit model that assumes that preferences are homogenous amongst respondents.[4] The RPL model allows for variation in preferences across individuals. Its application requires assumptions to be made about the distribution of preferences. Here it is assumed that preferences relating to the attributes are heterogeneous and follow a normal distribution while preferences towards cost are assumed to be homogeneous. Therefore, separate parameters are estimated for each individual for all attributes along with a single parameter for all respondents for cost. The result is that each random attribute has a mean value (interpreted as the average preference of respondents for the attribute) and a standard deviation value (interpreted as the magnitude of differences in respondents' preferences for the attribute). RPL models were estimated in all regions apart from Yorkshire and the Humber, where the conditional logit model with respondents' characteristics passed the IIA test. Table 4.4 presents the model coefficients and Table 4.5 explains the variable abbreviations used.

Some general findings emerge from the analysis of the model results. While the same questionnaire and specification of attributes are used in all regions, the factors that influence the choices made by respondents in different regions vary. Heather moorland and bog, mixed and broadleaved woodland and a large change in cultural heritage attributes are shown to be significant factors in respondents' choices in most regions. On the other hand, rough grassland, field boundaries and a small change in cultural heritage attributes are generally not significant factors in the choices. The only evidence that respondents might prefer what is already abundant in their region is that respondents in Yorkshire and the Humber were the only SDA GOR respondents to have their choices significantly affected by field boundaries. However, this GOR also has the greatest abundance of heather moorland and bog, and respondents were not shown to be particularly responsive to that attribute.

In terms of socio-economic variables, the level of education and the relative importance attached to environmental policy compared to other policy seem to be the variables that have a significant influence over respondents' choices most commonly across the regions. Note that two of the variables – ENVIMP and VISFREQ – have counterintuitive questionnaire rankings in reverse order of magnitude, so extra care must be taken over the interpretation of their coefficients. More specifically, a lower variable value implies that someone is more concerned about environmental policy, or that they visit SDAs more often.[5]

Where income could be included in models, it does not appear to have been a significant factor, a potential result of the high non-response rate to the income question resulting in fewer observations for that variable. However, among other factors such as awareness, education could also embody at least part of the impact income would have, given that education level is generally associated with income level.

Table 4.4 Attributes and socio-economic variables: model coefficients for each region

	NW	NW	YH	WM	EM	SW	SE
Model used	RPL	RPL	CL	RPL	RPL	RPL	RPL
Const	−0.485	0.248	2.915*	3.880*	2.225*	1.463	2.828*
	(0.933)	(1.238)	(0.722)	(0.861)	(0.819)	(0.957)	(0.641)
HMB	0.062*	0.006	0.011***	0.035*	0.016***	0.03*	0.025*
	(0.014)	(0.011)	(0.006)	(0.008)	(0.007)	(0.009)	(0.007)
RG	0.059*	0.004	0.011**	0.008	0.001	−0.002	0.016*
	(0.012)	(0.010)	(0.005)	(0.007)	(0.007)	(0.007)	(0.006)
BMW	0.049*	0.005	0.005	0.023*	0.015**	0.009	0.038*
	(0.012)	(0.014)	(0.006)	(0.01)	(0.007)	(0.006)	(0.007)
FB	0.000	0.000	0.001**	0.001	0.001	−0.001	0.002*
	(0.002)	(0.001)	(0.001)	(0.001)	(0.001)	(0.001)	(0.001)
CH1	0.082	−0.079	0.109***	0.033	0.119	0.187**	0.025
	(0.121)	(0.107)	(0.061)	(0.074)	(0.077)	(0.083)	(0.065)
CH2	0.391*	0.139	0.423*	0.214**	0.338*	0.291*	0.493*
	(0.143)	(0.138)	(0.066)	(0.098)	(0.087)	(0.108)	(0.071)
	−0.080*	−0.021*	−0.035*	−0.039*	−0.015*	−0.029*	−0.031*
TAX	(0.007)	(0.004)	(0.003)	(0.004)	(0.003)	(0.003)	(0.003)
	−0.463	0.121	−0.031	0.342***	−0.175	0.155	−0.047
AGE	(0.223)	(0.267)	(0.142)	(0.188)	(0.150)	(0.188)	(0.130)
	0.079	0.727**	0.231	−0.497**	0.261	0.903*	−0.122
GENDER	(0.276)	(0.316)	(0.154)	(0.232)	(0.194)	(0.240)	(0.164)
	−0.899*	−1.070*	−0.599*	−0.585*	−0.794*	−0.255	−0.381*
ENVIMP	(0.192)	(0.237)	(0.124)	(0.204)	(0.148)	(0.204)	(0.136)
	0.153*	0.085	−0.235*	−0.222*	−0.044	−0.125*	−0.250*
VISFREQ	(0.064)	(0.067)	(0.036)	(0.052)	(0.036)	(0.047)	(0.046)
	−0.022*	−0.02***	−0.006	−0.012	0.009	0.003	−0.001
LIVING	(0.009)	(0.012)	(0.007)	(0.008)	(0.007)	(0.142)	(0.006)
	−0.150	0.064	−0.196***	−0.204***	−0.446*	−0.127	−0.204**
REMAIN	(0.125)	(0.197)	(0.116)	(0.113)	(0.138)	(0.142)	(0.094)
	0.936**	0.019	0.437	0.564**	−0.059	−0.006	0.554*

MEMBER	(0.407)	(0.424)	(0.275)	(0.238)	(0.234)	(0.270)	(0.195)
	0.482*	0.275***	0.267*	0.126	0.393*	0.281*	0.286*
EDU	(0.109)	(0.149)	(0.082)	(0.082)	(0.109)	(0.105)	(0.067)
	1.343*	1.046*	0.148	−0.230	0.321	−0.059	0.089
EMPLOY	(0.336)	(0.328)	(0.162)	(0.250)	(0.201)	(0.280)	(0.171)
	−1.083**	2.862*	0.673*	−1.559*	0.325	−0.394	1.481*
RURAL	(0.514)	(0.613)	(0.280)	(0.435)	(0.214)	(0.261)	(0.232)
	0.166			0.109	0.095		
INCOME	(0.105)	n/a	n/a	(0.091)	(0.086)	n/a	n/a
Standard deviation values							
HMB	0.089*	0.072*	Not	0.054*	0.00001	0.062*	0.00002
	(0.021)	(0.017)	relevant	(0.014)	(0.00001)	(0.014)	(0.00002)
RG	0.080*	0.064*		0.050*	0.00002***	0.049*	0.00002
	(0.080)	(0.011)		(0.009)	(0.00001)	(0.009)	(0.00002)
BMW	0.031	0.097*		0.078*	0.000008	0.031*	0.00003**
	(0.127)	(0.016)		(0.012)	(0.00001)	(0.012)	(0.00001)
FB	0.010*	0.007*		0.003	0.000002	0.008*	0.00004*
	(0.002)	(0.002)		(0.002)	(0.00002)	(0.001)	(0.00001)
CH1	0.479*	0.183		0.199	0.000056	0.471*	0.0003**
	(0.167)	(0.219)		(0.169)	(0.00006)	(0.131)	(0.0001)
CH2	0.667*	1.034*		0.760*	0.000121	0.900*	0.00027***
	(0.163)	(0.152)		(0.099)	(0.00014)	(0.117)	(0.0002)
No obs	1073	813	1138	1157	846	1135	1255
LL	−760.9	−727.2	−1049.4	−1059.0	−821.9	−1032.4	−1134.3
Pseudo ρ^2	0.354	0.19	0.15	0.17	0.12	0.17	0.18

Notes:
RPL – random parameter logit model applied.
CL – conditional logit model applied.
The income variable had to be omitted from these models due to the high non-response rate.
Asterisks denote significance levels at 1% (*), 5% (**) and 10% (***) respectively.
See Table 4.5 for an explanation of the variables.

Table 4.5 Explanation of variable abbreviations used in Table 4.4

const	constant term (= 0 if the current policy is chosen, = 1 for alternatives A or B)
HMB	percentage change in area of heather moorland and bog
RG	percentage change in area of rough grassland
BMW	percentage change in area of broadleaf and mixed woodland
FB	change in the length of field boundaries (in metres restored)
CH1	small change in cultural heritage indicated (1 = yes, 0 = no)
CH2	Large change in cultural heritage indicated (1 = yes, 0 = no)
TAX	tax amount indicated in pounds
AGE	respondent's age in years
GENDER	respondent's gender (1 = male, 0 = female)
ENVIMP	importance of environmental policy to respondent (1 = very important, 4 = not important)
VISFREQ	respondent's frequency of visits to severely disadvantaged areas (1 = every day, 10 = never)
LIVING	number of years respondents have been living in the region
REMAIN	respondent's expected residence in the region (1 = less than 6 months, 5 = indefinite)
MEMBER	whether respondent belongs to an environmental, recreational, etc. organization (1 = yes, 0 = no)
EDU	respondent's education level (1= primary, 6= higher degree)
EMPLOY	whether respondent is an active worker (1 = yes, 0 = no)
RURAL	whether respondent is a rural dweller (1 = yes, 0 = no)
INCOME	household income per head

The only universally significant finding was that the cost of a policy option was a significant factor in making respondents less likely to choose an alternative policy, all else being equal.

Convergent Validity

Convergent validity examines whether the quantitative results are broadly comparable with the results of other studies valuing similar goods. From the choice experiment model coefficients reported in Table 4.4, it is possible to estimate utility-consistent welfare measures following the compensating surplus formula described by Hanemann (1984).[6] Compensating surplus estimates for various management scenarios of other environmental good, such as landscapes and wetlands, are also reported in Chapters 5 and 11, respectively. Table 4.7 shows the compensating surplus estimates and 95 per cent confidence intervals for the following scenarios:[7]

- **Scenario 1: Environment-agricultural.** Under Scenario 1, the strategic policy aims of the HFA reflect the importance of environmental and conservation objectives and the importance of maintaining upland farming systems to achieve these objectives. Eligibility for HFA support is dependent upon producers having all or part of their holding in an existing or new agri-environment scheme. The result would be more land being entered into agri-environment schemes than otherwise and the associated delivery of greater environmental outcomes.
- **Scenario 2: Environment only.** Under Scenario 2, the strategic aims for upland support are focused solely on achieving environmental goals. It is assumed that existing support amounting to £27 million per year is maintained but incorporated into the agri-environment scheme budget and ring-fenced for the uplands, specifically the SDAs. It is assumed that the funding schemes target specific activities such as active grazing, maintaining hefted flocks on the poorest grazing areas and moorland grip blocking.
- **Scenario 3: Abandonment-intensification.** Under Scenario 3, upland support is withdrawn entirely.

Note that all compensating surplus estimates are relative to the 'Business-As-Usual' scenario where the Hill Farm Allowance (HFA) scheme remains broadly the same as it is presently. There is no change in the strategic aims, structure and level of upland support, which remains focused on maintaining the upland farming system. Variations of the attribute levels under the different scenarios are presented in Table 4.6 and compensating surplus estimates in Table 4.7.

Note that Table 4.7 does not include results for the North East as the function that explains the WTP estimates for the North East returned insignificant coefficients for all upland attributes. This precludes estimation of WTP per attribute of compensating for this region, and similarly, compensating surplus for policy options.

These surplus estimates represent respondents' average WTP to move from the state of the world given in the 'Business-As-Usual' scenario to the state of the world given in Scenarios 1, 2 or 3 (note that in the choice cards, respondents were valuing 'end points' of landscape change following a policy choice, not annual increments or decrements in landscape features). Respondents show positive WTP for both Scenario 1 and Scenario 2, with a higher compensating surplus associated with the latter. This makes sense, since Scenario 2 implies a higher level for each landscape attribute than Scenario 1. Note that there is considerable regional variation in the values attached to both Scenario 1 and Scenario 2 ranging from £7.44 for Scenario

Table 4.6 Predictions of how the five CE landscape attributes would change under the three policy scenarios compared to the 'Business-As-Usual' scenario

Upland attribute	Scenario 1 Env-agri	Scenario 2 Env only	Scenario 3 Aband-intens
Heather moorland and bog	+2%	+4%	−3%
Rough grassland	−2%	−4%	+2%
Mixed and broadleaved woodland	+1%	+3%	+2%
Field boundaries	+1%	+5%	−3%
Cultural heritage	'Slow decline' rather than 'decline'	'No decline' rather than 'decline'	No difference

Source: Cumulus *et al.* (2005).

1 in the West Midlands region to £47.97 for Scenario 2 in the East Midlands. The compensating surplus for Scenario 3 is mostly negative and insignificantly different from zero, suggesting that respondents do not value the change under this policy option. The aggregate values for the South East region that might be generalised to other regions not containing SDAs (this requires the assumption of preference equality amongst these regions) are considered a sort of national-level 'non-resident' value. Such value may be added proportionally to the regional values to estimate a total economic value for conserving landscape features in the SDAs.

CS estimates of Scenario 1 and 2 can be compared with the WTP ranges found in other similar studies – this comparison is shown in Table 4.8. The only study with figures considerably lower than the CS figures found in this study is White and Lovett (1999). This is unsurprising as it valued only one small estate, whereas the other studies valued large upland areas comparable to the regional SDA areas valued in this study. The CS figures are broadly comparable to the figures found in Willis and Garrod (1993) and Hanley *et al.* (1998); they are on the low side compared to Bullock and Kay (1997).

CONCLUSIONS

The objective of this study was specifically to provide monetary estimates of the relative economic value of upland attributes in each Government Office Region (GOR) with Severely Disadvantaged Areas (SDAs). This

Table 4.7 Compensating surplus estimates for the three policy scenarios (relative to 'Business-as-Usual') for each GOR

	North West	Yorkshire and the Humber	West Midlands	East Midlands	South West	South East
Compensating surplus (£ per household per year)*						
Scenario 1 (agri-environment)	7.68 (2.59–13.33)	18.64 (12.28–25.56)	7.44 (0.39–14.42)	41.81 (22.27–81.34)	20.59 (9.28–32.83)	19.85 (12.47–27.66)
Scenario 2 (environment only)	9.17 (3.60–15.22)	20.54 (14.16–27.59)	10.04 (2.58–17.51)	47.97 (26.45–94.88)	21.74 (9.84–34.64)	25.40 (17.72–34.17)
Scenario 3 (abandonment)	0.21 (−1.41–1.88)	−1.20 (−2.78–0.63)	−1.50 (−3.36–0.42)	−2.73 (−9.06–3.83)	−0.92 (−3.76–2.20)	−0.89 (−3.12–1.15)
No. households (million)	2.81	2.07	2.15	1.73	2.09	3.29
Compensating surplus (aggregated across all households, £ million per year)						
Scenario 1 (agri-environment)	21.58 (7.28–37.46)	38.58 (25.42–52.91)	16.00 (0.84–31.00)	72.33 (38.53–140.72)	43.03 (19.40–68.61)	65.31 (41.03–91.00)
Scenario 2 (environment only)	25.77 (10.12–42.77)	42.52 (29.31–57.11)	21.59 (5.55–37.65)	82.99 (45.76–164.14)	45.44 (20.57–72.40)	83.57 (58.3–112.42)
Scenario 3 (abandonment)	0.59 (−3.96–5.28)	−2.48 (−5.75–1.30)	−3.23 (−7.22–0.90)	−4.72 (−15.67–6.63)	−1.92 (−7.86–4.60)	−2.93 (−10.26–3.78)

Notes:
* Average exchange rate £1=€1.42 in 2005.
Figures in brackets indicate 95% confidence intervals.

Table 4.8 Summary of per household WTP figures found by similar landscape valuation studies

Study / Location	**Geographical scope**	**Change valued**	**WTP per household per annum**[1]
Willis and Garrod (1993), Yorkshire Dales	Yorkshire Dales National Park (177 000 ha)	A range of alternative landscape changes, ranging from intensive/ agricultural to wild/abandoned	£18–35
Hanley *et al.* (1998), Bread-albane	An ESA[2] covering 179 000 ha	Change to the landscape from removing ESA subsidies	£22–27
Bullock and Kay (1997), Scottish Central Southern Uplands	An ESA covering 273 000 ha	Landscapes brought about by extensive or very extensive grazing	£41–82
White and Lovett (1999), North York Moors	The Levisham Estate (1359 ha)	Landscapes and habitat types brought about by reduced sheep grazing	Mean WTP £3.10
This study	SDAs in a given GOR	Landscape changes brought about by the hypothecated policy Scenarios 1–3 net of the BAU Scenario 0	£7–48

Notes:
1. Ranges are for different scenarios or sub-samples.
2. Environmentally Sensitive Area.

information was collected through a choice experiment survey applied in seven regions in England.

On the whole, people are willing to pay to contribute to improvements in the upland attributes of the SDAs included in the study. The lowest WTP is observed in the North West region. This fits in with attitudinal responses from the North West; respondents from that region had the highest percentage of genuine zero WTP responses, and the policy cost (increases in annual tax payments) attribute showed the most negative coefficient in the North West, indicating an unwillingness to pay. The North West results, along with the high WTP of South Eastern respondents, to some extent indicate that people either value what they do not already have in abundance, or that people in the North West are less willing to pay *alone* for what they consider to be a national asset (the Lake District).

There are, however, large variations in the values individuals place on landscape features across different regions, which cannot be explained fully on the basis of socio-economic differences between populations. Therefore there are regional differences which cannot presently be explained or included in a benefits transfer function. This could make the transfer error in a possible benefits transfer exercise unacceptably large. For this reason, we do not think it advisable to conduct a benefits transfer exercise from the South East results to the other two non-SDA regions of England as originally intended.

Notwithstanding the regional differences, on the whole, changes in cultural heritage (if a large improvement) and policy cost attributes seem to have played a role in the choices respondents made. The consistently large coefficients for a large improvement in cultural heritage could be purely because a large discrete change (from 'rapid decline' to 'much better conservation') was on offer. If we had been able to measure the cultural heritage attribute quantitatively, and hence vary it continuously, it may not have been as consistently important in affecting respondents' choices. That said, it was clear from the focus groups, valuation workshops and reasons respondents gave for being willing to pay for landscape improvements that cultural heritage is something that is highly valued. Therefore, the implications of any agricultural or environmental improvement scheme on this attribute should be considered carefully.

In terms of the other attributes, woodland was the next most likely to affect respondents' choices, followed by heather moorland and bog, rough grassland and field boundaries; the latter did not appear to be highly valued. It is possible that respondents saw field boundaries as an attribute which could be rebuilt or replanted, and which was not gone forever if lost.

On the basis of the South East survey, there is also evidence that those who live in regions without SDAs are likely to have positive preferences for the improvement of upland attributes in the SDAs. However, due to significant but not completely explainable differences in preferences across GORs, we cannot transfer the results of the South East to the London and East of England GORs, which also do not have SDAs.

A final piece of evidence for non-use values comes from the finding that many respondents in GORs with SDAs who said that they never visited SDAs were nevertheless willing to pay for improvements.

ACKNOWLEDGEMENTS

Preliminary work on the physical forecast changes to upland attributes by eftec was reviewed and expanded by Cumulus Consultants Ltd in association with the Institute for European Environmental Policy and the

Countryside and Community Research Unit. The study was funded by the UK Department for Environment, Food and Rural Affairs.

The study team would like to thank Professor Ian Bateman (University of East Anglia) who, as the peer reviewer, provided valuable comments at various stages of the work, as well as Dr Stavros Georgiou and Dr Tony Hyde, who moderated the focus groups and workshops.

NOTES

1. Please visit www.defra.gov.uk/farm/capreform/pdf/EnglandSDA.pdf for a map of the location of SDAs in England.
2. Multiplying the number of levels of each attribute together gives $3 \times 3 \times 3 \times 3 \times 3 \times 6 = 1458$.
3. Different numbers of choice cards were tested in the pilot survey to assess the optimum number of cards a respondent could cope with.
4. In any case, as firstly indicated by Louviere *et al.* (2002) and recently pointed out by Swait (2006, page 258), the use of a random parameter logit model implicitly requires the assumption of a constant scale parameter. If the scale is not constant across respondents there is a confounding between the distribution of the preference parameters and the distribution of the scale parameter. In this case, the RPL model is not able to identify correctly the preference distribution parameters, although model prediction is unaffected by this property of the model. If analysts are primarily interested in determining the parameter distributions, they should switch to the heteroskedastic RPL model, where the scale is free to vary among respondents and alternatives. However, specific software is required for this estimation.
5. Socio-economic and attitudinal variables being invariant across individual choices impede model estimation. To circumvent this problem they must interact with either the model constant or attributes. In this study we interacted the individual characteristic variables with the constant. The resulting coefficients have to be interpreted as the effect of the individual characteristics on the probability of choosing the current policy option or either policy A or B options.
6. In the compensating surplus estimation, all respondents' characteristics were set to the sample mean level.
7. The policy scenarios used and the attribute forecasts resulting from them are described in detail in a report submitted to Defra by a different set of authors (Cumulus *et al.*, 2005). It is not necessary to go into the complex details of the reasoning and assumptions behind the different forecast estimates here, so only basic descriptions of the policy scenarios and the forecast results are provided. The interested reader can refer to Cumulus *et al.* (2005).

REFERENCES

Bullock, C.H. and Kay, J. (1997), 'Preservation and Change in the Upland Landscape: The Public Benefits of Grazing Management', *Journal of Environmental Planning and Management*, 40(3): 315–334.

Cumulus Consultants Ltd, Institute for European Environmental Policy and the Countryside, and Countryside Research Unit (2005), *Assessment of the Impact of CAP Reform and Other Key Policies on Upland Farms and Land Use Implications in both Severely Disadvantaged and Disadvantaged Areas of England*, report to the Department for Environment, Food and Rural Affairs.

Hanemann, W.M. (1984), 'Welfare Evaluations in Contingent Valuation Experiment with Discrete Responses', *American Journal of Agricultural Economics*, 66: 332–341.
Hanley, N., MacMillan, D., Wright, R.E., Bullock, C., Simpson, I., Parsisson, D. and Crabtree, B. (1998), 'Contingent Valuation Versus Choice Experiments: Estimating the Benefits of Environmentally Sensitive Areas in Scotland', *Journal of Agricultural Economics*, 49(1): 1–15.
Hausman, J.A. and McFadden, D. (1984), 'Specification Tests for the Multinomial Logit Model', *Econometrica*, 55, 1219–1240.
Krinsky, I. and Robb, A.L. (1986), 'On Approximating the Statistical Properties of Elasticities', *Review of Economics and Statistics*, 68: 715–719.
Louviere, J.J., Hensher, D.A. and Swait, J.D. (2000), *Stated Choice Models: Analysis and Application*, Cambridge: Cambridge University Press.
Louviere, J.J., Street, D., Carson, R., Ainslie, A., Deshazo, J., Cameron, T., Hensher, D., Kohn, R. and Marley, T. (2002), 'Dissecting the Random Component of Utility', *Marketing Letters* 13(3): 177–193.
Street, D., Burgess, L. and Louviere, J. (2005), 'Quick and Easy Choice Sets: Constructing Optimal and Nearly Optimal Stated Choice Experiments', *International Journal of Research in Marketing* 22(4): 459–470.
Swait, J. (2006), 'Advanced choice models', in Kanninen, B. (ed.), *Valuing Environmental Amenities Using Stated Choice Studies: A Common Sense Approach to Theory and Practice*, Boston: Kluwer.
White, P.C.L. and Lovett, J.C. (1999), 'Public Preferences and Willingness-to-Pay for Nature Conservation in the North York Moors National Park, UK', *Journal of Environmental Management*, 55: 1–13.
Willis, K.G. and Garrod, G.D. (1993), 'Valuing Landscapes: A Contingent Valuation Approach', *Journal of Environmental Management*, 37(1): 1–22.

5. How can choice experiments inform public environmental policies: a French case study of landscape valuation

Jeanne Dachary-Bernard

INTRODUCTION

Even though the choice experiment method (CEM) has been applied to non-market environmental valuation since the 1990s (for example, Adamowicz *et al.*, 1994), applications of this method are still scarce in France. There is a wide gap between the use of traditional stated preference techniques such as the contingent valuation method (CVM) or revealed preference methods such as the hedonic pricing, and the use of CEM in the French economic literature (Josien and Rambonilaza, 2004). There are very few and recent French studies on choice experiments (Dachary-Bernard, 2004; Bonnieux *et al.*, 2006), and they focus on landscape conservation and forest management respectively. Yet French environmental valuation is increasingly being developed by technical ministries and public agencies which progressively take the initiative in financing a range of economic valuations. We can therefore assume that the use of the CEM in France is very likely to increase considerably.

Among the various environmental concerns of French policies, landscape is becoming a key issue in public debate. This concern for landscape emerged from the need to bring environmental research and policies into line with social demands. With the 1993 law on the protection and enhancement of landscape, which amended certain legal measures regarding public inquiries, France was equipped with a strong tool enabling it to democratise landscape management. The same has applied at European level, since the Council of Europe adopted the European Landscape Convention on 20 October 2000 (with a recent French ratification on 17 March 2006), 'to promote European landscape protection, management and planning, and to organise European co-operation on landscape issues' (Article 3 of the Convention). Resources are allocated and certain projects abandoned because of the importance attached to landscape quality. In particular, rural landscape changes are analysed in the context of the multifunctionality of agriculture, and landscape has become an object of agri-environmental policies. As also mentioned in Chapters 2, 3, 4 and 6, in 1992 the EU Common Agricultural Policy (CAP) was reoriented towards environmental conservation with the introduction of the agri-environmental measures (EC No. 2078/92 agri-environmental regulation). In France, application of this regulation created measures at two levels: national (PMSEE)[1] and regional (zonal and local operations). Rural landscape protection is the main object of local operations. Therefore, landscape policy makers need to know the benefits and costs associated with different programmes which have consequences for the quality of landscape amenities.

It consequently follows that application of CEM to landscape valuation would yield useful results. The main objective of this chapter is to present an application of the CEM to landscape valuation with an empirical case study undertaken in Brittany, France. The analysis pays particular attention to the perspective of public policy-making processes, with a view to answering the following question: does CEM supply helpful information to policy makers concerning landscape values?

The first part of the chapter considers the meanings of landscape in detail. The CEM is then presented. The second part applies the method to value landscape attributes of the Monts d'Arrée area in Brittany, by modelling people's landscape preferences. Finally, the last part of the chapter is devoted to constructing helpful indicators for policy makers and testing them on different hypothetical landscape policies.

A METHODOLOGICAL CHOICE FOR LANDSCAPE VALUATION

Characteristics of Landscape

Before illustrating the application of the choice experiment method to a French landscape valuation study, we need to explain the meaning of 'landscape'. We will then be able to justify our methodological choice and at the same time sum up the main characteristics of the method. Landscape is a non-market good because it has no market price and cannot be sold or bought. It is also considered to be an impure public good since it presents (imperfectly) the non-exclusion and non-rivalry properties. Finally, landscape is composed of several elements. This multidimensional property is translated into economic terms as a multi-attribute dimension. This particular point is the centre of our analysis, which relies on Lancaster's economic theory (Lancaster, 1971). According to this theory, a consumer's utility is explained by the consumption of the different attributes of the good and not by the consumption of the good itself.

One of the assumptions usually made about landscape is that the value individuals derive from it is mainly explained by their geographical origin: people who live in the countryside and those who live in urban areas do not have the same expectations with regard to rural landscapes (Mathieu, 2000). That is why we will look at both tourists' and main/second residents' valuations. Investigation of the valuations of different stakeholders is also carried out in Chapter 10 of this volume.

The Choice Experiment Method

This method is particularly appropriate here because it follows the Lancaster approach, which we used as the main theoretical basis to describe landscape (Louviere *et al.*, 2000). As introduced in Chapter 1, and also mentioned in other chapters of this volume, the CEM considers the environmental good as a set of attributes with different levels. From the combination of the different attribute levels, several scenarios are constructed, each representing the state of the environmental good resulting from a specific political measure. These scenarios are formed into choice sets, usually composed of two alternatives and the status quo. In our survey, the latter option describes the non-intervention state of the landscape that is actually different from the current state (since there is a current landscape intervention with regard to one of the attributes). In the survey these choice sets are presented to respondents, who choose the alternative they prefer in each choice set.

Respondents' choices enable us to infer the monetary values that people attach to the hypothetical changes of the good (via different scenarios). That is why CEM is mainly supported by the random utility theory (RUT) (Thurstone, 1927; McFadden, 1974; Manski, 1977). Adapted to our specific context, this theory assumes that, from different landscape scenarios, people choose the scenario that generates the highest utility. The following equation expresses the utility function for choice alternative i held by a respondent.

$$U_i = V_i + \varepsilon_i \tag{5.1}$$

where U_i is the utility for choice ith alternative, V_i is the systematic component and ε is the random term.

Because of the random component, it is not possible to explain and predict consumer preferences perfectly; this naturally leads to the use of choice probability. Thus, supposing that the random terms are independent and identically distributed with a Gumbel distribution, the probability of choosing the *i*th scenario from the choice set *C* follows a logistic distribution and involves use of the Conditional Logit model (Greene, 2003).

$$P(i/C) = \exp^{\lambda V_i} / \sum_j \exp^{\lambda V_i} \tag{5.2}$$

The method of modelling V_i depends on the case study, but we usually distinguish the choice attributes from the individual characteristics; the latter are used to take into account the heterogeneity of preferences. The indirect utility function (of individual *n* for choice alternative *i*) estimated is

$$V_{in} = A_i + \sum_k \beta_k x_{ik} + \sum_h \delta_{hi} z_{hn} \tag{5.3}$$

where A_i is the alternative specific constant (ASC) of the *i*th scenario, β_k is the parameter vector associated to the attributes k ($k=1 \ldots K$) of alternative i noted (x_{ik}), and δ_h is the parameter vector of the h ($h=1 \ldots H$) characteristics of individual n (z_{hn}).

The case study determines the attributes and characteristics we use in the models in order to estimate preferences. Attributes may be qualitative or quantitative. In the case study presented here they take qualitative levels. Therefore, the question is to code correctly the variables x_{ik}. As is usually done in stated preference models, we will use effects coding (EC) rather than dummy coding (Adamowicz *et al.*, 1994).[2] EC consists of creating $L-1$ variables for each attribute of L qualitative levels, the reference level (status quo) being assigned a value of -1. Thus, the effect coded variable for one qualitative level is set equal to 1 when the qualitative level is present, equal to -1 if the reference level is present and equal to 0 otherwise. In EC, the status quo is consequently defined as the negative sum of the estimated coefficients. Supposing the reference level (or status quo) at the level $l=1$, the general conditional logit equation (5.3) may be transformed from effects coding as follows:

$$V_{in} = A_i + \sum_k \left[\sum_{l=2}^{L} \beta_{kl} x_{ikl} \right] + \sum_h \delta_{hi} z_{hn} \tag{5.4}$$

where the x_{ikl} are the effects-coded variables whose values may be -1, 1 or 0.

In addition to its technical advantages, effects coding is also suitable for the valuation of landscape attributes since it reveals the utility level accorded to the landscape attribute levels; this could be useful information for landscape policy makers (McVittie *et al.*, 2001).

CHOICE EXPERIMENT IMPLEMENTATION

Case Study Description

The study area is the Monts d'Arrée landscape, in the Finistère region of Brittany (France). It stretches over about 43 000 ha and 14 municipalities of the Natural Regional Park of Armorique (NRPA), as shown in Figure 5.1. The nature of this landscape is twofold. To the south of the mountains one finds the symbolic Monts d'Arrée landscape with its wild moorland (in the

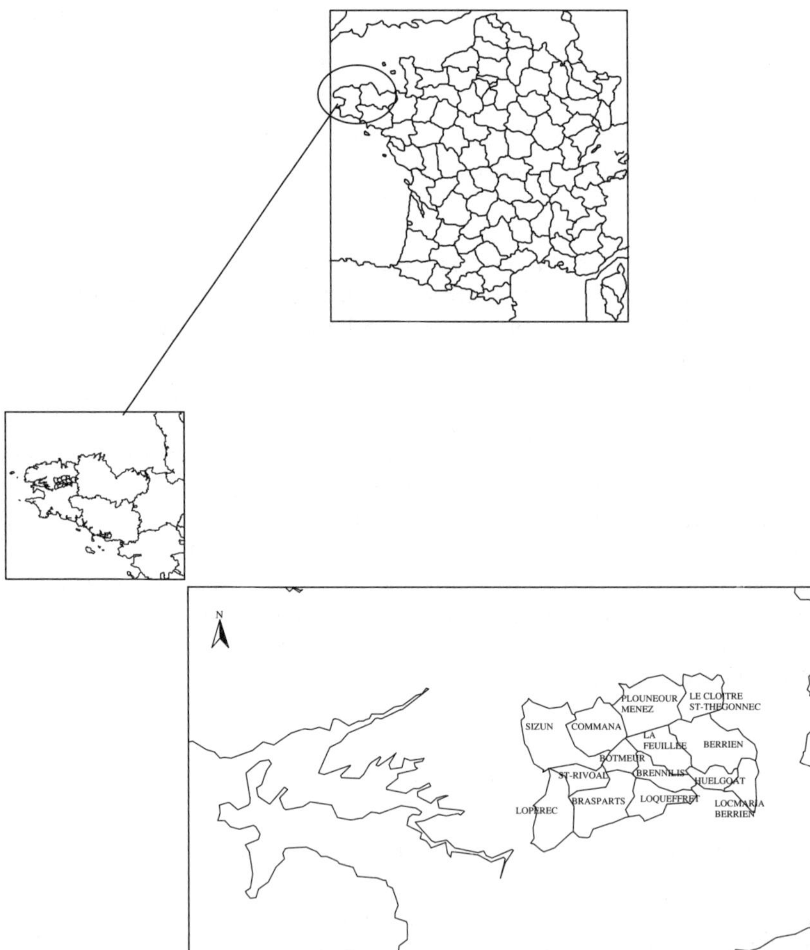

Figure 5.1 Study area of the Monts d'Arrée (Brittany)

Yeun Elez). This part of the region is associated with legends about death and Hell. In contrast, to the north of the mountains lies a farming zone, marked by an agricultural landscape and more precisely by hedged farmlands and farm buildings.

This part of Brittany has seen some striking landscape changes. First, in the southern zone, moorland is becoming less and less trimmed, with more and more trees, because the land has been abandoned and become overgrown. On the other hand, the northern part has seen the destruction of the hedged farmlands and an increase in the number of modern farm buildings due to the modernisation of the agricultural system.

In view of this situation, the NRPA has decided to take these two landscape issues into account in its landscape management policy (Parcs Naturels Régionaux de France, 2000). This local institution encourages the inhabitants and, more particularly, the owners of wild lands to continue the maintenance of the moorlands in order to preserve the traditional landscape of this zone. To this end, the Park presents the products of the moorland as a viable way of feeding farm animals. The NRPA is moreover seriously considering reconstructing the hedged farmlands in order to maintain the typical Breton landscape and to fight ecological problems due to their destruction.

In addition, in order to verify the assumption that landscape values differ depending on geographical origin (country or city), we interviewed tourists, second home residents and main home residents through face-to-face surveys. The survey was designed from the usual factorial fractional design (Zwerina *et al.*, 1996) using SAS software (Kuhfeld, 2004). The efficient design is composed of nine choice sets (or eighteen alternatives), but because of realistic considerations and of task complexity (Hanley *et al.*, 2000), we finally proposed six choice sets to each respondents. Each choice set is composed of two alternatives, each described by attribute levels and illustrated by photographs as shown in Appendix Figure A5.1. A total of 262 tourists were randomly interviewed in the summer of 2002; 345 residents, giving statistical sampling criteria, were interviewed over two months during the spring of 2003 (17 per cent were second home residents). It is interesting to note that among the tourists, about half of the sample was touring and therefore did not spend a night in the study area. However, 41 per cent of the tourists had already been to the area and 'knew' this landscape. We can deduce from these observations that tourist respondents were on the whole capable of understanding the landscape change scenarios proposed in the survey. Concerning the resident respondents, main and second home inhabitants had very good knowledge of the area, on the whole. Recreational activities were associated with landscape for 50 per cent of the second home residents and 35.5 per cent of the main home residents. Finally, we note that 78 per cent of second home residents had their main

Table 5.1 Choice experiment attributes and their levels in the Monts d'Arrée

Attributes	**Description**	**Levels**	**Status quo**
Moorland	Wide space of heath usually cut	1. With a lot of trees 2. With some trees 3. Trimmed (clean)	Lots of trees
Hedged farmland	Natural hedges defining small fields	1. Not dense 2. Slightly dense 3. Dense	No hedged farmland
Farm buildings	No traditional farm buildings	1. Not concealed 2. Slightly concealed 3. Well concealed	No farm building integration
Monetary attribute			
Local tax increase	Residents' monetary contribution to the corresponding landscape scenario	1. € 15 2. € 30 3. € 45	No additional tax
Tourist tax increase	Tourists' monetary contribution to the corresponding landscape scenario	1. € 0.10 2. € 0.20 3. € 0.30	No additional tax

residence in an urban area. This fact allows us to compare our data with the usual hypothesis mentioned in the introduction, on the impact of residential areas on landscape preferences.

In this context, it appears appealing to measure the welfare changes due to the modifications of the Monts d'Arrée landscape, in order to have an idea of the economic advantages of the NRPA measures planned. To implement CEM in this area we first have to express landscape in terms of its main attributes and levels of these attributes. Considering the description above, the main landscape attributes retained in this study are moorland, hedged farmlands and farm buildings. Both the scientific director of the NRPA and researchers from the Cemagref, who worked some years ago in this area on a similar subject, have scientifically validated these attributes. Moreover, they defined three different levels for each of the attributes as set out in Table 5.1, the third level being the closest to the traditional landscape of this area.

In order to estimate individual monetary values, CEM implies the integration of a cost attribute in the scenarios. This attribute represents the additional cost that people would have to pay in order to finance the proposed landscape policies. Because we are dealing with two different social groups of respondents, we cannot use the same cost attribute in both surveys. We have chosen to use a tax increase in both cases so that respondents associate the monetary attribute with a monetary constraint, and so that we have a comparable payment vehicle between tourists and residents. Thus, in the tourist survey this attribute is an increase in tourist tax, while in the residents' survey it is an increase in local income tax (Nielsen *et al.*, 2007). Both monetary attributes take three levels, determined according to the current tax levels on the national, regional and local scales.

Landscape Preferences Modelling

In relation to the specific study area in the Monts d'Arrée, we need to specify the different variables employed in the landscape preferences model.

Concerning the attributes, Table 5.1 details the possible levels they can take. Whereas the monetary attribute is a quantitative variable and can be included in the model with a quantitative variable p, landscape attributes are qualitative variables and need a specific treatment in order to be correctly taken into account. Instead of using dummy variables, we employ 'effects coding', as explained above.

Table 5.2 presents the variables included in the model with their respective values, according to the level under consideration and given that the base level is the status quo. For each of the three level attributes we create two effects-coded variables in the model. Thus, for example, if moorland is trimmed (level 3) ML_2 would take the value 0 (because level 2 is not present) and ML_3 the value 1. The opposite would be true if moorland were at the medium level. If this attribute is at its status quo level (or level 1), both effects-coded variables ML_2 and ML_3 would be set at value -1, to underline the presence of the reference level.

The 'price' variable is integrated into the model in a linear form, as are the other attributes. But there is no consensus on the appropriate functional

Table 5.2 Landscape attribute variables with effect coding

Landscape attributes	Number of levels	Effects coded variables	Values of variables
Moorland	3	ML_2	(0;1;−1)
		ML_3	(1;0;−1)
Hedged farmland	3	HF_2	(0;1;−1)
		HF_3	(1;0;−1)
Farm building	3	FB_2	(0;1;−1)
		FB_3	(1;0;−1)

form in choice experiments models (Hanley *et al.*, 1998). That is why, according to the first results estimation, we also experiment with a quadratic form for this price attribute.

Moreover, because we have decided to estimate a conditional logit model as presented in the general equation (5.4), we need to define the individual characteristics included in the model. Indeed, one way of accounting for preference heterogeneity is by including respondent's social and economic characteristics (Birol *et al.*, 2006), as Chapters 4, 12 and 13 in this volume also explain. From a microeconomic point of view, some usual socio-economic variables that are hypothesised to influence people's preferences for landscape include income, age, gender and number of children. Additionally, specific characteristics are considered according to the type of respondent: (i) for tourists, having already visited this area previously may be important, in addition to their length of stay in the Monts d'Arrée and the rural/urban environment of their main home; (ii) for residents, the type of residence (main or second home) may be important in the modelling, in addition to the locality of their residence (north or south of the zone) and family origin (from the Monts d'Arrée or not). Nevertheless, some econometric considerations lead us to retain finally only some of these characteristics in the model. Note that in relation to all the characteristics, type of residence is not significant. Yet we found that this characteristic is significant with regard to the moorland attribute. We therefore created new variables RL_2 and RL_3 defined as the product of the dummy variable 'residence' (coded 0 for second home residence and 1 for main home residence) with the moorland level 2 or 3 respectively.

Estimated models for both tourists and residents are expressed in the following equation (5.5) and their estimation results are presented in Table 5.3. Both linear and quadratic forms are estimated using LIMDEP 7.0 and both kinds of result are shown in order to analyse the economic signification of the quadratic form.

$$V_{in} = A_i + \beta_1 ML_2 + \beta_2 ML_3 + \gamma_1 HF_2 + \gamma_2 HF_3 + \eta_1 FB_2 + \eta_2 FB_3 + \pi_1 p + \sum_h \delta_{hi}(A_i z_{hn})$$

$$V_{in} = A_i + \beta_1 ML_2 + \beta_2 ML_3 + \gamma_1 HF_2 + \gamma_2 HF_3 + \eta_1 FB_2 + \eta_2 FB_3 + \pi_1 p + \pi_2 p^2 + \sum_h \delta_{hi}(A_i z_{hn}) \quad (5.5)$$

The overall fit of the models is given by the pseudo R^2 (ρ^2) and the log-likelihood statistics, and these measures show that quadratic models fit the data better. A log-likelihood ratio test is computed for each model testing

Table 5.3 Choice experiment estimation results

Variables	**(parameters)**	**Conditional Logit Model with effects coding**			
		Linear form of *p*		**Quadratic form of *p***	
		Tourists	**Residents**	**Tourists**	**Residents**
ML_2	(β_1)	−0.45***	+0.4***	+0.22**	+0.59***
ML_3	(β_2)	+0.56**	−0.15/	−0.29***	−0.34***
HF_2	(γ_1)	−0.34***	−0.09/	+0.04 /	−0.16*
HF_3	(γ_2)	+1.50***	+0.62***	+0.6***	+0.83***
FB_2	(η_1)	+0.50***	−0.18*	−0.19 /	−0.48***
FB_3	(η_2)	+1.59***	+0.43***	+0.73***	+0.2 /
p	(π_1)	+5.02***	+0.01*	+9.66**	+0.07***
p^2	(π_2)	–	–	−25**	−0.0009**
firstvisit (ACS_1)	(δ_{11})	−0.46*	–	−0.4 /	–
firstvisit (ACS_2)	(δ_{12})	−0.53**	–	−0.56**	–
Nbchild (ACS_1)	(δ_{31})	+0.23**	–	+0.24***	–
Nbchild (ACS_2)	(δ_{32})	+0.27***	–	+0.26***	–
Income (ACS_1)	(δ_{41})	–	+0.32***	–	+0.29***
Income (ACS_2)	(δ_{42})	–	+0.3***	–	+0.32***
RL_2 (ACS_1)	(δ_{51})	–	+0.14 /	–	+0.17 /
RL_2 (ACS_2)	(δ_{52})	–	−0.43**	–	−0.37*
RL_3 (ACS_1)	(δ_{61})	–	−0.33 /	–	−0.54***
RL_3 (ACS_2)	(δ_{62})	–	+0.07 /	–	+0.24 /
Pseudo R^2 (ρ^2)		0.17128	0.09029	0.17663	0.09173
Log L		−1097.417	−1643.08	−1095.16	−1640.49
LR test		–	–	4.52	5.20

Note: Alternative specific constants were also included in estimation in linear models but the results are not shown here. Other characteristics, of no significance, are not shown either. Estimates are 1 per cent (***), 5 per cent (**), 10 per cent (*) significant or non significant (/).

H_0: $\pi_2=0$. The test statistics are also given in Table 5.3. The critical value of $\chi^2_{(1)}$ is 3.84, so in both cases we prefer the quadratic functional form of the model.

Therefore, we can now focus on the quadratic models. From the estimates we can derive the attribute reference levels (noted β_0, γ_0 and η_0), given that the reference point is defined as the negative sum of the estimated coefficients. Because of the RL_2 and RL_3 variables, the real coefficients associated with moorland attribute levels are also calculated for residents (β_0, β_1, β_2). The corresponding t-student statistics[3] also appear in Table 5.4.

Based on the results reported in Tables 5.3 and 5.4, three main remarks can be made about the landscape attributes:

Table 5.4 Parameter calculations for reference level of landscape attributes and all levels of moorland

Variables	Global parameters	Main home residents	Second home residents	Tourists
***ML*$_1$**	β_0	$=-\beta_1-\beta_2-\gamma_{RL2}-\gamma_{RL3}=+0.67$ ($t=+1.86$)	$=-\beta_1-\beta_2=-0.25$ ($t=-2.57$)	$=-\beta_1-\beta_2=+0.07$ ($t=+0.85$)
***ML*$_2$**	β_1	$=\beta_1+\gamma_{RL2}=+0.22$ ($t=+1.17$)	$=\beta_1=+0.59$ ($t=+3.89$)	$=\beta_1=+0.22$ ($t=+1.95$)
***ML*$_3$**	β_2	$=\beta_2+\gamma_{RL3}=-0.88$ ($t=-2.97$)	$=\beta_2=-0.34$ ($t=-2.46$)	$=\beta_2=-0.29$ ($t=-2.9$)
***HF*$_1$**	γ_0	$=-\gamma_1-\gamma_2=-0.67$ ($t=-6.3$)	$=-\gamma_1-\gamma_2=-0.67$ ($t=-6.3$)	$=-\gamma_1-\gamma_2=-0.64$ ($t=-7.5$)
***FB*$_1$**	η_0	$=-\eta_1-\eta_2=+0.28$ ($t=+0.99$)	$=-\eta_1-\eta_2=+0.28$ ($t=+0.99$)	$=-\eta_1-\eta_2=-0.54$ ($t=-2.2$)

1. Concerning moorland, the three respondent groups significantly reveal a preference for moorland with trees. More precisely, main home residents prefer it with a lot of trees whereas second home residents and tourists prefer the medium state (some trees), which is closer to the traditional state of moorland.
2. For hedged farmlands, all interviewed individuals prefer to see them dense and negatively value the base level: they are against all hedged farmland destruction.
3. Finally, tourists are the only ones who prefer farm buildings to be well concealed in the landscape. Main and second home residents have a significant preference against partial integration of buildings (negative estimates for level 2) rather than a positive preference for any other level of the attribute.

Therefore, from Table 5.3, equation (5.5) may be written as follows:

$$V^T = 0{,}22ML_2 - 0{,}29ML_3 + 0{,}04HF_2 + 0{,}6HF_3 - 0{,}19FB_2 + 0{,}73FB_3 + 9{,}66p - 25p^2 + \theta^* A_1^*(- 0{,}4fv + 0{,}24nbc) + (1 - \theta)^* A_2^*(- 0{,}56fv + 0{,}26nbc) \quad (5.6)$$

$$V^R = + 0{,}59ML_2 - 0{,}34ML_3 - 0{,}16HF_2 + 0{,}83HF_3 - 0{,}48FB_2 + 0{,}2FB_3 + 0{,}07p - 0{,}0009p^2 + \theta^* A_1^*(0{,}29inc + 0{,}17RL_2 - 0{,}54RL_3) + (1 - \theta)^* A_2^*(0{,}32inc - 0{,}37RL_2 + 0{,}24RL_3) \quad (5.7)$$

Also interesting in the estimation results are the monetary attribute parameters. In the quadratic form of the model, 'price' is included in both its level form and its squared form. This specific functional form means that, all other things being equal, people have an increasing utility until a certain level of price and then have a decreasing utility. From our data, this optimal level of price for which utility is maximised is €0.19 for tourists and €37 for residents. Figure 5.2 illustrates this quadratic relation for both respondent groups.

Such information from estimates is surely interesting for policy makers, but needs to be expressed in another form in order to support public policy processes. That is why willingness-to-pay indicators and welfare measures need to be calculated. These are considered in the next section.

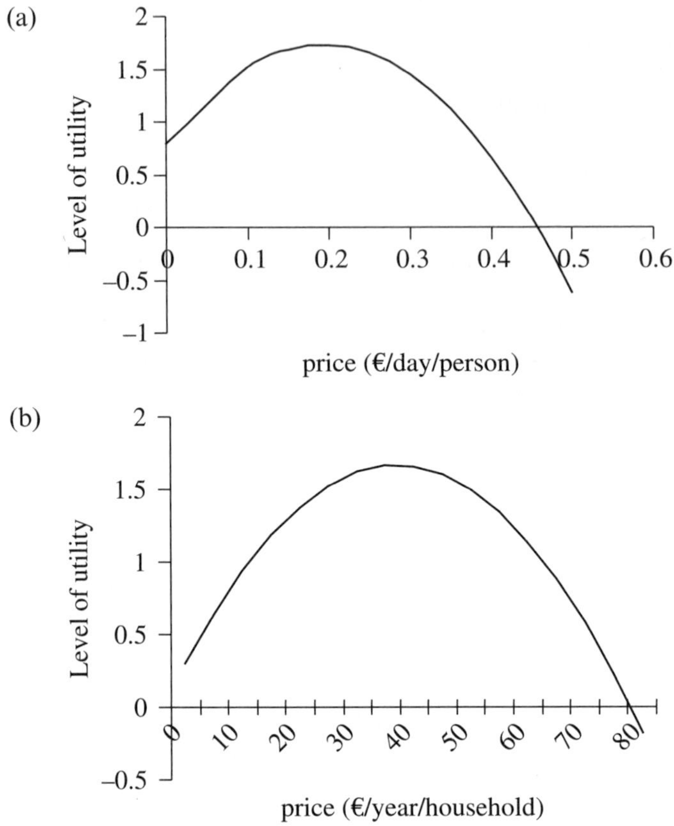

Figure 5.2 Quadratic relation between utility level and tax increase for tourists (a) and residents (b)

SUPPORT FOR PUBLIC POLICY MAKING

Policy-Making Processes: Context

Economic public policy making refers to rational choice, for which political theory usually distinguishes two approaches: the utilitarian conception and the deontological (or Kantian) one (Sagoff, 1998). Without going into detail, we can say that in the first approach, policy makers choose among alternatives whose valuation produces the maximum social well-being. The second conception considers individuals as citizens, and policy makers choose the alternative that is deemed the most appropriate for society as a whole. Since the utilitarian conception thinks of the individual as a consumer, whereas the Kantian approach sees the individual as a citizen, economic valuation such as that proposed in this chapter refers to the first conception of public choice. Therefore, until now, we have looked for public policy indicators in line with the utilitarian approach whose most useful technique is cost-benefit analysis (CBA). *Ex ante*, CBA implies the evaluation of both the costs and the benefits of a project in order to decide on its economic advantages. An application of CBA to water resource management is presented in Chapter 12 of this volume. Concerning landscape changes, policy makers need to know the benefits generated by different landscape change scenarios in order to decide if the landscape can be improved or not. In order to calculate such benefits, we must first calculate respondents' willingness to pay (WTP).

In CEM, one of the objectives is to supply WTP at the attribute level: we call this 'marginal'[4] willingness to pay (MWTP), which gives the measure of the benefits resulting from the transformations of the attribute from one level to another. Because of the specific functional form of the indirect utility function, the MWTP of the level *j* of attribute *i* has to be performed as follows:

$$MWTP_{ji} = -\frac{\partial V/\partial X_{ji}}{\partial V/\partial p} = -\frac{Vm_{ji}}{(\pi_1 + 2.\pi_2.p)} \tag{5.8}$$

The Vm_{ji} is the marginal indirect utility for the attribute *i* of level *j* (j=0,1,2). We need to specify that this marginal utility is the effects-coded variable's coefficient (γ_j, η_j), except for base levels (j=0) and for the moorland attribute (because of the presence of the *RL* variable), for which we take the global parameters β_j as calculated in Table 5.4. Because of a different payment vehicle for each survey, the monetary unit is not the same for these MWTP. They are presented in Table 5.5, with the 95 per cent confidence intervals calculated with parametric bootstrapping (Poe *et al.*, 1997; Foster and Mourato, 2003).

These results express the same preferences as the parameters. Nevertheless, MWTP gives more information about the amount of money people agree to spend to enjoy the landscape attribute at its corresponding level. Negative MWTP, or willingness to accept (WTA), means that people agree to be paid (and not to pay) to enjoy the attribute at the corresponding level. This is the case for both tourists and residents, for trimmed moorland and not dense hedged farmlands. Concerning the reference level of farm buildings (not concealed) we note a surprising WTP among residents. But analysis of Table 5.4 demonstrates that the corresponding parameters are not significant, so WTP for this attribute is not significant either. Moreover,

Table 5.5 Marginal WTP for landscape attribute levels for tourists and residents

Attribute levels	MWTP (*95% confidence intervals*)		
	Tourists (€/person/day)	Main home residents (€/household/year)	Second home residents (€/household/year)
ML_1	−0.007 (−0.28;0.26)	+31.6 (−121.9;192.8)	−11.9 (−59.9;37.2)
ML_2	+0.09 (−0.67;0.73)	+13.7 (−21.9;46.8)	+32.4 (−86.6;139.2)
ML_3	−0.16 (−1;1.05)	−47.8 (−222.4;137)	−18.7 (−83.3;50.8)
HF_1	−0.31 (−2.1;2.01)	−37.5 (−176;111.6)	
HF_2	+0.06 (−0.06;0.2)	−7.4 (−41.2;28.4)	
HF_3	+0.25 (−2.04;2)	+45 (−142.6;208.7)	
FB_1	−0.22 (−1.52;1.49)	+16.9 (−30.1;75.9)	
FB_2	−0.07 (−0.67;0.55)	−27 (−108.2;63.1)	
FB_3	+0.38 (−2.1;2.25)	+7.9 (−47.5;53.6)	

if we look at the highest MWTP (in absolute value) in each respondent group, we note that they underline different priorities: tourists have the highest WTP for good farm building integration; main home residents are more sensitive to moorland with trees (with a WTA for clean moorland); and second home residents have a WTP for dense hedged farmlands.

From these measures, we can look for economic surplus indicators helpful in the policy-making process.

Economic Surpluses for Different Specific Landscape Protection Policies

Considering that policy makers aim to increase social well-being, economic surplus has to be maximised. In the case of landscape quality improvement, we deal with WTP indicators and thus with compensating surplus (CS), which is estimated not by implicit prices (Bennett and Blamey, 2001, p 101) but by the following equation:

$$CS_N = \frac{-1}{\partial V / \partial p}(V_{SQ} - V_N) \tag{5.9}$$

where V_{SQ} and V_N are the utility of the status quo situation (*SQ*) and the new situation or scenario of landscape changes (*N*), respectively. Chapters 4 and 12 of this volume also calculate the CS measures for various environmental management scenarios by using this formula.

In order to calculate V_{SQ} and V_N, we need to replace the different variables in (5.6) and (5.7) by the value they are given in the appropriate scenario. The utility derived from the reference situation supposes that all landscape attributes are taken at the level −1; the price is null; and the alternative specific constant is equal to zero (so that individual characteristics are not relevant at this reference stage). Thus, using notations *T* and *R* for tourists and residents respectively, we find: ${V_{SQ}}^T = -1.1$ and ${V_{SQ}}^R = -0.66$. If there is no public intervention on landscape, tourists as well as residents have a negative benefit, that is, a cost.

We can therefore do the same for any specific landscape management scenario or programme. Different programmes can be implemented according to the number of attributes controlled for: (i) mono-attribute measures deal with a unique attribute of the study landscape; (ii) bi-attribute programmes aim to preserve simultaneously two of the landscape attributes, and (iii) complete measures concern changes in the levels of the three landscape attributes. In our particular case study, we focus on the scenarios which have been the most frequently chosen among the twelve presented in the survey experiences.

- Programme 1, called P_1, represents a bi-attribute measure which aims to reach simultaneously the attribute levels HF_3 and FB_3 and does not influence the moorland attribute: (ML_1, HF_3, FB_3).
- P_2 is a complete programme which aims to influence the three landscape attributes (ML_2, HF_2, FB_3) simultaneously.

The results can be found in Table 5.6

Results are given in € per household and per year. Tourists' and main home residents' expected benefits from programme P_1 are higher than that of P_2, while the opposite is true for second home residents. This is mainly explained by their preferences for the moorland attribute as reported above. Second home residents reveal a significant preference for moorland at its medium level, which is clearly the objective of the policy P_2. They are also the only ones to consider level 1 of this attribute negatively, whereas tourists and main home residents derive a positive value from this non-intervention state of moorland. That is why the policy P_1 gives us more important benefits (since moorland is kept at its 'natural' state in P_1) than the other potential policy.

Table 5.6 Compensating surplus for tourists and residents of two landscape programmes

	Status quo	P_1	P_2
Indirect utility of tourists	−1.1	2.18	1.70
compensating surplus of tourists (CS^T)	x	+9.6	+8.2
Indirect utility of main home residents	−0.64	2.23	2.06
compensating surplus of main home residents (CS^{MR})	x	+1435	+1351
Indirect utility of second home residents	−0.64	2.06	2.39
compensating surplus of second home residents (CS^{SR})	x	+1348	+1513

Note: Individual characteristics have estimated coefficients which are dependent on the order of appearance of the alternative (1 or 2) of the experiment. Thus, two calculations of utility and therefore two calculations of compensating surplus have been done for each programme. Only the lower in absolute value are presented here in order to have the information 'at the lowest' for expected benefits.

Such information is informative for policy makers, especially in the case of designing policies which seek to discriminate according to the population to be charged. To obtain more useful indicators, we need to consider the aggregation question of such individual benefits.

The Aggregated Benefits at Issue

At this stage, the available results are given at a disaggregated level, which means for tourists and residents. CBA needs aggregated benefits, which means all groups taken together, in order to compare them with the cost of the policy under consideration. The question of aggregation is still in debate in economic theory since it concerns the problem of equity (Bergson, 1938). However, following Arrow *et al.* (1996), we can consider the aggregated benefit as a factor of political choice rather than a decision rule.

In this context, we may propose a weighting system for the different groups studied in this choice experiment. Two aspects need to be taken into account: (i) the relative weight of the different populations, and (ii) their size, since the preceding benefits are reported for the average household in the population under consideration. The aggregated compensating surplus held by the landscape change (from status quo to new situation N desired by the policy) can be expressed as follows:

$$CS_N = (a.CS_N^{MR}.MR) + (b.CS_N^{SR}.SR) + (c.CS_N^{T}.T) \qquad (5.10)$$

where *T*, *MR* and *SR* are respectively the number of tourists, main home residents and second home residents. The weighting system used is (*a*, *b*, *c*), which we based on the following assumption: the time that people spend in contact with landscape influences the value they give to it.

Starting from statistical data concerning the length of visits to the area (for tourists and second home residents) and the leisure time which inhabitants spend in the area, we find the following weightings: (a=0.673; b=0.303; c=0.024). This system, which is totally dependent on the assumption made and which can be questionable in several respects, gives the most weight to inhabitants' preferences, then to second home residents and finally to tourists, even if the latter probably decided to visit the area because of its landscape.

The numbers of *MR* and *SR* are given in the national population census of 1999. Tourist statistics, however, are not available for this specific area. We therefore simulated different aggregated surplus values for different numbers of tourists (25 000; 50 000; 75 000). Because of the much lower weights given to this population, the size does not significantly influence the final results (gaps of 0.05 per cent). That is why we present the case of T = 50 000, with the aggregated compensating surplus as follows:

$$CS(P_1) = +€5\,401\,318$$

$$CS(P_2) = +€5\,197\,632$$

When all individuals are taken together, it is found that the expected benefits of policy P_1 are higher than those of programme P_2, by more than €5.4m. This result is not expected to provide a solution for policy makers, but it does give them very important and useful information to take into account in their policy-making process. We do not know the corresponding costs of P_1 and P_2, nor the other benefits of such policies, yet such results are informative for policy makers since they know which attributes and programmes are preferred by the different users. Moreover, we have only interviewed users, so the values we find are likely to be lower bound values in the sense that by also interviewing non-users, we could have come up with higher social welfare estimates.

With regard to these aggregated expected benefits, the programme P1 seems to generate the highest economic value from a utilitarian point of view. But if we come back to the Kantian approach presented earlier in the chapter, different policy-making processes may conclude differently. Some elements of social choice theory (Kreps, 1990) may enrich present reflection in this direction. Indeed, we consider that the WTP calculated in Table 5.5 reflects individual preferences. Thus, from these indicators we infer a ranking by giving points according to the individuals' order

Table 5.7 Preference ranking of attributes

	T	*MR*	*SR*
ML_1	6	8	4
ML_2	7	6	8
ML_3	3	1	3
HF_1	1	2	1
HF_2	5	4	5
HF_3	8	9	9
FB_1	2	7	7
FB_2	4	3	2
FB_3	9	5	6

Table 5.8 Preference ranking of policy P_1 and P_2 and consequent Borda scores

Alternatives	Prog. name	*T*	*MR*	*SR*	Borda scores
(ML_1, HF_3, FB_3)	P_1	23	22	19	64
(ML_2, HF_2, FB_3)	P_2	21	15	19	55

of preference for the attribute level: 9 points for the most preferred attribute level, through to 1 point for the least preferred one (Table 5.7). Hence, P_1 and P_2 may also be associated with a number of points as shown in Table 5.8.

As proposed by Martin *et al.* (1996), two different social choice rules may be applied: the Condorcet rule and the Borda rule. According to Martin *et al.*, 'a Condorcet winner is a candidate *a*, who defeats every other candidate in majority comparisons: for all *b* different from *a*, more voters prefer *a* to *b* than *b* to *a*'. In our case, policy P_1 should be the candidate chosen by decision makers since it is the 'Condorcet winner' for tourists and for main home residents (only second home residents give the same score to P_1 and P_2). In the light of the Borda rule, 'each voter reports his preferences by ranking the *p* candidates from top to bottom, and the Borda winner is the candidate with the higher score': *P*1 is also the policy 'Borda winner'. Both rules produce the same result.

Hence, a brief analysis of the democratic approach applied to our specific empirical data would lead policy makers in the same direction: towards policy P_1, which is more specific to agricultural attributes and leaves the moorland attribute in its 'natural' state (not trimmed). This is particularly interesting in the current political context of the area. Policy makers are used to cutting down moorland in order to keep it in its traditional state, which is a protection measure regarding this specific landscape attribute. But our results raise questions about the extent to which such a measure is really appreciated, and whether such a policy does generate social benefits among users. Is there some potential conflict over land use for this specific landscape attribute?

CONCLUSION

This French case study relating to landscape valuation suggests interesting conclusions with regard to the use of the choice experiment method. First, the use of choice experiments is at its beginnings in France, so this case study fills a gap in the economic valuation area by initiating such a stated preference technique. But, secondly and principally, the main interest is to present the way the results of a choice experiment valuation study may be used to support the public policy-making process with regard to landscape management.

On this point, our conclusions show an interesting divergence of preferences not among the users themselves but between the users on the one hand and the policy makers on the other. Tourists and residents prefer moorland with trees. Landscape managers, however, are taking actions to keep it trimmed and clean. Therefore taking into account the decreasing well-being that these measures involve for landscape users, the real cost of taking these measures are in fact even higher. This question of helpful indicators for decision makers raises the aggregation issue. Aggregated benefits are calculated for two different hypothetical landscape management policies. Results appear to be convergent with the Condorcet and Borda decision rules proposed by social choice theory.

Even if the results of the French case study are specific to local concerns, this example underlines the interest of using such a valuation method to investigate landscape management issues and, consequently, to help policy makers choose those landscape management programmes or multi-attribute measures that respect social choice rules.

ACKNOWLEDGEMENTS

The author would like to thank Patrick Point and Mbolatiana Rambonilaza for all their helpful comments. The French Ministry of Ecology and Sustainable Development provided funding for this research under the S3E (2002) programme.

APPENDIX

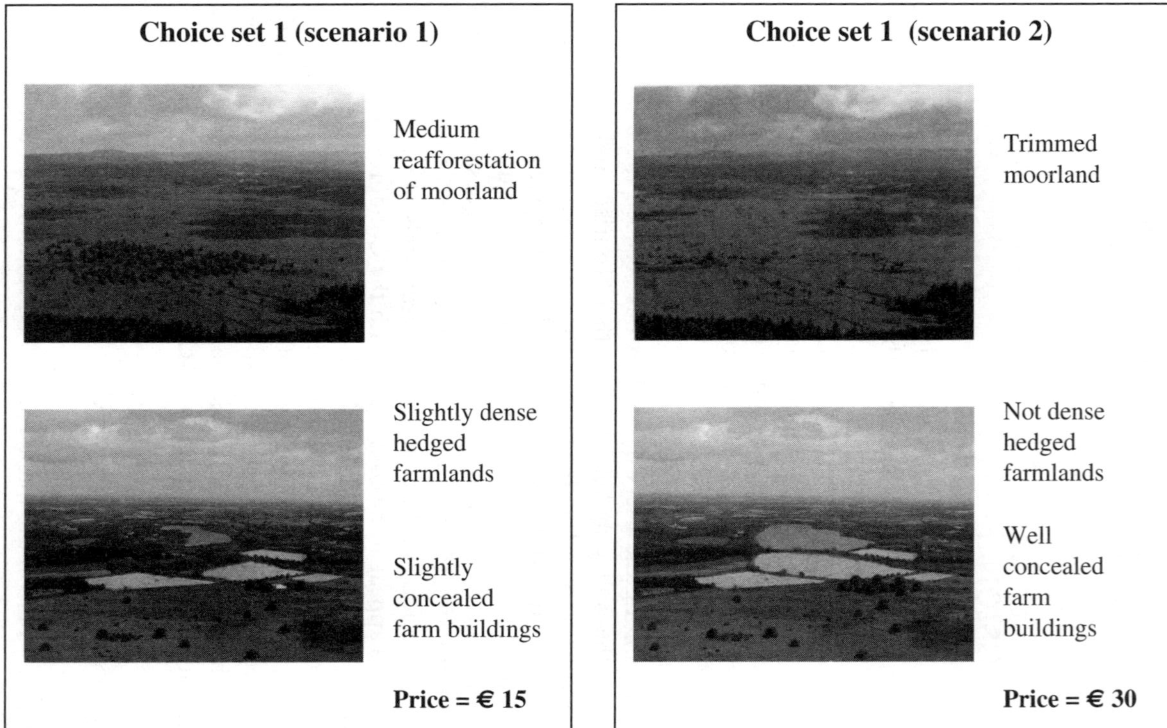

Figure A5.1 Photographs used in the choice set 1 (residents survey)

Figure A5.1 (continued)

NOTES

1. Premium for maintaining extensive breeding systems.
2. For detailed comparison between effect coding and dummy coding, see Bech and Gyrd-Hansen (2005).
3. T-student needs to be calculated because the status quo parameters are not estimated. The formula employed is the following (example taken for moorland):

$$Var(\beta_0) = Var(-\beta_1 - \beta_2) = (-1)^2 Var(\beta_1) + (-1) Var(\beta_2) + 2(-1)(-1) Cov(\beta_1, \beta_2)$$

   And so $se(\beta_0) = \sqrt{Var(\beta_1) + Var(\beta_2) + 2Cov(\beta_1, \beta_2)}$
4. The attribute transformations are not really marginal because they concern the progression from one level to another of the attribute, and in this sense the progression is not continuous but discrete.

REFERENCES

Adamowicz, W., J. Louviere and M. Williams (1994), 'Combining revealed and stated preference methods for valuing environmental amenities', *Journal of Environmental Economics and Management*, 26, 271–292.

Arrow, K. J., M. L. Cropper, G. C. Eads, R. W. Hahn, L. B. Lave, R. G. Noll, P. R. Portney, M. Russel, R. Schmalensee, V. K. Smith and R. N. Stavins (1996), 'Is there a role for benefit-cost analysis in environmental, health, and safety regulation?', *Science*, 27, 221–222.

Bech, M. and D. Gyrd-Hansen (2005), 'Effects coding in discrete choice experiments', *Health Economics*, 14(10), 1079–1083.

Bennett, J. and R. Blamey (2001), *The Choice Modelling Approach to Environmental Valuation*, Cheltenham, UK and Northampton, MA, USA: Edward Edgar.

Bergson, A. (1938), 'A reformulation of certain aspects of welfare economics', *Quarterly Journal of Economics*, 52, 310–334.

Birol, E., K. Karousakis and P. Koundouri (2006), 'Using a choice experiment to account for preference heterogeneity in wetland attributes: The case of Cheimaditida wetland in Greece', *Ecological Economics*, 60(1), 145–156.

Bonnieux, F., A. Carpentier and J. C. Paoli (2006), 'Priorités des résidents et des visiteurs pour la protection et l'aménagement de la forêt en Corse: Exemple de la forêt de Bonifatu', *Revue Forestière Française*, 58(2), 167–180.

Dachary-Bernard, J. (2004), 'Une évaluation économique du paysage: Une application de la méthode des choix multi-attributs aux Monts d'Arée', *Economie et Statistique*, 373, 57–74.

Foster, V. and S. Mourato (2003), 'Elicitation format and sensitivity to scope', *Environmental and Resource Economics*, 24, 141–160.

Greene, W. H. (2003), *Econometric Analysis*, New York: Prentice-Hall International, Inc.

Hanley, N., D. MacMillan, R. E. Wright, C. Bullock, I. Simpson, D. Parsisson and B. Crabtree (1998), 'Contingent valuation versus choice experiments: Estimating the benefits of environmentally sensitive areas in Scotland', *Journal of Agricultural Economics*, 49 (1), 1–15.

Hanley, N., R. E. Wright and G. Koop (2000), *Modelling Recreation Demand using Choice Experiments: Climbing in Scotland*, Economics Discussion Paper Series, University of Glasgow.
Josien, E. and M. Rambonilaza (2004), *Knowledge, Models, Techniques and Tools that Help to Explain and Forecast Multifunctionality of Agriculture. Country Report France*, Multagri Project, 46 pages.
Kreps, D. M. (1990), *A Course in Microeconomic Theory*, Princeton, New Jersey: Princeton University Press.
Kuhfeld, W. F. (2004), *Experimental Design and Choice Modeling Macros*, SAS Technical Support Documents – Statistical and Marketing Research no. TS-694I, SAS Institute.
Lancaster, K. J. (1971), *Consumer Demand: A New Approach*, New York: Columbia University Press.
Louviere, J., D. A. Hensher and J. D. Swait (2000), *Stated Choice Methods: Analysis and Application*, Cambridge: Cambridge University Press.
Manski, C. (1977), 'The structure of random utility models', *Theory and Decision*, 8, 229–254.
Martin, W. E., D. J. Shields, B. Tolwinski and B. Kent (1996), 'An application of social choice theory to U.S.D.A. forest service decision making', *Journal of Policy Modeling*, 18(6), 603–621.
Mathieu, N. (2000), 'Des représentations et pratiques de la nature aux cultures de la nature chez les citadins: Question générale et étude de cas', *Bulletin de l'Association Géographique Française*, 2, 162–174.
McFadden, D. (1974), 'Conditional logit analysis of qualitative choice behaviour', in P. Zarembka ed., *Frontiers in Econometrics*, New York: Academic Press, pp. 105–142.
McVittie, A., N. Hanley and D. Oglethorpe (2001), 'Choice experiments benefits transfer and the design of agri-environmental policy', in Agricultural Economics Society one day conference: Choice experiments: A new approach to environmental valuation, London, 9 April.
Nielsen, A. B., S. B. Olsen and T. Lundhede (2007), 'An economic valuation of the recreational benefits associated with nature-based forest management practices', *Landscape and Urban Planning*, 80(1–2), 63–71.
Parcs Naturels Régionaux de France (2000), *Paysages de Bocage*, Report, Paris: PNRF.
Poe, G. L., M. Welsh and P. Champ (1997), 'Measuring the difference in mean willingness to pay when dichotomous choice contingent valuation responses are not independent', *Land Economics*, 73(2), 255–267.
Sagoff, M. (1998), 'Aggregation and deliberation in valuing environmental public goods: A look beyond contingent pricing', *Ecological Economics*, 24(2–3), 213–230.
Thurstone, L. (1927), 'A law of comparative judgement', *Psychological Review*, 4, 273–286.
Zwerina, K., J. Huber and W. F. Kuhfeld (1996), *A General Method for Constructing Efficient Choice Designs*, SAS Technical Support Documents – Statistical and Marketing Research no. TS-650D, SAS Institute.

6. Valuing preferences towards cultural landscapes and rural heritage: a perspective from Northern Spain

Maria L. Loureiro and Edelmiro López

INTRODUCTION

As already mentioned in Chapters 3 and 4 of this volume, agricultural policies in the European Union (EU) have dramatically changed in the last few decades, increasing the importance of measures aiming to preserve the traditional agricultural landscape. Until the end of the 1980s, price and market support policies were oriented towards increasing agricultural production and productivity. However, the publication of the Green Book of the European Community in 1985 announced a change in the Common Agricultural Policy (CAP) doctrine. As part of the Mac Sharry 1992 reforms, the guaranteed section of the European Agricultural Guidance and Guarantee Fund (EAGGF) took responsibility, for the first time, for the financing of certain measures to stimulate environmental protection and rural development. In particular, Regulation (EEC) 2078/92 was established as one of the so-called 'accompanying measures', providing a framework for the implementation of 'agricultural production methods compatible with the requirements of the protection of the environment and the maintenance of the countryside'. Later, in 1999, the Berlin European Council reaffirmed that Agenda 2000 would secure a multifunctional, sustainable and competitive agriculture, maintaining the landscape and the countryside, contributing to the vitality of rural communities, and responding to consumer concerns and demands regarding food quality and safety, environmental protection and animal welfare.

Currently, the redeployment of the agricultural budget to multifunctional aspects of agriculture remains a matter for debate in the EU. Some Member States, backed up by most agricultural lobbies, argue that supporting agricultural production is a good way to reach multifunctional objectives. However, others are in favour of targeting aid on identified multifunctional agricultural services. The Mid-Term Review of the CAP in 2003 explicitly proposed making payments conditional on environmental protection, food safety, animal welfare, health and occupational safety standards, and on the requirement to keep all farmland in good condition. In addition, more money was allocated to rural development policy and to new measures geared towards promoting product quality, animal welfare and meeting EU production standards. Therefore, designing multifunctional policies has become a very challenging task. On the one hand, it is necessary to give economic incentives to producers to provide these joint outputs of agricultural production and environmental amenities, while on the other hand, these economic incentives should not discriminate among final outputs, nor create market distortions, particularly against imports.

There has been extensive research on different multifunctional practices, and whether they may or may not be profitable for adoption. Consequently, future policy adoptions may provide an opportunity to help protect agricultural landscapes, open space and cultural heritage whilst enhancing profitability opportunities. Therefore, in this chapter we wish to evaluate societies' demand for such multifunctional attributes. As is well known, the new agricultural policy should be designed to facilitate local rural development while promoting sustainable tourism initiatives and preserving the local heritage.

In this study we deal with the possible alternatives of intervention in a specific area of Galicia, the Ribeira Sacra region of Spain (Figure 6.1). Thus, understanding societal preferences towards multifunctional attributes is relevant for policy-making purposes, given that new green payments should be in line with social preferences. With the aim of knowing visitors' preferences towards multifunctional attributes derived from the local cultural landscapes, we surveyed a sample of 173 tourists. They were presented with a face to face survey containing questions related to their travelling experience, their preferences towards different landscape elements, and a set of choice experiment (CE) questions with different policy scenarios aimed at preserving the local cultural landscape and environmental amenities. The current study is expected to provide useful information to policy makers working on the green payments designs.

The structure of this chapter is as follows. First, a review of previous studies closely related to the present objectives of analysis is presented. Then, there follows a description of the geographical area and the main characteristics of the area. The next section contains a description of the methodology, followed by the data and the main results sections. The chapter concludes with some policy implications derived from the findings.

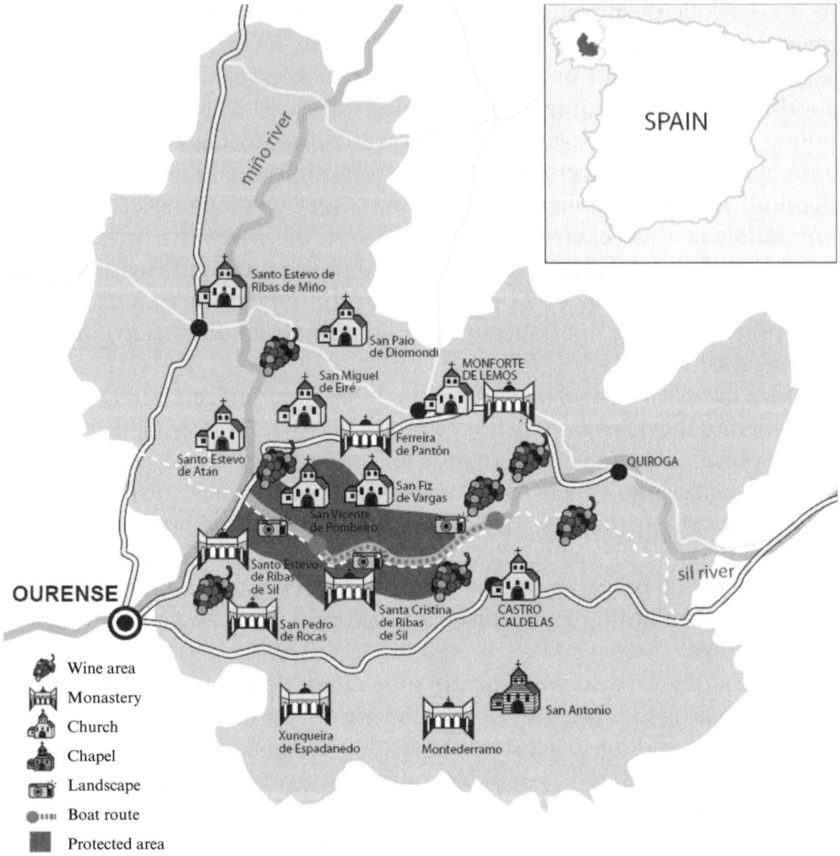

Figure 6.1 *Location of the study area (Ribeira Sacra) and its main characteristics*

PREVIOUS STUDIES

A review of the literature offers interesting references regarding the valuation of multifunctional policies and joint outputs derived from agriculture. However, most of the previous studies have employed contingent valuation (CV) methods, while in the present chapter we use choice experiments (CE). One of the first studies of valuation of agricultural non-market outputs was undertaken by Drake (1992), who estimated the monetary value that the Swedish population were willing to pay to preserve the traditional landscape. Drake's results suggest that even though this study reveals a considerable aggregate willingness to pay (WTP), the amount would probably not suffice to maintain farmers in mountainous regions. Santos (1998) and Madureira (2006) show that Portuguese society has a significant willingness to pay for landscape preservation. Pruckner (1995) evaluated the economic value that tourists place on environmental benefits provided by the agricultural sector in Austria. Although he concluded that the value given was fairly high, it may not have been sufficiently high to maintain agricultural activities in mountain areas. Alvarez-Farizo *et al.* (1999) studied the conservation benefits associated with the preservation of Environmentally Sensitive Areas (ESAs) in Scotland, finding that users and non-users were willing to pay significant amounts to preserve such sensitive areas. Following the same line of analysis, Yrjölä and Kola (2004) estimated the value of multifunctional agriculture in a representative sample of Finnish households. As in the previous study, the authors concluded that the willingness to pay (WTP) for these attributes is fairly large, and in this particular case, well above the per capita support in Finland.

Other references in Southern European countries include the work done in Portugal by Santos (1998) and more recently by Madureira (2006). Agricultural systems in Southern European countries are characterized by the abandonment of agriculture, instead of the intensification process typical of their Northern European counterparts. In his evaluation, Santos (1998) used CV to assess the value of the Pennine Dales ESA scheme in England in comparison with the Penade-Gerês national park in Portugal. His methodology was closely followed by Madureira (2006), who assessed tourists' preferences toward wine landscapes in the Porto region. In Italy, Cicia and Scarpa (2000) investigated the potential benefits derived by tourists from the implementation of a programme aimed at preserving the traditional agricultural landscape in the National Park of Cilento (Southern Italy). Their results show that visitors would be willing to pay at least €1 per day of visit to preserve the traditional landscape of this region.

As stated earlier, we employ a choice modelling or choice experiment (CE) approach. One of the advantages of choice modelling with respect to contingent valuation is that it becomes possible to value independently each of the specified attributes contained in a particular good or programme being valued. In the literature related to multifunctionality studies, Hanley *et al.* (1998a) estimated the benefits derived from agriculture, employing both CV and CE. More recently, Bennett, van Bueren and Whitten (2004) also employed a CE approach to measure the benefits derived from maintaining the population in their rural communities in Australia. Hanley *et al.* (1998b) also offered an example of how to value environmental amenities with choice experiments. We employ these previous studies as bases for the current chapter, which aims to contribute to the literature of multifunctional agriculture in the Northwest of Spain. As far as we know, this is the first application of CE to measure multifunctional and cultural landscape benefits derived from Spanish agricultural areas.

THE CASE STUDY AREA

The Ribeira Sacra (literally the Sacred Riverbank) is an area on the confluence of the rivers Miño and Sil between the provinces of Lugo and Ourense (see Figure 6.1). The area is marked by the deep depressions formed by the rivers. The local landscapes are characterized by very lofty slopes which top out at heights of between 500 and 900 metres, with multiple granite fractures intertwined with autochthonous forests. This geology favours the existence of climatic conditions which are characterized by high temperatures in the summer and warmer temperatures in winter.

It is a documented fact that the name Ribeira Sacra referred to shelters for monks and hermits in the gorges of the rivers Sil and Miño. During the Middle Ages there were about a dozen monasteries located in spots that even nowadays invite reflection, forming the greatest concentration of monasteries and Romanesque churches of this region. These monks, helped by the benign climate, improved and developed the culture of the grapevine, which was introduced by the Romans. The families of this area have carried on the wine-making tradition over the centuries, and as a consequence, the landscape has a human dimension developed by the vineyards planted on terraces (*socalvos*) on the hillsides exposed to the sun.

Typical products from this area are the Ribeira Sacra's red wines, which date from Roman times. It is said that the spiced wines of this area were so highly prized that they were dispatched to Caesar. Remarkably, wine making in this area is still on a farm scale, with each producer making just a few thousand bottles. The grapes are organically grown on tiny strips of land scattered around the Sil Valley, whose slopes run from steep to precipitous. As a consequence, the quantities of wine are limited by the unique locations needed for the best wines, where the very best grapes grow only on the spurs of slopes which receive long hours of direct sunlight. These densely cultivated areas make a dizzying abstract landscape that represents centuries of hard toil. However, the traditional landscape and production methods in this area may be changing soon. The local designation 'Ribeira Sacra' has recently been upgraded from a regional to a national denomination of origin (DO). Winemakers hope that with DO status, the Ribeira Sacra growers will win higher premiums while holding on to traditional organic methods. This DO aims to protect the name and the quality of the wine produced in this region, in the same way as do the Protected Designations of Origin (PDO) created following the Council Regulation EC No 2081/92 for many other European products.

For the past ten years, the regional government of Galicia has aimed to attract tourists to this region, applying different EU rural development programmes. Tourist development of this area has focused on exploring the value of the local amenities, mainly the cultural vineyard landscapes, the natural canyons of the rivers, the monasteries and other historical and cultural sites. To protect and preserve at the same time these three main elements of the local cultural landscape (traditional wine landscapes, historical sites and local environmental amenities) seems to be a challenging task for the public administration. The main reason is that the rural population of this area is decreasing and getting older. This phenomenon contributes to the abandonment of agriculture landscapes and local traditions, which results in the disuse of local cultural and historical sites. At the same time, the remaining population seeks ways of obtaining a better quality of life, which at times drives them to industrialize all their production processes, even if they are in conflict with the preservation of the local environment and the local economy.

Given the current struggle to attract tourists and at the same time preserve these natural areas with a well-managed landscape, we assess tourists' preferences towards different cultural landscape and rural heritage preservation programmes. The responses gathered from the tourists' preferences provide information for policy makers regarding the most preferred elements of this complex cultural rural landscape. This information could be helpful in prioritizing actions or rural development policies. The next sections describe the methodology and sample used in our analysis. We conclude with some policy recommendations based on our findings.

METHODOLOGY: CHOICE MODELLING

In order to elicit tourists' preferences, we use a choice modelling framework, which allows individuals to select between two alternative options (two types of cultural landscape and rural heritage preservation programmes) that contain a number of attributes at different levels. As recommended by Adamowicz *et al.* (1998b) a non-choice option was also presented to participants, since this is an obvious element of choice behaviour. Similar exercises to the one here presented have been employed in food marketing, transportation economics and environmental economics studies (see for example, Adamowicz *et al.*, 1998a and 1998b). Thus, instead of asking individuals whether they would be willing to pay a certain amount of money for preserving Ribeira Sacra's cultural landscape, in this application they were asked to select their preferred preservation alternative from two programmes aiming to protect the local landscape.

Formally, this attribute-based choice method is based on Lancastrian consumer theory (Lancaster, 1966), which proposes that utilities for goods can be decomposed into separate utilities for their component characteristics or attributes, and random utility theory (see McFadden, 1974; Hanemann and Kanninen, 1999). The basic assumption of random utility theory is that individuals act rationally, selecting the alternative that yields the highest utility. Consequently, the probability of selecting a given alternative will be higher if the utility provided by such alternative is the highest among the different choices.

Therefore, a conditional (multinomial) logit model can represent the ith visitor's probability of selecting the jth programme choice, given that the conditional logit model is choice conditional on the attributes of choice (Greene 1997, pp. 913–914; Maddala [1983] 1999, pp. 42),

$$\text{Prob}\,(y_i = j) = \frac{e^{X_i \beta_j}}{\sum_{k=1}^{J} e^{X_i \beta_j}} \quad \text{for } j = 1, \ldots, J, \tag{6.1}$$

where β_j refers to parameters that weight exogenous variables in determining the utility of choice j; and X_i is a row vector of exogenous variable values corresponding to the programme characteristics and socio-demographics of the ith tourist.

The log likelihood of the conditional (multinomial) logit is given by:

$$L = \prod_{i=1}^{n} \prod_{j=1}^{J} \text{Prob}\,(y_i = j)^{y_{ij}}, \tag{6.2}$$

where $y_{ij} = 1$ if alternative j is chosen by the ith individual, and zero otherwise.

DATA

During early summer 2006, data were gathered using a face to face survey of visitors to Ribeira Sacra. Respondents were approached to complete the survey at different locations of this study area, including the tourist information centre, the biggest monastery of the area (today remodelled and used as a hotel), and the boating port where tourists get tickets for catamaran excursions through the rivers. After using the information gathered in the pre-test to make slight modifications, the final survey contained questions about the frequency of visits, the length and travelling mode of their trip, the subjective importance given to the different landscape elements, the activities in which tourists spend their time while visiting the area, general attitudes towards different landscape scenarios, choice experiment questions, and finally, some ethical and socio-economic questions about the respondent's characteristics.

In the choice modelling questions, individuals were asked to select between two types of public programmes with different lines of action aiming to preserve the local cultural landscape and rural heritage which carried different associated costs to visitors and had different objectives. Information regarding the meaning of each of the actions considered was also presented to tourists just before the choice experiment. The different measures and their corresponding values are displayed in Table 6.1. Given that the larger number of attributes the programme contains, the more difficult the selection becomes, five different attributes were employed to minimize the number of choice sets required, without losing relevant information for the purposes of this study. The selection of the attributes included was based on the results obtained in the pre-test regarding

Table 6.1 Variable definition, levels and coding

Variable	**Definition**	**Levels**	**Coded**
Price	Expected price increment in a daily trip per person	€11.5, €22.5, €37.5	11.5, 22.5, 37.5
History	Lines of action focused on preservation of historical monuments	Yes vs No	−1, 1
Tradition	Lines of action focused on preservation of local traditions, local foods and rural settlements	Yes vs No	−1, 1
Environment	Lines of action focused on preserving the local environment and keeping it clean	Yes vs No	−1, 1
Agri-forestry landscape	Lines of action focused on preserving the agricultural and forestry traditional landscape	Yes vs No	−1, 1

the most significant characteristics of the local area according to the visitors.

The selected lines of action contained in the programmes presented were: preservation of traditional customs, food products, and rural settlements; protection of the local environment (maintaining clean rivers, cleaning open spaces and collecting and recycling trash); protection of the traditional agro-forestry landscape (including wine terraces, autochthonous forests and autochthonous livestock); and preservation of the historical-cultural heritage (restoration of cultural and historical sites). It was indicated that the implementation of these public programmes would be costly; and in order to put them into action, costs would have to be paid by society as a whole, including also a share that would be transferred to the visitors. In the survey, it was explained that the regional government would have to tax establishments more heavily to raise sufficient budget to provide the programmes described, so that tourists and locals would face higher final prices for many products and services.

The proportional costs to be paid by tourists were presented as a percentage increment of the current average daily expenditures that a regular tourist faces when visiting this area. Recent tourist statistics indicate that the average daily expenditure per tourist in this area amounts to €113 per day of stay (IGE, 2006). Therefore, in our application the increments on average daily expenditures if the selected programmes were applied would amount to an increase of 10 per cent, 20 per cent and 33 per cent on the daily expenditures if the cultural landscape and rural development programmes were implemented.

The choice set design was created employing fractional factorial design generation. Specifically, we generated full factorial design for five attributes, each with two levels, except for the price increase, which contained three levels. The procedure called *proc optex* in SAS was used to find a design that maximizes the D-Efficiency and A-Efficiency scores. The goal of D-optimality is to maximize the determinant of the information matrix, while A-optimality attempts to minimize the sum of the variances of estimated coefficients. Later, the DETMAX algorithm of Mitchell (1974) was performed to search for this design, where the starting point was determined by random seeds. Thus, the final design was selected based on the optimal combination of high D-Efficiency (91.008) and A-Efficiency (81.576), fewer choice sets (12 choice sets), and minimal correlation between factors. In order to ensure that earlier questions did not affect tourists' responses to later questions in a systematic way, the order of the choice sets was randomized. The correlation of the factors was calculated to assess estimability of the main effects.

EMPIRICAL SPECIFICATION

The empirical specification of the utility levels underlying the conditional multinomial logit makes references to the attributes of each choice and was formulated as follows:

$$U_{ij} = \beta_1 \text{Pr}\,ice_{ij} + \beta_2 Tradition_{ij} + \beta_3 Environment_{ij} + \beta_4 AgForestLandscape_{ij} + \beta_5 History_{ij} + \varepsilon_{ij} \quad (6.3)$$

Since U_{ij} is the latent unobservable utility level that the ith individual obtains from choosing the jth programme, the observed choice is a reflection of this latent unobservable utility. Note that *Price, Tradition, Environment, AgForestLandscape* and *History* are programme attributes considered in the choice set. The model described in (6.3) was formulated given the attribute levels and the responses to the choice experiment survey. Table 6.1 contains the definitions and coding of the programme attributes under consideration.

A conditional (multinomial) logit model was estimated with the LIMDEP NLOGIT 3.0 version within a maximum likelihood framework to analyse tourists' choice behaviour under the condition that different public programmes enhance different multifunctional elements.

RESULTS

A total of 173 completed surveys were collected from a random sample of tourists. The response rate was about 44 per cent, the majority of respondents being female (58.38 per cent), with an average age of about 41 years, and 84 per cent of all respondents having children under the age of 18 years in their household. The household income was well distributed between the lowest interval (household income below €11 999) and the highest interval (with income above €60 000). The median household income was calculated to be between €24 000 and €29 999 for the 2005 calendar year, while the average educational attainment in the sample was fairly high, given that about 40 per cent of the total sample had a college degree.

In the survey, each participant was asked to choose between two alternative public programmes aiming to preserve the Ribeira Sacra, programmes A and B, and the 'neither of them option' on repeated choice occasions, providing a total of 1038 responses. The literature disagrees on whether to include 'no choice' or 'neither A or B' responses because they do not provide much information in the analysis (Hensher and Bradley, 1993). However, recent contributions to choice analysis seem to caution against eliminating

Table 6.2 Summary statistics sample

Variable Name	Description (Coding)	Mean	St. Dv.
Age	In years	41.51	12.12
Gender	1 if female, 0 if male	0.583	0.504
Education			
	1 = No formal education	0.005	0.075
	2= Elementary school	0.156	0.363
	3 = HS diploma	0.161	0.368
	4 = Professional degree	0.150	0.357
	5 = College (3-year degree)	0.144	0.351
	6= College (5-year degree)	0.329	0.470
	7=College (Postgraduate education)	0.052	0.222
Children	1 if children <18 living in the household, 0 otherwise	0.843	0.964
Family Size	Number of family members living in the household	1.904	0.745
Household Income	1 = <€11 988	0.10	0.300
	2= €12 000–€17 988	0.146	0.353
	3= €18 000–€23 988	0.166	0.372
	4= €24 000–€29 988	0.160	0.366
	5= €30 000–€35 988	0.160	0.366
	6= €36 000–€59 988	0.133	0.340
	7= >=€60 000	0.126	0.332

such options from experiments because they may have significant impacts on the resulting designs (Louviere *et al.*, 2000, p. 302). In the empirical estimation of the choice selection, ignoring option C produces inconsistent results with the principles of economic theory. Figure 6.2 gives an example of one of the multiple-choice sets that participants evaluated.

Results obtained from the empirical specification of equation (6.3) are reported in Table 6.3. All coefficients are statistically significant at conventional critical levels, and their relationship with the utility function is as expected. Thus, increments on price decrease the associated utility level provided by the programme, whereas increments on any of the other lines of action considered increase tourists' utility. The highest utility increment occurs where there is action related to preserving the Ribeira Sacra's environment, followed by actions in favour of preserving the local agricultural and forestry landscape, the historical sites, and finally, local traditions.

18.2	Option A	Option B	Option C
Estimated price increase (€/day per visitor)	37.5	22.5	Neither option A nor option B= Current situation
Protection of local food products and rural settlements	NO	YES	
Protection of local environment	NO	NO	
Protection of traditional agricultural and forestry landscape (wine terraces, autochthonous forests and autochthonous livestock)	YES	NO	
Protection of historical and cultural sites	NO	YES	
I would select: (Please select the correct one)	☐	☐	☐

Figure 6.2 Choice set example

Table 6.3 Conditional (multinomial) logit results

	Coefficients	Std Error
Price	−0.03423***	0.00727
History	0.76592***	0.13888
Tradition	0.25504**	0.11464
Environment	1.1106***	0.10943
Agri-forestry landscape	0.83604***	0.10957
Observations	1038	
R^2 adjusted	0.449	
Log-likelihood	−275.25	

Note: *** denotes statistical significant coefficients at a 1% level or less and ** denotes statistical significance at a 5% level or less.

ESTIMATING WTP FOR PROGRAMME ATTRIBUTES

In the conditional (multinomial) logit the coefficients cannot be directly interpreted as the direct effects of the respective explanatory variables on the probability of choosing each particular programme alternative. Rather, they represent the direct effects associated with each of the explanatory variables on the (unobservable) utility function, which can be used to calculate the mean willingness-to-pay estimates (WTP) for each of the attributes. Each of

Table 6.4 WTP for each attribute

Attribute	WTP estimate for attribute (€/day)	90% C.I.*
History	22.39	(22.41, 22.36)
Tradition	7.45	(7.46, 7.42)
Environment	32.47	(32.50, 32.44)
Agri-forestry landscape	24.44	(24.46, 24.41)

Note: * Confidence intervals have been calculated employing the delta method, where:

$$a\ \mathrm{var}\left(\frac{-\alpha}{\beta}\right) = \frac{1}{\beta^2}\left[\left(\frac{\alpha}{\beta}\right)^2 \mathrm{var}(\alpha) + \mathrm{var}(\beta) - 2\left(\frac{\alpha}{\beta}\right)\mathrm{cov}(\alpha,\beta)\right]$$

the WTP estimates is calculated as the ratio of the coefficient associated with the attribute of interest over the Price coefficient (see Hanemann and Kanninen, 1999). Therefore, in order to calculate the mean WTP estimates for each line of action included in the cultural landscape and rural development programmes, we estimate the corresponding ratios. Each of these ratios is understood as a price change associated with a unit increase in a given programme characteristic.

These mean WTP estimates obtained with the coefficients reported in Table 6.3 and the asymptotic standard errors obtained via the delta method for each attribute are reported in Table 6.4. Results indicate that the initiatives most praised by visitors are those related to preservation of the local environment. On average, visitors are willing to pay about €32.47/day extra for a public programme which contains actions related to the preservation and enhancement of local environmental amenities. The conservation of agricultural landscape, in which the wine terraces are predominant, is the second most praised attribute, with an associated WTP estimate of €24.44/day extra. Initiatives linked to the preservation of historical monuments and cultural sites are the third most preferred line of action. Visitors are willing to pay an average of €22.39/day for a public programme aiming to protect and restore existing historical monuments and sites. Finally, the less preferred restoration actions are those linked to the preservation of local traditional food products and production processes, and local population settlements. Elicited WTP for this last attribute amounts to €7.45/day. These results are justifiable and according to previous results; for example, Gonzalez and León (2003) indicated that the consumption process of different attributes plays a crucial role in their valuation.

Our results imply that visitors value more the attributes they experience, such as the nature of the area, the vineyard landscape and the historical sites, and less the local traditional products (such as the local wines and typical foods). Furthermore, average length of stay in this area is limited to just one single day, so tourists value more policy actions such as restoration of the environment and agricultural landscape which may have a very quick visual impact. However, other actions encouraging the preservation of local foods and wines may provide less utility to visitors, since some of them may pass by without enjoying the typical food products of the area. Future studies should study local inhabitants' preferences and their divergences from those of the visitors.

CONCLUDING REMARKS

In this study, a random sample of visitors of the geographical area named Ribeira Sacra was interviewed. This area is located in the north-west of Spain (Galicia), and has a very complex landscape and multiple possibilities to improve agricultural and forestry multifunctional programmes. Due to the population collapse and the abandonment of the agricultural sector, policies in this area need to focus on specific lines of action: maintaining the local settlements of rural population, keeping the local traditions, preserving the natural open spaces and traditional agricultural and forestry landscapes, among others. Given that information is needed regarding social preferences towards these rural development options, a survey was conducted among tourists with the objective of assessing their preferences regarding different public interventions to protect and recover the area of study. Our results show that visitors place more value on programmes containing actions related to the preservation of the environment and local landscapes of the area of study, followed by other actions aiming to maintain the historical sites. The less preferable policy actions are those linked to maintaining local traditions. This information should be of interest to policy makers aiming to keep rural settlements alive and conserve rural landscapes.

Currently, the natural scenary of the river canyons and forests is quite spectacular, but public investments are needed to preserve this natural landscape from degradation. The traditional agricultural landscape (mainly formed by wine terraces) is also highly prized by visitors, and policy options aiming to improve it are also justifiable, based on the previous WTP estimates. Furthermore, our results also suggest that educational campaigns promoting the high quality of the local traditional foods and wines may be necessary in order for tourists to increase their consumption during their visit. It is surprising that local products historically considered to be of high quality are not so admired by tourists. The quick travelling time around this area may be an explanation for these results. However, there might be some room for better promotion of these quality wines and local products using the PDO (Protected Designation of Origin) instruments for effective marketing. Thus, there is room for better managing of traditional cultural landscapes and recreational alternatives in Ribeira Sacra in order to maximize all that this area has to offer to potential visitors.

ACKNOWLEDGEMENT AND NOTE

Acknowledgment: The authors wish to thank *Fundación Caixa Galicia* for funding support for this project.

Note: The views expressed in this chapter are those of the authors, and do not represent in any way the views of the Galician Rural Development Agency.

REFERENCES

Adamowicz, W., P. Boxall, M. Williams and J. Louviere (1998a), 'Stated Preference Approaches for Measuring Passive Use Values: Choice Experiments and Contingent Valuation', *American Journal of Agricultural Economics*, 80, 64–75.

Adamowicz, W., J. Louviere and J. Swait (1998b), *An Introduction to Stated Choice Methods for Resources Based Compensation*, prepared by Advanis Inc. for the National Oceanic and Atmospheric Administration, U.S. Department of Commerce.

Alvarez Farizo, B., N. Hanley, R. E. Wright and D. Macmillan (1999), 'Estimating the Benefits of Agri-Environmental Policy: Econometric Issues in Open-ended Contingent Valuation Studies', *Journal of Environmental Planning and Management*, 42(1), 23–43.

Bennett, J., M. van Bueren and S. Whitten (2004), 'Estimating Society's Willingness to Pay to Maintain Viable Rural Communities', *The Australian Journal of Agricultural and Resource Economics*, 48(3), 487–512.

Cicia, G. and R. Scarpa (2000), *Willingness to Pay for Rural Landscape Preservation: A Case Study in Mediterranean Agriculture*, working paper, Milan: Fondazione Eni Enrico Matei.

Drake, L. (1992), 'The Non-Market Value of the Swedish Agricultural Landscape', *European Review of Agricultural Economics*, 19, 351–364.

Greene, W. (1997), *Econometric Analysis*, New York: Prentice Hall (third edition).

Gonzalez, M. and C. J. León (2003), 'Consumption Process and Multiple Valuation of Landscape Attributes', *Ecological Economics*, 45, 159–169.

Hanemann, W. M. and B. Kanninen (1999), 'The Statistical Analysis of Discrete-Response Data', in I. Bateman and K. Willis (eds), *Valuing the Environment: Preferences: Theory and Practice of the Contingent Valuation Method in the US, EC and Developing Countries*, Oxford: Oxford University Press.

Hanley, N., D. MacMillan, R. Wright, J. Simpson, D. Parsisson, C. Bullock and R. Crabtree (1998a), 'Choice Experiments versus Contingent Valuation: Estimating the Benefits of Environmentally Sensitive Areas in Scotland', *Journal of Agricultural Economics*, 49(1), 1–15.
Hanley, N., R. E. Wright and V. Adamowicz (1998b), 'Using Choice Experiments to Value the Environment', *Environmental and Resource Economics*, 11(3–4), 413–428.
Hensher, D. A. and M. Bradley (1993), 'Using Stated Response Choice Data to Enrich Revealed Preferences Discrete Choice Models', *Marketing Letters*, 4, 139–51.
IGE (Instituto Galego de Estasítica) (2006), *Estatística do Gasto do Turimo que Pernoita en Establecementos Hoteleiros*, Santiago de Compostolea, Spain: IGE.
Lancaster, K. (1966), 'A New Approach to Consumer Theory', *Journal of Political Economy*, 74, 132–157.
Louviere, J. J., D. A. Hensher, and J. D. Swait (2000), *Stated Choice Methods: Analysis and Application*, Cambridge: Cambridge University Press.
Maddala, G. S. ([1983] 1999), *Limited-Dependent and Qualitative Variables in Econometrics*, Cambridge: Cambridge University Press.
Madureira, L. (2006), 'Multi-Attribute Valuation of Douro Valley Winescape based upon Qualitative Data for Individual's Attitudes Regarding Nature-Related and Rural Heritage Attributes', paper presented at the *II AERNA conference*, Lisbon, 2–3 June.
McFadden, D. (1974), 'Conditional Logit Analysis of Qualitative Choice Behavior', in P. Zarembka (ed.), *Frontiers in Econometrics*, New York: Academic Press, 105–142.
Mitchell, T. J. (1974), 'An Algorithm for the Construction of "D-optimal" Experimental Design', *Technometrics*, 16(2), 210.
Pruckner, G. J. (1995), 'Agricultural Landscape Cultivation in Australia: An Application of the CVM', *European Review of Agricultural Economics*, 22, 173–190.
Santos, J. M. L. (1998), *The Economic Valuation of the Landscape Change*, Cheltenham, UK and Northampton, MA, USA: Edward Elgar.
Yrjörlä, T. and J. Kola (2004), 'Society's Demand for Multifunctional Agriculture', Paper presented at the 90th European Association of Agricultural Economists Seminar *Multifunctional Agriculture, Policies and Markets: Understanding the Critical Linkages*, Rennes, 28–29 October.

7. Latent market segmentation analysis of choice experiment data and implications for the EU's GM labelling policy

Andreas Kontoleon and Mitsuyasu Yabe

INTRODUCTION: GM LABELLING POLICY AND CONSUMER MARKET SEGMENTATION

Over the past ten years the EU's policy for regulating GM foods has moved from a moratorium-based policy to one based on labelling. This shift in EU GM policy – from an effective ban of GM foods to a regime where such foods can be sold if appropriately labelled – largely reflects an attempt to balance its obligations towards the World Trade Organization and the apparent concerns of portions of the European public (Kalaitzandonakes, 2004). The EU's most recent GM labelling regime (established in Directives No. 1829/2003 and 1830/2003) has been in effect since April 2004 and is considered to be one of the most rigid and strict GM labelling regimes worldwide (Kalaitzandonakes, 2004). There are four main points of disparity between the EU's labelling policies and those followed in other countries (Phillips and McNeill, 2000; Sheldon, 2004; Food Standards Agency, 2005). First, the EU has developed a much more stringent, strict and lengthy protocol for the scientific testing and authorisation of each new crop prior to its introduction into the market. Secondly, the EU has opted for a mandatory scheme as opposed to voluntary labelling schemes found in other countries such as the US and Canada. Thirdly, the EU has embraced a much wider range of food products that are to be included in its labelling scheme by requiring the labelling of certain (but not all) foods derived from GM crops irrespective of whether genetically modified DNA is detectable in the final products. Hence, foods such as refined maize oil or glucose syrup produced from GM maize starch are required to be labelled under the latest EU directives governing the labelling of GM foods. Moreover, the same EU directives also require animal feed (such as soybean meals) that have been produced from genetically modified organisms

(GMOs), to be labelled so that farmers can make an informed choice over the inputs they use. The rationale, therefore, of the EU's new regime is 'process driven' and moves away from detectability towards traceability, whereby parties/agents involved in each link in the food production chain (from the production of seeds to the sale of a final food product) must keep records of the GM inputs used. Lastly, the EU has tended to adopt a lower minimum threshold of GM traces that are permissible for a food product to be considered GM free. In the EU, such minimum threshold of adventitious contamination is set at 1%, whereas other countries such as Japan have set this level to 5% (Kalaitzandonakes, 2004).

The EU's relatively hard-line labelling stance has not been without its critics both within and outside the EU. Economists have debated the necessity, efficiency and cost-effectiveness of the regime (for example, Giannakas and Fulton, 2002; Carter and Gruère, 2003; Gray *et al.*, 2004; Kalaitzandonakes, 2004); genetic engineers have questioned the scientific legitimacy of the EU's policy as they argue that there is no evidence that GM and GM-derived foods differ in any way from their conventional counterparts (for example, AgBioWorld, 2003; Bertoni and Marsan, 2005); while several governments outside the EU have contested its legality and have argued that it constitutes a form of covert protectionism (for example, Lapan and Moschini, 2001; Sheldon, 2004). The central theme of the EU's response to such criticisms is that the evolution of its GM food labelling policies simply reflects the widespread aversion towards GM foods amongst European consumers. It has been frequently argued that these policies are welfare enhancing as they simultaneously satisfy the 'precautionary', the 'consumer sovereignty' and the 'consumer right to know' principles, all of which are reflected in European preferences and are embodied in the fundamental treaties of the EU (European Commission, 2002). The EU is in essence making a welfarist argument in that its GM policy-making process has elevated the relative importance of consumer preferences over other considerations or over other stakeholder interests (Fulton and Giannakas, 2004). Given the importance that has been placed on consumer aversion towards GM foods in determining the course of the EU's GM labelling regime, it is particularly important to have accurate and meaningful information over the degree of this aversion. Economic analysis has shown that this requires an assessment both of the level of aversion as well as how this aversion is distributed across different segments of the population (Bureau *et al.*, 1998; Giannakas and Fulton, 2002; Lusk and Hudson, 2003; Nielsen *et al.*, 2003; Kalaitzandonakes, 2004; Lusk *et al.*, 2005b; Giannakas and Yiannaka, 2006).

With respect to assessing the level of European consumer aversion towards GM foods, the empirical evidence that is often evoked in support of the EU's welfarist argument is mostly derived from numerous opinion polls and attitudinal studies.[1] Though such studies can offer useful information, they may not provide a sound basis to make judgements over the welfare impacts of GM labelling policies. Instead responses derived from such survey-based studies reflect societal beliefs, voting intentions or general perceptions and not individual consumer purchasing behaviour (Noussair *et al.*, 2004; Owen *et al.*, 2005). Such behavioural information can best be derived from preference data that is collected from individuals operating within a market (that is, incentive-compatible) setting. Since due to current market thinness, obtaining such data from revealed preference sources (for example, supermarket scanner data) is extremely rare in Europe, researchers have mostly been confined to using data from hypothetical and experimental survey-based methods.[2] Two such methods that have been shown to better simulate actual market transactions are choice experiments and experimental auctions (Ben-Akiva *et al.*, 2002a; Huffman *et al.*, 2004; Lusk and Schroeder, 2004). There is now a plethora of such studies that have assessed the intensity and determinants of European consumer preferences over GM foods under alternative experimental and informational, institutional and regulatory conditions.[3]

The second component in assessing the degree of aversion towards GM foods is to evaluate how this aversion is distributed across segments of the market. As GM content cannot be currently distinguished by consumers via 'search' prior or 'experience' after the purchase of a particular food, it is by definition a 'credence' attribute similar to 'nutritional value' or 'preservative content'. A labelling scheme would thus aim at overcoming this informational asymmetry. One of the necessary conditions for such a scheme to be viable and desirable is that the consumer market is sufficiently segmented. This requires consumers to perceive that the labelled and non-labelled alternatives are significantly differentiated and that there exist sufficiently distinct and behaviourally consistent preferences for each good across the different segments of the market. Hence, it is particularly important for the meaningful assessment of GM policies to enhance our understanding of the likely number of market segments that exist with respect to GM foods, the size (market share) of each segment, the nature and determinants (for example, socio-economic and attitudinal characteristics) of each segment and how preferences vary across each segment. Despite the large policy relevance of such information there are surprisingly very few economic studies that have undertaken such a detailed segmentation analysis on European consumers. This chapter undertakes the first detailed market segmentation analysis of the demand for GM foods in Europe with the aim of illustrating how this analysis can provide distinct information that can assist in evaluating the welfare impacts of proposed changes to the

EU's GM labelling policy. In particular, the chapter makes three main contributions.

First, the chapter shows how segmentation analysis provides distinctively useful information that can assist in the assessment of the welfare implications of specific proposals made for further enhancing the scope and strictness of the EU's labelling regime. With respect to the former, there are calls for extending the scope of the current labelling regime to include GM-derived animal products. These refer to eggs, meat and dairy products that are derived from animals that have been fed with GM animal feed.[4] With respect to the latter proposal over enhancing the strictness of the EU labelling regime, there are persistent voices for lowering the certification threshold from its current 1 per cent level to one close (if not equal) to zero. In many EU Member States there are large campaigns underway lobbying European legislators for the urgency of such changes. The UK is at the forefront of these campaigns, where many major consumer and environmentalist fora have been most active (for example, the National Consumer Council, the Consumers Association, the European Consumer Organisation, Consumers' International, Friends of the Earth and Greenpeace). The adoption by European legislators of such appeals for increasing the scope and strictness of the EU labelling regime would have serious cost repercussions for the production and commercialisation of foods (Food Standards Agency, 2001; Kalaitzandonakes *et al.*, 2001). Advocacy groups acknowledge the cost-raising implications of such changes but argue that they are required if consumers are to be given a real choice between GM and non-GM foods and if the labelling regime is to truly reflect European consumers' preferences. It is thus vital to accumulate information that can aid our assessment of the efficiency and distributional implications of such proposed legislative changes.

In this chapter we present the results of a choice experiment study undertaken in the UK that was purposefully designed to evaluate the welfare implications of these proposals. Though there is some preliminary empirical evidence to suggest that EU consumers would support labelling of GM-derived foods such as bread or biscuits (for example, Burton *et al.*, 2004; Noussair *et al.*, 2004), there has not been sufficient analysis of European preference heterogeneity with respect to labelling GM-derived animal products.[5] In the study discussed in this chapter we analyse the preferences for one such widely consumed product, namely eggs.[6] By examining the magnitude of the discount that would have to be given to each segment of consumers in order to purchase eggs derived from chickens fed with GM animal feed, we were able to assess whether there are welfare enhancing reasons for extending the scope of the new labelling regime to include such animal products. Similarly, despite the policy significance of determining the optimal threshold level for non-GM certification, there has been very little consumer research on this issue.[7] In the present study, this issue is examined by assessing the welfare implications of altering the GM content in animal feed used in the production of eggs.

The second contribution of this chapter is the method employed to undertake an analysis of consumer choice and segment membership – the latent segment (LS) method. It is argued that this modelling approach may provide more policy-relevant information when analysing welfare impacts in highly segmented consumer markets (as may be the case for GM foods). The model is well understood and has been tested in other areas of consumer research and marketing and has been employed in various environmental and agricultural economic contexts (Wedel and Kamakura, 2000; Vriens, 2001; Boxall and Adamowicz, 2002). Yet despite its familiarity and its likely usefulness for providing information over the nature and degree of consumer market segmentation with respect to GM foods, the LS model has not been utilised for this purpose. We thus explore the usefulness of this particular model in assessing UK consumer welfare impacts from changes in GM food labelling policies.

Thirdly, the modelling framework employed is based on the work by McFadden (1986), Ben-Akiva *et al.* (1997) and McFadden (1999), and attempts to enrich the analysis of consumer data by introducing motivational and attitudinal drivers of individual behaviour. The analysis thus contributes to our understanding of incorporating insights from behavioural sciences (such as psychometric variables) in micro-econometric choice models as a means for providing a more accurate and enriched explanation of complex human decision making processes (Ashok *et al.*, 2002). In particular, by employing purposefully designed psychometric variables in our analysis, we extend previous stated preference based research on GM foods, which has so far mainly focused on exploring demographic variables (such as age, income and education levels) as sources of preference heterogeneity. The need to include psychometric variables in the analysis of GM food choice data was in fact identified as one of the central research priorities in a recent comprehensive assessment of the body of applied research on the demand for GM foods conducted by Marks *et al.* (2003). The study discussed in this chapter is the first attempt to develop and incorporate such psychometric variables in a segmentation analysis of consumer preferences for GM foods.

The chapter is structured as follows. The next section discusses the conceptual and statistical foundations of the latent segment model as well as its potential usefulness for informing GM policy makers and stakeholders. The following two sections describe the design of the study and present the results of the analysis. The final section concludes and highlights the contributions and policy implications of the analysis.

THE LATENT SEGMENT MODEL

The latent segment model belongs to the family of latent class finite mixture models which are currently considered as providing the most powerful avenue for market segmentation analysis (Wedel and Kamakura, 2000, p. 26). Such models assume that sampled observations can be classified into two or more groups that are mixed in unknown proportions. At the limit, the number of groups may equal the sample size, which motivates the use of a random parameter mixed logit model (Greene and Hensher, 2002). The aim of these models is to 'unmix' the sample by identifying the stochastic structures governing segment membership and the behaviour of each individual (Wedel and Kamakura, 2000). There are various such models that identify segments and estimate the response functions within each segment. These models have a relatively long track record in the marketing literature and have revealed consumer heterogeneity in various markets and types of behaviour (for extensive reviews see Novak and MacEvoy, 1992; Dillon and Kumar, 1994; Wedel and DeSarbo, 1994; McLachlan and Peel, 2000; Wedel and Kamakura, 2000). The various models differ with respect to the behavioural framework they are derived from and the mechanism that determines segment membership, as well as the nature of the dependent variable under investigation. Latent class models that are able to deal with multinomial choice data include the linear logistic model of Formann (1992), the cluster-wise logit model of Kamakura and Russell (1989), the paired comparisons model of Dillon *et al.* (1993) and the mixture regression method for metric conjoint analysis data of DeSarbo *et al.* (1992). The specific latent class model utilised here has been adapted to deal with choice experiment data. The model has been developed by Swait (1994) and is based on the conceptual framework developed in the work by McFadden (1986), Ben Akiva *et al.* (1997) and McFadden (1999).

The next sections present the LS model as one avenue for accounting and explaining preference heterogeneity. Though the model cannot *a priori* be considered the most appropriate approach to be used in all applications, it is argued that for the specific problem at hand (that is, assessing the welfare impacts of GM foods) it does present specific attractive features that produce information that is more actionable and relevant to policy decision making.

Conceptual Framework of the LS model

The LS model identifies sources of preference heterogeneity by revealing a finite number of latent segments of consumers that are characterised by relatively common tastes. Yet unlike other latent class modelling approaches where segments are determined purely in a statistical manner, the LS model employed here is based on more sound behavioural microeconomic foundations. This allows for a less *ad hoc* specification of the econometric model. Further, whereas other latent class models impose the restriction that segment membership depends solely on one's individual characteristics and is independent from one's choice decisions, the LS model is much more flexible in that it allows the analyst to perform market segmentation and simultaneously explain choice for a given segment of the population.

In addition, the framework presented in this chapter for determining the sources of preference heterogeneity does not rely merely on information from socio-demographic data but also utilises the information from psychographic constructs. There is an emerging literature in the analysis of discrete choice data that emphasises the importance of the explicit treatment of latent individual characteristics in the decision-making processes (for example, McFadden, 1986; Ben Akiva *et al.*, 1997; McFadden, 1999; Ben Akiva *et al.*, 1999; Ben Akiva *et al.*, 2002b; Fennell *et al.*, 2003). One of the central outcomes of this research is that the incorporation of latent attitudinal, perceptual and motivational constructs leads to a behaviourally realistic representation of the choice process, and consequently, provides better explanatory power. Moreover, the same body of work has shown that in many cases psychometric data captures taste heterogeneity more adequately than demographic characteristics. Complementary findings have been derived by the stated preference literature. For example the US National Oceanic and Atmospheric Administration panel has recommended the use of such variables when modelling stated values in order to assess the construct validity of the results (Arrow *et al.*, 1993, p. 4609), while several studies have shown that attitudinal indexes (as opposed to socio-economic or demographic indicators) can in many cases be the primary drivers of stated preferences (for example, Langford *et al.*, 2000).

Under the LS model, the mechanism that leads to the realisation of choice is as follows:

1. Individual latent attitudes, perceptions and motives (approximated by observed attitudinal indexes) together with the individual's socio-demographic traits determine one's segment membership likelihood function.
2. Through a latent segment classification mechanism, the membership likelihood function determines the latent segment to which an individual belongs.

3. Individuals' preferences over a set of choices are influenced by (i) the latent class to which they belong, (ii) their (observable) socio-demographic traits (iii) their subjective perceptions of the (observable) choice objective attributes and (iv) exogenous market and institutional conditions.
4. These preferences are then processed according to a decision protocol (utility maximisation) which leads to the observation of the final choice.

This model of choice, therefore, implies that preferences are indirectly affected by attitudes, perception and motives through membership of a particular latent segment.

The Econometric Model

The choice process described above is operationalised within the random utility framework.[8] The model postulates a composite utility function of the following form (assuming linearity):

$$U_{ni/s} = \beta_s X_{in} + \varepsilon_{ni/s} \tag{7.1}$$

This basic expression gives the utility for the nth individual that belongs to a particular segment s of choosing an alternative i from a finite set C. The vector, $X_{ni/s}$, consists of choice-specific attributes but could also include individual-specific characteristics. Within this framework preference, heterogeneity implies that each segment has its own utility parameter vector (that is, $\beta_s \neq \beta_k; \forall s \neq k, \forall k \in S$). By assuming that the disturbances ε_{ni} are independent and identically distributed (iid) and follow a Type I (or Gumbel) distribution, we can derive the probabilistic response function:

$$\pi_{n/s}(i) = e^{\mu_s(\beta_s X_{in})} \Big/ \sum_{j \in C} e^{\mu_s(\beta_s X_{jn})} \tag{7.2}$$

The scale parameter μ_s may vary across segments, although in practice it is usually assumed that $\mu_1 = \mu_2 = \ldots \mu_s = 1$. In order to construct a segment membership function, it is assumed that there exist a finite number of segments $S(S \leq N)$ in which each individual can be classified with some probability W_{ns}. The actual number of segments is itself a latent variable and will have to be recovered from the estimation processes. Let Y^*_{ns} represent a latent variable that determines segment classification of all N individuals into one of the segments in S. According to the behavioural framework presented above, Y^*_{ns} was described as being a function of both observable and unobservable (latent) individual characteristics. Following

Ben-Akiva *et al.* (1997) and Swait (1994), this relationship can be formulated as:

$$Y^*_{ns} = \alpha_s Z_n + \zeta_{ns} \tag{7.3}$$

where Z_n contains both the psychographic and demographic characteristics of the individual and a_s is the corresponding parameter vector. An individual will be classified in a particular segment s as opposed to any other segment $k \in S$ according to the classification mechanism:

$$Y^*_{ns} = \max\{Y^*_{nk}\}, k \neq s, k = 1,..,S \tag{7.4}$$

Since, Y^*_{ns} is a latent random variable, we can assess the probability that a particular individual belongs to a specific segment by specifying the distribution and nature of the residual terms in equation (7.3). By assuming that the ζ_{ns} are independently distributed across individuals and segments (as well as independent of the error terms associated with the estimation of the latent psychometric variables), and that they follow a Gumbel distribution with scale parameter λ, we can derive the probability function for segment membership:

$$W_{ns} = e^{\lambda(a_s Z_n)} \Big/ \sum_{k=1}^{S} e^{\lambda(a_k Z_n)} \tag{7.5}$$

In order to derive a model that simultaneously accounts for choice and segment membership, the models of equations (7.2) and (7.5) are brought together to construct a mixed-logit model that consists of the joint probability that individual n belongs to segment s *and* chooses alternative i:

$$P_{isn} = (\pi_{in/s}) \cdot (W_{ns}) = \left[e^{\mu_s(\beta_s X_{in})} \Big/ \sum_{j \in C} e^{\mu_s(\beta_s X_{jn})} \right] \cdot \left[e^{\lambda(a_s Z_n)} \Big/ \sum_{k=1}^{S} e^{\lambda(a_k Z_n)} \right] \tag{7.6}$$

Note that if we impose the restrictions $\alpha_s = 0, \beta_s = \beta$, $\mu_s = \mu$, $\forall s$ we are in essence assuming homogeneity in tastes (that is, the population is characterised by a single segment) and the model in equation (7.5) collapses to the standard multinomial logit model. Alternatively, Swait (1994) points out that as $S \rightarrow N$ (that is, the number of segments approaches the number of individuals in the sample or population) the LS model becomes more akin to the random parameter logit model. Finally, it is worth noting that mixture models such as that in equation (7.6) also have the attractive feature of not requiring the restrictive independence of irrelevant alternatives (IIA) assumption (Shonkwiler and Shaw, 2003).

The likelihood function of equation (7.6) is repeatedly estimated for several segments until a reasonable number of segment solutions is attained (roughly more than three and less than ten). Determining the optimal number of latent segments, S^*, requires the balanced assessment of multiple statistical criteria as well as personal subjective judgement dictated by the objectives of the study. The optimal number of segments is reached when additional segments provide little extra information or are simply superfluous. Hence, the aim is to attain 'segment parsimony' (Swait, 1994). Various statistical criteria for deciding on the optimal number of latent segments have been suggested (Louviere *et al.*, 2000; Wedel and Kamakura, 2000; Andrews and Currim, 2003). In the current study we employ three criteria: the minimum Bayesian Information Criterion (BIC), the minimum Bozdogan Akaike Information Criterion (AIC3) and the maximum Akaike Likelihood Ratio Index ($\bar{\rho}^2$). These criteria are calculated as follows:

$$BIC = -L(\hat{\beta},\hat{\alpha}/s) + \left[\left(\frac{(S\cdot K_\beta + (S-1)\cdot K_\alpha)}{2}\right)(\ln(N))\right] \quad (7.7)$$

$$AIC3 = -2LL + 3\cdot(S\cdot K_\beta + (S-1)\cdot K_\alpha) \quad (7.8)$$

$$\bar{\rho}^2 = 1 - \frac{-2(L(\hat{\beta},\hat{\alpha}/s) + (S\cdot K_\beta + (S-1)\cdot K_\alpha))}{2\hat{L}(0,0/1)} \quad (7.9)$$

where $L(\hat{\beta},\hat{\alpha}/s)$ is the estimated log-likelihood, $L(0,0/1)$ is the log-likelihood evaluated at zero, K_β the number of parameters in β and K_α the total number of parameters in α. In order to attain a more conservative estimate of the BIC criterion, we followed the suggestion of Louviere *et al.* (2000) and used the number of respondents, N, instead of the number of choice responses as the total number of observations.

Using the LS Model for Evaluating GM Labelling Policies

The latent segment model is simply one way of accounting for and explaining preference heterogeneity when dealing with data generated via a random utility framework. The unwarranted imposition of preference homogeneity may lead to biased utility parameter estimates as well as to misleading implications about the distributional and other impacts of policy decisions (Greene, 1997). Other approaches for accounting for preference heterogeneity in random utility models include the use of multinomial logit models with interacted individual characteristics (where conditional taste heterogeneity is explored) and the random parameter logit model (where both conditional and unconditional taste heterogeneity are explored). For example, choice modelling studies that have employed the random parameter logit approach for accounting for preference heterogeneity with respect to GM foods include Lusk *et al.* (2002), Carlsson *et al.* (2004), Bruno *et al.* (2004), Kontoleon and Yabe (2004), Rigby and Burton (2004), Rigby and Burton (2005) and Tonsor *et al.* (2005). Whereas these modelling approaches allow utility parameters to vary across each individual, the latent segment model assumes that these parameters vary across segments of individuals.

Whether preference heterogeneity is best addressed at the individual or segment level is an empirical question that depends on the data set at hand (Greene and Hensher, 2002; Andrews *et al.*, 2002; Magidson *et al.*, 2003). Beyond comparing models on statistical grounds, however, Greene and Hensher (2002) point out that there are other criteria for choosing the most appropriate econometric approach relating to the specific policy questions that are being explored by the analyst. In the case of GM foods, the LS model can possibly provide more actionable, operationally meaningful and policy-relevant information compared to other approaches for accounting for preference heterogeneity, as it possesses certain attractive features for the question at hand. First, the model is particularly suited for dealing with data derived from populations that are suspected to have an inherent segmented structure (Wedel and Kamakura, 2000). Second, the approach is well suited for analysing preferences for novel goods (such as GM foods) since it can cope with situations where the analyst does not have *a priori* knowledge of the number of likely segments of the particular market nor of the membership of individuals in each segments. Thirdly, the model is better suited to explain the sources (determinants) of segmentation membership, which has been shown to be vital for the formation of policies related to GM labelling (Boxall and Adamowicz, 2002). Fourth, the model is more flexible than the RPL model in that it does not restrict the choice and segmentation processes to be determined by the same function, namely the utility function. In fact, there is evidence to suggest that directly including individual characteristics in the utility function is generally not a sufficient way to capture heterogeneous choices, especially in low budget purchases such as foods (Fennell *et al.*, 2003; Hu *et al.*, 2004).

Despite the potential usefulness of the LS model for contributing to the assessment of the EU's contested GM labelling policies, it has so far not been utilised in Europe. There are however two applications of the LS model on consumer demand for GM foods, undertaken in Canada and in Australia by Hu *et al.* (2004) and Owen *et al.* (2005) respectively. The first of these studies undertook a CE on the consumption of GM bread in Canada. As the authors did not manage to obtain FIML (full information maximum livelihood) convergence of the model, they identified segments through a two-stage estimation process. Four segments were revealed. They found that 52 per cent of the sample (consisting of 'value seeking' and 'fringe' consumer segments) are indifferent towards purchasing GM bread while 48 per cent (consisting of 'traditional' and 'anti-GM' consumers) are against. The second application, by Owen *et al.* (2005), employed the LS model on data obtained from a CE study undertaken in Australia on a series of food products, including one animal-derived product, namely milk. They found that the data supports the existence of three segments of milk consumers, of which only one of these (consisting of 26 per cent of the sample) would not purchase GM milk (that is, would require a prohibitively large discount – of about 85 per cent – for purchase to take place). The other two segments would buy GM milk if offered an average discount of around 30 per cent. Beyond this information, however, the segments derived from the Owen *et al.* (2005) study are not readily interpretable.[9]

STUDY DESIGN AND IMPLEMENTATION

The CE study presented in this chapter examining preferences for GM-derived eggs was part of a larger survey-based study on the demand for GM foods that was implemented via post in the UK and completed in 2004.[10] The response rate was approximately 35 per cent, which is in accordance with (if not considerably higher than) that reported in other CE studies conducted in the UK. Moreover, the overall representativeness of the sample was highly satisfactory when comparing our sample descriptive statistic results from variables such as age, education, family size, number of children and income with national figures. Also, the data received on actual egg consumption patterns was highly representative as compared to the data published by the British Egg Information Service. Moreover, the CE survey also included five attitudinal questions that were taken from a recent Eurobarometer questionnaire that sought to examine European perceptions and attitudes towards GM foods (European Commission, 2003). Comparison of the sample responses to these questions with those from the Eurobarometer revealed that our respondents exhibited highly representative attitudinal characteristics. Finally, with respect to item non-response, only 5.5 per cent of the sample did not complete the CE questions while the missing data on socio-economic variables were quite low (between 2 per cent and 10 per cent on key variables). Observations with missing data were excluded from the sample. The total final number of usable questionnaires was 582.

For the design of the CE, several attributes and levels were explored through a series of focus group sessions with consumers and interviews

Table 7.1 Attribute and levels of eggs profiles

Attribute	Description	Levels	Expected sign on utility
Living conditions	Referred to the conditions in which hens were raised.	Free range vs battery cage	Positive
Pesticides	Refers to whether pesticides were used in the production of animal feed.	Pesticides not used vs pesticides used	Positive
Health information	Refers to whether each box of eggs contained a health information label such as the 'Lion seal', which is readily identified by UK consumers as a health quality certification label (providing assurance over the absence of bacteria such as salmonella).	Included vs not included	Positive
GM content	Refers to the GM content in animal feed.	0%, 1%, 5%, 30%	Negative
Price	Price of box of six medium-sized eggs.	£0.38, £0.68, £0.98 and £1.28	Negative

with food industry experts and food psychologists, followed by a large-scale pilot study. The final set of attributes and levels that were used in the design of the CE as well as the expected sign on utility are presented in Table 7.1. The use of an animal food such as eggs in the current CE study, coupled with the inclusion of the 'GM content' attribute, would enable us to assess the welfare implications of altering the scope and strictness of the EU's labelling regime. The other attributes that were included in each choice profile aimed at making the choice process as realistic as possible. Following past research on European consumers, in the absence of any benefit from GM foods, an increase in GM content is assumed to impact negatively on the utility function. The price variable is also expected to have a negative impact on utility while the presence of all remaining attributes ('free range', 'no pesticides used', 'health information included') is assumed to have a positive impact on utility.[11]

The experimental design consisted of a series of profiles for a box of six medium-sized eggs. The choice sets provided to respondents included two varying 'unbranded' egg profiles, A and B, a third fixed egg profile, C, and an opt-out option, D. A fractional factorial design following Louviere *et al.* (2000) and Louviere (1998) was adopted to create 32 choice sets. In order to reduce task complexity it was decided to present each individual with only eight choice sets or occasions. Hence, the set of 32 choice sets was randomly blocked into four versions. The sample was then randomly divided into four groups, with each sub-sample receiving one version. After accounting for missing data and for individuals who do not consume eggs, the sample size provided data for 4283 usable choices.

ESTIMATION

Latent Perceptual and Attitudinal Variables

Estimation of the LS model required first the specification of the vector of individual latent perceptual and attitudinal constructs in equation (7.3), underpinning segment membership and choice behaviour. To determine this vector we initially undertook an extensive review of food attitudinal constructs. We then undertook several focus group sessions to determine which of these were most relevant for our target population (the UK public) as well as for the specific case study at hand. The final set of latent constructs that was chosen included both general concerns over food purchasing decisions as well as specific concerns over GMOs in particular.

The next step of the estimation process consisted of constructing observable proxy indicators of these latent attitudinal constructs. A total of 40 attitudinal and behavioural questions were included in the survey. The responses to these questions (obtained on a five-point Likert scale) were subjected to exploratory factor analysis. The factor analysis method is also employed in the following chapter of this volume. Following Child (1990), rotated factor loadings above 0.40 were considered as factoring together. Based on this criterion, the following five factors were identified:

1. Ethical resistance: captures moral concerns about GM technology that may affect one's food-purchasing decisions. These concerns convey the idea that GM foods may be objectionable as a matter of principle and can be distinguished from more teleological or utilitarian sentiments against GM foods.
2. Mistrust and disbelief: captures how risky the individual believes GM foods are and how much the individual trusts the authorities, scientists and the industry when handling/managing this new technology. Also, this factor captures the level of trust or confidence in the information on the risks and benefits of GM foods that the individual receives from media.

3. Environmental concerns: these refer to concerns over the impact of GM foods on the state of the environment as well as on the welfare of livestock.
4. Cost and bargain concerns: captures the attitudinal construct of ‘bargain-proneness’. It is qualitatively different from ‘price sensitivity’ since it may not be necessarily associated with low-income individuals or segments.
5. Food safety concerns: refers to a more specific type of latent variable that is more related to food safety consciousness than to overall health concerns.

Factor scores were obtained for every observation using the regression method suggested by Child (1990). This process produced data for five new variables that were then used to parameterise the vector Z_n.

Estimation of the Latent Segment Model

Using the Swait-Louviere log-likelihood test as well as the higher log-likelihood value criterion, we explored the best fit specification for both the utility and segment membership components of the LS model. The best-fit functional form and specification for the choice or utility portion of the model ($\beta_s X_{in}$) was found to be that in which: (a) the binary attributes of ‘living conditions’, ‘pesticides’ and ‘information’ were effects coded; (b) the price attribute was coded as cardinal-linear (the use of quadratic terms was explored and rejected); and (c) the GM content attribute was entered as a ‘mixed’ specification such that the change from 0 per cent to 1 per cent GM content was coded with a binary variable (GM_{zero}), while each subsequent level of GM content was coded as a cardinal, continuous variable ($GM_{content}$). The use of this mixed specification captures the idea that there is a qualitative difference between 0 per cent and 1 per cent levels of GM content. It allowed us to assess the welfare implications and viability of extending the scope and increasing the strictness of the current EU labelling regime.[12] Finally, specifications that included individual characteristics in the utility portion of the model were also explored but were rejected in favour of the more parsimonious specification. This finding provides additional insights as to the joint ‘segmentation’ and ‘product choice’ process, indicating that individual characteristics impact primarily on the former. Also, this is in line with findings from other related research that demographic variables do not have strong explanatory power for GM preferences (for example, Baker and Burnham, 2001; Li *et al.*, 2002; Li *et al.*, 2004; Noussair *et al.*, 2004; Owen *et al.*, 2005).

Table 7.2 Criteria for determining optimal number of segments

Number of segments	Parameters (P)	Log-Lik. (LL)	$\bar{\rho}^2$	BIC	AIC3
1	8	−2061.61	0.144	2083.18	4147.22
2	24	−1704.45	0.281	1769.17	3480.9
3	40	−1630.74	0.322	1738.61	3381.48
4	56	−1607.51	0.328	1758.53	3383.02
5	72	−1578.03	0.331	1772.20	3372.06

After experimentation with various specifications for the segment membership component, the best fit specification was to include the five attitudinal variables extracted in the factor analysis along with the socio-economic characteristics of income (in logarithmic form) and education (in dummy variable form such that '1' indicates a university degree held by at least one household head and '0' otherwise).[13]

In total, we estimated up to the five-segment model.[14] Determination of the solution with the optimal number of segments requires a balanced assessment of the log-likelihood, $\bar{\rho}^2$, *AIC3* and *BIC* statistics for each of the five models estimated. These statistics are presented in Table 7.2.

First, we can see that the log-likelihood and $\bar{\rho}^2$ statistics improve as more segments are added, which supports the presence of multiple segments in the sample. We can observe that though the AIC3 statistic decreases as more segments are added to the model, the rate of decrease is much smaller after the third segment. Further, the increase in the $\bar{\rho}^2$ statistics is substantially levelled off after the three-segment solution. Finally, the BIC criterion is minimised at segment three. We can thus conclude with a reasonable degree of confidence that the three-segment solution provides the best fit to the data.

Interpretation of Best-Fit Specification

Having selected the model with the optimal number of segments, we now turn to its interpretation. Table 7.3 displays the results from both the segment membership and utility coefficients. The model exhibits an overall highly satisfactory fit, with most of the coefficients being highly significant and an Akaike Likelihood Ratio Index of $\bar{\rho}^2 = 0.32$. The labelling of each segment is based on the overall fit of the model and the relative significance and magnitude of the coefficients in the latent segment membership function. The segment membership coefficients for the first segment were normalised to zero in order to be able to identify the remaining coefficients of

Table 7.3 Three Latent Segment Model

	Segment function coefficients		
	Segment 1 Food Optimists	**Segment 2 Food Cautious**	**Segment 3 GM Opponents**
Constant	-	−0.2517***	−4.4874***
		(0.0775)	(0.3975)
Ethical resistance	-	0.1856**	4.3309***
		(0.0980)	(0.9575)
Mistrust and disbelief	-	1.6259***	1.4175***
		(0.1837)	(0.5517)
Environment concerns	-	0.7506***	2.1525***
		(0.1800)	(0.4865)
Cost and bargains	-	−0.3612	−1.1883***
		(0.2197)	(0.5908)
Food safety concerns	-	1.5731***	0.1443
		(0.2518)	(0.7967)
Education (1 = university)	-	−1.3073***	2.8957***
		(0.2393)	(0.9778)
Income	-	−0.1290***	0.8936**
		(0.0560)	(0.5040)
	Utility function coefficients		
	Segment 1 Food Optimists	**Segment 2 Food Cautious**	**Segment 3 GM Opponents**
ASCs	1.0327***	−1.0277***	−0.5924***
	(0.1855)	(0.1845)	(0.1990)
Living conditions	0.6923***	4.2152***	0.0190
	(0.0610)	(0.2836)	(0.3103)
Pesticides	0.3048***	3.1320***	3.2077***
	(0.0902)	(0.6036)	(1.0721)
GM_{zero}	0.0006	−0.4710*	−3.2564***
	(0.2317)	(0.2602)	(1.0372)
$GM_{Content}$	−0.0110*	−2.6402***	−2.1867***
	(0.0065)	(0.7424)	(0.6076)
Information	0.1607	2.1106***	0.9108**
	(0.1604)	(0.2630)	(0.4409)
Price	−1.4267***	−5.7319***	−4.7093***
	(0.1745)	(0.7516)	(1.6783)
Log of Likelihood: −1630.74			
Number of Observations: 4283			

Note: Standard errors in parenthesis; *** significance at 1–4%; ** significance at 5–7%; * significance at 8–10%

the model. All other coefficients are to be interpreted relative to the normalised or baseline first segment (Boxall and Adamowicz, 2002).

Observing first the membership coefficients in Segment 2 we can see that the likelihood of belonging to this segment is highly influenced by pro-environmental concerns, concerns over food and health safety, ethical concerns against the use of biotechnology in food production and mistrust and disbelief over the information received about GM foods. This segment is also characterised by low propensity to seek food bargains (though the effect is insignificant) as well as by relatively lower income and education levels. The segment may thus be labelled the 'food cautious' segment on account of the relatively stronger influence of the 'food safety' and 'mistrust' variables. In fact, these two factors have been found to be major determinants of consumer willingness to purchase GM foods in several European studies (for example, Harrison *et al.*, 2004).

Segment 3 is characterised by very strong ethical concerns against the use of biotechnology as well as high environmental and animal welfare concerns. The segment also displays a high level of mistrust over GM information received by the government, scientists and the industry. However, it does not appear to be influenced by food safety concerns in making food purchasing decisions. Also, individuals in this segment are characterised by weak bargain proneness, relatively low income and higher education levels. The segment is labelled 'GM opponents' on account of the relatively strong ethical opposition to GM foods. Before moving on to the discussion of Segment 1, it is interesting to note that though the coefficients of the psychometric attributes all have the same signs in both segments 2 and 3, the coefficients on 'income' and 'education' have the reverse signs between these two segments. This is an interesting finding as it suggests that concerns over issues of food safety or mistrust of information are not associated with specific income or education groups. This is consistent with evidence from the communications literature, where it has been shown that individual predispositions towards GM foods are not correlated with demographic and socio-economic attributes in any clear manner (for example, MORI, 2003). Instead, the impact of perceptual constructs appears to be much more revealing and informative for policy purposes.

Turning now to the segment membership coefficients from Segment 1, these can be implicitly interpreted by observing the signs from the estimated parameters obtained from the other two segments. Yet this can only be unambiguously achieved in cases where the estimated membership coefficients have the same sign across these two segments. It can thus be seen that individuals in this first segment are mostly characterised by low ethical barriers against GM goods, a high degree of trust in the information received about GM foods, low environmental and food safety concerns and high bargain proneness. We can thus label this group as 'food optimists'. Interestingly, the direction of the education and income parameters is indeterminate for this segment. Overall, the results reveal the relative importance of using psychometric constructs (in addition to demographic and socio-economic variables) in the explanation of preference heterogeneity. Lastly, it is worth noting that no segment is characterised purely by one type of attitudinal concern. The model allows for attitudes to overlap since it acknowledges that individuals (or segments of individuals) are complex and multifaceted entities.

Turning to the utility parameters of Segment 1 we see that the coefficient of the GM_{zero} attribute is insignificant while that of $GM_{content}$ is only significant at the 8 per cent level. Hence, individuals in this segment will receive only a moderate disutility from an increased percentage of GM content while they are not affected at all by the presence of small traces of GM content (below 1 per cent). Further, the 'information' attribute is insignificant for this segment, which is consistent with the group's overall high degree of trust and optimism with respect to managing the risks involved in GM food production and consumption.

The utility component of the 'food cautious' segment is strongly influenced by concerns over the treatment of animals ('living conditions') and use of pesticides in food production processes. This is consistent with the strong pro-environmental, food safety and health concerns determining membership in this segment. Moreover, the individuals in this segment would receive disutility from having 1 per cent GM content in chicken feed (compared to 0 per cent) as well as from further increases in GM content. Notice that the negative impact on utility from a percentage increase in GM content beyond the 1 per cent level is larger than the impact of totally eliminating GM content (as indicated by the larger coefficient and significance level of '$\mathrm{GM}_{\mathrm{content}}$' compared to the $\mathrm{GM}_{\mathrm{zero}}$ attribute). This is consistent with the overall make-up of this segment, which is characterised by more teleological motivations (such as personal health) rather than deontological precepts such as ethical opposition to GM technology in the production of foods.

In contrast, in the 'GM opponent' segment, the $\mathrm{GM}_{\mathrm{zero}}$ parameter has a relatively larger impact on utility that seems to dwarf the importance of other attributes such as the 'living conditions' attribute (see next section). This is consistent with individuals in this segment being opposed to GM foods on ethical grounds and being thus more strongly in favour of the elimination of all traces of GM content in the food production process. Also, note that the ASC is positive in the 'food optimist' while it is negative in the other two segments, indicating that the first segment would be more likely to choose a box of eggs that contains GM than to go without the good while the other two segments would be inclined not to choose any of the alternative egg profiles offered to them if they contained GM content.

Lastly, the relative size of each segment (or market share) can be calculated by inserting the estimated segment coefficients into equation (7.5). This will provide a series of probabilities that each individual *n* belongs to each of the three segments. Individuals are assigned to one of the three segments on the basis of their largest probability score. We thus find that 51.1 per cent of the sample can be classified in the 'food optimist' segment, 41.3 per cent in the 'food cautious' segment and 7.6 per cent in the 'GM opponents' segment.[15] Hence, it appears that just over half of the sample is more open to the possibility of consuming eggs derived from hens fed with GM animal feed, while the remaining sample has a rather negative predisposition towards such food products. This finding, derived from an economic segmentation analysis of preferences, is in stark contrast to the results obtained from attitudinal studies that report uniformly widespread aversion towards GM-derived foods.

Assessing the Relative Importance of Choice Attributes

As the raw coefficients of the choice attributes do not provide a clear indication of their relative importance, we calculate the 'part-worth' (Table 7.4) as well as the 'relative factor score' (Table 7.5) of each attribute coefficient for each segment. Part-worth values represent the marginal WTP (or WTA) for a change in each of the attributes, keeping all other attributes constant.[16] The relative factor score of each attribute represents a measure of the relative importance of the variation in each attribute over the variation of all other attributes.

Initial inspection of these tables shows that the relative importance of each attribute changes from one segment to the other, which illustrates the richness and distinctiveness of the results obtainable from the LS model. We can see that choices for the 'food optimist' segment are mainly determined by the 'living conditions', 'pesticides' and 'price' attributes while the 'GM' and 'food safety information' attributes have low impact. On balance, the most influential attributes in the second 'food cautious' segment are $GM_{content}$, and 'living conditions'. Interestingly the 'GM_{zero}' variable has a low relative weight in this segment. The choices of the third 'GM opponent' segment are influenced mostly by the 'GM' and 'pesticides' attributes.

We can further use the information from Table 7.4 to gain some insight over the welfare impacts of extending the scope and strictness of the EU's labelling regime. First, the estimates on the $GM_{content}$ part-worth can be used to assess the discount that would need to be offered to consumers in each segment in order to exclude eggs from the EU labelling regime (that

Table 7.4 Part-worth values for alternative multinomial choice models

	Three-Segment LS Model		
	Food Optimist Segment	**Food Cautious Segment**	**GM Opponent Segment**
Living conditions	0.970***	1.471***	0.008
Pesticides	0.427***	1.093***	1.362***
GM_{zero}	0.0004	−0.082	−1.383***
$GM_{content}$	−0.008	−0.461**	−0.929***
Information	0.225*	0.736***	0.387**

Notes:
Values in UK£, £1=€1.42 (1 January 2005)
Standard errors were calculated using the Wald procedure
*** Significant at 5% or less
The MNL and RPL were estimated with the same individual characteristics as those included in the LS model.

Table 7.5 Relative factor score of attributes

	Three-Segment LS Model					
	Food Optimist Segment		**Food Cautious Segment**		**GM Opponent Segment**	
	%	**Rank**	%	**Rank**	%	**Rank**
Living conditions	25.09	2	4.47	3	0.02	5
Pesticides	11.05	3	3.32	4	4.16	3
GM_{zero}	0.02	6	0.50	6	4.22	3
$GM_{content}$	11.98	4	84.06	1	84.99	1
Information	5.83	5	2.24	5	1.18	4
Price	46.03	1	5.41	2	5.43	2

is, the welfare change from introducing a mandatory labelling of eggs derived from chickens that have been given feed that contains at least 1 per cent of GM crops). These discounts are approximately £0.07, £4.15 and £4.20 for each segment respectively. The discount for the 'food optimist' segment is not statistically significant indicating that they are indifferent towards the presence of GM content in animal feed. For a box of six medium free-range, organic eggs with food safety information (for example, Lion Seal) these values translate to a price discount of 3.28 per cent for the first segment and between 125 per cent and 234 per cent for the other two segments.

Further, from Table 7.5 we see that in the 'food cautious' and 'GM opponents' segments, the $GM_{content}$ attribute receives the highest factor score (with a considerable difference from all other attributes). Taken together, these findings suggest that the market is sufficiently segmented to lend support for extending the scope of the EU's labelling regime to include animal-derived products such as eggs.

Examining the value for eliminating all traces of GM content in chicken feed, we can see that individuals in both the 'food optimist' and 'food cautious' segments would not require compensation for purchasing a box of six eggs that had been produced from animal feed that contained traces of GM content (the GM_{zero} part-worth is insignificant). Individuals in the 'GM opponents' segments would require compensation of £1.40, which for a box of six medium free-range eggs translates to a discount of nearly 100 per cent. This finding in essence places these individuals entirely out of the GM food market. Also, from the ranking of attributes based on relative factor scores presented in Table 7.5, we can see that the 'food cautious' and 'food optimists' segments assign a very low relative weight to the GM_{zero} variable compared to the 'GM opponent' segment. It is thus clear that it is only the last segment (comprising less than 8 per cent of the sample) that exhibits a strong preference for eliminating all traces of GM content in the derivation of animal foods. This finding is in-line with the attitudinal make-up of each segment group. For example, the 'GM opponents' group was found to have strong ethical reservations and mistrust for the government with respect to using GM technology for the production of food. Also, this segment assigns a relatively higher importance to whether the food product is organic or not, which signals that they may be associated with the marginal segment of the consumer food market consisting of 'high frequency' or 'loyal' organic consumers.

CONCLUDING REMARKS: MARKET SEGMENTATION ANALYSIS AND IMPLICATIONS FOR THE EU'S GM LABELLING REGIME

The debate surrounding the EU's rigid and strict GM labelling policy has been largely led by concerns over the degree of European consumer aversion towards GM foods. It is thus of high policy relevance to improve our understanding of the level and distribution of this aversion. It has been argued in this chapter that due to the inherently segmented nature of the market, such an assessment would best be undertaken via a segmentation analysis of consumer preferences with respect to GM foods. This chapter presented the results from the first such detailed segmentation analysis undertaken in Europe. The specific application aimed at illustrating the relative usefulness of the segmentation analysis in providing distinct information for assessing the welfare impacts of specific proposed changes to the EU's GM labelling policy.

The study used data from a purposefully designed choice experiment study and elicited the preferences of UK consumers for eggs that may have been derived from chickens fed with animal feed that contained varied percentages of GM content. The specific modelling approach employed was the latent segment (LS) model, which allows for the simultaneous determination and explanation of both segment membership and product choice. Based on psychometric and demographic variables as well as choice data, the LS model was able to identify three distinct and coherent consumer segments: 'food optimists' (51.1 per cent), 'food cautious' (41.3 per cent) and 'GM opponents' (7.6 per cent). These results question reported findings from previous empirical studies undertaken in Europe that do not account for consumer differences across segments of the market and which portray an almost uniform consumer aversion towards GM foods. Our findings thus contribute to the limited but gradually growing body of economic studies undertaken in Europe that has revealed considerable heterogeneity with respect to preferences for GM foods. The study advances this literature by exploring the relative merits of accounting for and explaining preference heterogeneity directly at the segment level. In particular, our analysis displays how the LS model, which simultaneously accounts for segment membership and product choice, can provide a richer and clearer representation of the complex consumer food market. Considering our findings from the UK together with those from the two other known applications of the LS model on GM foods undertaken in North America (Hu *et al.*, 2004) and Australia (Owen *et al.*, 2005) we can identify clear advantages of such a direct segmentation method compared to alternative approaches. Clearly, further research on the manner in which European food markets are segmented is required for more efficient and equitable GM labelling policy formation. Among other things, this research agenda should include an analysis of the dynamics of segments (that is, how they change) as well as research that fuses stated and revealed preference data.

Moreover, the current chapter contributes to the growing body of literature on incorporating latent attitudinal and perceptual variables in the analysis of consumer choices. Our results clearly suggest that motivational psychometric variables have a greater and clearer influence in explaining segment membership than demographic and socio-economic variables. This adds to similar findings from the general food safety literature as summarised in Baker and Burnham (2001). Yet for the latent constructs used in segmentation analysis to have adequate explanatory power, they must be relevant to the choice context being examined (Fennell *et al.*, 2003). This highlights the need for further interdisciplinary research between economists and other behavioural scientists in order to understand better latent GM food-related attitudes and perceptions as well as to develop more robust proxy indicator variables (Ben-Akiva *et al.*, 1997). Another important avenue for further research highlighted by Boxall and Adamowicz (2002) as one of the key challenges to social science research agendas is how to deal with out-of-sample prediction when using choice models that incorporate psychographic information.

Lastly, we display how segmentation analysis yields important and distinctive policy implications that can assist both policy makers in the design of welfare enhancing regulatory frameworks as well as the industry in its planning of sound marketing strategies. First, on the basis of this study we can conclude that there are strong welfare enhancing arguments for extending the EU labelling regime to include food products derived from animals fed with GM feed. The magnitude of the net welfare gains coupled with the sizes of each of the segments appears to justify the establishment of viable separate production tracks (Caswell, 2000; Carter and Gruère, 2003; Noussair *et al.*, 2004). Yet our study results suggest that – contrary to the expectations of advocacy groups – there is insufficient market segmentation to support a policy change of reducing the percentage of allowable traces of GM foods in non-GM certified foods substantially below the 1 per cent level.

Secondly, our results illustrate how likely purchasing patterns across segments can provide information on the possible future prospects for the development of GM foods. For example, the sizeable 'food optimist' segment was found to be 'bargain prone' and 'price sensitive', which suggests that they could form the basis for the niche market of initial consumers of GM foods if these were offered at a reasonably low discount. In time, the relevant market signals over the safety of these products and their equivalence to conventional foods may be transferred to other market segments. In essence, the experience gained by the 'food optimists' from consuming GM-derived foods can over time serve as a means for transforming 'safety' and 'equivalence' from a 'credence' to an 'experience' characteristic and subsequently increase the market share for GM-derived products (Noussair *et al.*, 2004; Owen *et al.*, 2005).

Thirdly, our results show how latent segment analysis can assist governments to plan more effectively their communication strategies by reaching segments, such as the 'food cautious' segment, that are potentially more open to GM-derived foods but who have been shown to be particularly concerned about the safety of such products and have low levels of trust in the information they receive on the use of GM technology. Similarly, as the next generation of GM 'functional' foods are fully tested and developed, the food retail and biotechnology industry can undertake more targeted marketing campaigns by stressing the personal direct benefits to consumers beyond the possible lower price (for example, health benefits). Further segmentation analysis will be required to ascertain the magnitude and nature of the niche markets for such functional GM foods before the relevant labelling policies can be put into place.

ACKNOWLEDGEMENTS

This chapter is based on an article originally published in the *Journal of Agricultural and Food Industrial Organization* (JAFIO), available http://www.bepress.com/jafio/vol4/iss 1/art8. The current chapter has been reprinted with permission from the publishers of JAFIO, The Berkeley Electronic Press, 2006.

The authors would like to thank Professor David W. Pearce, Professor Ian Bateman, Professor Nick Hanley and Dr Dan Rigby for their helpful comments.

NOTES

1. Recent European studies include Zechendorf (1998), Marris *et al.* (2001), Consumers Association (2002), DEFRA (2002), IFIC (2002), Shaw (2002), EC (2003), MORI 2003 and PIFB (2003). Reviews of this voluminous body of work are provided by Hoban (2004) and Marks *et al.* (2003).
2. A rare study using revealed preference data on GM foods derived from consumers in the Netherlands is by Marks *et al.* (2004).
3. For a review see Marks *et al.* (2003) while a meta-analysis of such WTP GM studies is provided by Lusk *et al.* (2005a).
4. Other products that are also excluded from the EU's labelling regime are foods such as cheese produced from GM enzymes as well as animal feed additives derived from GMOs (FSA, 2005).
5. There has been some work on examining European preferences for GM-derived salmon (Chern *et al.* 2003) and beef (Lusk *et al.*, 2002; Tonsor *et al.*, 2005) but these studies do not provide a segmentation analysis of the distribution of these preferences.
6. Following received knowledge from consumer research, in order to minimise various cognitive biases, we did not undertake the CE on a bundle of animal products (for example, 'poultry' or 'dairy') but instead chose a single product that is very familiar and fundamental to UK consumers.
7. A notable exemption is the work by Noussair *et al.* (2004).
8. This section is based on Swait (1994), Louviere *et al.* (2000) and Boxall and Adamowicz (2002).
9. Comparison of the results from these studies with those reported from the present study should be made with caution for two reasons. First, neither of the aforementioned studies explores the impact of psychometric variables on segment membership and choice. Secondly, these studies apply the LS model in a very different context (mainly to explore trade-offs between costs (risks) and benefits from GM consumption).

10. A nationwide representative sample of 2000 households was selected based on the multistage sampling procedure suggested by Lynn and Lievesley (1991), which is tailor-made for drawing samples in the UK. The list of postal addresses was extracted from the UK Info-Disk Professional (2001 edition). The 'Total Design Method' of Dillman (2000) and the prescriptions of Mangione (1995) for administering a postal survey were closely adhered to in order to maximise response rates, minimise item non-response and enhance sample representativeness. The survey asked for the household member who most frequently undertook the weekly shopping to be identified and to complete the questionnaire.
11. The only other stated preference study on eggs that we are aware of is by Bennett and Blamey (2003), who used the contingent valuation method to assess UK preferences for legislation to phase out battery cages from egg production. In line with our results, the authors found that hen living conditions have a significant welfare impact on UK consumers.
12. The current study design did not aim to induce respondents to trade off different benefits and risks associated with the use of GM technology for the production of food products. This is an equally important area of research for enhancing our understanding of consumer preferences for GM foods (for example, recent studies include Burton and Pearce (2002), Chern and Kaneko, 2003; Hu *et al.*, 2004; Trail 2004; Loureiro and Bugbee, 2005; Owen *et al.*, 2005). Therefore, we provided respondents with no extra information about risks or benefits that might have altered their preconceived views about the use of GM technology in the production of food.
13. We also explored additional demographic variables in the segment membership portion of the model, namely age and gender of household member normally undertaking grocery shopping and number of children in the household. The impact of all such variables was insignificant, while their inclusion did not alter (either quantitatively or qualitatively) the 'best fit' results discussed below. Further, likelihood ratio tests for the contribution of such variables did not reject the null hypothesis that their coefficients were statistically equal to zero.
14. The programme for maximising the likelihood of the LS model was coded in GaussX for Windows. We chose this approach instead of using a pre-canned routine (such as that in LIMDEP) as this provided greater control over the estimation process. Both the BHHH and the BFGS algorithms for maximising the log-likelihood function were used. Starting values were obtained by using the BFGS algorithm. Also, following Swait (1994) and Boxall and Adamowicz (2002), we assumed independence across multiple responses from the same individual.
15. As noted by Boxall and Adamowicz (2002), this assignment method is dependent upon the segment membership function parameters, which were jointly estimated with the utility parameters. This entails that the choice experiment information influenced the segment membership probabilities. This in turn implies that the quality of the assignment method is reflected in the overall robustness of the model with the optimal number of segments.
16. The effects coded variables were calculated as in Hu *et al.* (2004).

REFERENCES

AgBio World Foundation (2003), *Sound Science, Not Silence: An Open Letter to World Leaders, Scientists, Media and other Stakeholders*, available at www.agbioworld.org/biotech-info/articles/agbio-articles/soundscience-agbo.html, accessed 21 September 2007.

Andrews, R. L., A. Andrew and I. S. Currim (2002), 'An Empirical Comparison of Logit Choice Models with Discrete Versus Continuous Representations of Heterogeneity', *Journal of Marketing Research*, 39, 479–487.

Andrews, R. L. and I. S. Currim (2003), 'A Comparison of Segment Retention Criteria for Finite Mixture Logit Models', *Journal of Marketing Research*, 40, 235–243.

Arrow, K., R. Solow, E. Leamer, P. Portney, R. Radner and H. Schuman (1993), 'Report of the NOAA Panel on Contingent Valuation', *Federal Register* 58, 4601–4614, available at www.darp.noaa.gov/library/pdf/cvblue.pdf, accessed 21 September 2007.

Ashok, K., W. R. Dillon and S. Yuan (2002), 'Extending Discrete Choice Models to Incorporate Attitudinal and Other Latent Variables', *Journal of Marketing Research*, 39, 31–46.

Baker, G. A. and T. A. Burnham (2001), 'Consumer Response to Genetically Modified Foods: Market Segment Analysis and Implications for Producers and Policy Makers', *Journal of Agricultural and Resource Economics*, 26, 387–403.

Ben-Akiva, M., J. Walker, A. T. Bernardino, D. A. Gopinath, T. Morikawa and A. Polydoropoulou (1997), 'Integration of Choice and Latent Variable Models', paper presented at the *International Association of Travel Behavior Research Conference (IATBR)*, Austin, Texas, 21–25 September 1997.

Ben-Akiva, M., D. McFadden, T. Gärling, D. Gopinath, J. Walker, D. Bolduc, A. Boersch-Supan, P. Delquié, O. Larichev, T. Morikawa, A. Polydoropoulou and V. Rao (1999), 'Extended Framework for Modeling Choice Behavior', *Marketing Letters*, 10, 187–203.

Ben-Akiva, M., D. McFadden, K. Train, J. Walker, C. Bhat, M. Bierlaire, D. Bolduc, A. Boersch-Supan, D. Brownstone, D. Bunch, A. Daly, A. de Palma, D. Gopinath, A. Karlstrom and M. Munizaga (2002a), 'Hybrid Choice Models: Progress and Challenges', *Marketing Letters*, 13, 163–175.

Ben-Akiva, M., T. Morikawa and D. McFadden (2002b), 'Discrete Choice Models Incorporating Revealed Preferences and Psychometric Data', in P. H. Franses and A. L. Montgomery (eds) *Econometric Models in Marketing: Advances in Econometrics*, Vol. 16 Amsterdam: Elsevier Science Ltd.

Bennett, R. M. and R. J. P. Blaney (2003), 'Estimating the Benefits of Farm Animal Welfare Legislation Using the Contingent Valuation Method', *Agricultural Economics*, 29, 85–98.

Bertoni, G and P. Marsan (2005), 'Safety Risks for Animals Fed Genetic Modified (GM) Plants', *Veterinary Research Communications*, 29, 13–18.

Boxall, P. C. and W. L. Adamowicz (2002), 'Understanding Heterogeneous Preferences in Random Utility Models: A Latent Class Approach', *Environmental and Resource Economics*, 23, 421–446.

Bruno, L., G. E. West, C. Gendron and R. Lambert (2004), 'Consumer Response to Functional Foods Produced by Conventional, Organic or Genetic Manipulation', *Agribusiness*, 20, 155–156.

Bureau, J., S. Marette and A. Schiavina (1998), 'Non-tariff Trade Barriers and Consumers' Information: The Case of the EU–US Trade Dispute over Beef', *European Review of Agricultural Economics*, 25, 437–462.

Burton, M. and D. Pearce (2002), 'Consumer Attitudes Towards Genetic Modification, Functional Foods and Microorganisms: A Choice Modeling Experiment for Beer', *AgBioForum*, 5, 51–58.

Burton, M., D. Rigby and T. Young (2004), 'UK Consumer, Regulation and the Demand for GM Food', paper presented at the *EnvCon Conference*, Royal Society, London, 26 March 2004.

Carlsson, F., P. Frykblom and C. Lagerkvist (2004), *Consumer Benefits of Labels and Bans on Genetically Modified Food: An Empirical Analysis Using Choice Experiments*, working paper, Department of Economics, Gothenburg University.

Carter, C. A. and G. P. Gruère (2003), 'Mandatory Labeling of Genetically Modified Foods: Does it Really Provide Consumer Choice?', *AgBioForum*, 6, 68–70.

Caswell, J. A. (2000), 'Labelling Policy for GMOs: To Each His Own?', *AgBioForum*, 3, 53–57.

Chern, W. and N. Kaneko (2003), 'Contingent Valuation of the Willingness to Pay for Selected Genetically Modified Foods: A Multi-country Analysis', paper presented at the *7th International ICABR Conference*, Ravello, Italy, 29 June–3 July 2003.

Chern, W. S., K. Rickertsen, N. Tsuboi and T. Fu (2003), 'Consumer Acceptance and Willingness to Pay for Genetically Modified Vegetable Oil and Salmon: A Multiple-country Assessment', *AgBioForum*, 5, 105–112.

Child, D. (1990), *The Essentials of Factor Analysis*, London: Cassell Educational Limited.

Consumers Association (CA) (2002), *GM Dilemmas: Consumers and Genetically Modified Foods*, Policy Report, September 2002, available at www.which.co.uk/files/application/pdf/0209gmdilemmas_br-445-55292.pdf

Department for Environment, Food and Rural Affairs (DEFRA) (2002), *Survey of Public Attitudes to Quality of Life and to the Environment*, available at www.defra.gov.uk/environment/statistics/pubatt.download/survey2001.pdf, accessed 21 September 2007.

DeSarbo, W. S., M. Wedel, M. Vriens and V. Ramaswamy (1992), 'Latent Class Metric Conjoint Analysis', *Marketing Letters*, 3, 273–288.

Dillman, D. A. (2000), *Mail and Internet Surveys: The Tailored Design Method*, New York: John Wiley.

Dillon, W. R. and A. Kumar (1994), 'Latent Structure and Other Mixture Models in Marketing: An Integrative Survey and Overview', in R. P. Bagozzi (ed.), *Advanced Methods of Marketing Research*, Oxford: Blackwell Publishers, pp. 295–351.

Dillon, W. R., M. A. Kumar and M. Smith de Borrero (1993), 'Capturing Individual Differences in Paired Comparisons: An Extended BTL Model Incorporating Descriptor Variables', *Journal of Marketing Research*, 30, 42–51.

European Commission (EC) (2002), *Economic Impacts of Genetically Modified Crops on the Agri-Food Sector*, prepared by the Directorate-General for Agriculture, Brussels: European Commission.

European Commission, (EC) (2003), *Europeans and Biotechnology*. *Eurobarometer* 58.0, prepared by the Methodology Institute of London School of Economics and the project 'Life Sciences in European Society', March 2003, available at http://ec.europa.eu/public_opinion/archives/eb/ebs_177_en.pdf, accessed 21 September 2007.

Fennell, G., G.M. Allenby, S. Yang and Y. Edwards (2003) 'The Effectiveness of Demographic and Psychographic Variables for Explaining Brand and Product Use', *Quantitative Marketing and Economics*, 1, 223–244.

Food Standards Agency (FSA) (2001), *Economic Appraisal of Options for Extension of Legislation on GM Labelling*, prepared by NERA Economic Consulting, available at http://archive.food.gov.ukpdf_files/gmlablag.pdf, accessed 27 September 2007.

Food Standards Agency (FSA) (2005), *GM Labelling*. Food Standards Agency, available at www.food.gov.uk/gmfoods/gm_labelling, accessed 27 September 2007.

Formann, Anton K. (1992), 'Linear Logistic Latent Class Analysis for Polytomous Data, *Journal of the American Statistical Association*, 87, 476–486.
Fulton, M. and K. Giannakas (2004), 'Inserting GM Products into the Food Chain: The Market and Welfare Effects of Different Labeling and Regulatory Regimes', *American Journal of Agricultural Economics* 86, 42–60.
Giannakas, K. and M. Fulton (2002), 'Consumption Effects of Genetic Modification: What if Consumers are Right?', *Agricultural Economics*, 27, 97–109.
Giannakas, K. and A. Yiannaka (2006), 'Agricultural Biotechnology and Organic Agriculture: National Organic Standards and Labelling of GM Products', *AgBioForum*, 9, 84–93.
Gray, R., C. B., Moss and A. Schmitz (2004), 'Genetically Modified Organisms: Rights To Use Commodity Names and the Lemons Problem, *Journal of Agricultural and Food Industrial Organization*, 2, Article 7, available at: www.bepress.com/jafio/vol2/iss 2/art7.
Greene, W. (1997), *Econometric Analysis*, New York: Prentice Hall.
Greene, W. and D. A. Hensher (2002), *A Latent Class Model for Discrete Choice Analysis: Contrasts with Mixed Logit*, Working Paper, ITS-WP-02-08, Institute of Transport Studies, University of Sydney and Monash University. Available at: http://stern.nyu.edu/nwgreene/latent-class.pdf, accessed 27 September 2007.
Harrison, R. W., S. Boccaletti and L. House (2004), 'Risk Perceptions of Urban Italian and United States Consumers for Genetically Modified Foods', *AgBioForum*, 7, 195–201.
Hoban, T.J. (2004), *Public Attitudes Towards Agricultural Biotechnology*, ESA Working Paper No. 04-09, Agricultural and Development Economic Division, The Food and Agriculture Organization of the United Nations, available at www.fao.org/docrep/fao/007/ae064e/ae064e00.pdf, accessed 27 September 2007.
Hu, W., A. Huennemeyer, M. Veeman, W. Adamowicz and L. Srivastava (2004), 'Trading off Health, Environmental and Genetic Modification Attributes in Food', *European Review of Agricultural Economics*, 31, 389–408.
Huffman, W. E., M. Rousu, J. Shogren and A. Tegene (2004), 'Consumers' Resistance to Genetically Modified Foods: The Role of Information in an Uncertain Environment, *Journal of Agricultural and Food Industrial Organization*, 2, Article 8, available at: www.bepress.com/jafio/vol2/iss 2/art8.
International Food Information Center (IFIC) (2002), *US Consumer Attitudes toward Food Biotechnology*, prepared by Cogent Research Washington DC: IFIC.
Kalaitzandonakes, N. (2004), 'Another Look at Biotech Regulation', *Regulation*, 27, 44–50.
Kalaitzandonakes, N., R. Maltsbarger and J. Barnes (2001), 'The Costs of Identity Preservation in the Global Food System', *Canadian Journal of Agricultural Economics*, 49, 605–615.
Kamakura, W. and G. Russell (1989), 'A Probabilistic Choice Model for Market Segmentation and Elasticity Structure', *Journal of Marketing Research*, 26, 379–390.
Kontoleon, A. and M. Yabe (2004), 'Assessing the Impacts of Alternative "Opt-out" Formats in Choice Experiment Studies', *Journal of Agricultural Policy Research*, 5, 1–32.
Langford, I., R. Day, S. Georgiou and I. Bateman (2000), *A Cognitive Social Psychological Model for Predicating Individual Risk Perception and Preferences*, working paper, CSERGE, University of East Anglia and University College London.

Lapan, H. and G. Moschini (2001) 'GMO Labeling and Trade: Consumer Protection or, (Just) Protectionism?', paper presented at *Globalization, Biotechnology and Trade, International Agricultural Trade Research Consortium, (IATRC) annual meeting*, Tucson, AZ, 14 December 2001.

Li, Q., K. Curtis, J. McCluskey and T. Wahl (2002), 'Consumer Attitudes Towards Genetically Modified Foods in Beijing, China', *AgBioforum*, 5, 145–152.

Li, Q., J. McCluskey and T. Wahl (2004), 'Effects of Information on Consumer Willingness to Pay for GM-Corn-Fed Beef', *Journal of Agricultural and Food Industrial Organization*, 2, Article 9, available at www.bepress.com/jafio/vol2/iss 2/art9.

Loureiro, M. L. and M. Bugbee (2005), 'Enhanced GM Foods: Are Consumers Ready to Pay for the Potential Benefits of Biotechnology?', *The Journal of Consumer Affairs*, 39, 52–70.

Louviere, J. J. (1998), *Analyzing Decision Making: Metric Conjoint Analysis*, Newbury Park, CA: Sage Publications Inc.

Louviere, J. J., D. A. Hensher, J. D. Swait and W. Adamowicz (2000), *Stated Choice Methods: Analysis and Applications*, Cambridge: Cambridge University Press.

Lusk, J. L. and D. Hudson (2003), 'Willingness-to-Pay Estimates and Their Relevance to Agribusiness Decision Making', *Review of Agricultural Economics*, 26, 152–169.

Lusk, J. L., J. Roosen and J. A. Fox (2002), 'Demand for Beef from Cattle Administered Growth Hormones or Fed Genetically Modified Corn: A Comparison of Consumers in France, Germany, the United Kingdom, and the United States', *American Journal of Agricultural Economics*, 85, 16–29.

Lusk, J. L. and T. C. Schroeder (2004), 'Are Choice Experiments Incentive Compatible? A Test with Quality Differentiated Beef Steaks', *American Journal of Agricultural Economics*, 86, 467–482.

Lusk, J. L., M. Jamal, L. Kurlander, M. Rouca and Lesley Taulman (2005a), 'A Meta Analysis of Genetically Modified Food Valuation Studies', *Journal of Agricultural and Resource Economics*, 30, 26–44.

Lusk, J. L., L. O. House, C. Valli, S. R. Jaeger, M. Moore, B. Morrow and W. B. Traill (2005b), 'Consumer Welfare Effects of Introducing and Labelling Genetically Modified Food', *Economic Letters*, 88, 382–388.

Lynn, P. and D. Lievesley (1991), *Drawing General Population Samples in Great Britain*, London: Social and Community Planning Research.

Magidson, J., T. Eagle and J. K. Vermunt (2003), 'New Developments in Latent Class Choice Models', *Sawtooth Software Conference Proceedings*, 89–112, available at www.statisticalinnovations.com/articles/choice_developments.pdf, accessed 27 September 2007.

Mangione, W. (1995), *Mail Surveys: Improving the Quality*, Applied Social Research Methods Series, Volume 40, London: Sage Publications.

Marks, L. A., N. Kalaitzandonakes and S. S. Vickner (2003), 'Evaluating Consumer Response to GM Foods: Some Methodological Considerations', *Current Agriculture, Food and Resource Issues*, 4, 80–94.

Marks, L. A., N. Kalaitzandonakes, and S. S. Vickner (2004), 'Consumer Purchasing Behavior Towards GM Foods in the Netherlands', in R. D. Evenson and V. Santaniello (eds), *Consumer Acceptance of Biotechnology Foods*, Wallingford, UK: CABI Publishers Ltd, pp. 23–39.

Marris, C., B. Wynne, P. Simmons and S. Weldon (2001), *Public Perceptions of Agricultural Biotechnologies in Europe: Final Report of the PABE Project*, Lancaster, UK: Lancaster University.

McFadden, D. (1986), 'The Choice Theory Approach to Marketing Research', *Marketing Science*, 5, 275–297.

McFadden, D. (1999), 'Rationality for Economists, *Journal of Risk and Uncertainty*, 19, 73–105.

McLachlan, Geoffrey and David Peel (2000), *Finite Mixture Models*, New York: John Wiley & Sons, Inc.

MORI (2003), *Continuing Opposition to GM Foods*, available at www.ipsos-mori.com/polls/2003/meb2.shtml, accessed 27 September 2007.

National Consumer Council (NCC) (2002), *GM Labelling and Traceability: The Consumer View*, available at www.ncc.org.uk/food/gm_label_trace.pdf.

Nielsen, C. P., K. Thierfelder and S. Robinson (2003), 'Consumer Preferences and Trade in Genetically Modified Foods', *Journal of Policy Modeling*, 25, 777–794.

Noussair, C., S. Robin and B. Ruffieux (2004), 'Do Consumers Really Refuse To Buy Genetically Modified Food?', *Economic Journal*, 114, 102–120.

Novak, T. P. and J. B. MacEvoy (1992), 'Richness Curves for Evaluating Market Segmentation', *Journal of Marketing Research*, 29, 254–267.

Owen, K., J. Louviere and J. Clark (2005), *Impact of Genetic Engineering on Consumer Demand*, Kingston, ACT, Australia: Rural Industries Research and Development Corporation, available at www.rirdc.gov.au/reports/GLC/05-015.pdf, accessed 27 September 2007.

Pew Initiative on Food and Biotechnology (PIFB) (2003), *Public Sentiment about Genetically Modified Foods*, Pew Initiative on Food and Biotechnology, available at http://pewagbiotech.org/research/2003update/, accessed 27 September 2007.

Phillips, P. W. B. and H. McNeill (2000), 'A Survey of National Labelling Policies for GM Foods', *AgBioForum*, 3, 219–224.

Rigby, D. and M. Burton (2004), 'Modeling Indifference and Dislike: A Bounded Bayesian Mixed Logit Model of the UK Market for GM Food', paper presented at *The Agricultural Economics Society 78th Annual Conference*, Imperial College, London, 2–4 April 2004.

Rigby, D. and M. Burton (2005), 'Preference Heterogeneity and GM Food in the UK', *European Review of Agricultural Economics*, 32(2), 269–288.

Shaw, A. (2002), 'It Just Goes Against the Grain: Public Understanding of Genetically Modified (GM) Food in the UK', *Public Understanding of Science*, 11, 273–291.

Sheldon, I. (2004), 'Europe's Regulation of Agricultural Biotechnology: Precaution or Trade Distortion?', *Journal of Agricultural and Food Industrial Organization*, 2, Article 4.

Shonkwiler, J. S. and W. D. Shaw (2003), 'A Finite Mixture Approach to Analyzing Income Effects in Random Utility Models', in N. D. Hanley (ed.) *The New Economics of Outdoor Recreation*, Cheltenham, UK and Northampton, MA, USA: Edward Elgar.

Swait, J. R. (1994), 'A Structural Equation Model of Latent Segmentation and Product Choice for Cross-sectional Revealed Preference Choice Data', *Journal of Retailing and Consumer Services*, 1, 77–89.

Tonsor, G. T., T. C. Schroeder, J. A. Fox and A. Biere (2005), 'European Preferences for Beef Steak Attributes', *Journal of Agricultural and Resource Economics*, 30, 367–380.

Traill, W. B. (2004), 'Effect of Information About Benefits of Biotechnology on Consumer Acceptance of Genetically Modified Food: Evidence from

Experimental Auctions in the United States, England, and France, *European Review of Agricultural Economics*, 31, 179–204.
Vriens, M. (2001), *Market Segmentation: Analytical Developments and Application Guidelines*, Technical Overview Series, Millward Brown IntelliQuest.
Wedel, M. and W. S. DeSarbo (1994), 'A Review of Recent Developments in Latent Class Regression Models', in R.P. Bagozzi (ed.) *Advanced Methods of Marketing Research*, Oxford: Blackwell Publishers, pp. 352–388.
Wedel, M. and W. Kamakura (2000), *Market Segmentation: Conceptual and Methodological Foundations*, Boston, MA: Kluwer Academic Publishers.
Zechendorf, B. (1998) 'Agricultural Biotechnology: Why Do Europeans Have Difficulty Accepting It?, *AgBioForum*, 1, 8–13.

8. Use of choice experiments in assessing the role of policy instruments in social acceptability of forest biodiversity conservation in Southern Finland

Paula Horne

INTRODUCTION

The last decade has seen an increase in the use of choice experiments in the examination of complex preference and choice situations in environmental valuation. Choice experiments or choice modelling offer a wide range of information on benefit trade-offs even between qualitative and quantitative attributes (Adamowicz *et al.* 1994, Bennett and Blamey 2002). The method also allows flexibility in examining the welfare impacts of different policy scenarios. The choice experiment enables valuation of non-use values in multi-attribute choice settings and thus potentially provides a useful tool for assessing changes in biodiversity policies. While valuation studies on citizens' preferences for nature conservation have abounded since the early 1990s (the early applications including for example Kriström 1990, Pope and Jones 1990, Veisten *et al.* 1993), there are few empirical results of the impacts on employment losses (for example Rogers and Sinden 1994) and fewer still on the impact of conservation policy instruments on preferences and their distributional impacts (Rolfe *et al.* 2005, Milon and Scrogin 2006). Most of the applications on nature conservation have used techniques other than choice experiment valuation. The main purpose of this chapter is to contribute to the relatively scarce choice experiment literature on heterogeneity in public preferences for conservation policy options.

In the present study, the choice experiment method was applied to determine whether the use of incentive-based policy instruments would increase the level of acceptance of nature conservation in Southern Finland and how the welfare of different segments of society would be affected by the policy change.

The growing interest in biodiversity conservation has created a need to develop socially and economically sustainable as well as ecologically efficient conservation policies. Economically and socially sustainable conservation policy can be achieved when the policy instruments are effective and acceptable to the general public as well as to the forest owners (Borrini-Feyerabend 1997, Polasky and Doremus 1998, Manning *et al.* 1999, Innes 2000). One aspect of social sustainability is the general acceptance of the goals, impacts and implementation of the policy.

During the last decade, requirements for biodiversity conservation in forests have increased through EU commitment to halt the decrease of biodiversity by 2010, thereby exceeding the requirements of the Rio Convention. The EU has left it to its Member States to decide upon the policies and instruments to achieve this goal.

Albeit economic literature strongly supports the use of incentive-based instruments in environmental governance, they have not yet been widely applied in practice for a number of reasons (Dijkstra 1999). Research findings support the use of incentives to promote biodiversity conservation in privately owned land (for example Kline *et al.* 2000, Horne 2006, Langpap 2006). From the viewpoint of social acceptability, this is especially important in Finland, where almost 70 per cent of forest land is non-industrial private forest (NIPF), and almost 20 per cent of households own a forest holding (*Finnish Statistical Yearbook of Forestry*, 2005). In 2002, the state accepted an action programme called the Forest Biodiversity Programme for Southern Finland (METSO). Three actions in the METSO programme focus on incentive-based mechanisms for non-industrial private forests. NIPF owners themselves can offer sites for fixed-term conservation contracts or for land purchases by the state. A third type of action in the programme investigates the potential to establish a forest conservation foundation based on voluntary donations by citizens and companies. The actions were evaluated in 2006 in order to provide information for designing a new biodiversity policy programme in 2007. This present study was conducted at the time when the new actions were tested in the pilot studies and thus provides timely results on the preferences and views of Finnish citizens on biodiversity conservation. It can also shed light on general aspects of the acceptability of market-based instruments in the governance of non-market natural resources.

According to earlier studies, some Finnish citizens would prefer to have more conservation areas while others stress the commercial use of forests or prefer multifunctional forest management (Hänninen and Karppinen 1996, Kangas and Niemeläinen 1996). Citizens pay the conservation compensation to forest owners through taxes. According to the results of valuation studies, Finnish people would be willing to pay for conservation programmes, at least hypothetically (Kuuluvainen *et al.* 2002, Siikamäki 2001). However, conservation policies also have potential socio-economic impacts such as effects on employment in the forest sector and on the ownership rights of private forest owners. Biodiversity conservation may potentially have adverse impacts on employment. Even though the forest sector employs only 4 per cent of the total labour force in Finland, in some regions its share of offered employment rises above 10 per cent (*Finnish Statistical Yearbook of Forestry*, 2005). Most citizens are also concerned with justice towards forest owners and their sovereignty (Horne *et al.* 2004). The economic and social implications of forest protection fall especially upon this sector. A clear majority of citizens are in favour of full compensation to the forest owners for lost revenues and possible costs of biodiversity conservation action, and support forest owners' sovereignty in forest management decisions. These trade-offs between the benefits of biodiversity conservation and adverse socio-economic impacts should be incorporated into preference studies on nature conservation.

When considering the social acceptability and trade-offs of additional conservation, it should be recognised that the aggregate values tell nothing about the distribution of preferences or welfare among citizens. In order to identify potential opposition and support and to get an idea of the breadth and distribution of variability in preferences, it helps to segment the respondents according to their values and their relation to the forest environment. Previously, empirical valuation studies often ignored the taste variations in the sample, and used models where the respondents were treated as a homogenous group. However, if the quantity and/or quality of environmental good demanded varies significantly between individuals, this might lead to misinformed policy conclusions on the basis of the results. Some recent studies have accounted explicitly for heterogeneity in preferences by the use of econometric techniques. In an early example, Adamowicz *et al.* (1997) interacted respondent-specific attributes with the design attributes. Since then, econometric techniques have been widely used, for example Train's (1998) random parameter logit model that was first applied to demonstrate preference heterogeneity for fishing site choices. Latent class models were developed to account for psychographic differences (for example Boxall and Adamowicz 2002). This study took the approach of segmenting respondents according to their values related to nature, running models separately for these segments and examining the welfare impacts of a nature conservation policy scenario on these different segments of the society (for an earlier example see Hanley *et al.* 2001). We created hypothetical policy scenarios where different attributes, like the policy instrument, the level of conservation and the monetary attribute could be altered in order to find out their effect on respondents' welfare. The welfare impacts were investigated for the two attitude segments separately in order to examine welfare distribution in different policy scenarios.

The next two sections present data collection and background information on respondents, and the segmentation of respondents according to their attitudes towards forest management and biodiversity conservation. In the following section this segmentation is used in choice modelling to examine the welfare impacts of different policy scenarios. Finally, the last section discusses the conclusions and policy implications of the results.

DATA COLLECTION

The data were collected by a mail survey in the early summer of 2002. A simple random sample of 3000 was made by the Population Register Centre to represent 15–74 year-old Finnish citizens. The response rate was 45 per cent.

The questionnaire consisted of questions on the respondent's background, their nature activities, knowledge about biodiversity and attitudes towards compensating forest owners for costs of conservation. The respondents were also presented with two sets of attitude statements concerning forest use and management in general and particularly in privately owned forests. A five-step Likert-scale was used for response alternatives. In the last part of the questionnaire, the respondents were asked both in an open-ended format and in a choice experiment setting about their opinions on the extent of nature conservation areas, policy instruments used in conservation and some socio-economic effects of conservation.

The descriptive statistics of the background information on the respondents show that they represented the population well (Horne *et al.* 2004). Almost 20 per cent of the respondents' households were forest owners with more than five hectares of land. The average size of the forest holding was 40 hectares.

In order to control for a bias brought about by potential differences between those that responded and those that did not, we examined a sample of non-respondents. In Autumn 2002, 70 recipients who had not answered the questionnaire were interviewed on the telephone. They were asked their reason for not responding. The most common single reason was generally lack of interest in surveys. The non-respondents did not differ significantly from the respondents in their backgrounds. About 40 per cent of non-respondents were not willing to reveal their preference for biodiversity conservation and its socio-economic impacts. Those that did were somewhat more content with the current amount of nature conservation areas, less willing to pay more taxes to cover the costs of increased protection and less willing to forsake employment than the respondents. While the average size of the forest holding in the non-respondent group was slightly larger, the forest property had more economic significance for those that had answered the questionnaire.

HETEROGENEITY OF PREFERENCES FOR FOREST MANAGEMENT AND NATURE CONSERVATION

Factor Analysis

Values explain people's behaviour and attitudes towards nature and conservation in general, and they can also be expected to be demonstrated in their preferences and choices related to forests. More frequently, abreast with demographic measures, psychometric measures are also used in explaining differences in values (for example Milon and Scrogin 2006).

We used attitude statements on nature conservation and forestry issues as a basis for examining the heterogeneity of preferences in the sample. The questionnaire included a set of attitude statements developed in Canada (McFarlane and Boxall 2000), that presents 17 statements concerning citizens' relationships with forests and their use. The latent value dimensions were based on Pietarinen's (1987) typology of the human relationship to forest and nature in Finland. Karppinen (2000) has applied the same value typology in analysing Finnish NIPF owners' goals in their forest management and ownership. The typology divides latent values towards nature into four dimensions. Utilitarianism and humanism can be classified as anthropocentric, and mysticism and primitivism as principally ecocentric value dimensions. Utilitarianism emphasises the material benefits of nature while humanism covers different aspects of multiple use of forests including cultural and social values. Mysticism comprises nature's sacredness and the intuitive connection between humans and nature. In primitivism, the core is the intrinsic value of nature and equality between all forms of life.

The attitude statements were answered on a five-step scale from 'very important' to 'not important at all' and the answers were analysed using factor analysis and latent attitude values (Table 8.1) with the software SPSS 13.0. This approach is similar to the one employed in the previous chapter. Five variables had communalities below 0.3, which means that the proportion of their variance explained by the factor structure was relatively

Table 8.1 Results of the factor analysis on respondents' relationship with nature (maximum likelihood method, varimax rotation, n=1258)

	Mysticism	Utilitarian	Primitivism	Humanism
Forests rejuvenate the human spirit	**0.727**			
Forests let us feel close to nature	**0.705**			
Forests give humans a sense of peace and well-being	**0.582**			
Humans should have more respect and admiration for our forests	**0.500**		0.262	
Forests are sacred places	**0.495**		0.288	
The primary use of forests should be for products that are useful to humans		**0.785**		
Forests that are not used by humans are a waste of our natural resources		**0.669**	−0.259	
Forests exist mainly to serve human needs		**0.652**		
A forest owner should have the right to manage his/her forest the way he/she wants		**0.481**		
Forest conservation actions should be limited to conservation areas, not be applied in all forests		**0.471**		
Forests should be left to grow, develop and succumb to natural forces without being managed by humans			**0.767**	
Forests should have the right to exist for their own sake, regardless of human concerns and uses		−0.203	**0.678**	
Forests should be managed to meet the needs of as many people as possible				**0.762**
As many uses (e.g. forestry, wildlife habitat, recreation) should be made of as much forested land as possible				**0.597**
Expectations of forest recreationists should be taken into account in all forest planning			0.217	**0.412**
Wildlife, plants and humans should have equal rights to live and develop	0.261		0.285	0.205
It is important to maintain our forests so that future generations will enjoy the same benefits that we enjoy	0.356	−0.215		

Notes:
1. Loadings smaller than +/− 0.2 are not shown.
2. Bold font indicates that the loading has been used in the interpretation of the factor.

low. These variables were, however, included in the analysis since they loaded to the factors according to the latent attitudes. Maximum likelihood was used as the extraction method. The number of factors was selected on the basis of Eigen values above 1, which is the typical threshold and resulted in four factors with an explanatory power of 41 per cent. The factor solution was obtained using varimax rotation. The first factor was interpreted as mysticism according to Pietarinen's theory (2000). Those statements that related positively to the factor concerned experiencing nature. Statements relevant to the second factor related to exploitation of forest for human benefit and to the sovereignty of forest owners. This factor was interpreted as utilitarianism. The third factor was primitivism, with statements emphasising the intrinsic value of nature relating strongly to it. The fourth factor, humanism, included the statements that emphasised multiple use and, the social function of forest. Two of the statements did not relate clearly to any of the factors. The statement defending equal rights of all living organisms related weakly to other factors but not to utilitarianism. The rights of future generations related positively to mysticism and negatively to utilitarianism.

Cluster Analysis

In relation to forests, people have been divided into anthropocentric and ecocentric segments (Oksanen 1997, Pietarinen 2000, McFarlane and Boxall 2000). The anthropocentric segment views nature from the human point of view and gives nature only instrumental value. For example, biodiversity can be seen as valuable if it is beneficial to people. The ecocentric segment emphasises the intrinsic value of nature. The segments are not homogenous within themselves but rather emphasise the different latent value dimensions people hold toward nature.

In this study, respondents were segmented using K-means clustering on the factors representing the latent value dimensions. This procedure attempts to identify relatively homogeneous groups of cases based on selected characteristics, using an algorithm that can handle large numbers of cases. However, the algorithm requires a pre-specified number of clusters. The analysis was tested using different numbers of clusters. Theoretically and also for interpretation purposes, the best result was attained using two clusters (Table 8.2).

Respondents belonging to the first segment emphasised human needs and the role of forests as a source of raw materials in accordance with a human-centred and utilitarian view. This segment, named anthropocentric, consisted of 46 per cent of the respondents. Respondents in the other segment regarded forests as spiritually inspiring and sacred (mysticism) and

Table 8.2 Value dimensions by segments reflecting respondents' relationship with nature

	Anthropocentric	**Ecocentric**
Share of respondents, %	46	54
Mysticism	−0.40065	0.33838
Utilitarianism	0.50475	−0.42630
Primitivism	−0.46937	0.39642
Humanism	−0.11055	0.09337

emphasised the right of forests to exist without human intervention (primitivism). Fifty-four per cent of the respondents belonged to this segment. The humanistic view, emphasising multiple use and social values, did not fit clearly into either of the two segments.

The segments were characterised by cross-tabulating them with the background information on the respondents. The significance level of cross-tabulation was tested using Pearson's χ^2 test. Variables that were significantly related ($p<0.05$) were forest ownership, current and childhood place of residence, gender, age, education, occupation and most of the recreational activities. Family income and size and some of the recreational activities (tending meadows, picking berries and mushrooms, working in forests) did not differ between the segments.

Respondents in the anthropocentric segment were typically men, forest owners, above the average age, farmers or pensioners and practised hunting, fishing or leisure time forest management. Their current and childhood place of residence was typically rural.

Those emphasising immaterial values, the ecocentric segment, were mainly women, younger than the average age, had a secondary level or university degree and were clerical employees or students by occupation. Characterising recreational activities in this segment were nature observation, hiking and walking, nature literature, visiting nature reserves and activism in environmental organizations.

These characteristics represent the attributes that predict which segment a respondent would most likely belong to, not necessarily a typical segment member. For example, those emphasising immaterial values were typically women and practised hiking but overall men practised hiking more than women.

The focus of this study was to examine the distribution of welfare impacts among different segments of society, and thus the welfare impact was calculated separately for each segment instead of using statistical procedures to incorporate the heterogeneity into a model.

RESULTS

Choice Modelling

The choice experiment method was used to investigate public preferences for policy instruments and socio-economic impacts of conservation. The respondents were presented with six choice sets where they had to consider the trade-offs between conservation percentages in different parts of the country and their socio-economic impacts, and make a choice from the given alternatives described by these attributes (Figure 8.1). One of the alternatives in each choice set represented the present situation, the status quo, and the two others were alternatives where the conservation percentage was increased. The six attributes and their different levels are listed in Table 8.3. A separate glossary explained the attributes and their levels to the respondents and also gave instructions for answering.

Three of the attributes were ecological in nature: conservation percentage in southern Finland, conservation percentage in northern Finland and a calculated number of threatened species for the combined conservation percentages. The number of threatened species correlated strongly with the conservation percentages, and therefore only one or the other was used in the model at a time. The conservation percentages in the southern and northern parts of Finland were selected as ecological attributes because

Choice set 2	Alternative 1 (present situation)	Alternative 2	Alternative 3
Percentage of protected forest area in Southern Finland	Present 1.8%	1.5x present (2.7%)	1.5x present (2.7%)
Percentage of protected forest area in Northern Finland	Present 17%	Present 17%	1.25x present (21%)
Number of threatened species	Present 958	675	654
Impact of protection on employment	No change	2000 jobs less	1000 jobs more
Annual cost to households over 10 year period	No change	600 mk (€100)	180 mk (€30)
Policy instrument	Land acquisitio n	Conservation contracts	Extension and planning
	↓ ☐	↓ ☐	↓ ☐

Please choose the best alternative from these three alternatives by ticking **one** of the above boxes.

Figure 8.1 Example of a choice set

Table 8.3 Attributes used in the choice experiment

Attributes	**Levels**
Percentage of protected forest area in Southern Finland	Present 1.8% (only in the status quo) 1.25 × present (2.3%) 1.5 × present (2.7%) 2 × present (3.6 %) 4 × present (7.2%)
Percentage of protected forest area in Northern Finland	Present 17% 1.25 × present (21%) 1.55 × present (25%) 2 × present (34%)
Number of threatened species	Calculated from previous
Impact of protection on employment	−5000 −2000 No change +1000
Annual cost to households over 10 year period	No change 60 mk €10 180 mk €30 600 mk €100 900 mk €150 1800 mk €300
Policy instrument	Land acquisition Conservation contracts Advising and planning

currently there is a great disparity between them (Figure 8.2). The pressure for protecting threatened species falls on southern Finland, where there is a richer fauna and flora and more intensive land use. The METSO programme targeted biodiversity protection in southern Finland, where the pilot projects of incentive-based policy instrument are also located. The levels of attributes were determined on the basis of current conservation percentages, literature, public discussion and the responses to questionnaire testing.

Attributes representing socio-economic impacts included impacts of conservation on employment and the amount of annual extra taxes per household over the next 10 years. The three optional policy instruments were land acquisition, conservation contracts and a nature management plan. As the policy instrument was a qualitative attribute it was effects

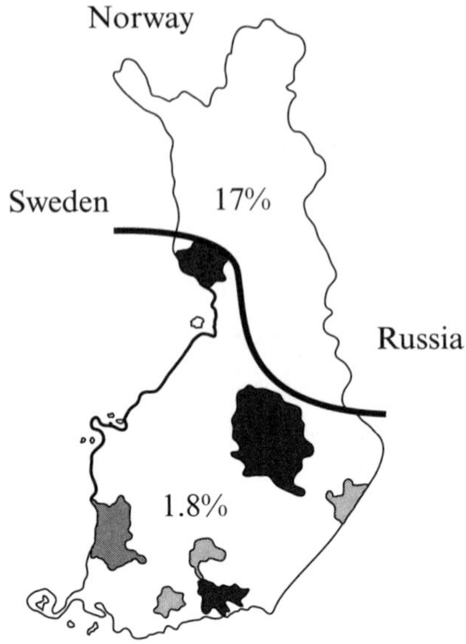

Note: The METSO pilot areas for market-based instruments are marked with different shadings

Source: Ministry of Agriculture and Forestry

Figure 8.2 Map showing the percentages of forest biodiversity conservation in Southern and Northern parts of Finland

coded in the analysis, the base value being land acquisition. The glossary explained the three policy instruments in terms of their effects on the land ownership and the certainty of conservation status:

- **Land acquisition**. A traditional policy instrument where the land owner sells the land voluntarily or it is subject to compulsory purchase by the State, which pays compensation. The land owner loses his/her proprietary rights. The fulfilment of conservation is certain.
- **Conservation contract**. The land owner enters into a contract with a governmental organisation to set aside land for a fixed term. The State pays compensation to the forest owner for economic losses. The owner maintains his/her proprietary rights but the contract restricts forest utilisation. The fulfilment of conservation is certain for the duration of the contract.
- **Advising and planning**. The State pays for drawing an ecologically oriented nature management plan for an individual forestry holding. The plan instructs the forest owner in the management and conservation

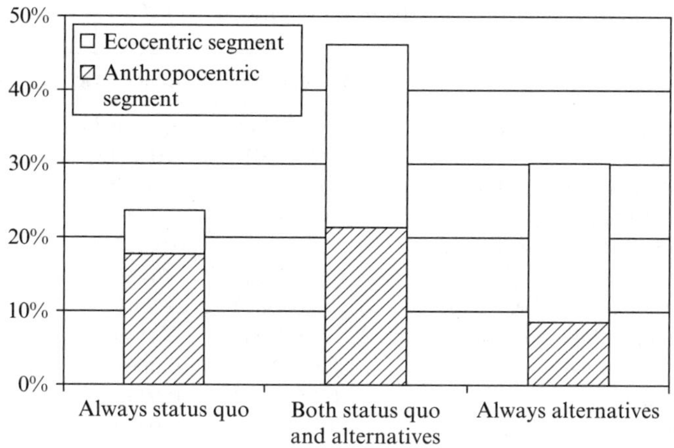

Figure 8.3 *Division of respondents according to their choices between the status quo and the alternatives with increased biodiversity conservation*

of ecologically important sites. The forest owner maintains his/her proprietary rights and the right of final decision in management practices. The fulfilment of conservation goals is uncertain.

Preferences for Forest Biodiversity Conservation by Attitude Segments

One out of four respondents chose the status quo alternative in all choice situations, and about a third always preferred one of the alternatives with increased conservation (Figure 8.3). The rest chose the status quo alternative or one of the conservation alternatives alternately. Most of the respondents always choosing the status quo alternative belonged to the anthropocentric segment, whereas the majority of those always choosing an alternative with increased conservation were ecocentrics.

Conditional logit models were used to model preferences for nature conservation by attitude segments, and also for all data combined (Table 8.4). The analysis was run with the software Limdep Nlogit 3.0. The alternative specific constant (ASC) in the model describes the tendency to choose the present 'no additional conservation' alternative. Its coefficient reflects the relative utility of the status quo to any additional conservation regime. This constant clearly reflects the attitude differences between the segments: the constant was statistically significant but negative for one and positive for the other. The positive constant for the anthropocentric segment reflects a high probability of choosing the 'no additional conservation' alternative.

Table 8.4 Estimated model parameters (and standard errors)

Variable	Anthropocentric	Ecocentric	All data
Alternative specific constant	0.6187***	−0.5290***	0.0311
(status quo)	(0.1310)	(0.1118)	(0.0802)
Annual additional cost to households	−0.0025***	−0.0020***	−0.0021***
over 10 year period (tax)	(0.0005)	(0.0004)	(0.0003)
Conservation area of forest land	−0.0468*	0.0492*	0.0067
in Southern Finland	(0.0236)	(0.0200)	(0.0144)
Conservation area of forest land	−0.0198**	−0.0129*	−0.0187***
in Northern Finland forest	(0.0075)	(0.0062)	(0.0045)
Impact of conservation on	0.0002***	0.0003***	0.0002***
employment	(<0.0001)	(<0.0001)	(<0.0001)
Policy instrument: Conservation	0.1607**	0.0401	0.0833*
contract	(0.0619)	(0.0503)	(0.0374)
Policy instrument: Nature	0.0889	0.0087	0.0305
management plan	(0.0654)	(0.0553)	(0.0403)
Policy instrument: Land acquisition	−0.2496	−0.0488	−0.1138
	–	–	–
Log-likelihood	−1483.50	−1874.05	−3698.54
n	1665	1855	3711
ρ2	0.1873	0.0787	0.0920

Note: *** significant at 1%; ** significant at 5%; * significant at 10%.

Among the ecocentric segment, this alternative was unpopular, as indicated by the negative coefficient. The importance of analysing the segments separately is reflected in the non-significant coefficient for the ASC in the all data model.

The difference between the segments was also pronounced in attitudes towards conservation in southern Finland. An increase in the conservation percentage resulted in a decrease in acceptability in the anthropocentric segment and an increase among the ecocentrics. Because of this difference in the preferences of the two segments, the coefficient for the all data model was, again, non-significant.

Both segments held a similar view with regard to increased conservation in northern Finland: a higher conservation percentage decreased the probability of choosing the alternative. The unanimity was reflected in the negative and significant coefficient of the all data model. It must be noted, though, that in the open-ended questions, only one-third of the respondents preferred the conservation percentage in northern Finland to reach more than 20 per cent of forest area (Horne *et al.* 2004). Since all the proposed levels of additional conservation percentages in the alternatives were more than 20 per cent (except in the status quo) the results do not indicate whether a smaller increase would be acceptable.

Impacts of increased nature conservation on employment and taxes were both considered important and the coefficients were statistically significant. For the alternatives where employment was decreased or taxes were increased from the present level, the probability of being chosen decreased significantly in both segments. The same trend is shown in the results for the all data model.

Attitudes towards policy instruments differed notably between the two segments. The ecocentrics preferred conservation contracts over land acquisition but the preference is not statistically significant. Among the anthropocentric segment, conservation contracts (significant) and nature management plans (non-significant) were preferred, while land acquisition was highly unpopular. In the all data model, the signs and the preference order was the same as for the segments but the heterogeneity in preference intensity was lost.

Welfare Impacts of Conservation Scenarios

The base scenario with conservation contracts and taxes

The welfare impacts of a policy change can be estimated by comparing welfare in the situation before (the status quo) and after a policy change. The welfare impacts of policy changes and the trade-offs between attributes can be studied with scenarios where the levels of attributes are shifted in order to examine their impacts on welfare. Using the coefficients of the estimated models, we can calculate the welfare changes in monetary terms.

In the base scenario for all data, the policy change examined an increase in the conservation area in southern Finland to 4.2 per cent, which is more than double the area currently protected. This percentage was selected for the scenario as it was the average of answers to an open-ended question about the conservation percentage (Horne *et al.* 2004). The conservation area in northern Finland was maintained at its present level in the scenario. The policy instrument used was a fixed-term contract and no changes in employment would occur. The point of interest was the amount of money the respondents would pay as increased taxes for additional conservation while their welfare still remained at the original level. In this case, the benefits of the increased level of conservation would equal the costs of increased taxes. Over the 10 years, annual payments by households would equal €142. An aggregated willingness to pay of the Finnish citizens was calculated on the basis of this result.

In addition to the base scenario, the welfare impacts on the two attitude segments were examined separately in order to examine the welfare distribution among different segments of society. Also, the effects of different policy instruments on welfare were investigated to examine the role of the policy instrument in the acceptability of biodiversity conservation. The potential of conservation trusts as a funding tool was examined by first calculating the sum the ecocentric segment would need to pay for the aggregate sum to equal that collected through taxes and then estimating the welfare distribution for the two segments. Results of these scenarios are presented in the following section.

Welfare impacts on different segments

In the base scenario, the data were treated as homogenous. However, as seen in the earlier results of factor and cluster analyses, respondents differed in terms of their relation to nature. The ecocentric segment wanted the percentage of the protected area increased while anthropocentrics did not (Horne *et al.* 2004). A scenario with increased biodiversity conservation level in southern Finland would thus increase the welfare of ecocentrics and decrease that of the anthropocentric segment. Both segments would suffer from increased tax. The net welfare impact of the base scenario on the anthropocentric segment was –€270 and for the ecocentric segment €226 (Figure 8.4, base scenario, vertically and horizontally striped bars respectively).

Land acquisition as the policy instrument

In the base scenario for the two segments we used fixed-term conservation contracts as the policy instrument and found that the welfare impact would

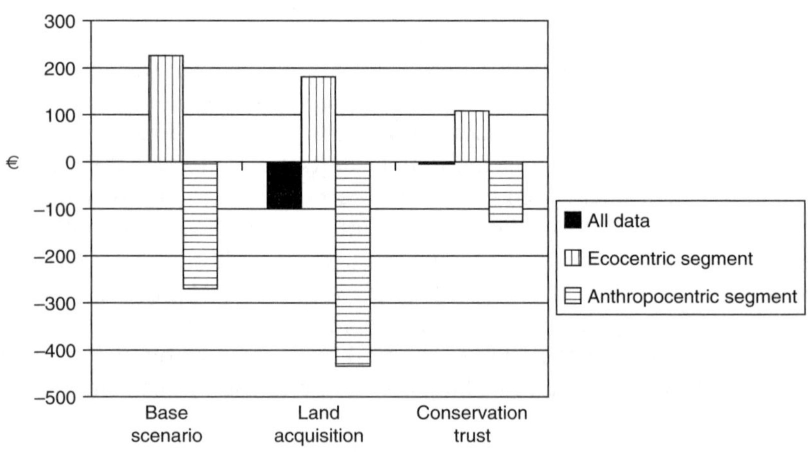

Figure 8.4 Welfare impact on all data and on the attitude segments of different conservation scenarios

be positive for the ecocentric segment and negative for the anthropocentric segment. The average welfare was set to remain at the level prior to the conservation policy change. If, instead of contracts, land acquisition was used as the policy instrument, average welfare would decrease by €100 (Figure 8.4, land acquisition, black bar). In the anthropocentric group the decrease would be €434 and in the ecocentric group the gain €181 on average (Figure 8.4, land acquisition, vertically and horizontally striped bars respectively). All other attributes were the same as in the base scenario.

Voluntary payments as the payment vehicle

In principle, a part of the costs of conservation could be covered by voluntary payments instead of taxes. We created a scenario to simulate the collection of funds needed for conservation through voluntary payments to a conservation foundation. We first calculated the sum the ecocentric households would need to pay in order for the aggregate sum to equal that collected through taxes in the base scenario, and then estimated the welfare distribution for the two segments. It should be noted, though, that the payment vehicle given in the questionnaire was household taxes instead of voluntary payments and thus the results are only indicative. The policy instrument used in the scenario was a fixed-term contract and all other attributes were the same as in the base scenario.

The same amount as in the base scenario could be collected if all the respondents in the ecocentric segment donated annually €260 per household. The anthropocentric segment faced no payment in this scenario. The net welfare impact on the ecocentric segment was now lower than in the base scenario, €108, but still positive, while that of the anthropocentric segment was still negative, –€128, but less so than in the base scenario (Figure 8.4, conservation trust, vertically and horizontally striped bars respectively). Thus this scenario would decrease the absolute value of the welfare impacts in the segments and even out the welfare distribution between the segments while the average impact would still remain at €0 as in the base scenario (Figure 8.4, conservation trust, all data €0).

CONCLUSIONS AND POLICY IMPLICATIONS

The study examined the public demand for biodiversity in Finnish forestlands. Biodiversity values were explicitly presented in a trade-off setting with socio-economic costs using a choice experiment method. Use of a welfare analysis based on choice experiment results gives more information on preferences relating to policy choice than a referendum with simple 'no' or 'yes' answers. In welfare analysis, we can obtain information on the intensity of preferences, not simply whether the option is preferable or not. Assessing welfare distribution is also possible. As people hold different values in relation to nature and forest issues, respondents were divided into two attitude segments according to their stated values in order to study the impact of respondent heterogeneity in the results. The analysis clearly indicates the importance of examining heterogeneity in data. The policy conclusion on the basis of the all data model would have been that citizens are indifferent with regard to additional forest conservation overall and in Southern Finland. However, the opposite results emerged from segmented models that showed that respondents have strong and polarised views on these issues.

Even though Finnish people's relation to forests is commonly characterised by multiple values, the respondents were heterogeneous in the weights given to different aspects. A little less than half of the respondents emphasised utility aspects and the role of forests as providers of goods for human needs. A good half of the respondents, on the other hand, put more emphasis on the spiritual well-being experienced in the forest environment and the existence value of forests. In this ecocentric segment there were relatively more women, younger people and urban residents, whereas in the anthropocentric segment there were more forest owners and older people. This is in good accordance with previous studies. The results show that an increase in the percentage of protected forests would have a different impact on the welfare of these segments. For those who are not in favour of increased conservation, welfare would decrease, whereas in the other segment, welfare would increase despite increased costs accrued by conservation measures. The latter would also accept a loss of jobs more readily.

The new trend in conservation policy is to use incentive-based mechanisms such as voluntary contracts with full compensation to forest owners. With the conservation contracts, the forest owner will agree to set aside a designated area for a predetermined period, and he or she will receive compensation for the conservation values. The focus of the study was to examine the welfare impacts on different segments of society when the policy measure was changed from conventional land acquisition to voluntary conservation contracts.

While the increase of biodiversity protection in Finnish forests divided opinions, consensus was found in the choice of conservation instruments. Policy instruments based on voluntariness of forest owners like planning and conservation contracts were preferred to a more authoritarian approach of land acquisition. If conservation measures are funded by additional taxes, the costs would be paid by all citizens. The funding based on voluntary payments to a conservation foundation would shift the financial burden to those (the segment of population) that would experience the most benefits from conservation.

In these results it should be noted that some of the respondents choosing the status quo scenario have probably done so as an easy way out of answering. Also, it is unlikely that all the respondents who expressed willingness for voluntary payments would actually do so. Thus further research is needed in order to increase the reliability of the results in this aspect.

ACKNOWLEDGEMENTS

I would like to extend my gratitude to several people who greatly assisted in completing this research project. Ms Eeva Ylinen assisted in data handling and study design while doing her MSc thesis in the project. Dr Heimo Karppinen gave valuable insight on the psychographic analysis. Professor Vic Adamowicz and Professor Peter Boxall greatly helped throughout the study design. Professor Ilkka Hanski and Mr Juha Siitonen kindly estimated the number of threatened species on the basis of the protected areas. Ms Michel Haener, Professor Jari Kuuluvainen, Dr Eija Pouta and Dr Mika Rekola gave valuable comments on the questionnaire. The discussions with Dr Ville Ovaskainen helped in clarifying problematic issues in the welfare analysis. Dr Taina Horne and Professor Jari Kuuluvainen improved the manuscript with their comments. The study was financed by Metla, the Finnish Biodiversity Research Programme and the Environment and Law Research Programme (FORBID 206020) of the Finnish Academy.

REFERENCES

Adamowicz, W.L., J. Louviere and M. Williams (1994), 'Combining revealed and stated preference methods for valuing environmental amenities', *Journal of Environmental Economics and Management*, **26**, 271–292.

Adamowicz, W.L., J. Swait, P.C. Boxall, J. Louviere and M. Williams (1997), 'Perceptions versus objective measures of environmental quality in combined revealed and stated preference models of environmental valuation', *Journal of Environmental Economics and Management*, **32**, 65–84.

Bennett, J. and R. Blamey (eds) (2002), *The Choice Modelling Approach to Environmental Valuation*, Cheltenham, UK and Northampton, MA, USA: Edward Elgar.

Borrini-Feyerabend, G. (1997), *Beyond Fences: Seeking Social Sustainability in Conservation. Volume 1: A Process Companion*, Cambridge, UK: IUCN.

Boxall, P. and W. Adamowicz (2002), 'Understanding heterogeneous preferences in random utility models: a latent class approach', *Environmental and Resource Economics*, **23**, 421–446.

Dijkstra, B.R. (1999), *The Political Economy of Environmental Policy: A Public Choice Approach to Market Instruments*, Cheltenham, UK and Northampton, MA, USA: Edward Elgar.

Finnish Statistical Yearbook of Forestry (2005), Vantaa, Finland: Finnish Forest Research Institute.
Hänninen, H. and H. Karppinen (1996), 'Kansalaismielipide metsien suojelusta ja talouskäytöstä', *Metsätieteen aikakauskirja*, **1**, 27–39.
Hanley, N., S. Mourato and R. Wright (2001), 'Choice modelling approaches: a superior alternative for environmental valuation?', *Journal of Economic Surveys*, **15**(3), 1–25.
Horne, P. (2006), 'Forest owners' acceptance of incentive based policy instruments in forest biodiversity conservation: A choice experiment based approach', *Silva Fennica*, **40**(1), 169–178.
Horne, P., T. Koskela and V. Ovaskainen (eds) (2004), *Metsänomistajien ja Kansalaisten Näkemykset Metsäluonnon Monimuotoisuuden Turvaamisesta*, Metsäntutkimuslaitoksen Tiedonantoja 933, Vantaa, Finland: Finnish Forest Research Institute.
Innes, R. (2000), 'The economics of takings and compensation when land and its public use value are in private hands', *Land Economics*, **76**(2), 195–212.
Kangas, J. and P. Niemeläinen (1996), 'Opinion of forest owners and the public on forests and their use in Finland', *Scandinavian Journal of Forest Research*, **11**(3), 269–280.
Karppinen, H. (2000), *Forest Values and the Objectives of Forest Ownership*, Metsäntutkimuslaitoksen Tiedonantoja 757, Vantaa, Finland: Finnish Forest Research Institute.
Kline, J., R. Alig and R. Johnson (2000), 'Forest owner incentives to protect riparian habitat', *Ecological Economics*, **33**(1), 29–43.
Kriström, B. (1990), *Valuing Environmental Benefits Using the Contingent Valuation Method: An Econometric Analysis*, Umeå Economic Studies 219, Umeå, Sweden: University of Umeå.
Kuuluvainen, J., E. Lehtonen, E. Pouta, M. Rekola and C.-Z. Li (2002), *Etelä-Suomen ja Pohjanmaan Metsien Suojelun Hyötyjen Taloudellinen Arvottaminen*, Tutkimusraportteja 22, Helsinki, Finland: Helsingin yliopisto, Metsäekonomian laitos.
Langpap, C. (2006), 'Conservation of endangered species: Can incentives work for private landowners?', *Ecological Economics*, **57**, 558–572.
Louviere, J.J., D.A. Hensher and J.D. Swait (2000), *Stated Choice Methods: Analysis and Applications*, Cambridge, UK: Cambridge University Press.
Manning, R., W. Valliere and B. Minteer (1999), 'Values, ethics, and attitudes toward national forest management: An empirical study', *Society and Natural Resources*, **12**, 421–436.
McFarlane, B.L. and P.C. Boxall (2000), 'Factors influencing forest values and attitudes of two stakeholder groups: The case of the Foothills Model Forests, Alberta, Canada', *Society and Natural Resources*, **13**, 649–661.
Milon, J.W. and D. Scrogin (2006), 'Latent preferences and valuation of wetland ecosystem restoration', *Ecological Economics*, **56**, 162–175.
Oksanen, M. (ed) (1997), *Arvot ja Luonnon Arvottaminen*, Helsinki, Finland: Yliopistopaino.
Pietarinen, J. (1987), 'Ihminen ja metsä: Neljä perusasennetta', *Silva Fennica*, **21**(4), 323–331.
Pietarinen, J. (2000), 'Ihmislähtöiset luontoarvot ja luonnon omat arvot', in A. Haapala and M. Oksanen (eds), *Arvot ja Luonnon Arvottaminen*, Helsinki, Finland: Yliopistopaino.

Polasky, S. and H. Doremus (1998), 'When the truth hurts: Endangered species policy on private land with imperfect information', *Journal of Environmental Economics and Management*, **35**, 22–47.

Pope, C.A. III and J.W. Jones (1990), 'Value of wilderness designation in Utah', *Journal of Environmental Management*, **30**, 157–174.

Rassi, P., A. Alanen, T. Kanerva and I. Mannerkoski (eds) (2001), *Suomen Lajien Uhanalaisuus 2000*. Helsinki, Finland: Ympäristöministeriö and Suomen Ympäristökeskus.

Rogers, M.F. and J.A. Sinden (1994), 'Safe minimum standard for environmental choices: old-growth forest in New South Wales', *Journal of Environmental Management*, **41**, 89–103.

Rolfe, J., J. Wake and P. Donaghy (2005), *Designing Incentive Mechanisms to Improve Water Quality in Sandy Creek*, Rockhampton, Australia: Central Queensland University.

Siikamäki, J. (2001), *Discrete Choice Experiments for Valuing Biodiversity Conservation in Finland*, PhD Dissertation. Department of Environmental Sciences and Policy, Davis, USA: University of California.

Train, K.E. (1998), 'Recreation demand models with taste differences over people', *Land Economics*, **74**, 230–239.

Veisten, K., H. Hoen, S. Navrud and J. Strand (1993), *Valuing Biodiversity in Norwegian Forests: A Contingent Valuation Study with Multiple Bias Testing*, Memorandum from Department of Economics 7. Oslo, Norway: Oslo University.

Virkkala, R., K.T. Korhonen, R. Haapanen and K. Aapala (2000), *Metsien ja Soiden Suojelutilanne Metsä- ja Suokasvillisuusvyöhykkeittäin Valtakunnan Metsien 8. Inventoinnin Perusteella*, Suomen ympäristö 395, Helsinki, Finland: Metsäntutkimuslaitos, Suomen ympäristökeskus.

9. Value inference using contingent valuation and choice experiments in Spanish forests

Pere Riera, Joan Mogas and Jeff Bennett

INTRODUCTION

Forest ecosystems generate a wide variety of goods and services not only for the forest owners, but for society at large. They provide a number of public goods, like enjoyment from recreational opportunities, non-timber products (for example, mushrooms, berries, aromatic herbs), carbon sequestration, erosion prevention and biodiversity preservation, among others.

In order to make sound decisions for the whole society, forest planning and management ought to take into account the value of forests for both the landowner and the other affected persons. The field of economics helps in this process by being able to estimate the value, in monetary units, of the forest at stake. While the value for the owner – or private value – is expressed in terms of market prices, tools to estimate the forest value to the whole society – often called social value or total economic value – have been developed in the last few decades. The most commonly used non-market valuation technique is the contingent valuation method (CVM), with other stated preference methods, like choice experiments (CE), becoming more popular in recent years.

Non-market methods are time-consuming and relatively expensive to undertake, especially if they are to be applied to a large number of forests. A consequence of high cost is a reduction in the likelihood of undertaking such valuation studies. To some extent, this has been mitigated in areas like transportation or health by 'borrowing' or 'transferring' already obtained values to estimate the value of a relatively similar good (Galbraith and Hensher, 1982; Koppelman *et al.* 1985; Ben-Akiva and Bolduc, 1987). However, relatively less attention has been paid to this approach in environmental economics, and even less in forest economics (Xu and Adamowicz, 1997; Haener *et al.*, 2001; Rosenberger and Loomis, 2001;

Rolfe and Bennett, 2006). Most interesting in these fields has been the reliability of the procedure: whether the new values obtained from existing ones are similar or significantly different from the value that would be obtained from specifically targeted valuation exercises (Loomis, 1992; Bergland *et al.*, 1995; Kirchhoff *et al.*, 1997; Morrison and Bennett, 2000; Morrison *et al.*, 2002).

This chapter proposes a way to infer values from existing ones and conducts a test of predictability of forest social value inference that uses two non-market valuation methods, CVM and CE. This value inference process is related to benefit transfer, although it is different in the sense that there is no transfer between sites. Rather the process involves the inference of values between goods and attributes at the same site. In brief, the process involves the use of CVM to provide the value of a specific change in forest management (the 'base value') and CE-derived values of changes in the supply of particular attributes of the forest (the 'marginal values') to infer the values of a range of other alternative forest management outcomes. To our knowledge, no similar tests have been conducted combining CVM and CE.

The procedure is empirically tested in an afforestation case study in Catalonia, a region in the Northeast of Spain with 1.3 million ha of forests or about 40 per cent of its total area. Although the composition of the forest varies from the coastal areas to the Pyrenees and the inland plains, most are composed of Mediterranean species. Commercial forests in Catalonia represent only 2 per cent of the agrarian production (García, 1997). However, the Catalan forest provides society with a variety of goods and services, including a large number of forest externalities and public goods. These have seen an increase in their demand due to the economic development of the last decades and consequently higher incomes per capita (Merlo and Rojas, 1999).

The main conclusion from the application is that the null hypothesis of equality between the CVM value of a forest and the value predicted from inference cannot be rejected. Given that one objective of forestry policy is to maximise the social value of forestry, it is important to know how different elements of the forest landscape contribute to this social value, that is, knowing the marginal benefits of extending or reducing certain landscape features within the forest. The result suggests that the combination of CVM and CE (that is, base and marginal values) would constitute a reliable alternative to valuing relatively similar environmental goods.

The policy relevance of this result covers different aspects. For instance, knowing the base and marginal values for different forestation alternatives would allow forest planners to evaluate different management schemes and to use the values in their optimisation studies. For subsidy schemes that aim to account for forest-positive externalities, such as the Farmland Foresting Programme based on Regulation 2080/1992, and regulated by Royal Decree 152/1996 (Spanish Ministry of the Environment, 2002), it would aid in evaluating farmers' applications. Also, value information would facilitate policy makers' efforts to estimate the optimal amount of subsidies. Likewise, undertaking cost-benefit analyses of alternative forest management strategies would be easier. Geographically, value inference would seem, intuitively, to work better in areas where types of forests are similar. Finally, the procedure does not need to be restricted to forest goods and products. It could be applied to other agricultural aspects and outside agriculture, to goods where it would be relevant to know values according to their different compositions.

VALUE INFERENCE AND BENEFIT TRANSFER

The closest literature to the study presented here is that relating to benefit transfer (BT). Following Desvouges *et al.* (1992), benefit or value transfer is the use of the monetary value of a good obtained in a given context (often called the study or source site), to estimate the value of a similar good under a different context (policy or target site). For instance, the value of a forest can be estimated from the known value of another similar forest located elsewhere. Sometimes, however, it is the good itself that varies in one way or another. This would be the case when estimating the value of a forest with a given composition from a forest in the same area but with a different composition or management programme. This case is what is called here 'value inference' to distinguish it from value or benefit transfer.

Obtaining values from transfer exercises has pros and cons. On the negative side, transferred values are subject to different measurement errors (Bergstrom and De Civita, 1999). This could be the case when the study and policy sites differ significantly in some characteristics. Potential statistically significant discrepancies between transferred values and values obtained directly have raised concerns about the reliability of transferring benefits (Brouwer, 2000). On the positive side, if reliable, transferability (inference) would be a cost-effective way to estimate the social value of forests. Applying previous research findings might be an attractive alternative to expensive and time-consuming original research.

Transferring is standard practice for some practitioners, especially in cost-benefit analysis (Bergstrom and De Civita, 1999), and it has been suggested that benefit transfer approaches will become even more widespread (Desvouges *et al.*, 1992; OECD, 1993). One reason for this practice is that since the 1990s, more rigorous approaches to benefit transfer have been proposed with the use of better protocols, guidelines and common practice recommendations (Boyle and Bergstrom, 1992; Desvouges *et al.*, 1992; Smith, 1992; Kask and Shogren, 1994; Brouwer, 2000; Economics for the Environment, 2000; Rosenberger and Loomis, 2001; Ruijgrok, 2001). The growth in the number of source site value estimates has also facilitated benefit transfer.

Most of the comments above can be applied to value inference. It shares the basic advantages and disadvantages of BT and different implementation approaches are possible, similar to BT. The rest of this section is devoted to illustrating the way value inference could work in a forest valuation context and to introduce the test to be undertaken in the case study application reported here.

Considerer two forests, Forest A and Forest B, located in the same region, but with different characteristics (attributes). The idea of the test is to see whether the value of Forest B can be predicted (inferred) from the CVM-derived value of Forest A using the marginal values of the attributes that vary from one forest to the other estimated with a choice experiment.

The indirect utility for Forest A and Forest B can be expressed respectively as:

$$v(p, y, z^0(z_j)) = v(p, y - CV^A, z^A(z_j)) \tag{9.1}$$

$$v(p, y, z^0(z_j)) = v(p, y - CV^B, z^B(z_j)), \tag{9.2}$$

where v is the indirect utility level of the individual, p is the vector of prices of private goods, z^0 is the level of the public good before the proposed change (marginal agricultural use of the land, in the case study below), z^1 is the new level of the good, and z_j denotes the j relevant attributes of good z, z^A and z^B denote the goods Forest A and Forest B, and compensating variations CV^A and CV^B reflect the maximum willingness to pay (WTP) of the individual to obtain each good.

In the application below, CV^A for Forest A and CV^B for Forest B are estimated by CVM. In addition, CV^B is also estimated from inference by adding to CV^A the corresponding value of attribute variations between both forests (CV_J). The values of these attributes are estimated using CE. To distinguish between the two estimates of CV^B, the one corresponding to the mean of the maximum willingness to pay calculated from CVM will be denoted $\mu_{CVM}{}^{B}$, while the one obtained by value inference will be denoted as $\mu_{VI}{}^{B}$.

The null and alternative hypothesis for the predictability (or convergence between specifically targeted and inferred values) test can then be expressed as

$$H_0: \mu_{CVM}{}^{B} = \mu_{VI}{}^{B}$$
$$H_1: \mu_{CVM}{}^{B} \neq \mu_{VI}{}^{B} \quad (9.3)$$

If the null hypothesis cannot be rejected at a given confidence level, the reliability of obtaining values from value inference cannot be discarded, when estimated by the methods used in the empirical exercise.

AFFORESTATION IN CATALONIA AND THE RESEARCH DESIGN

Choice Experiment Method

The number of papers dealing with BT and choice experiments is rather modest. The closest applications to the one presented here are those of Morrison *et al.* (1998), Morrison and Bennett (2000) and Hanley *et al.* (2006). The first two papers estimated the marginal WTP for some attributes of Australian wetlands, using the choice experiment method in three sub-samples, and tested the equality among those marginal WTP values. They concluded that choice experiments estimated similar marginal values when applied to goods with different levels of their attributes. On the other hand, Hanley *et al.* (2006) evaluated whether the implicit prices for some attributes selected to represent the ecological status for two rivers in the UK were the same: they rejected the benefit transfer test because the implicit prices differed across rivers.

The valuation exercise presented in this chapter involves the estimation of the impact of alternative afforestation programmes on non-market forest values. The afforestation programme concerned was in Catalonia, a region in the Northeast of Spain, which has 1.3 million ha of forests, composed mainly of Mediterranean species. The pine is the dominant species, covering 50 per cent of the forested area, followed by the holm oak with some 10 per cent (Ministerio de Medio Ambiente, 1996). The majority (77 per cent) of the forest is privately owned. The programme being proposed involves an increase in forest coverage from the current 40 per cent of the Catalonian area to 50 per cent. The additional 10 per cent of forest area would be at the expense of marginal agricultural land. Each questionnaire contained a sequence of four choice sets with three alternatives. The alternatives varied from questionnaire to questionnaire, as will be explained below. One of the three alternatives was always the status quo situation, that is, no afforestation and no payment required. The other two reflected 10 per cent afforestation with different attribute levels.

The first step in implementing the CE exercise was the determination of the attributes to be used to describe each afforestation alternative. Discussions with experts working in forestry research, focus groups and repeated interviews with samples of the Catalan population were conducted to determine the non-market attributes associated with the forest. The attributes chosen for the analysis were some recreational activities – such as picnicking, picking mushrooms and driving motor vehicles on forest way – CO_2 sequestration and erosion prevention. A payment vehicle of an annual contribution that the Catalan citizens would have to make to a fund exclusively dedicated to the afforestation programme was also used as an attribute. Payment values were originally expressed in Spanish pesetas, although in this chapter they are reported in euros. In the focus groups, this payment vehicle was viewed as a realistic payment mechanism. The attributes and their levels are shown in Table 9.1.

Table 9.1 Attributes and levels used in the choice experiment

Attribute	Description	Levels
Picnic	Picnicking allowed in the new forests	Yes No
Drive	Driving by car through the new forests would be allowed	Yes No
Mushrooms	Picking mushrooms allowed in the new forests	Yes No
CO_2	CO_2 sequestered annually by the new forests. Equivalent to the pollution produced annually by a city of . . .	300 000 people 400 000 people 500 000 people 600 000 people
Erosion	Erosion decrease (If not afforested, land would become unproductive. . . .)*	After 100 years After 300 years After 500 years After 700 years
Cost#	The afforestation cost per person and year	€6 €12 €18 €24

Note:
\# Payment values were originally expressed in Spanish pesetas, although in this chapter they are reported in euros.
* If afforested, erosion would be prevented indefinitely.

The final design selected 64 pairs of alternative afforestation compositions out of a universe of $(2^3 \times 4^3) \times (2^3 \times 4^3)$ possible combinations, following a fractional factorial design (Louviere, 1988). The 64 pairs were then blocked into 16 versions of four choice sets of two alternatives plus the status quo. In this way, there were a total of 16 questionnaire versions, each one assigned randomly to a sub-sample out of a larger sample of 1200 individuals representative in terms of location, age and gender of the Catalan population over 18 years old. Appendix 9A displays one of the resulting choice sets.

Contingent Valuation Method

A second valuation exercise was undertaken, to find the maximum willingness to pay for two given new forest compositions: Forest A and Forest B. The new forests had the same expansion area as in the CE exercise, that is, covering an additional 10 per cent of Catalonia, replacing marginal agricultural land. The method used was the Contingent Valuation Method (CVM), which was applied in a similar way to the CE, but without varying the physical attributes of the forest, only the monetary payments. CVM is a stated preference method where respondents are asked for their maximum willingness to pay (or minimum willingness to accept compensation) to get or avoid a given increase or decrease in environmental quality (see, for instance, Mitchell and Carson, 1989). CVM has been used to estimate the value of a wide variety of environmental resources. However, its use has been subject to criticism in terms of its ability to deliver reliable and accurate estimates of the willingness to pay and the correct design of CVM surveys (Diamond and Hausman, 1994).

Following the guidelines of the National Oceanic and Atmosphere Administration blue ribbon panel (Arrow *et al.*, 1993), a binary dichotomous choice format was used where each forest was offered to individuals at a given price (bid). Thus, after describing the particular forest composition, the respondents were given the option of choosing to pay the bid (annual compulsory payment for the rest of their life) and accepting the afforestation programme, not paying the cost amount and not accepting the programme (status quo option) or responding 'I don't know'. The monetary amounts were €6, €12, €18, €36, €48 and €72. The bid vector was derived based on the distribution of WTP expressed as an open-ended answer in a pre-test, following Duffield and Patterson (1991) and Kanninen (1993). A bid was assigned to each questionnaire version, making a total of six versions per type of afforestation. Table 9.2 shows the attribute levels of both forests. It is assumed from the differences in physical attribute levels that Forest B is preferred to Forest A. Appendix 9B shows a card corresponding to the Forest A CVM exercise.

Table 9.2 Attributes and levels used in the CVM exercises

Attribute	Forest A	Forest B
Picnic	Yes	Yes
Drive	Yes	Yes
Mushrooms	Yes	Yes
CO_2	400 000 people	600 000 people
Erosion	After 500 years	After 100 years
Bid	€ 6	€ 6
	€ 12	€ 12
	€ 18	€ 18
	€ 36	€ 36
	€ 48	€ 48
	€ 72	€ 72

A total sample of 1000 people, representative in terms of location, age and gender of the Catalan population over 18 years old, was divided into two roughly equal sub-samples.[1] Each sub-sample was assigned a given afforestation project (Forest A or Forest B), and one of the six CVM questionnaire versions was randomly allocated to respondents within each sub-sample.

Sample

Interviews were conducted face-to-face in households, in the Fall of 1999. The average valid response rate was 95 per cent across all sub-samples for the CE application and 84 per cent for the CVM survey. The difference is explained by a higher number of protest answers in the CVM version. The most common motives for protesting were that the 'government should pay', and the belief that the provision of the good would be ineffectual. Protest answers were excluded from the value estimation.

The socio-demographics of the respondents who completed the CE surveys and who completed the CVM questions with valid responses for each one of the afforestation programmes are summarized in Table 9.3. The age and gender of the survey sample are not statistically different from the Catalonian average. However, respondents' incomes and educational qualifications are lower than the average population. In the CVM, the sub-sample corresponding to Forest A tends to be representative of the urban areas whereas for Forest B, it tends, to some extent, to be self-selected towards rural areas.

Table 9.3 Socio-demographics of the survey respondents in the CE and CVM

Variable	Definition	CE Sample	CVM Sample Forest A	CEM Sample Forest B	Catalonia Average	Codification
Age	Respondent's age:					Respondent's age minus mean age of sample (45.64)
	>18 years	21%	22%	24%	20%	
	18–29 years	31%	29%	28%	31%	
	30–44 years	30%	27%	30%	27%	
	45–64 years	18%	22%	18%	22%	
	65 or over					
Gender	Gender of the respondents: % Male	50%	48%	52%	49%	1 for male 0 for female
Income	Average gross monthly income of the respondent in euros	552.25	392	305	940.66	Income of the respondent in euros
Visits	% respondents that have gone to the forest in the last year	57%	61%	63%	Not available	1 if the respondent had used the forest during the last year 0 otherwise
Rural	Village size < 10 000 inhabitants	21%	14%	36%	20%	1 if <10 000 inhabitants 0 if >10 000 inhabitants

Source: Institut d'Estadistica de Catalunya, 2002. Instituto Nacional de Estadística, 2002

EQUIVALENCE TEST OF THE MODELS

Before proceeding with the test of the hypothesis for the predictability (or convergence of values described above and the estimation of welfare measures, the preference equality across the three sets of data (CE and CVM for Forest A, and CVM for Forest B) is considered. Since the CE and CVM approaches share the same random utility maximization theory, and the choices are being made over the same goods, it is possible to combine the three data sets for a joint estimation to identify the relative scale factors (Swait and Louviere, 1993; Adamowicz *et al.*, 1994; Adamowicz *et al.*, 1998; Rolfe *et al.*, 2002).

To see whether the preferences reflected in the CE and CVM exercises are the same, the equivalence test originally proposed by Swait and Louviere (1993) was conducted. Preference equality across data sources involves pooling the three data sources under the restriction that the common parameters across the models are equal, while controlling for the scale parameters. Although it is not possible to identify the three scale parameters, a relative scale parameter can be computed across separate data sets. The scale factor will account for differences in the variation of the unobserved effects, that is, error variance heterogeneity (Swait and Louviere, 1993). The scale parameter for the CE data set is set to 1, while the scale parameters for CVM (from Forest A and Forest B) are unconstrained. Therefore, two relative scale parameters with respect to the CE data scale could be estimated: the ratio of the scale parameter of the Forest A data set relative to the scale parameter of the CE data (ω_A) and the scale factor of Forest B relative to the CE data (ω_B).

The hypothesis to be tested is H_0: $\beta = \beta^{CE} = \beta^{CVMA} = \beta^{CVMB}$, where β^{CE}, β^{CVMA} and β^{CVMB} are utility parameters for the common attributes between the three data sets. Under this hypothesis, the relative scale factors between models can be estimated by stacking the three data sets and conducting a one-dimensional search using a range of values for the scale parameters. The value of the scale parameter is found when the log-likelihood of the conditional logit model using the stacked data is maximized. The joint model is presented in Table 9.4. LIMPDEP 7.0 was the software used for the econometric analysis. The maximum log-likelihood value of the joint or 'stacked' model was achieved when ω_A assumed a value of 1.45 and ω_B a value of 1.61.

The Swait and Louviere (1993) test is used to determine whether the null hypothesis should be rejected. This test statistic is asymptotically chi-squared distributed with k–1 degrees of freedom, where k is the number of attributes that are forced to be the same across data sets. The estimated chi-squared statistic is 4.724 (5 d.f.), and the critical value of the χ^2 statistic

Table 9.4 Joint model estimation (scaled)

Variable	Coefficient	Statistics	Value
Constant	1.146***	Scale parameters	
Picnic	0.073**		
Mushrooms	0.106***	ω_A	1.45
Drive	−0.166***	ω_B	1.61
CO_2	0.730E-06***		
Erosion	−0.264E-03***	Log. Likelihood	−5046.064
Cost	−0.0180E-01***	Pseudo-R^2	0.15
Age	−0.010***	(McFadden, 1974)	
Gender	−0.290***	χ^2	1737.72
Income	0.3195E-05**	Observations	5411
Visitation	0.374***		
Rural	0.607***		

Note: *** Significant at 1% level; ** Significant at 5% level

at the 5 per cent significance level is 11.07, implying that the null hypothesis of equality of parameters cannot be rejected. In other words, the hypothesis of preference equality between the three data sources can be retained.

RESULTS

Choice Experiment Results

A conditional logit model was specified and estimated from the choice data using a maximum likelihood approach (McFadden, 1974). The results of the logit analysis of the stated preference data are presented in Table 9.5. The signs of the parameters are consistent with *a priori* expectations, and all attributes are statistically significant at the 95 per cent confidence level. The intercept term indicates that the respondents systematically prefer the afforestation programme, *ceteris paribus*. Picnicking, picking mushrooms and the CO_2 sequestered by the new forests are factors that positively affect utility, while respondents place a negative value on allowing the use of cars in forest ways and increases in erosion if the afforestation was not undertaken. The coefficient of the annual contribution is also negative, as expected, which indicates that it is perceived as a cost.

Focusing on the socio-demographic characteristics, being female, living in a rural area, having higher income and using the forest for recreation,

Table 9.5 Conditional logit model estimation for the CE application

Variable	Coefficient	Statistics	Value
Constant	1.0446***	Log. Likelihood	−4515.908
Picnic	0.0809**	Pseudo-R^2	0.10
Mushrooms	0.1079***	(McFadden, 1974)	
Drive	−0.1649***	Pseudo-R^2	0.27
CO_2	0.8110E-06***	(Veall-Zimmermann, 1996)	
Erosion	−0.3030E-03***		
Cost	−0.0187***	χ^2	1005.60
Age	−0.0105***	Observations	4576
Gender	−0.3712***		
Income	0.840E-03***		
Visits	0.4174***		
Rural	0.7385***		

Note: *** Significant at 1% level; ** Significant at 5% level

increase significantly the probability of choosing the afforestation programme alternatives. Also, ages between 25 and 65 tend to be more willing to pay for the programme than younger or older populations.

The fit of the model is rather low,[2] although in line with some other CE applications (Adamowicz *et al.*, 1998; Christie and Azevedo, 2002; Morrison *et al.*, 2002; Rolfe *et al.*, 2002). It would be advisable, however, to replicate the value inference test with higher fit statistics.

The β coefficients from the conditional logit model were used to estimate the marginal WTP for each attribute, or implicit price. The marginal annual WTP for each attribute can be inferred by calculating the ratio $-\beta_i/\beta_{COST}$, where β_i is the regression coefficient of the physical attribute and β_{COST} represents the monetary attribute coefficient. The confidence intervals for the different marginal WTP estimations were obtained following the Krinsky and Robb (1986) bootstrapping procedure and the percentile method of Efron and Tibshirani (1993) with 1000 random extractions.[3] Table 9.6 shows the main results.

The marginal WTPs indicate, for each attribute, the average amount of euros that a person would be prepared to pay annually, indefinitely, for an increase (or decrease) of one unit in the attribute level. A positive (negative) marginal value for an attribute denotes that the average person would be better off with an increase (decrease) in the level of the attribute. The values of Picnic, Mushrooms and Drive correspond to a discrete change, from being able to picnic, pick mushrooms or drive cars in the new forests, to not being able to do those recreational activities. The marginal WTP for CO_2

Table 9.6 Marginal annual WTP for the CE attributes (in € of 1999)

Variable	Marginal WTP
Picnic	4.33#
	(0.039, 9.96)
Drive	−8.83
	(−15.91, −4.18)
Mushrooms	5.78
	(1.07, 12.00)
CO_2	4.345E-05
	(2.18E-05, 7.66E-05)
Erosion	0.017
	(0.0064, 0.032)

Note: # Non-significant coefficient in the conditional logit estimation. In brackets, confidence intervals at 95%.

reflects the value that a new forest provides to society by sequestering the CO_2 emissions that a citizen of Catalonia generates annually in production and consumption activities.[4] Similarly, the marginal WTP for Erosion is interpreted as the average maximum WTP for increasing by one year the time horizon of land productivity due to the prevention of erosion with the land use change. The value is reported with a positive sign, although the sign is negative in Table 9.5 due to the way the question was framed.

Contingent Valuation Results

The coefficients of the two CVM exercises were estimated using a binary logit regression (Hanemann, 1984). Table 9.7 shows the model estimation results for Forest A and Forest B, with the dependent variable reflecting the decision whether to accept the proposed annual payment (bid). As expected, the sign of the Price coefficient is negative and significant, which indicates that the probability of people agreeing to pay the proposed amount decreases as the demanded payment increases. In both CVM models, those who have more income, those who have used the forest for recreation during the last year and those who live in a rural area, are more likely to pay. The chi-square statistic indicates that each model is significant at the 99 per cent level.

Table 9.8 shows the estimation of the mean WTP based on the information from Table 9.7. Since the assumed distribution for WTP in the logit model is a symmetrical one, the mean and median WTP coincide and can be estimated from the ratio $-\alpha/\beta$, where β is the value of the coefficient of

Table 9.7 Logit model estimation for Forests A and B

Variable	Forest A Coefficient	Forest B Coefficient
Constant	0.577 ***	0.802**
Cost	−0.033***	−0.018***
Gender	−0.215E-02	−0.458**
Income	4.261E-4***	4.128E-4**
Visits	0.581***	0.482**
Rural	1.091***	0.405*
Maximum Log Likelihood	−289.469	−238.325
% of correct predictions	68%	63%
χ^2	64.856	22.586
Number of valid observations	464	371

Note: *** Significant at 1% level; ** Significant at 5% level; * Significant at 10% level

Table 9.8 Mean annual WTP for Forest A and Forest B (in euros of 1999)

Welfare specification	WTP Forest A	WTP Forest B	P-value (Poe *et al.*)
Mean CVM	37.5 (31.57, 45.97)	60.95 (47.28, 100.62)	0.00

Note: 9.5 per cent confidence intervals for 1000 extractions.

the cost variable in the estimated logit equation, and α is the sum of all other terms in the equation evaluated at the mean values of the explanatory variables (Hanemann, 1984; Hanemann and Kanninen, 1999). Table 9.8 reports the mean WTP for both forests, as well as the confidence intervals. The confidence intervals were calculated using the Krinsky and Robb (1986) bootstrapping procedure with 1000 extractions.

The mean WTP for Forest B (WTP_B) is greater than the WTP for Forest A (WTP_A), by a difference of about €23. The sign of this result is consistent with expectations, since the Forest B type was supposed to be more desirable than Forest A because it sequesters more CO_2 and prevents erosion for a longer period of time (Table 9.2).

To see, however, if the difference is statistically significant, the one-tail non-parametric test proposed by Poe *et al.* (1997) was applied. This test was constructed following a Krinsky and Robb (1986) bootstrap procedure, with a thousand extractions. The 95 per cent confidence intervals and the probability value for the test of equality among means are shown in

Table 9.8. For a 95 per cent confidence level, the null hypothesis of equal WTP for Forests A and B is rejected.

VALUE INFERENCE TEST

The value inference test checks whether $\mu_{CVM}{}^{B}$ is significantly different from $\mu_{VI}{}^{B}$. The value of $\mu_{CVM}{}^{B}$ in equation (9.3) is the WTP for Forest B reported in Table 9.8 (€60.95 per year and person, in 1999 values). The value of Forest B inferred from Forest A, $\mu_{VI,}{}^{B}$, is calculated from the WTP for Forest A and the marginal values obtained through the CE of the two attributes that vary between forests (CO_2 and Erosion), as shown in Table 9.6 (€52.70).

For the inference test, both the values for the increase in CO_2 sequestration of Forest B compared to Forest A – which is the annual equivalent of a city of 200 000 people – and the improvement in erosion prevention – for an extra 400-year period – were treated as if they responded to a linear function. This is a usual hypothesis in the literature and implies the assumption that marginal unitary values would be constant within the limited segments of level variation examined.

Table 9.9 shows the abovementioned results and their confidence intervals using the Krinsky and Robb (1986) bootstrap procedure with 1000 extractions. It also shows the results of the test for equation (9.3), based on the non-parametric indicator proposed by Poe *et al.* (1997), with 1000 bootstrapping extractions. In this particular context, equation (9.3) takes the form:

$$H_0: \mu_{CVM}{}^{B} - \mu_{VI}{}^{B} = 0$$

$$H_1: \mu_{CVM}{}^{B} - \mu_{VI}{}^{B} \neq 0.$$

The result implies that the null hypothesis of equality between the transferred predicted value and the one obtained with an *ad hoc* estimation cannot be rejected at a 95 per cent confidence level (the *p* value is above the 5 per cent threshold level). These results suggest that the marginal WTP values

Table 9.9 Predictability test for Forest B (in euros of 1999)

Welfare specification	WTP Forest B $\mu_{CVM}{}^{B}$	WTP Forest B predicted $\mu_{VI}{}^{B}$	P-value (Poe *et al.*)
Mean CVM	60.95 (47.28, 100.62)	52.70 (46.14, 64.29)	0.20

obtained from a choice experiment may constitute an acceptable option for estimating the value of new forests where attributes of the good vary, instead of undertaking successive CVM studies to find the value of each forest.

CONCLUSIONS

In their decision making, public administrations or private agents may be interested in knowing the economic value of environmental assets, like forests. This value can be obtained by applying the contingent valuation method (CVM) or some other valuation method. If the process of estimating such values were less expensive and time consuming, environmental values would probably influence decisions more often, contributing to their rationality. A possible cost-effective way of obtaining non-market values for a number of environmental assets (like forests) would be through a procedure with similarities to benefit transfer, named here 'value inference'. In other words, if by value inference the analyst could obtain approximately the same value as with a specifically commissioned CVM *ad hoc* study, the procedure would be a cost-effective alternative.

This chapter has proposed the combined use of CVM and CE to obtain a base value and marginal attribute values respectively to be used in the inference exercise. Furthermore, it has presented an application between forests that vary in some attribute levels. The main conclusion has been that the null hypothesis of equality between the CVM value of a forest and the value predicted from inference cannot be rejected. The result suggests that, if it could be further replicated, the combination of CVM and CE (base and marginal values) would constitute a reliable alternative to valuing relatively similar environmental goods.

Wherever it is important to know the benefits from policies, the evaluation of forest plans can benefit from the flexibility provided by this instrument. Forest planners can use the approach to include public good values in their optimization studies for forest management. The methodology can potentially be applied to other fields in agriculture, the environment and other goods, and those values can vary according to their characteristics. It is not clear whether the positive results from the empirical exercise would still hold in a more diverse context, such as the whole of Spain instead of Catalonia, or the entire Mediterranean region, or for different types of European forests. Further research could focus on the suitability of this approach in larger contexts.

On a more methodological aspect, future work could test whether assuming other than a linear relation between attribute level and value, or using discrete instead of marginal values of attributes, could improve the accuracy of the inference. Additionally, using CE only, without relaying in CVM, could also be considered.

ACKNOWLEDGEMENTS

We would like to thank the Spanish Ministerio de Agricultura, Pesca y Alimentación (CICYT INIA FOA97-1646) and MEDFOREX programme for partial financial support.

NOTES

1. The sample of 1000 respondents used in the CVM exercises was a sub-sample of the total sample used in the CE. Each respondent faced a questionnaire that contained a description of the positive and negative effects of the afforestation programme, the choice experiment questions, the dichotomous choice CVM question, a part devoted to debriefing and a socio-demographic section.
2. Two Pseudo-R^2's based on different construction criteria are used following the recommendations of Amemiya (1981).
3. It involves the simulation of an asymptotic distribution of the coefficients that are generated in a CE, from which confidence intervals can then be computed. The distribution is achieved by taking repeated random draws of the coefficient vectors from the multivariate normal distribution defined by the coefficient estimates and their associated covariance matrix. Implicit prices can then be calculated from each of the random draws of coefficients, and confidence intervals estimated by identifying the values at each tail of the distribution of implicit prices (Rolfe *et al.*, 2002).
4. This estimation was based on the total of CO^2 emissions added to the atmosphere in Catalonia in 1995, equivalent to 6.8 tonnes per year (Departament de Medi Ambient de la Generalitat de Catalunya, 1996).

REFERENCES

Adamowicz, W.L., Louviere, J.J. and M. Williams (1994), 'Combining stated and revealed preference methods for valuing environmental amenities', *Journal of Environmental Economics and Management*, 263, 271–292.

Adamowicz, W.L., Boxall, P.C., Williams, M. and J.J. Louviere (1998), 'Stated preference approaches for measuring passive use values: choice experiments and contingent valuation', *American Journal of Agricultural Economics*, 80, 65–75.

Arrow, K., Solow, R., Portney, P., Leamer, E., Radner, R. and H. Schuman (1993), 'Report of the NOAA Panel on contingent valuation', *Federal Register*, 58, 4602–4614.

Amemiya, T. (1981), 'Qualitative response models: a survey', *Journal of Economic Literature*, 19, 1483–1536.

Ben-Akiva, M. and D. Bolduc (1987), 'Approaches to model transferability and updating: the combined transfer estimator', *Transportation Research Record*, 1139, 1–7.

Bergland, O., Magnussen, K. and S. Navrud (1995), *Benefit transfer: testing for accuracy and reliability*, Discussion Paper #D-03/1995, Department of Economics and Social Sciences, University of Norway.

Bergstrom, J.C. and P. De Civita (1999), 'Status of benefit transfer in the United States and Canada: a review', *Canadian Journal of Agricultural Economics*, 47, 79–87.

Boyle, K.J. and J.C. Bergstrom (1992), 'Benefit transfer studies: myths, pragmatism and idealism', *Water Resources Research*, 28, 657–663.

Brouwer, R. (2000), 'Environmental value transfer: state of the art and future prospects', *Ecological Economics*, 32, 137–152.

Christie, M and C. Azevedo (2002), 'Testing the consistency in benefit estimates across contingent valuation and choice experiments: a multiple policy option application', paper presented at the *2nd World Congress of Environmental and Resource Economists*, June, Monterey, California.

Departament de Medi Ambient de la Generalitat de Catalunya (1996), *Les emissions a l'atmosfera a Catalunya 1996: una aproximació quantitativa*, Quaderns de Medi Ambient, 5, Barcelona: Generalitat de Catalunya.

Desvousges, W.H., Naughton, M.C. and G.R. Parsons (1992), 'Benefit transfer: conceptual problems in estimating water quality benefits using existing studies', *Water Resources Research*, 28, 675–683.

Diamond, Peter A. and Jerry A. Hausman (1994), 'Contingent valuation: is some number better than no number?', *Journal of Economic Perspectives*, 8, 45–64.

Duffield, W. and Patterson, D. (1991), 'Inference and optimal design for a welfare measure in dichotomous choice contingent valuation', *Land Economics*, 67, 225–239.

Economics for the Environment Consultancy (EFTEC) (2000), *Guidance on using stated preference techniques for the economic valuation of non-market effects*, report to the Department of the Environment, Transport and the Regions (DETR), UK.

Efron, B. and R.J. Tibshirani (1993), *An Introduction to the Bootstrap*, New York: Chapman and Hall.

Galbraith, R. and D.A. Hensher (1982), 'Intra-metropolitan transferability of mode choice models', *Journal of Transport Economics and Policy*, 16, 7–29.

Garcia, C. (1997), *Estimació de les macromaginituds agràries de les comarques de Catalunya, 1993*, Lleida: Serveis de Publicacions, Universitat de Lleida.

Haener, M., Boxall, P.C. and W.L. Adamowicz (2001), 'Modeling recreation site choice: do hypothetical choices reflect actual behavior?', *American Journal of Agricultural Economics*, 83, 629–642.

Hanemann, W.M. (1984), 'Welfare evaluations in contingent valuation experiments with discrete responses', *American Journal of Agricultural Economics*, 66, 332–341.

Hanemann, W.M. and B.K. Kanninen (1999), 'The statistical analysis of discrete-response CV data', *Valuing environmental preferences: theory and practice of the contingent valuation method in the US, EC, and developing countries*, Oxford: Oxford University Press, 302–441.

Hanley, N., Wright, R. and B. Alvarez-Farizo (2006), 'Estimating the economic value of improvements in river ecology using choice experiments: an application to the water framework directive', *Journal of Environmental Management*, 78, 183–193.

Institut d'Estadística de Catalunya (2002), *Web de l'Institut d'Estadística de Catalunya*, available from www.idescat.net accessed 27 September 2007.

Instituto Nacional de Estadística (2002), *Web del Instituto Nacional de Estadística*, available from www.ine.es, accessed 27 September 2007.
Kanninen, B. (1993), 'Optimal design for double-bounded dichotomous choice contingent valuation', *Land Economics*, 69, 138–146.
Kask, S.B. and J.F. Shogren (1994), 'Benefit transfer protocol for long-term health risk valuation: a case of surface water contamination', *Water Resources Research*, 30, 2813–2823.
Kirchhoff, S., Colby, B.G. and J.F. LaFrance (1997), 'Evaluation of the performance of benefit transfer: an empirical inquiry', *Journal of Environmental Economics and Management*, 33, 75–93.
Koppelman, F.S., Kuah, G. and C.G. Wilmot (1985), 'Transfer model updating with disaggregate data', *Transportation Research Record*, 1037, 102–107.
Krinsky, I. and L.A. Robb (1986), 'On approximating the statistical properties of elasticities', *The Review of Economics and Statistics*, 68, 715–719.
Loomis, J.B. (1992), 'The evolution of a more rigorous approach to benefit transfer: benefit function transfer', *Water Resources Research*, 28, 701–705.
Louviere, J.J. (1988), 'Conjoint analysis modeling of stated preferences: a review of theory, methods, recent developments and external validity', *Journal of Transport Economics and Policy*, 22(1), 93–119.
McFadden, D. (1974), Conditional *logit analysis of qualitative choice behaviour*, New York: Academic Press, pp. 105–142.
Merlo, M. and E. Rojas (1999), 'Policy instruments for promoting positive externalities of Mediterranean forests', paper presented at the *European Forest Institute Sixth Annual Conference*, Chartreuse, Ittingen, 4–6 September.
Ministerio de Medio Ambiente (1996), *Segundo Inventario Nacional, 1986–1996*, Madrid: Dirección General de Conservación de la Naturaleza, Ministerio de Medio Ambiente.
Mitchell, R.C. and R.T. Carson (1989), *Using surveys to value public goods: the contingent valuation method*, Washington, DC: Resources For the Future.
Morrison, M. and J. Bennett (2000), 'Choice modelling, non-use values and benefit transfer', *Economics Analysis and Policy*, 30, 13–32.
Morrison, M., Bennett, J., Blamey, R. and J. Louviere (1998), *Choice modelling and test of benefit transfer*, Choice Modelling Research Report 8, Canberra, Australia: University College, The University of New South Wales.
Morrison, M., Bennett, J., Blamey, R. and J. Louviere (2002), 'Choice modeling and tests of benefit transfer', *American Journal of Agricultural Economics*, 84, 161–170.
Organisation for Economic Co-operation and Development (OECD) (1993), *Project and policy appraisal: integrating economics and environment*, ENV/EPOC/GEEI(93) 14, Paris, France: Group on Economic and Environmental Policy Integration, Environment Directorate, Environmental Policy Committee.
Poe, G., Welsh, M. and P. Champ (1997), 'Measuring the difference in mean willingness to pay when dichotomous choice contingent valuation responses are not independent', *Land Economics*, 73, 255–267.
Rolfe, J. and J. Bennett (2006), *Transferring Environmental Values from Choice Modelling Applications*, Cheltenham, UK and Northampton, MA: Edward Elgar.
Rolfe, J. Bennett, J. and J. Louviere (2002), 'Stated values and reminders of substitute goods: testing for framing effects with choice modelling', *The Australian Journal of Agricultural and Resource Economics*, 46, 1–20.

Rosenberger, R.S. and J.B. Loomis (2001), *Benefit transfer of outdoor recreation use values: a technical document supporting the Forest Service Strategic Plan (2000 revision)*, Gen. Tech. Rep. RMRS-GTR-72, Fort Collins, CO: U.S. Department of Agriculture, Forest Service, Rocky Mountain Research Station.

Ruijgrok, E.C.M. (2001), 'Transferring economic values on the basis of an ecological classification of nature', *Ecological Economics*, 39, 399–408.

Smith, V.K. (1992), 'On separating defensible benefit transfer from "Smoke and Mirrors"', *Water Resources Research*, 28, 685–694.

Spanish Ministry of the Environment (2002), 'Environment-related cross-sector policies under the jurisdiction of other ministries and public administrations', *Actuaciones Públicas en materia de medio ambiente*, available from www.mma.es/portal/secciones/el_ministerio/actuaciones_publicas.

Swait, J. and J. Louviere (1993), 'The role of the scale parameter in the estimation and comparison of multinomial logit models', *Journal of Marketing Research*, 30, 305–314.

Veall, Michael, Zimmermann, R. and F. Klaus (1996), 'Pseudo-R^2 measures for some common limited dependent variable models', *Journal of Economic Surveys*, 10, 241–259.

Xu, X. and W. Adamowicz (1997), *Modelling non-timber benefits via benefit transfer*, Network of Centres of Excellence, Project Report SES-1. Edmonton, Alberta, Canada: University of Alberta.

APPENDIX 9A EXAMPLE OF A PAIR OF AFFORESTATION ALTERNATIVES USED IN THE CE EXERCISE

Of these two ways of afforesting 10% of the area of Catalonia [SHOW CARD AND EXPLAIN THE MEANING OF THE LEVELS AND ATTRIBUTES]

FOREST UTILITY	**AFFORESTATION A**	**AFFORESTATION B**
RECREATIONAL ACTIVITIES ALLOWED	 • DRIVING BY CARS IN DESIGNATED TRAILS	 • DRIVING BY CARS IN DESIGNATED TRAILS  • PICNICKING
GAS CO_2 SEQUESTERED PER YEAR (Pollution produced by....	 CITY OF 400 000 INHABITANTS	 CITY OF 500 000 INHABITANTS
NEW FOREST IN...	Soil eroded A LITTLE (Unproductive in 500 years)	Soil eroded A LITTLE (Unproductive in 500 years)
ECONOMIC COST		
ANNUAL CONTRIBUTION	€18 /year	€24 /year

Would you choose A, B, or neither? [**ALLOW INDIFFERENCE**]

AFFORESTATON A...........1

AFFORESTATION B..........2

NEITHER.............................3

INDIFFERENT....................4

DOESN'T KNOW...............8

DOESN'T ANSWER..........9

APPENDIX 9B EXAMPLE OF THE QUESTION USED IN THE CVM CORRESPONDING TO THE FOREST B

The afforestation that the administration is thinking about carrying out is the afforestation corresponding to the card **[SHOW CARD]**, *i.e., they would do an afforestation with these effects* **[EXPLAIN THE MEANING OF THE LEVELS AND ATTRIBUTES OF THE CARD]**

FOREST B

FOREST UTILITY

RECREATIONAL ACTIVITIES ALLOWED	 • DRIVING BY CARS IN DESIGNATED TRAILS  • PICNICKING  • PICKING MUSHROOMS
GAS CO_2 SEQUESTERED PER YEAR (Pollution produced by....	 CITY OF **400 000** INHABITANTS
NEW FOREST IN......	Soil eroded **A LITTLE** (Unproductive in 500 years)

ECONOMIC COST

ANNUAL CONTRIBUTION	**€36 /year**

Would you accept this afforestation?

YES 1
NO 2
DOESN'T KNOW........ 8
DOESN'T ANSWER.... 9

10. Evaluation of heterogeneous preferences for forest recreation in the UK using choice experiments

Michael Christie and Nick Hanley

INTRODUCTION

Outdoor recreation has been a significant stimulant for the conception and development of environmental valuation techniques. Clawson's seminal work to measure the demand and value of outdoor recreation led to the development of the travel cost model (Clawson 1959), while four years later Davis's doctoral thesis, which utilised questionnaires to estimate the benefits of outdoor recreation in the Maine backwoods area, was instrumental in the development of the contingent valuation method (Davis 1963). More recently, choice experiments, which originated in the fields of transport and marketing research (Louviere 1988), were first applied to environmental resources in 1994 when Adamowicz *et al.* (1994) used the technique to examine the values for a range of attributes of water-based recreation. Since their conception, much research effort has been undertaken to validate and refine these methods. The result of this effort is that it is now generally recognised that these methods can provide useful information on the value of environmental resources for policy analysis (Arrow *et al.* 1993; HM Treasury 2003).

In this chapter, we aim to demonstrate the use of choice modelling in the context of valuing forest recreation. The majority of existing environmental valuation research on forests has either simply valued forest recreation in a generic sense (Bishop 1992) or forest recreation as a single attribute of wider forests values (Willis *et al.* 1988; Hanley 1989; Willis and Benson 1989; Hanley and Ruffell 1993; Chapter 9 in this volume). However, to date, few studies have actually examined the economic value of specific recreational activities that take place in the forest (such as walking, cycling), nor does current research rigorously explore heterogeneity of consumers' surplus values between alternative uses and user groups. This research therefore aims to fill this knowledge gap through the use of a choice experiment study that explores, in detail, the heterogeneity of people's values for forest recreation in terms of (i) eliciting values for the component attributes of the forest recreation resource and (ii) how these values vary between different uses and users. Thus, in this study, we aim to demonstrate how choice experiments may be adopted to provide a much more rigorous and detailed examination of the value of forest recreation than has been undertaken to date. It is envisaged that the results from this research will help forest managers and planners to identify discrete market segments for forest recreation, which in turn will allow them to develop specific recreational facilities for different user groups either within or between forests. On a more strategic level, the research will also provide useful information to feed into the implementation of the EU Forestry Action Plan (Commission of the European Communities 2006) in that it will help to demonstrate how forest recreation can 'contribute to the quality of life', as well as provide evidence on the value of forest recreation in enhancing the sustainable use of forests.

IMPROVING FACILITIES FOR FOREST RECREATION

Forests and woodlands are an important destination for outdoor recreation. For example, in Great Britain, there are an estimated 252 million leisure day trips made to forest and woodlands each year (TNS Travel and Tourism 2004). This accounts for 5 per cent of all leisure day trips or 20 per cent of all leisure day trips in the countryside (ibid.). People have a wide range of motivations for visiting forests. Some will be attracted by the forest itself and the nature that resides within it, while others may simply find it a convenient place to, for example, walk their dog. Others will be attracted by the recreational facilities provided within the forest, which might include, for example, dedicated walking or mountain bike trails, wildlife hides, or simply a forest picnic area.

In this research, we are interested in identifying which types of improvement to the forest recreation resource may result in the greatest gains in welfare, and how these welfare gains are distributed across different uses and user groups. Existing research highlights that there are a wide range of activities currently taking place within forests (Forestry Commission 2004a). Following a series of focus group meetings with forest visitors and forest managers, four types of recreation activities were identified as being important: cycling, horse riding, nature watching and a catchall group for general forest visitors. The selection criteria used to identify these activities included: those activities that attract a significant number of users; those activities where the numbers of users is expanding most rapidly; those activities that have specific facility, infrastructure and/or management needs; and those activities that are important to future forest policy.

Cycling was selected as it represents an interesting and unique case study for this research. Over the past ten years or so, there have been a number of significant investments in mountain bike centres, which provide a range of specifically built technical single track trails for mountain biking. More recently, there have been moves to extend this provision to provide more 'hard core' facilities such as downhill, 4 cross and dirt jumps. These mountain bike centres attract a high number of users (Forestry Commission 2002) and represent an increasingly important use of forest. However, constraining the examination of cycling to mountain biking alone would be restrictive since forests also attract large numbers of casual and family cyclists. These cyclists are likely to have different needs from mountain bikers.

Horse riding presents a second interesting case study for this research. Horse riding currently takes place in 22 per cent of Great Britain's main forest sites (Forestry Commission 2004a), and accounts for around 2 per cent of forest users (TNS Travel and Tourism 2004). Currently, horse riding takes place on existing forest trails, but further horse-specific facilities are generally not provided. One prominent exception to this is in the forests of Dyfnant and Lake Vyrnwy, located in mid Wales. Here, the local riding group, in partnership with the Forestry Commission, has developed a suite of facilities aimed to meet the specific needs of horse riders. Facilities provided include corrals, horsebox-friendly parking, mounting blocks, horse-friendly trail surfaces and optional challenges such as jumps. The facilities are now in much demand and serve to demonstrate the potential of providing horse-specific facilities. It was suggested during developmental focus groups with forest managers that efforts to promote horse riding in forests could potentially follow the success of the mountain biking centres and therefore there was interest to examine whether this is the case or not.

Nature watching was also identified as an activity of interest for this research. 'Specialist' nature watching currently takes place in 15 per cent of forests (Forestry Commission 2004b); however, there are also opportunities within most forests to view nature. An interesting finding from forest visitor studies is that whilst only a small proportion of visitors visit forests specifically to watch nature, many visitors reported that seeing nature enhanced their visit. Thus, the third case study examined people's values for enhancing opportunities to appreciate nature in forests. Facilities examined included specialist facilities such as interpretation centres, wildlife hides and nature walks, as well as less formal provisions such as forest management that increases opportunities for wildlife and for viewing wildlife.

Finally, it was recognised that limiting the study only to cover the three activities outlined above might be restrictive in that the views and values of other types of forest users would not be captured. It was therefore considered that it would be appropriate to group all other non-specialist forest users into a single 'general forest visitor' category, which would also cover forest visitors undertaking multiple activities during the trip to the forest.

THE CHOICE EXPERIMENT METHOD

Choice experiments (CE) are a stated preference valuation technique that is capable of measuring the economic benefits associated with the attributes of an environmental policy. CE relies on surveys to gather data. Within the survey, respondents are usually presented with a series of choice tasks in which they are asked to choose their preferred policy option from a list of three options; one of which normally includes the status quo or 'do nothing' option. An alternative, but rarely used approach is to use frequency-of-use data in the choice task instead of choice data. This frequency-based choice task was utilised in this application. Specifically, respondents were asked to allocate their next five recreation trips to forests (to be undertaken within a year) between two hypothetical forests and a 'stay at home' option. Figure 10.1 provides an example of a typical frequency-based choice task used in this research. Frequency-based approaches potentially have a number of advantages for this application over the more traditional choice-based questions in terms of realism and efficiency of data collection. In terms of realism, the frequency-based question appears to be better suited to capture the dynamic nature of people's actual recreation behaviour, which often involves numerous trips to a number of different forests. Note that in contrast, the majority of valuation studies address one-off policy programmes, which are likely to be more suited to the traditional choice-based choice task. A further advantage of the frequency-based approach is that it allows respondents who (in reality) would plan to make say only two trips to forests that year to account for this behaviour by allocating up to two trips (out of the five possible) to the hypothetical forests and then allocate the remaining trips to the 'stay at home' option. In addition, the frequency-based approach also enables the researcher to capture a common behaviour pattern where an individual might visit a (distant) forest on a small number of occasions to 'see what it is like', and then go to local forests on a more regular basis. Thus the

	Forest A	Forest B
Type of trail	Multi-use trails + dedicated way marked, long distance (+ 20 miles) cross country bike trails. 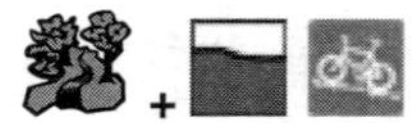	Multi-use trails + dedicated technical single track mountain bike trails. 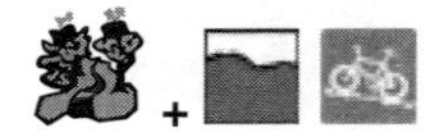
Optional trail obstacles	No optional trail obstacles. 	A range of optional trail obstacles provided including jumps, drop-offs, and north shore. 
Bike wash facilities	Bike washing facilities available. 	No bike wash facilities. 
Changing and shower facilities	Changing / shower facilities available. 	No changing / shower facilities. 
General facilities	Facilities included car parking, toilets, BBQ / picnic area, café and forest shop. 	Facilities include car parking and toilets only. 

Information	Only basic information on the forest, trails, and wildlife provided. 		Detailed and up-to-date information on the forest, trails and wildlife provided at forest centre, in leaflets, along trails and on website. 
Surrounding	Forest not managed to increase opportunities to view wildlife, points of interest and view points. 		Forest enhanced to increase opportunities to view wildlife, features of interest and view points. 
Distance	Forest located **300 miles** from your home.		Forest located **150 miles** from your home.
I would allocate my next 5 trips (to be taken within the next year) to:	**Forest A** ☐	**Forest B** ☐	**Stay at home** ☐

Figure 10.1 Example of a choice experiment choice task

frequency-based choice task is capable of capturing a much richer depth of information on forest visitor's intended behaviour than might be possible using a traditional choice-based choice task.

Similar to the traditional choice-based choice task, the analysis of a frequency-based CE model is based on Hanemann's (1994) random utility maximisation (RUM) theory. Accordingly, it is assumed that the forest visitor's utility function can be broken down into two parts, one deterministic (V) and one which is a random error term (ε). It is also assumed that the forest visitor chooses how often to visit each site from the set of all possible sites (C) according to the relative utility they obtain from each site, which in turn depends on the characteristics of that site. The deterministic part of utility is assumed to be a linear function of site characteristics:

$$V_{ij} = \beta_1 + \beta_2 X_{ij2} + \beta_3 X_{ij3} + \ldots + \beta_n X_{ijn} + \mu TC_{ij} \tag{10.1}$$

where X_{ij} represent the attributes of site j and β its parameters, and TC_{ij} is travel costs of visiting site j for individual i and μ its parameter. The probability that site j will be selected over other sites in C depends, for individual i, on:

$$\pi_i(j) = \text{Prob}\,[V_{ij} + \varepsilon_{ij} \geq V_{ik} + \varepsilon_{ik}; \forall\, k \in C] \tag{10.2}$$

If we assume that the error term is independent and identically distributed (IID) with an extreme-value Gumbel distribution, then this gives us the familiar conditional logit model (Louviere *et al.* 2000). Assuming that the independence of irrelevant alternatives (IIA) hypothesis holds:

$$\pi_i(j) = \frac{\exp(V_{ij})}{\sum_{k \in C} \exp(V_{ik})} \tag{10.3}$$

Compensating variation welfare measures can then be obtained, using the standard Hanemann (1994) formula, where V_0 is (deterministic) utility in the initial situation, and V_1 is utility in some different situation: for example, when forest characteristics have been improved.

$$CV = -\frac{1}{\mu}[ln(\Sigma_{j \in C} \exp(V_{j0})) - ln(\Sigma_{j \in C} \exp(V_{j1}))] \tag{10.4}$$

Utility changes are converted into money-metric using the inverse of the marginal utility of income, which here is the parameter on the travel cost variable (μ). Finally, implicit prices for a change in the provision of a particular recreation activity may be established by dividing the coefficient of the attribute with the negative of the travel cost coefficient (μ).

The forest recreation attributes and levels examined in the CE study were developed from information gathered during a review of relevant literature and from forest user and forest manager focus groups. For each of the four recreation activities examined in this research, eight attributes were specified (see Tables 10.1a and b for a summary of attributes and attribute levels). The first four attributes (Table 10.1a) were activity-specific (for example, for cycling, the activity-specific attributes were 'type of trail', 'optional trail obstacles', 'bike wash facilities' and 'changing and shower facilities'), while the remaining four attributes (Table 10.1b) used were identical over all four activity groups ('general facilities', 'information', 'surroundings', and 'distance' attributes). Five of the attributes were specified with two levels of provision and three attributes with four levels of provision. A complete $2^5 \times 4^3$ factorial design would involve 2048 combinations. Following Street *et al.* (2005), the attributes and levels were allocated to choice tasks according to an orthogonal main effects fractional factorial design, which resulted in 16 choice cards. These were subsequently split into four sub-samples, each containing four choice tasks. Thus, each respondent was asked to complete a series of four choice tasks based on the main recreation activity undertaken during the day of interview. A similar experimental design was applied to all four recreation activities investigated.

Data for this research was collected using on-site, in-person interviews – the recommended format for stated preference valuation studies (Arrow *et al.* 1993). Up to 24 days of interviews were undertaken at seven forests located throughout Great Britain: Glentress, Dyfnant, Cwm Carn, Thetford, New Forest, Rothiemurchus and Whinlatter. These forests were selected to cover the range of recreational activities examined in the research, as well as providing a geographic sample of British forests (see Figure 10.2).

The format of the survey questionnaire followed standard guidelines for the design of the stated preference valuation survey instruments (Arrow *et al.* 1993; Bateman *et al.* 2002; Hensher *et al.* 2005). Survey respondents were therefore provided with some background information on the study and then asked to outline how they use forests for recreation. Next, they were presented with information on how the forest might be improved for recreation. Respondents were then presented with a series of four CE choice tasks (see Figure 10.1 for an example). Before making their choices, respondents were presented with a series of statements that reminded them to answer truthfully and account for their personal budget constraints. A follow-up question was also asked to identify respondent's motivations when answering the choice tasks. Finally, socio-economic, demographic and attitudinal data were collected from the respondents.

Table 10.1a Summary of variable attributes used in the CE model

CYCLING	HORSE RIDERS	NATURE WATCHERS	GENERAL VISITORS
TYPE OF TRAIL	**TYPE OF TRAIL**	**TYPE OF TRAIL**	**WALKING TRAIL**
Only multi-user trails (walkers, cyclists and horse riders) available. No dedicated cycle trails.	Only multi-user trails (walkers, cyclists and horse riders) available. No dedicated cycle trails.	Only multi-user trails (walkers, cyclists and horse riders) available.	Only multi-user trails (walkers, cyclists and horse riders) available.
Multi-use trails + dedicated way marked, long distance (+ 20 miles) cross country bike trails.	Multi-use trails + dedicated horse riding trails with horse friendly trail surfaces.	Multi-use trails + short dedicated, easy access nature trails.	Multi-use trails + short dedicated, easy access walking trails.
Multi-use trails + dedicated technical single track mountain bike trails.	Multi-use trails + dedicated horse riding trails, which are also suitable for carriage driving.	Multi-use trails + dedicated medium length nature trails with many information boards on forest wildlife.	Multi-use trails + art / sculpture walks.
Multi-use trails + dedicated steep and technical downhill/ 4 cross bike trails.	Multi-use trails + dedicated long distance (+ 20 miles) horse riding trails.	Multi-use trails + quiet 'off the beaten track' trails into areas of high wildlife interest.	Multi-use trails + dedicated long distance (+ 20 miles) walking routes.
OPTIONAL TRAIL OBSTACLES	**OPTIONAL TRAIL OBSTACLES**	**HIDES**	**MOUNTAIN BIKE TRAILS**
No optional trail obstacles.	No optional obstacles provided.	No wildlife hides.	No dedicated technical single track mountain bike trails.
A range of optional trail obstacles provided including jumps, drop-offs, and north shore.	A range of optional obstacles provided including jumps, ditches.	Wildlife hides available.	Dedicated technical single track mountain bike trails in forest.

Table 10.1a (continued)

CYCLING	HORSE RIDERS	NATURE WATCHERS	GENERAL VISITORS
BIKE WASH FACILITIES	**HORSE-FRIENDLY PARKING**	**WILDLIFE VIEWING CENTRES**	**HORSE RIDING TRAILS**
No bike wash facilities.	Horse-friendly parking NOT provided.	No wildlife viewing centre.	No dedicated horse riding trails
Bike washing facilities available.	Horse-box-friendly parking provided at forest.	A wildlife viewing centre available for unique species.	Dedicated horse riding trails in forest.
CHANGING AND SHOWER FACILITIES	**HORSE CORRALS AND TIE-UP POINTS**	**GUIDED NATURE WALKS**	**NATURE TRAILS / WILDLIFE HIDES**
No changing / shower facilities.	No horse corrals and tie-up points available.	No guided nature walks available.	No nature trails / wildlife hides.
Changing / shower facilities available.	Horse corrals and tie-up points available at forest.	Guided nature walks available.	Nature trails / wildlife hides in forest.

Table 10.1b Summary of common attributes used in the CE model

GENERAL FACILITIES	GENERAL FACILITIES	GENERAL FACILITIES	GENERAL FACILITIES
Facilities include car parking and toilets only.	Facilities include car parking and toilets only.	Facilities include car parking and toilets only.	Facilities include car parking and toilets only.
Facilities included car parking, toilets and BBQ / picnic areas.	Facilities included car parking, toilets and BBQ / picnic areas.	Facilities included car parking, toilets and BBQ / picnic areas.	Facilities included car parking, toilets and BBQ / picnic areas.
Facilities included car parking, toilets, BBQ / picnic area, café and forest shop.	Facilities included car parking, toilets, BBQ / picnic area, café and forest shop.	Facilities included car parking, toilets, BBQ / picnic area, café and forest shop.	Facilities included car parking, toilets, BBQ / picnic area, café and forest shop.
Facilities included car parking, toilets, BBQ / picnic areas, café, forest shop and children's play areas.	Facilities included car parking, toilets, BBQ / picnic areas, café, forest shop and children's play areas.	Facilities included car parking, toilets, BBQ / picnic areas, café, forest shop and children's play areas.	Facilities included car parking, toilets, BBQ / picnic areas, café, forest shop and children's play areas.
INFORMATION	**INFORMATION**	**INFORMATION**	**INFORMATION**
Only basic information on the forest, trails, and wildlife provided.	Only basic information on the forest, trails, and wildlife provided.	Only basic information on the forest, trails, and wildlife provided.	Only basic information on the forest, trails, and wildlife provided.
Detailed and up-to-date information on the forest, trails and wildlife provided at forest centre, in leaflets, along trails and on website.	Detailed and up-to-date information on the forest, trails and wildlife provided at forest centre, in leaflets, along trails and on website.	Detailed and up-to-date information on the forest, trails and wildlife provided at forest centre, in leaflets, along trails and on website.	Detailed and up-to-date information on the forest, trails and wildlife provided at forest centre, in leaflets, along trails and on website.

Table 10.1b (continued)

GENERAL FACILITIES	GENERAL FACILITIES	GENERAL FACILITIES	GENERAL FACILITIES
SURROUNDINGS	**SURROUNDINGS**	**SURROUNDINGS**	**SURROUNDINGS**
No special management to increase opportunities to view wildlife, points of interest and view points.	No special management to increase opportunities to view wildlife, points of interest and view points.	No special management to increase opportunities to view wildlife, points of interest and view points.	No special management to increase opportunities to view wildlife, points of interest and view points.
Forest enhanced to increase opportunities to view wildlife, features of interest and view points.	Forest enhanced to increase opportunities to view wildlife, features of interest and view points.	Forest enhanced to increase opportunities to view wildlife, features of interest and view points.	Forest enhanced to increase opportunities to view wildlife, features of interest and view points.
DISTANCE	**DISTANCE**	**DISTANCE**	**DISTANCE**
20 miles, 75 miles, 150 miles, or 300 miles	20 miles, 75 miles, 150 miles, or 300 miles	20 miles, 75 miles, 150 miles, or 300 miles	20 miles, 75 miles, 150 miles, or 300 miles

Figure 10.2 Map of forest locations

RESULTS

A total of 1568 on-site, personal interviews were undertaken during this research across the seven forests. General forest users accounted for just under half (47.5 per cent) of the total sample, while cyclists accounted for 37.3 per cent. Horse riders and nature watchers were less well represented, accounting for 7.1 per cent and 8.1 per cent respectively. These low numbers reflect the fact that there were often very few people in the forests undertaking these two activities.

The NLOGIT econometrics software package was used to run a series of conditional logit models for the forest recreation data. These models are reported in Tables 10.2, 10.4, 10.6 and 10.8 respectively for cyclists, horse riders, nature watchers and general forest users. The implicit prices generated from these models can be found in Tables 10.3, 10.5, 10.7 and 10.9 respectively. In each of these tables, Model 1 is based on all users within the specified recreation activity, while Models 2 and beyond relate to subgroups of users in that activity group. We now report the key findings from the four recreation activities in turn.

Cyclists

Table 10.2 reports a series of CE models for cyclists, while Table 10.3 reports the implicit prices generated from these models. Model 1 includes all respondents who indicated that cycling was the main activity undertaken during the trip to the forest. In Model 1 all of the cycle-specific attributes are significant and positive, suggesting that cyclists considered these attributes to be important and that they were more likely to visit a forest if these attributes were provided. The highest implicit prices are found for 'dedicated downhill trails' (£9.74), 'dedicated single track trails' (£8.40) and 'obstacles' (£7.56). Other significant attributes include 'dedicated cross country trails' (£5.81), 'bike wash facilities' (£4.27) and 'changing and shower facilities' (£1.58). Interestingly, the 'multi-purpose trails' attribute is significant but negative (−£23.95). This suggests that cyclists did not want to share trails with other users. None of the other non-cycle-specific attributes (such as 'general facilities', 'information' and 'enhance surroundings') are significant in Model 1, suggesting that cyclists did not consider these attributes to be important to their choice of forest. The alternative specific constant (ASC), which took a value of 1 if the 'stay at home' option was chosen or 0 if either of the forest options was chosen, is significant and negative. This indicates that cyclists generally preferred options that involved a cycle trip as opposed to staying at home. Finally, the distance attribute is (as expected) significant and negative; cyclists were less likely to choose a forest if the distance required to travel was greater. The validity of the choice model was assessed using various test statistics. The LL ratio test statistic for Model 1 is significant ($\chi^2 = 1936$), indicating that the inclusion of the forest attribute parameters adds to the predictive power of the model. The pseudo-Rho^2 goodness-of-fit statistic is estimated as 0.08 in Model 1, which is close to the acceptable value of 0.1 (Louviere *et al.* 2000). Finally, 42.9 per cent of choices are correctly predicted by the model, which is considered satisfactory for this type of model (Hensher *et al.* 2005).

Models 2, 3, and 4 in Table 10.2 relate to different sub-groups of cyclists, while the implicit prices generated from these models are reported in Table 10.3. Model 2 is based on 'leisure cyclists', that is, those cyclists who stated that they were not partaking in mountain biking or downhill biking activities. Within this Model, only three parameters are significant: the ASC (stay at home), the 'bike wash facilities' and the 'distance' parameters. The parameter on the 'bike wash facilities' is positive (implicit price = £3.32), indicating that leisure cyclists would prefer forests with bike wash facilities. The parameter on the 'distance' attribute is significant and negative, indicating that respondents were less likely to choose an option if the

Table 10.2 Choice experiments models – cyclists

	Model 1 All cyclists	Model 2 Leisure cyclists	Model 3 Mountain bikers	Model 4 Downhill riders
ASC	−0.324***	−0.532***	−0.369***	−0.427***
	(−6.246)	(−2.800)	(−6.544)	(−4.639)
Trails (dedicated cross country)	0.106***	0.033	0.125***	0.018
	(4.550)	(0.386)	(4.934)	(0.456)
Trails (dedicated single track)	0.154***	0.083	0.182***	0.002
	(6.488)	(0.981)	(7.122)	(0.060)
Trails (dedicated downhill)	0.178***	−0.053	0.162***	0.342***
	(7.334)	(−0.597)	(6.15)	(8.298)
Obstacles (jumps and drop-offs)	0.138***	0.030	0.134***	0.192***
	(11.512)	(0.681)	(10.346)	(9.365)
Bike wash facilities	0.078***	0.092**	0.073***	0.045**
	(6.386)	(2.010)	(5.572)	(2.160)
Changing and shower facilities	0.029**	−0.001	0.031**	−0.011
	(2.451)	(−0.028)	(2.444)	(−0.544)
Parking, toilets, picnic	0.014	0.031	0.023	0.051
	(0.497)	(0.320)	(0.734)	(1.004)
Parking, toilets, picnic, café, shop	0.019	0.010	0.006	0.042
	(0.669)	(0.108)	(0.181)	(0.842)
Parking, toilets, picnic, café, shop, play areas	0.029	0.103	0.033	−0.033
	(0.991)	(1.064)	(1.035)	(−0.633)
Detailed information	0.003	0.004	0.007	0.050**
	(0.269)	(0.096)	(0.556)	(2.437)
Enhanced surroundings	−0.004	0.039	−0.011	−0.069***
	(−0.335)	(0.871)	(−0.842)	(−3.358)
Distance	−0.018***	−0.028***	−0.018***	−0.015***
	(−35.555)	(−13.962)	(−6.544)	(−17.371)
LL model	−11181.10	*−1061.04*	*−9416.237*	*−3607.905*
LL (Constants only)	−12149.13	−1202.45	−10244.06	−3888.635
LL ratio test (χ^2)	1936.00	282.81	1655.65	561.46
p-value	0.000	0.000	0.000	0.000
Pseudo-Rho^2	0.08	0.12	0.08	0.07
Correct predictions	0.429	0.418	0.414	0.411
Number of respondents	566	54	480	183

Notes:
t-stats in parenthesis
** significance at p=0.05
*** significance at p=0.01

Table 10.3 Implicit prices for forest improvements – cyclists

	Model 1 All cyclists	Model 2 Leisure cyclists	Model 3 Mountain bikers	Model 4 Downhill riders
Trails (multi-purpose)	**−£23.95**	−£2.27	**−£25.90**	−£24.77
	(1.48)	(3.24)	**(1.63)**	(3.165)
Trails (dedicated cross-country)	**£5.81**	£1.19	**£6.89**	£1.26
	(1.28)	(3.07)	**(1.40)**	(2.76)
Trails (dedicated single track)	**£8.40**	£2.99	**£10.07**	£0.17
	(1.30)	(3.06)	**(1.42)**	(2.84)
Trails (dedicated downhill)	**£9.74**	−£1.91	**£8.93**	**£23.34**
	(1.33)	(3.20)	**(1.46)**	**(3.01)**
Obstacles (jumps and drop-offs)	**£7.56**	£1.09	**£7.39**	**£13.14**
	(0.66)	(1.60)	**(0.71)**	**(1.50)**
Bike-wash facilities	**£4.27**	**£3.32**	**£4.04**	**£3.05**
	(0.66)	**(1.63)**	**(0.72)**	**(1.40)**
Changing and shower facilities	**£1.58**	−£0.04	**£1.71**	−£0.75
	(0.64)	(1.57)	**(0.70)**	(1.38)
Parking, toilets only	−£3.40	−£5.18	−£3.42	−£4.14
	(1.56)	(3.50)	(1.73)	(3.45)
Parking, toilets, picnic	£0.79	£1.13	£1.29	£3.48
	(1.60)	(3.52)	(1.76)	(2.87)
Parking, toilets, picnic, café, shop	£1.03	£0.36	£0.31	£2.87
	(1.54)	(3.30)	(1.72)	(3.41)
Parking, toilets, picnic, café, shop, play areas	£1.58	£3.70	£1.81	−£2.22
	(1.59)	(3.50)	(1.76)	(3.51)
Detailed information	£0.18	£0.16	£0.40	**£3.41**
	(0.66)	(1.63)	(0.72)	**(1.43)**
Enhanced surroundings	−£0.22	£1.42	−£0.60	**−£4.71**
	(0.66)	(1.63)	(0.72)	**(1.40)**

Notes:
Standard errors in parenthesis
Implicit prices shown in bold were significant in the models; non-bold implicit prices were not significant and therefore were considered as being unimportant to respondents' choices.

distance required to travel to the forest was greater. None of the other forest attributes are significant in Model 2, suggesting that leisure cyclists did not have strong preferences for the facilities provided at a forest.

Model 3 in Table 10.2 is based on mountain bikers. In this model, all of the cycle-specific attributes are positive and significant, demonstrating that such facilities were considered to be important in mountain bikers' choice of forest. Table 10.3 demonstrates that positive implicit prices are found for 'dedicated single track trails' (£10.07), 'dedicated downhill trails' (£8.93), 'obstacles' (£7.39), 'bike wash facilities' (£4.04) and 'changing and shower facilities' (£1.71). 'Multipurpose trails' are again significant but negative (implicit price = −£25.90), providing evidence that mountain bikers in particular did not want to share trails with other users. The 'distance' attribute is again significant and negative as expected. None of the general facilities attributes are significant in this model, and thus were not considered to be important to mountain bikers' choice of forest.

Finally, in the 'downhill riders' model (Model 4), the 'dedicated downhill trails', 'obstacles' and 'bike wash facilities' attributes are all significant and positive. Of note is the fact that the implicit prices associated with 'dedicated downhill trails' (£23.34) and 'obstacles' (£13.14) are the highest over all models and activities. The 'detailed information' attribute is also positive and significant (£3.41), while the 'enhanced surroundings' attribute is significant but negative (−£4.71) suggesting that downhill riders did not want to cycle in forests where the opportunities to view wildlife and points of interest have been enhanced. It is speculated that the reason for this is that downhill riders may not have considered their activity as being compatible with nature. The 'distance' attribute is again significant and negative.

In terms of the significance of the three cyclist sub-group models, the LL ratio tests indicate that the inclusion of the forest attributes significantly improves the overall LL function of the models. The pseudo-Rho^2 values are 0.12, 0.08 and 0.07 respectively for Models 2, 3 and 4. Finally, the number of correct predictions of all models is around 41 per cent.

Horse Riders

Table 10.4 reports the CE models for horse riders, while Table 10.5 reports the implicit prices generated from these models. Model 1 reports the findings from all horse riders, while Models 2 and 3 respectively report models for 'family / leisure riders' and 'endurance riders or carriage drivers'.

In Model 1 (all horse riders) the 'distance' attribute is significant and negative as expected. In terms of the provision of horse-specific facilities, the provision of 'dedicated carriage driving' facilities is positive and significant, increasing utility (£8.88), while the provision of 'dedicated long distance routes' is found to reduce utility (−£5.85). The other horse riding specific attributes ('obstacles', 'horse friendly parking' and 'horse corrals and tie-up') are insignificant in the model and therefore appear to have been unimportant to horse riders' choice of forest. The 'general facilities' attribute is significant; however, there appears to be some inconsistencies within this attribute. The provision of 'parking, toilets and picnic areas' increases

Table 10.4 Choice experiments models – horse riders

	Model 1 All horse riders	Model 2 Family / leisure riders	Model 3 Endurance riders/ carriage drivers
ASC	−0.067	−0.009	−1.425***
	(−0.474)	(−0.061)	(−2.957)
Trails (dedicated horse riding)	0.062	0.092	−0.089
	(0.982)	(1.390)	(−0.410)
Trails (dedicated carriage driving)	0.235***	0.220***	−0.212
	(3.894)	(3.483)	(−0.893)
Trails (dedicated long distance)	−0.155**	−0.165**	0.110
	(−2.360)	(−2.378)	(0.576)
Obstacles (jumps and ditches)	0.033	0.027	−0.151
	(1.055)	(0.830)	(−1.404)
Horse-friendly parking	−0.004	0.009	0.131
	(−0.138)	(0.277)	(1.166)
Horse corrals and tie-ups	0.018	0.031	−0.177*
	(0.557)	(0.897)	(−1.708)
Parking, toilets, picnic	0.426***	0.506***	−0.640***
	(6.654)	(7.556)	(−2.789)
Parking, toilets, picnic, café, shop	−0.219***	−0.309***	0.701***
	(−3.103)	(−4.187)	(2.944)
Parking, toilets, picnic, café, shop, play areas	0.181***	0.236***	−0.638***
	(2.721)	(3.360)	(−2.865)
Detailed information	0.028	−0.020	0.466***
	(0.893)	(−0.609)	(4.056)
Enhanced surroundings	0.063**	0.028	0.426***
	(1.997)	(0.837)	(3.718)
Distance	−0.027***	−0.026***	−0.040***
	(−18.718)	(−17.456)	(−7.433)
LL model	−2022.282	*−1829.171*	*−217.618*
LL (Constants only)	−2296.042	−2075.314	−284.432
LL ratio test (χ^2)	547.52	492.29	133.63
p-value	0.000	0.000	0.000
Pseudo-Rho²	0.12	0.12	0.23
Correct predictions	0.422	0.421	0.500
Number of respondents	105	95	10

Notes:
t-stats in parenthesis
* significance at p=0.1
** significance at p=0.05
*** significance at p=0.01

Table 10.5 Implicit prices for forest improvements – horse riders

	Model 1 All horse riders	**Model 2 Family / leisure riders**	**Model 3 Endurance / carriage drivers**
Trails (multi-purpose only)	−£5.37 (2.42)	−£5.67 (2.62)	£4.79 (4.71)
Trails (dedicated horse-riding)	£2.33 (2.38)	£3.55 (2.57)	−32.23 (5.46)
Trails (dedicated carriage driving)	**£8.88** **(2.28)**	**£8.48** **(2.43)**	−£5.32 (5.80)
Trails (dedicated long-distance)	**−£5.85** **(2.45)**	**−£6.36** **(2.65)**	£2.76 (4.80)
Obstacles (jumps and ditches)	£1.25 (1.18)	£1.06 (1.28)	−£3.80 (2.63)
Horse-friendly parking	−£0.17 (1.23)	£0.37 (1.33)	£3.29 (2.74)
Horse corrals and tie-ups	£0.69 (1.24)	£1.20 (1.33)	**−£4.44** **(2.61)**
Parking, toilets only	**−£14.64** **(2.80)**	**−£16.67** **(3.04)**	**£14.48** **(5.68)**
Parking, toilets, picnic	**£16.06** **(2.27)**	**£19.52** **(2.69)**	**−£16.07** **(6.04)**
Parking, toilets, picnic, café, shop	**−£8.25** **(2.68)**	**−£11.95** **(2.90)**	**£17.61** **(6.19)**
Parking, toilets, picnic, café, shop, play areas	**£6.83** **(2.52)**	**£9.10** **(2.73)**	**−£16.03** **(5.61)**
Detailed information	£1.05 (1.17)	−£0.77 (1.27)	**£11.70** **(2.62)**
Enhanced surroundings	**£2.39** **(1.51)**	£1.09 (1.30)	**£10.69** **(2.62)**

Notes:
Standard errors in parenthesis
Implicit prices shown in bold were significant in the models; non-bold implicit prices were not significant and therefore were considered as being unimportant to respondents' choices.

utility (£16.06), while the added provision of a café/shop reduces utility (−£8.25): a strange result. A further increase in general facilities to include play areas then increases utility again (£6.83). Thus it would appear that horse riders preferred forests that only had the more basic facilities. The enhancement of the forest surroundings for viewing features of interest also increases utility (£2.39). The ASC is not significant in this model. The

LL ratio test statistic is significant at $p = 0.05$, indicating that the inclusion of the forest attributes significantly improves the overall LL function of the model. The pseudo-Rho^2 measure of goodness-of-fit is 0.12, which is higher than the recommended value of 0.1. Finally, approximately 42 per cent of choice outcomes are correctly predicted.

Model 2 (family and leisure horse riders) is very similar to Model 1 both in terms of attribute coefficients, implicit prices and goodness-of-fit. This, however, is not surprising since the majority of horse riders (95 out of the 105 in the full sample) were included in this sub-group. Perhaps the main difference in Model 2 is that the 'enhanced surroundings' attribute is not significant.

Model 3 includes only those riders who were participating in endurance rides or carriage driving. Only 10 respondents were included in this sub-sample, and therefore the explanatory power of the model is likely to be low. In this model, the 'dedicated carriage driving trails' and 'dedicated long distance trails' are not significant, while the 'horse corrals and tie-up points' attribute is significant and negative (implicit price = −£4.44). The 'detailed information' and 'enhance surroundings' attributes are significant and positive in this sub-group: implicit prices are £11.70 and £10.69 respectively. The ASC is significant and negative, indicating that endurance riders and carriage drivers would prefer to go to a forest than 'stay at home'. Finally, the goodness-of-fit measure for this sub-group indicates that the model is within the recommended levels with a pseudo-Rho^2 value of 0.23. Furthermore, the number of correct choice predictions is increased to 50 per cent.

Nature Watchers

Table 10.6 reports the CE models for nature watchers, while Table 10.7 reports the implicit prices. In Model 1 (all nature watchers), the 'wildlife hides' (£6.83), 'wildlife viewing centres' (£5.65) 'enhanced surroundings' (£3.62) and 'off the beaten track nature trails' (£6.48) are positive and significant, suggesting that the provision of these facilities would increase the likelihood that a nature watcher would visit a forest. However, the ASC attribute is significant and positive, indicating that, in general, nature watchers would prefer to stay at home as opposed to visiting one of the forests: this may be the result of the use of a simplifying decision heuristic. As expected, the 'distance' attribute is negative and significant in the model. Model 2 is restricted to include only those nature watchers who indicated that they were undertaking 'nature watching – general', that is, they were appreciating nature at the forest without the use of specific nature watching facilities such as wildlife hides. The significant attributes within this

Table 10.6 Choice experiments models – nature watchers

	Model 1 All nature watchers	Model 2 Nature watchers general	Model 3 Nature watchers – centres & nature trails
ASC	0.450***	0.462***	0.622***
	(4.098)	(3.642)	(4.685)
Trails (dedicated easy access nature trails)	−0.008	−0.005	0.010
	(−0.150)	(−0.083)	(0.137)
Trails (dedicated nature trails with information)	0.075	0.046	0.058
	(1.348)	(0.714)	(0.806)
Trails ('off the beaten track' nature trails)	0.115**	0.117*	0.114
	(2.087)	(1.832)	(1.599)
Wildlife hides	0.121***	0.152***	0.102***
	(4.180)	(4.504)	(2.695)
Wildlife viewing centres	0.100***	0.131***	0.181
	(3.406)	(3.783)	(4.723)
Guided nature walks	0.010	0.019	0.036
	(0.357)	(0.557)	(0.987)
Parking, toilets, picnic	0.084	0.106	0.095
	(1.400)	(1.537)	(1.195)
Parking, toilets, picnic, café, shop	0.009	−0.053	−0.074
	(0.162)	(−0.777)	(−1.006)
Parking, toilets, picnic, café, shop, play areas	−0.033	−0.012	0.054
	(−0.527)	(−0.171)	(0.671)
Detailed information	0.029	0.002	−0.002
	(1.003)	(0.047)	(−0.064)
Enhanced surroundings	0.064**	0.071**	0.071*
	(2.199)	(2.067)	(1.851)
Distance	−0.018***	−0.020***	−0.018***
	(−15.163)	(−14.222)	(−12.044)
LL model	−2496.812	*−1895.11*	*−1578.538*
LL (Constants only)	−2654.437	−2039.41	−1683.511
LL ratio test (χ^2)	315.25	288.60	209.95
p-value	0.000	0.000	0.000
Pseudo-Rho^2	0.06	0.07	0.06
Correct predictions	0.385	0.396	0.396
Number of respondents	123	95.0	79.0

Notes:
t-stats in parenthesis
* significance at p=0.1
** significance at p=0.05
*** significance at p=0.01

Table 10.7 Implicit prices for forest improvements – nature watchers

	Model 1 All nature watchers	Model 2 Nature watchers general	Model 3 Nature watchers – centres & nature trails
Trails (multi-purpose only)	−£10.25	−£8.02	−£9.95
	(3.21)	(3.41)	(4.08)
Trails (dedicated easy access nature trails)	−£0.47	−£0.27	£0.53
	(3.13)	(3.26)	(3.90)
Trails (dedicated nature trails with information)	£4.24	£2.35	£3.19
	(3.17)	(3.30)	(3.99)
Trails ('off-the-beaten-track, nature trails)	**£6.48**	**£5.94**	£6.23
	(3.11)	**(3.24)**	(3.86)
Wildlife hides	**£6.83**	**£7.70**	**£5.60**
	(1.67)	**(1.75)**	**(2.10)**
Wildlife-viewing centres	**£5.65**	**£6.63**	£9.89
	(1.66)	**(1.76)**	(2.10)
Guided nature walks	£0.57	£0.94	£1.99
	(1.61)	(1.69)	(2.02)
Parking, toilets only	−£3.44	−£2.07	−£4.13
	(3.31)	(3.42)	(4.04)
Parking, toilets, picnic	£4.75	£5.35	£5.19
	(3.43)	(3.53)	(4.41)
Parking, toilets, picnic, café, shop	£0.53	−£2.66	−£4.02
	(3.25)	(3.44)	(4.04)
Parking, toilets, picnic, café, shop, play areas	−£1.84	−£0.61	£2.96
	(3.49)	(3.59)	(4.43)
Detailed information	£1.66	£0.08	−£0.13
	(1.65)	(1.72)	(2.10)
Enhanced surroundings	**£3.62**	**£3.57**	**£3.87**
	(1.66)	**(1.74)**	**(2.11)**

Notes:
Standard errors in parenthesis
Implicit prices shown in bold were significant in the models; non-bold implicit prices were not significant and therefore were considered as being unimportant to respondents' choices.

model are the same as in Model 1 and implicit prices are similar. Finally, Model 3 is restricted to include those nature watchers who stated that they were using a viewing centre, nature trail or guided walk. Within this model only the 'Wildlife hides' and 'Enhanced surroundings' attributes are significant and positive. Implicit prices for these attributes are similar to those found in Models 1 and 2.

In terms of the overall performance of the nature watchers' models, all of the LL ratio tests are significant, indicating that the inclusion of the attributes increases the performance of the models compared to the constants-only model. The pseudo-Rho^2 values for the models are around 0.06, which is lower than the recommended values. Finally, around 40 per cent of the choices are correctly predicted.

General Forest Users

The final group of forest users are the general forest visitors. Four CE models are generated for this group (Tables 10.8 and 10.9). In Model 1 (all general forest users), attributes that are significant and positive include 'single track mountain bike trails' (£4.59), 'nature trails / wildlife hides' (£1.56), 'art / sculpture trails' (£2.90), 'parking, toilets and picnic' (£6.95), 'parking, toilets, picnic, café, shop and play areas' (£4.37), and 'enhance surroundings' (£2.70). It should be noted that these implicit prices are generally lower than those found in the activity-specific models. Attributes that are significant and negative are 'parking and toilets' (−£5.45), 'parking, toilets, picnic, café and shop' (−£5.87), and 'distance'. Insignificant attributes include 'easy access trails', 'long distance walking trails', 'horse riding trails' and 'detailed information'.

Models 2, 3 and 4 are based on sub-groups of the general forest users. Model 2 (active general visitors) includes those general visitors who indicated that they partook in either a cycling, horse riding or nature watching activity whilst in the forest, but not as the single main activity undertaken during the trip to the forest. Within this group, 'single track mountain bike trails' (£5.26), 'parking, toilets and picnic' (£8.43) and 'enhanced surroundings' (£3.37) are found to be significant and positive. 'Long distance walking trails', 'parking, toilets, picnic, café, shop', 'detailed information' and 'distance' are all significant and negative.

Model 3 is based on general forest users who indicated that they went on a walk during their visit to the forest. Significant and positive attributes include 'single track mountain bike trails' (£3.79), 'nature trails / wildlife hides' (£1.36), 'parking, toilets and picnic' (£10.03), 'parking, toilets, picnic, café, shop and play areas' (£4.65) and 'enhanced surroundings' (£2.03). Significant and negative attributes included 'horse riding trails', 'parking, toilets, picnic, café and shop' and 'distance'.

Finally, Model 4 is based on those general forest visitors who did not cycle, ride horses, nature watch or walk during their trip to the forest. Significant and positive attributes included 'art / sculpture walks' (£4.38), 'single track mountain bike trails' (£4.40), 'nature trails / wildlife hides' (£1.95), 'parking, toilets and picnic' (£3.04), 'parking, toilets, picnic,

Table 10.8 Choice experiments models – general forest users

	Model 1 All general visitors	Model 2 Active general visitors	Model 3 Walkers	Model 4 Non-active general visitors
ASC	0.153***	0.024	0.068	0.164***
	(3.368)	(0.395)	(1.310)	(2.801)
Trails (easy access)	0.011	0.018	−0.003	0.039
	(0.455)	(0.562)	(−0.099)	(1.346)
Trails (art / sculpture walks)	0.055**	0.048	0.040	0.088***
	(2.384)	(1.501)	(1.510)	(3.031)
Trails (long-distance walking)	−0.015	−0.080**	−0.022	−0.042
	(−0.620)	(−2.420)	(−0.816)	(−1.396)
Single-track mountain bike trails	0.088***	0.098***	0.071***	0.088***
	(7.351)	(5.966)	(5.211)	(5.894)
Horse-riding trails	−0.004	−0.017	−0.028**	−0.030*
	(−0.288)	(−0.995)	(−2.022)	(−1.897)
Nature trails / wildlife hides	0.030**	0.015	0.025*	0.039**
	(2.473)	(0.908)	(1.848)	(2.571)
Parking, toilets, picnic	0.133***	0.157***	0.187***	0.061**
	(5.410)	(4.617)	(6.737)	(1.963)
Parking, toilets, picnic, café, shop	−0.112***	−0.102***	−0.160***	−0.051
	(−4.450)	(−2.952)	(−5.530)	(−1.620)
Parking, toilets, picnic, café, shop, play areas	0.084***	0.043	0.087***	0.107***
	(3.367)	(1.231)	(3.059)	(3.496)
Detailed information	−0.002	−0.029*	−0.018	0.007
	(−0.181)	(−1.730)	(−1.347)	(0.489)
Enhanced surroundings	0.052***	0.063***	0.038***	0.050***
	(4.263)	(3.776)	(2.757)	(3.263)
Distance	−0.019***	−0.019***	−0.019***	−0.020***
	(−38.601)	(−27.402)	(−33.191)	(−31.822)
LL model	*−14281.98*	*−7428.155*	*−11038.29*	*−9114.99*
LL (Constants only)	−15235.14	−7916.58	−11741.4	−9770.897
LL ratio test (χ^2)	1906.32	976.85	1406.22	1311.81
p-value	0.000	0.000	0.000	0.000
Pseudo-Rho^2	0.06	0.06	0.06	0.07
Correct predictions	0.387	0.385	0.386	0.390
Number of respondents	706	365.5	544	452.3

Notes:
t-stats in parenthesis
* significance at p=0.1
** significance at p=0.05
*** significance at p=0.01

Table 10.9 Implicit prices for forest improvements – general forest users

	Model 1 All general visitors	Model 2 Active general visitors	Model 3 Walkers	Model 4 Non-active general visitors
Trails (multi-purpose)	−£2.68 (1.23)	£0.76 (1.72)	−£0.81 (1.42)	−£4.23 (1.49)
Trails (easy access)	£0.56 (1.22)	£0.97 (1.73)	−£0.14 (1.44)	£1.96 (1.46)
Trails (art / sculpture walks)	**£2.90 (1.22)**	£2.58 (1.72)	£2.14 (1.41)	**£4.38 (1.44)**
Trails (long-distance walking)	−£0.77 (1.25)	**−£4.31 (1.78)**	−£1.19 (1.46)	−£2.11 (1.51)
Single-track mountain bike trails	**£4.59 (0.63)**	**£5.26 (0.89)**	**£3.79 (0.73)**	**£4.40 (0.75)**
Horse-riding trails	−£0.19 (0.65)	−£0.90 (0.91)	**−£1.52 (0.76)**	**−£1.47 (0.78)**
Nature trails / wildlife hides	**£1.56 (0.63)**	£0.81 (0.89)	**£1.36 (0.74)**	**£1.95 (0.76)**
Parking, toilets only	**−£5.45 (1.31)**	**−£5.28 (1.85)**	**−£6.11 (1.53)**	**−£5.84 (1.59)**
Parking, toilets, picnic	**£6.95 (1.30)**	**£8.43 (1.84)**	**£10.03 (1.51)**	**£3.04 (1.55)**
Parking, toilets, picnic, café, shop	**−£5.87 (1.33)**	**−£5.46 (1.86)**	**−£8.58 (1.57)**	−£2.55 (1.58)
Parking, toilets, picnic, café, shop, play areas	**£4.37 (1.30)**	£2.31 (1.87)	**£4.65 (1.52)**	**£5.35 (1.53)**
Detailed information	−£0.11 (0.63)	**−£1.54 (0.89)**	−£0.99 (0.74)	£0.37 (0.75)
Enhanced surroundings	**£2.70 (0.64)**	**£3.37 (0.90)**	**£2.03 (0.74)**	**£2.47 (0.76)**

Notes:
Standard errors in parenthesis
Implicit prices shown in bold were significant in the models; non-bold implicit prices were not significant and therefore were considered as being unimportant to respondents' choices.

café, shop and play areas' (£5.35) and 'enhanced surroundings' (£2.47). 'Horse riding trails' and 'distance' are again significant but negatively valued.

In terms of the overall performance of the general visitor models, all of the LL ratio tests are significant. The psuedo-Rho^2 values are around 0.06, and the numbers of correct predictions are around 38 per cent.

POLICY IMPLICATIONS

This research has provided a wealth of information on the value of improvements to the forest recreation resource. Such information is likely to have implications for the development of forest policy in terms of the management of forests to maximise social benefits, and in particular provide evidence in support of some of the key objectives of the EU Forest Action Plan (Commission of the European Communities 2006). For example, this study provides evidence of the welfare benefits associated with recreational use of forests. Such benefits clearly illustrate the contribution that forests have in terms of enhancing people's quality of life; a key goal of the EU Forest Action Plan.

The results from this study also allow us to make specific recommendations for the future management of forests for specific recreation activities. For example, it is clear from the data that the more specialist forest users attain greater marginal value from the provision of activity-specific facilities than non-specialist users: mountain bikers had higher implicit price values than general cyclists and indeed general forest visitors (although numerically they are much less than more general visitors). This evidence suggests that policies aimed to increase benefits per visitor from forest recreation would be best to target the provision of specialist recreation facilities. The research also provides evidence on the benefits associated with four different recreational activities in forests. In terms of cycling, there is overwhelming support for further investments to create and enhance mountain bike centres, and in particular to provide additional 'hard core' facilities such as downhill courses (£23.34; €34.56) and optional obstacles such as jumps and drop-offs on existing trails (£13.14; €19.46). Furthermore, there is general support for the provision of bike wash facilities at forests where any form of cycling takes place (£4.27; €6.32). There is, however, little evidence in support of the provision of horse-specific facilities within forests. Information gathered in debriefing interviews identified that the main reason for this lack of demand stems from the relative difficulties associated with transporting horses to and from forests. Furthermore, evidence from other users groups indicate that any new riding facilities, if developed, should be developed away from areas used by the general public, who appear to be opposed to sharing the forest with horses. There is general support for increased investment in wildlife hides (£6.83; €10.11) and viewing centres (£5.65; €8.37) where appropriate. This detail of data on public preferences will help forest managers and planners to target investments in recreational facilities better in their forests. This in turn will help ensure that forests are economically viable and sustainable in the future, thus again helping to contribute to the

EU Forest Action Plan objective 'to enhance the sustainable use of forest products and services'.

Finally, it should be noted that the above data relate only to those improvements that generated the highest per-trip welfare gains. Recommendations for future investment should also take account of the number of potential users of these new facilities. This question was not fully addressed in this research. In addition, any future investment in facilities should also be assessed in terms of both the costs and benefits. This research provides information on the benefits, but information on the costs would be required in order to conclude whether investment would be recommended.

CONCLUSIONS

This research aimed to provide a unique insight into the value that different groups of forest users have for a range of enhancements to the forest recreation resource. Novel aspects of this research include the fact that this study is one of the first valuation studies to utilise an attribute-based valuation method to value the component attributes of forest recreation. Furthermore, we analyse this data according to different groups of forest users, thus providing significant detail on the heterogeneity of values for enhancements to forest recreation. Another novel aspect to this research is that we utilised a frequency-based choice task in the CE model. It is argued that this approach has advantages over the more traditional choice-based task for recreational use applications since (i) the choice task more closely reflects actual behaviour and (ii) it would appear that survey respondents take more considered account of the travel cost attribute in a frequency-based task than in a choice-based task. Finally, this research has produced a wealth of information on the relative values of a range of improvements to the forest recreation resource by different user groups. It is considered that this information will be invaluable to the future management of forests in terms of enabling forest managers to best target resources to different forests and forest users.

ACKNOWLEDGEMENTS

The authors acknowledge with gratitude the generous support of the Forestry Commission for this research. The views expressed in this chapter are those of the authors alone and not necessarily of any funding agency.

REFERENCES

Adamowicz, W., J. Louviere and M. Williams (1994), 'Combining Revealed and Stated Preference Methods for Valuing Environmental Amenities', *Journal of Environmental Economics and Management*, 26(3), 271–292.

Arrow, K., R. Solow, H. Schuman, R. Radner and P. Portney (1993), 'Report to the NOAA-Panel on Contingent Valuation. Report to the General Council of the United States National Oceanic and Atmospheric Administration', *U.S. Federal Register*, 58(10), 4601–4614.

Bateman, I.J., R.T. Carson, B. Day, W.M. Hanemann, N. Hanley, T. Hett, M. Jones-Lee, G. Loomes, S. Mourato, E. Özdemiroğlu, D. Pearce, R. Sugden and J. Swanson (2002), *Economic Valuation with Stated Preference Techniques: A Manual*, Cheltenham, UK and Northampton, MA, USA, Edward Elgar.

Bishop, K.D. (1992), 'Assessing the Benefits of Community Forests: An Evaluation of the Recreational User Benefits of Two Urban Fringe Woodlands', *Journal of Environmental Planning and Management*, 35(1), 63–76.

Clawson, M. (1959), *Methods of Measuring the Demand for and Value of Outdoor Recreation*, Washington D.C., Resources for the Future.

Commission of the European Communities (2006), *Communication from the Commission to the Council and the European Parliament on an EU Forest Action Plan*. Com(2006) 302 final.

Davis, R. (1963), 'Recreation Planning as an Economic Problem', *Natural Resources Journal*, 3(2), 239–249.

Forestry Commission (2002), *Wales Mountain Bike Survey 2002*, Edinburgh, Forestry Commission.

Forestry Commission (2004a), *Forest Visitor Surveys 2002*, Edinburgh, Forestry Commission.

Forestry Commission (2004b), *Forestry Statistics 2004*, Edinburgh, Forestry Commission.

Hanemann, W.M. (1994), 'Valuing the Environment through Contingent Valuation', *Journal of Economic Perspectives*, 4, 19–44.

Hanley, N. (1989), 'Valuing Rural Recreation Benefits: An Empirical Comparison of Two Approaches', *Journal of Agricultural Economics*, 40, 361–374.

Hanley, N. and R. Ruffell (1993), 'The Valuation of Forest Characteristics', Adamowicz, W.L., W. White and W.E. Phillips (eds) *Forestry and the Environment: Economic Perspectives*, Wallingford, CAB International, 171–197.

Hensher, D.A., J.M. Rose and W.H. Greene (2005), *Applied Choice Analysis: A Primer*, Cambridge, Cambridge University Press.

HM Treasury (2003), *The 'Green Book': Appraisal and Evaluation in Central Government*, London, HM Treasury.

Louviere, J.J. (1988), 'Conjoint Analysis Modeling of Stated Preferences: A Review of Theory, Methods, Recent Developments and External Validity', *Journal of Transport Economics and Policy*, 22(1), 93–119.

Louviere, J.J., D.A. Hensher and J.D. Swait (2000), *Stated Choice Methods: Analysis and Application*, Cambridge, Cambridge University Press.

Street, D.J., L. Burgess and J. Louviere (2005), 'Quick and Easy Choice Sets: Constructing Optimal and Nearly Optimal Stated Choice Experiments', *International Journal of Research in Marketing*, 22(4), 459–470.

TNS Travel and Tourism (2004), *Leisure Day Visits: Report of the 2002–3 GB Day Visits Survey*, Cheltenham, The Countryside Agency.

Willis, K.G. and J.F. Benson (1989), *Values of User Benefits of Forest Recreation: Some Further Site Surveys*, Edinburgh, Forestry Commission.
Willis, K.G., J.F. Benson and M.C. Whitby (1988), *Values of User Benefits of Forest Recreation and Wildlife*, Edinburgh, Forestry Commission.

11. Using a choice experiment to inform implementation of the European Union Water Framework Directive: the case of Cheimaditida Wetland in Greece

Ekin Birol, Katia Karousakis[1] and Phoebe Koundouri

INTRODUCTION

Water resources include surface water, groundwater, wetlands, inland waters, rivers, lakes, transitional waters, coastal waters and aquifers (Chave, 2001). Together these water resources are crucial to human health, the natural environment and the functioning of any economy in the world, since they are necessary inputs to agriculture, industry, domestic consumption and tourism (UNEP, 2000).

The quality and quantity of water resources have been deteriorating globally at alarming rates however. Though the situation is most severe in developing countries, two-thirds of which are expected to face water shortages by 2030 (FAO, 2003), the situation for water resources in Europe is also far from satisfactory. According to the European Commission's (EC) recent statistics, 20 per cent of all surface water in the European Union (EU) is seriously threatened by pollution. Sixty-five per cent of all Europe's drinking water is provided by groundwater resources, which are being exploited by 60 per cent of European cities. The area of irrigated land in Southern Europe has increased by 20 per cent since 1985, contributing to increasing water scarcity (EC, 2002). In the past century, Europe has lost 50 to 60 per cent of its wetlands, an integral part of water resources which generate an array of important economic functions and services including flood protection, water supply, improved water quality, commercial and recreational fishing and the mitigation of global climate change (Barbier *et al.*, 1997; Woodward and Wui, 2001; Brouwer *et al.*, 2003; Brander *et al.*, 2006). The EC reports that 50 per cent of all remaining European wetlands have 'endangered status' due to groundwater overexploitation (EC, 2002).

In response to the increasing pressures on the quality and quantity of European water resources, the EU established the Water Framework Directive in 2000 (WFD, 2000/60/EC). The WFD aims to tackle the water resource problems and to secure these resources for future generations by employing an integrated environmental management approach. This approach considers both water quality and quantity issues, as well as those related to all forms of water resources (Chave, 2001; EC, 2002). According to this Directive, member states are obliged to restore and upgrade the quality and quantity of their water resources to a 'good status', and to ensure their sustainable use by 2015. For surface waters, 'good status' is considered to be 'good ecological quality' and 'good chemical status', whereas for groundwaters, 'good status' implies 'good quantitative status' and 'good chemical status'. To ensure a 'good status' for European wetlands, the WFD calls for the protection, restoration and enhancement of the water needs of wetlands and stresses the EU's involvement in wetland protection and enhancement and its commitment to setting up strategic policies for these purposes. Further, the EU calls for active participation and consultation of all stakeholders in water management activities, including local communities and citizens groups (Chave, 2001; EC, 2002).

In relation to other EU countries, Greece is generously endowed with freshwater resources although these are unevenly distributed across the country. Some 85–90 per cent of freshwater resources are in the form of surface water and 10–15 per cent are groundwater (OECD, 2000). Like other EU countries, the quality and quantity of water resources have been deteriorating in Greece. Water demand has increased significantly over the past 30 years, with serious water imbalances due to temporal and regional variations in precipitation (Angelakis and Diamandopoulos, 1995). Intensive agricultural production and an ever-growing tourism sector are considered among the major sources of water resources deterioration. Some 35 per cent of the country is in danger of land damage through drought, largely because of wasteful irrigation, which constitutes about 87 per cent of total freshwater withdrawals (WWF, 2003). As a result of tourism, which accounts for over 18 per cent of Greece's GDP, more than thirty Greek islands are facing serious water supply problems (US Water News, 2006). Lake water quality degradation has been apparent for decades such that today, most Greek lakes (except deep ones) are eutrophic.

In addition, between 1920 and 1991, Greece lost 63 per cent of its wetlands (Barbier *et al.*, 1997). Most remaining inland wetlands are threatened, including some rare types. Coastal wetlands suffer particularly heavy pressure from human activities. The main factors causing wetland degradation are: construction of irrigation projects and diversion of watercourses, causing changes in water flow; overpumping, land clearing and illegal hunting, causing depletion of water resources and wildlife; agricultural run-off and municipal waste water, causing water pollution; and urban development and expansion of cultivated areas, causing loss of wetland area. Eutrophication occurs in coastal wetlands near big cities and in inland wetlands in areas with intensive farming (OECD, 2000).

As an EU member country, Greece is obliged to ensure sustainable integrated management of all of its water resources, according to the requirements of the WFD. The existing management of water resources is neither integrated nor adequate however (WWF, 2003), and there is an urgent need for development and implementation of an efficient institutional structure and economic instruments for the sustainable management of water resources in accordance with the WFD. In addition to the WFD, there are other EU regulations Greece must abide by, such as the EU Birds Directive (1979/409/EC) and the EU Habitats Directive (1992/43/EC), which aim to conserve several ecological functions that are provided by water resources, predominantly by wetlands.

The aim of this chapter is threefold. First, to demonstrate that the choice experiment method can be employed to capture the total economic values of water resources, such as wetlands, which generate both use and non-use values. To this end, the value of the economic benefits generated by sustainable management of the Cheimaditida Wetland in Greece is estimated using data from 407 respondents located in 10 cities and towns in Greece. The results reveal that the choice experiment method is suitable for valuation of the various use and non-use values generated by water resources, such as wetlands.[2] The second aim of this chapter is to provide policy makers with much-needed information for efficient, effective and sustainable management of this wetland, in accordance with the EU WFD, as well as the Habitats and Birds Directives. Consequently, the estimated total economic benefits generated by various alternative wetland management options are weighted against their corresponding costs. The results reveal the wetland management strategy that maximises social welfare, and these findings have implications for sustainable, efficient and effective management of similar wetlands in Greece and other EU countries.

The final aim of this chapter is to adapt the latent class model introduced in Chapter 7 of this volume, to the estimation of the economic value of wetlands. The aim of this exercise is to reveal that estimation of preference heterogeneity is important not only for private goods, that is, genetically modified food as investigated in Chapter 7, but also for pure or impure public goods, such as water resources. The results of the latent class model reveal that overall the Greek public derive positive and significant benefits

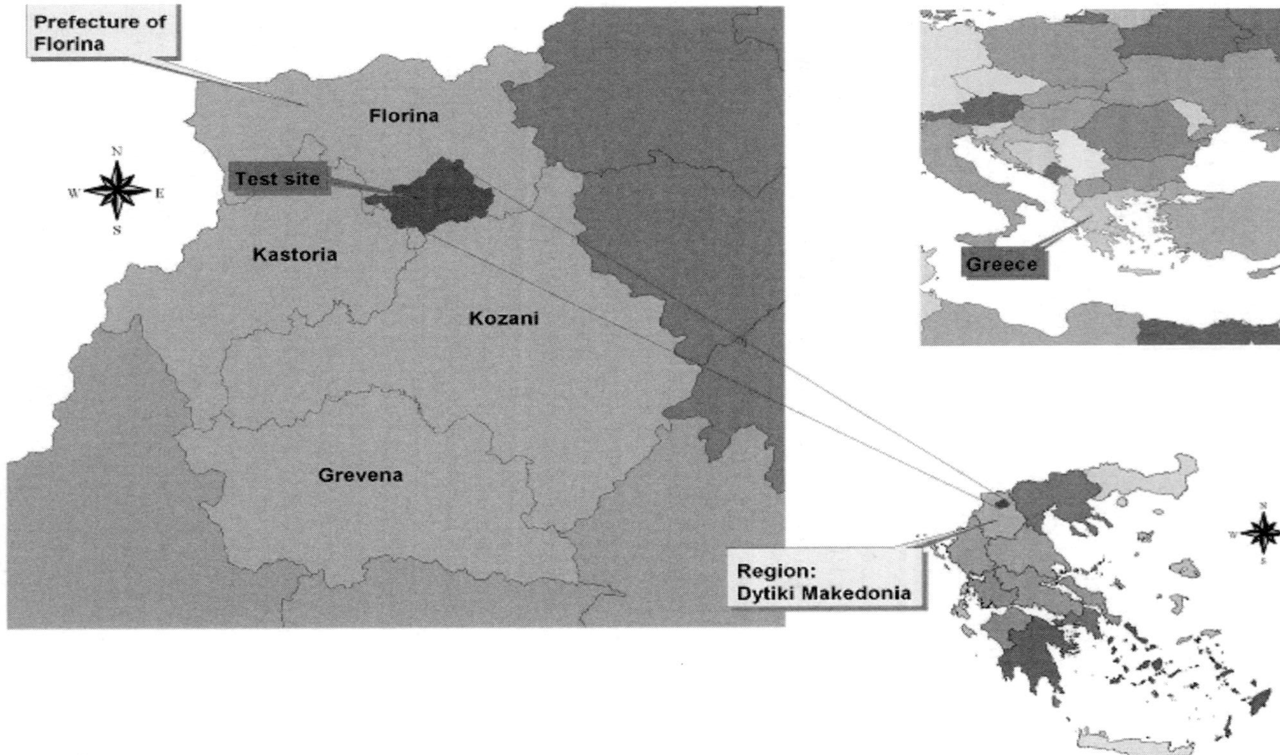

Figure 11.1 Location of Cheimaditida Wetland

from sustainable management of several ecological, social and economic functions of the wetland, including biodiversity, open water surface area, research and educational opportunities from the wetland, and locals retrained in environmentally friendly employment. There is, however, a considerable level of heterogeneity in the public's preferences for these functions, which should be taken into consideration when designing efficient, effective and equitable wetland management programmes, targeted at different segments of the population.

The chapter is organised as follows: The next section describes the Cheimaditida case study site, followed by a description of the choice experiment design and administration. The results of the econometric analysis are then reported; the final section concludes the chapter and draws out policy implications for implementation of the European Union's Water Framework Directive, as well as the Habitats and Birds Directives in Greece and in other EU countries.

THE CHEIMADITIDA WETLAND

The case study reported in this chapter is the Cheimaditida Wetland, located 40 km southeast of Florina in Northwest Greece (Figure 11.1). It includes Lake Cheimaditida, one of the few remaining freshwater lakes in Greece, and constitutes a total wetland area of 168 sq. km surrounded by extensive marshes with reeds (*Phragmites sp.*). The wetland is rich in flora, fauna and habitat diversity. It supports six habitat types listed under Annex I of the EU Habitats Directive, one of which is a priority natural habitat under Article 1, namely habitat type 7210 Calcareous fens with *Cladium mariscus* and *Carex davalliana*. Of the 150 relatively rare plant species in the wetland, 8 are Balkan endemic, 12 are only found in the Mediterranean region and 6 are listed under the Convention on International Trade in Endangered Species of Wild Fauna and Flora (CITES). The wetland also supports a wide array of fauna diversity, including 11 mammals, 7 amphibians, 7 reptiles and 8 fish, most of which are listed under Annexes II and IV of the EU Habitats Directive. Further, the Cheimaditida Wetland is recognised as an 'Important Bird Area' with approximately 140 identified bird species. Most of these are under protection, including the globally threatened species Dalmatian pelican (*Pelecanus crispus*), the ferruginous duck (*Aythya nyroca*) and the lesser kestrel (*Falco naumanni*) (M. Seferlis, personal communication, 2004).

Within the wetland, the main economic activities include agriculture, forestry and fishing. Agriculture is a vital activity where alfalfa and maize are the main cash crops whose production is water- and fertiliser-intensive.

Water opportunities from the lake for irrigation in agriculture, and pollution due to run-off from agricultural production, have adverse effects on water quantity and quality. These in turn affect the level of biodiversity that the wetland is able to support. Current local employment in agriculture supported by the wetland is estimated at 1470 persons. This is expected to fall, as the declining quality and quantity of water will no longer be able to support the current number of locals (M. Seferlis, personal communication, 2004; Psychoudakis *et al.*, 2005).

CHOICE EXPERIMENT DESIGN AND APPLICATION

Choice Experiment Design

The first step in choice experiment design is to define the good to be valued in terms of its attributes and their levels. The good to be valued in this choice experiment study is the wetland management scenario. Significant wetland management attributes pertaining to the Cheimaditida Wetland were identified in consultation with ecologists and hydrologists at the Greek Centre for Biotopes and Wetlands (EKBY) and agricultural and environmental economists at the Aristotle University of Thessaloniki. Three focus groups were then conducted with members of the Greek public to determine the final attributes and their levels that are important to them, as well as the vocabulary and language to be used in the survey.

The selected attributes and their levels are reported in Table 11.1. Economic benefits may be derived from social and economic factors in addition to the ecological factors (Portney, 1994). Several studies have included social and economic factors, such as number of farmers employed or living in the countryside, in choice experiment studies to capture the economic benefits enjoyed by the wider public from provision of such factors (for example, Morrison *et al.*, 1999; Bennett *et al.*, 2004; Othman *et al.*, 2004; Colombo *et al.*, 2005; Bergmann *et al.*, 2006; Birol and Cox, 2007). In the choice experiment presented here, two ecological and two social and economic attributes were selected to reflect the variety of economic benefits generated by the wetland. The former are biodiversity and open water surface area, and the latter are the inherent research and educational values that can be provided by the wetland, and the social values associated with re-training locals in environmentally friendly employment. Many species of animals, plants and their habitats depend on wetlands for their continued existence. To date the majority of the economic values associated with wetlands have been attributed to biodiversity (see, for example Brouwer *et al.*, 2003; Brander *et al.*, 2006). Open water surface areas and the natural vistas

Table 11.1 Wetland management attributes and levels used in the CE

Attribute	Definition	Management levels
Biodiversity	The number of different species of plants, animals, their population levels, the number of different habitats and their size.	Low: Deterioration from current levels High: A 10% increase in population and size of habitats
Open water surface area (OWSA)	The surface area of the lake that remains uncovered by reed beds.	Low: Decrease from the current open water surface area of 20% High: Increase open water surface area to 60%
Research and education	The educational, research and cultural information that may be derived from the existence of the wetland, including visits by scientists, students, and school children to learn about ecology and nature.	Low: Deterioration from the current levels of opportunities High: Improve the level of educational and research opportunities by providing better facilities
Retraining of farmers	Re-training of local farmers in environmentally friendly employment such as eco-tourism and arid-crop production.	Number of farmers re-trained in environmentally friendly employment: 30, 50, 75, 150
Payment	A one-off payment to go to the 'Cheimaditida Wetland Management Fund'.	Four payment levels from the pilot CV: €3, €10, €40, €80

associated with them are expected to create benefits through feelings of serenity and tranquillity. Further, higher open water surface areas provide the water quantity required for sustaining the wetland's biodiversity. Research and educational opportunities from the wetland are expected to contribute to social and economic values associated with cultural heritage and scientific knowledge. Finally, re-training locals in environmentally friendly employment is expected to generate social and economic values for the wider public.

The fifth attribute included in the choice experiment is a monetary one, which is required to estimate welfare changes. The levels of the monetary attribute used in the CE and the payment vehicle employed were determined through an open-ended pilot contingent valuation survey (Birol *et al.*, 2006b). The payment vehicle was a one-off increase in taxes for the year 2006–2007 to be channelled to a 'Cheimaditida Wetland Management

Fund', which would be managed by a trustworthy and independent body. Taxation was preferred over voluntary donations since respondents may have the incentive to free-ride with the latter (Whitehead, 2006), a point which was also brought up by the focus group participants, who did not reveal any major objections to the payment vehicle employed. The payment levels used are €3, €10, €40 and €80.

A large number of unique wetland management scenarios can be constructed from this number of attributes and levels.[3] Experimental design techniques (see Louviere *et al.*, 2000) and SPSS Conjoint software were used to obtain an orthogonal design, which consisted of only the main effects, and resulted in 32 pair-wise comparisons of alternative wetland management scenarios. These were randomly blocked to four different versions, each with eight choice sets. Each set contained two wetland management scenario profiles and an option to select neither scenario. Such an 'opt out' option can be considered as a status quo or baseline alternative, whose inclusion in the choice sets is instrumental in achieving welfare measures that are consistent with demand theory (Louviere *et al.*, 2000; Bennett and Blamey, 2001; Bateman *et al.*, 2003). The respondents were told that if they chose the 'opt-out' option, they would not be expected to pay, but there would not be any active wetland management, in which case the condition of the wetland would deteriorate to low levels for the biodiversity, open water surface area and research and education attributes (as defined in Table 11.1), and no locals would be re-trained in environmentally friendly employment. An example of a choice set is presented in Figure 11.1.

Choice Experiment Data Collection

The CE survey was administered in February and March of 2005 with face-to-face interviews. The survey design consisted of two stages. In the first stage, eight small towns (Amyntaio, Ptolemaida, Florina, Edessa, Kozani, Veroia, Naoussa, Chalkithona) and two cities (Athens and Thessaloniki) were selected. These locations were chosen to represent a continuum of distances from the Cheimaditida Wetland, as well as rural and urban populations. This design encompasses 60 per cent of the Greek adult population, with a sampling frame of 5 383 560. This stratified design enables testing of the hypotheses about the impacts of the respondents' social, economic and attitudinal characteristics and location on their valuation of the changes in conditions of the Cheimaditida Wetland.

In the second stage, randomly selected individuals were surveyed in each of the city and town centres. The choice experiment survey was administered to be representative of the Greek population in terms of gender and age, and only individuals aged 18 years or older were surveyed. During the

Which of the following wetland management scenarios do you favour? Option A and option B would entail a cost to your household. No payment would be required for 'Neither management scenario' option, but the conditions at the wetland would deteriorate to low levels for biodiversity, open water surface area and research and education attributes, and no locals would be retrained.

	Wetland management Scenario A	Wetland management Scenario B	Neither management scenario A nor management scenario B: I prefer NO wetland management
Biodiversity	Low	High	
Open water surface area	Low	Low	
Research and education	High	Low	
Re-training of locals	50	50	
One-off payment	€ 3	€ 10	
I would prefer: (Please tick as appropriate)	Choice A ☐	Choice B ☐	Neither ☐

Figure 11.2 Sample choice set

interviews a map of the wetland location and colour photographs were shown to each respondent. Enumerators described the Cheimaditida Wetland, its location, ecological importance and threats to its existence, and reminded the respondents of their budget constraints and of alternative wetlands and other environmental goods in Greece. Finally, the enumerators also explained that the attributes of the wetland management scenarios were selected as a result of prior research and were combined artificially, and each attribute was defined to ensure uniformity in understanding. A total sample of 700 respondents was envisaged, distributed between the 10 locations proportionately to their population levels. Across the 10 locations, overall 58 per cent of the sample approached agreed to take part in the survey, and a total of 407 respondents were interviewed.

In addition to the choice experiment questions, data on the respondents' social and economic characteristics and environmental attitudes were collected. This information is required to assess the representativeness of the sample of the Greek public, as well as to use these data as explanatory variables to investigate heterogeneity in preferences. The descriptive statistics of the sample reveal that the social and economic characteristics of the sample are similar to those of the Greek population with the exception of income, employment, the percentage of respondents with children, and education. The first is partly due to the fact that incomes in Athens and Thessaloniki are significantly higher than the Greek average. With respect to the percentage of respondents with children, the sample average is lower because a large proportion of the respondents were students, which also explains the high proportion of respondents with university degrees.

The attitudes of the respondents on environmental issues were elicited through a series of questions on their purchase of organic produce, environmental publications and fair-trade and environmentally friendly products, and recycling. These were measured on a scale ranging from zero (never) to four (always). Respondents were also asked whether they belonged to an environmental group. An environmental consciousness index (ECI), ranging from 0 to 20, was calculated using these scores and environmental group membership.

THEORETICAL FRAMEWORK

As mentioned in the other chapters of this volume, the choice experiment approach has a theoretical grounding in Lancaster's model of consumer choice (Lancaster, 1966), and an econometric basis in models of random utility (Luce, 1959; McFadden, 1974). Lancaster proposed that consumers derive satisfaction not from goods themselves but from the attributes they provide. The random utility approach is the theoretical basis for integrating behaviour with economic valuation in the choice experiment. In this approach, the utility of a choice is comprised of a deterministic component and an error component, which is independent of the deterministic part and follows a predetermined distribution. The error component implies that predictions cannot be made with certainty. Choices made among alternatives will be a function of the probability that the utility associated with a particular option is higher than that associated with other alternatives.

Earlier applications of the approach assumed homogeneous preferences across respondents, though preferences are in fact heterogeneous. Accounting for heterogeneity, however, enables unbiased estimates of individual preferences, enhancing the accuracy and reliability of estimates of demand, participation and marginal and total welfare (Greene, 1997). Furthermore, accounting for heterogeneity enables the prescription of policies that take equity concerns into account. Information on who will be affected by a policy change and the aggregate economic value associated with such changes is necessary for making efficient and equitable policies (Boxall and Adamowicz, 2002).

As explained in Chapter 7, the latent class model (LCM) is one of the most recent models to be employed to investigate preference heterogeneity. The LCM casts heterogeneity as a discrete distribution, a specification based on the concept of endogenous (or latent) preference segmentation (Wedel and Kamakura, 2000). The approach depicts a population that consists of a finite and identifiable number of segments, or groups of individuals. Preferences are relatively homogeneous within segments but differ substantially from one segment to another. The number of segments is determined endogenously by the data. Belonging to a specific segment is probabilistic, and depends on the social, economic and demographic characteristics of the respondents, as well as their perceptions and attitudes with regard to environmental goods and resources. Respondent characteristics affect choices indirectly through their impact on segment membership.

Formally, in the LCM employed here, the utility that the respondent i, who belongs to a particular segment s, derives from choosing wetland management scenario alternative $j \in C$ can be written as

$$U_{ij/s} = \beta_s X_{ij} + \varepsilon_{ij/s}, \tag{11.1}$$

where X_{ij} is a vector of attributes associated with wetland management scenario alternative j and respondent i, and β_s is a segment-specific vector of taste parameters. The differences in β_s vectors enable this approach to capture heterogeneity in preferences for the wetland management scenario attributes across segments. Assuming that the error terms are identically and independently distributed (iid) and follow a Type I (or Gumbel) distribution, the probabilistic response function is given by:

$$P_{ij/s} = \frac{\exp(\beta_s X_{ij})}{\sum_{h=1}^{C} \exp(\beta_s X_{ih})} \tag{11.2}$$

Consider a segment membership likelihood function M^* that classifies the respondent into one of the S finite number of latent segments with some probability P_{is}. The membership likelihood function for respondent i and segment s is given by $M^*_{is} = \lambda_s Z_i + \xi_{is}$, where Z represents the observed characteristics of the respondent, such as their social, economic and demographic characteristics, and their perceptions and attitudes. Assuming that the error terms in the respondent membership likelihood function are iid across respondent and segments, and follow a Gumbel distribution, the probability that respondent i belongs to segment s can be expressed as

$$P_{is} = \frac{\exp(\lambda_s Z_i)}{\sum_{k=1}^{S} (\lambda_k Z_i)}, \tag{11.3}$$

where $\lambda_k (k = 1,2, \ldots S)$ are the segment-specific parameters to be estimated. These denote the contribution of the various respondent characteristics to the probability of segment membership. A positive (negative) and significant λ implies that the associated respondent characteristic, Z_i, increases (decreases) the probability that the repondent i belongs to segment s. P_{is} sums to one across the S latent segments, where $0 \leq P_{is} \leq 1$.

In order to derive a mixed-logit model that simultaneously accounts for wetland management scenario choice and segment membership, (11.2) and (11.3) are brought together. The joint probability that respondent i belongs to segment s and chooses wetland management scenario alternative j is given by:

$$P_{ijs} = (P_{ij/s})*(P_{is}) = \left[\frac{\exp(\beta_s X_{ij})}{\sum_{h=1}^{C}\exp(\beta_s X_{ij})}\right]*\left[\frac{\exp(\lambda_s Z_i)}{\sum_{k=1}^{S}\exp(\lambda_k Z_i)}\right]. \quad (11.4)$$

RESULTS

As explained above, the LCM assumes that respondent characteristics affect choice indirectly through their impact on segment membership. After extensive testing with the respondent characteristics that were collected in the survey, the variables that affect segment membership the most were found to be the education level of the respondents, their environmental attitudes (that is, the ECI), income, distance to the wetland, whether they have children and if they visited the wetland in the past. The LCM was estimated using LIMDEP 8.0 NLOGIT 3.0, and models with two, three and four segments were run. The log likelihood, $\bar{\rho}^2$, Bozdogan Akaike Information Criterion (AIC3) and Bayesian Information Criterion (BIC) statistics for these LCMs are reported in Table 11.2.

Determination of the optimal numbers of segments requires a balanced assessment of the statistics reported in Table 11.2 (Louviere *et al.*, 2000; Wedel and Kamakura, 2000; Andrews and Currim, 2003). The log likelihood decreases and $\bar{\rho}^2$ increases as more segments are added, supporting the presence of multiple segments in the sample. The BIC and AIC3 statistics decreases monotonically as the number of segments increases but all four statistics flatten out from the two-segment model. Both AIC3 and BIC

Table 11.2 Criteria for determining the optimal number of segments

No. of Segments	Log likelihood	$\bar{\rho}^2$	Parameters (P)	AIC3	BIC
1	−3325.7	0.07	6	6669.4	3343.7
2	−2538.98	0.29	18	5131.96	2593.07
3	−2428.2	0.321	30	4946.4	2518.35
4	−2423.8	0.322	42	4973.6	2550.01

Note: AIC3 (Bozdogan AIC) is $(-2LL+3P)$; BIC(Bayesian Information Criterion) is $-LL+(P/2)*ln(N)$.

statistics are minimised at three segments, indicating a three-segment model as the optimal solution. It has, however, been demonstrated that the AIC3 and BIC criteria never under-fit the number of segments but sometimes over-fit, and over-fitting the true number of segments produces larger parameter bias than under-fitting (Andrews and Currim, 2003). Therefore the two-segment model provides the best fit to the data.

The results of the two-segment model are reported in Table 11.3. The first part of the table displays the utility coefficients from wetland management attributes and the second part reports segment membership coefficients. The segment membership coefficients for the second segment are normalised to zero in order to identify the remaining coefficients of the model. All other coefficients are interpreted relative to this normalised segment. For segment 1 the utility coefficients for all of the four wetland attributes are significant, indicating that respondents in this segment prefer wetland management which provides higher levels of each one of these attributes.

Table 11.3 Two-segment LCM estimates for wetland management attributes

	Segment 1	**Segment 2**
Utility function: Wetland management scenario attributes		
ASC	2.4*** (0.095)	−1.19*** (0.17)
Biodiversity	0.27*** (0.026)	0.08 (0.08)
OWSA	0.16*** (0.028)	0.29*** (0.085)
Research and education	0.14*** (0.027)	−0.08 (0.08)
Re-training	0.003*** (0.0007)	0.003** (0.0019)
Payment	−0.015*** (0.001)	−0.042*** (0.005)
Segment function: Respondents' social and economic characteristics		
Constant	−0.38 (0.37)	-
Education	0.44** (0.25)	-
ECI	0.06* (0.035)	-
Income	0.0002** (0.0001)	-
Child	0.25 (0.27)	-
Visit	0.005 (0.3)	-
Distance	0.004*** (0.001)	-
Log likelihood	2538.98	
ρ^2	0.29	
Sample size	3256	

Note: *** 1% significance level, ** 5% significance level, * 10% significance level with two-tailed tests

Source: Cheimaditida Wetland Management Choice Experiment Survey, 2005

The segment membership coefficients for this segment reveal that higher income, ECI, distance from the wetland and having a university degree increase the probability that the respondent belongs to the first segment, For the second segment, the biodiversity and research and education attributes are insignificant determinants of choice, whereas the other two attributes, that is, open water surface area (OWSA) and re-training of locals in environmentally friendly employment increase the likelihood that respondents in segment 2 choose a wetland management scenario with higher levels of these attributes.

The relative size of each segment is estimated by inserting the estimated coefficients into equation (11.3). This provides the series of probabilities that each respondent belongs to either one of the two segments. The respondents are assigned to one of the segments on the basis of their largest probability score. It is found that the majority of the sample, 57.24 per cent, belong to the first segment and 42.76 per cent belong to the second segment. The descriptive statistics for the social, economic and attitudinal characteristics of each segment are reported in Table 11.4.

As expected, respondents in segment 1, who derive significant and positive values from all four of the wetland management attributes, have statistically significantly higher levels of income, ECI, education and full-time employment. A higher proportion of respondents in segment 1 have children, and they also have a higher number of dependent children in the household, revealing 'bequest motives' (Krutilla, 1967) as found by previous wetland valuation studies (for example, Kosz, 1996). Finally, respondents in segment 1 live significantly closer to the wetland than those in segment 2, thereby revealing distance decay for valuation of this environmental resource, similar to the results of previous wetland valuation studies (for example, Bateman *et al.*, 1995).

Estimation of Willingness To Pay (WTP)

As explained in the previous chapters, the choice experiment method is consistent with utility maximisation and demand theory (Bateman *et al.*, 2003), so when the parameter estimates are obtained by the use of the appropriate model, welfare measures can be estimated using the following formula:

$$WTP = \frac{\ln \sum_k \exp(V_k^1) - \ln \sum_k \exp(V_k^0)}{\beta_{monetaryattribute}} \tag{11.5}$$

where WTP is the welfare measure, $\beta_{monetaryattribute}$ is the marginal utility of income represented by the coefficient of the monetary attribute in the CE,

Table 11.4 Profiles of respondents belonging to the two segments in LCM

Social and economic characteristics	**Segment 1 N=233**	**Segment 2 N=174**
Heard of the wetland	30.6%	31.2%
Visited the wetland**	13.7%	21.2%
ECI***	7 (3.5)	4.3 (3.2)
Gender***	61.5%	43.3%
Age	38.9 (13.4)	40.2 (15.3)
Household size***	3.6 (1)	2.9 (1.3)
Children***	67.6%	45%
Number of dependents***	1.2 (0.9)	0.6 (0.9)
Education***	88%	32.9%
Employment***	66.4%	57%
Tenure	80%	80.3%
Income***	2701.5 (1319.5)	1470.7 (735.2)
Distance **	193.1 (165.8)	241.2 (225.3)
Urban*	51.8%	46.3%

Note: T-tests and Pearson Chi square tests show significant differences (*) at 10% significance level; (**) at 5% significance level, and (***) at 1% significance level.

Source: Cheimaditida Wetland Management Choice Experiment Survey, 2005

and V_k^0 and V_k^1 represent indirect utility functions before and after the change in wetland management. For the linear utility index, the marginal value of change in a single binary wetland management attribute can be represented as a ratio of coefficients, reducing equation (11.5) to:

$$WTP = -2\left(\frac{\beta_{wetlandattribute}}{\beta_{monetaryattribute}}\right) \tag{11.6}$$

(see, Hu *et al.*, 2004) This part-worth (or implicit price) formula represents the marginal rate of substitution between income and the binary attribute in question, that is, the marginal WTP for a change in the attribute. As explained in Chapters 4 and 5, compensating surplus welfare measures can be obtained for different wetland management scenarios associated with multiple changes in attributes, that is, equation (11.5) simplifies to:

$$Compensating\ surplus = -(V^0 - V^1)/\beta_{monetaryattribute} \tag{11.7}$$

Table 11.5 reports the implicit prices, or marginal WTP values, for each of the wetland management attributes estimated using the Wald procedure (Delta method) in LIMDEP 8.0 NLOGIT 3.0.

Table 11.5 Marginal WTP for wetland management attributes (€ / respondent and 95% C.I.)

Attribute	Segment 1	Segment 2	Weighted
Biodiversity***	17.8 (16.10–19.5)	-	7.7 (6.96–8.44)
OWSA***	10.01 (8.25–11.88)	7.25 (5.13–9.38)	8.45 (6.48–10.46)
Research & education***	9.1 (7.34–10.84)	-	3.93 (3.17–6.15)
Re-training (per person)***	0.195 (0.149–0.24)	0.075 (0.03–0.12)	0.127 (0.066–0.172)

Note: T-tests show significant differences among at least one pair of models (*) at 10% significance level; (**) at 5% significance level and (***) at 1% significance level.

Source: Cheimaditida Wetland Management Choice Experiment Survey, 2005.

The implicit prices reported in Table 11.5 do not provide estimates of compensating surplus (CS) for the alternative management scenarios. In order to estimate the respondents' CS for improvements in wetland management over the status quo, three possible options were created.

- **Current scenario – status quo:** Biodiversity is managed at a low level; open water surface area is low; research and educational opportunities are low; and no local farmers are re-trained.
- **Scenario 1 – Low impact management scenario:** Biodiversity is managed at a low level; open water surface area is increased to a high level; research and educational opportunities are low; and 30 local farmers are re-trained.
- **Scenario 2 – Medium impact management scenario:** Biodiversity is managed at a high level; open water surface area is low; research and educational opportunities are high; and 75 local farmers are re-trained.
- **Scenario 3 – High impact management scenario:** Biodiversity is managed at a high level; open water surface area is high; research and educational opportunities are high; and 150 local farmers are re-trained.

To obtain the CS associated with each of the above scenarios, the differences between the welfare measures under the status quo and the three management scenarios are calculated. Note that in order to estimate overall WTP for wetland management, it is necessary to include the ASC, which captures the systematic but unobserved information about respondents' choices.

Table 11.6 Compensating surplus for each scenario (€ / respondent)

Scenario	Segment 1	Segment 2	Weighted
1 - Low impact	170	57.75	107.59
2 - Medium impact	195.67	53.88	116.49
3 - High impact	220.3	66.75	134.46

Source: Cheimaditida Wetland Management Choice Experiment Survey, 2005.

The estimates of WTP for the three scenarios are reported in Table 11.6. For comparisons, CS estimates are calculated for all four models. As expected, the CS for the change from the status quo to the scenarios considered increases as we move towards improved ecological, social and economic conditions in the wetland. The mean WTP for the Low impact scenario is €107.59, whereas greater improvements in ecological, social and economic conditions in the wetland under the Medium impact scenario increase the mean WTP to €116.49, and under the High impact scenario to as high as €134.46.

Cost-Benefit Analysis

The results can be used to design socially efficient wetland management policies by estimating the cost of improving the different attributes of the wetland and by comparing these to the benefits they generate (Carlsson *et al.*, 2003). The cost estimates for improvements in the different attributes are reported in Table 11.7. The total cost of providing the Low impact scenario is €500 872 per annum; the total cost of providing the Medium impact scenario is €6 314 179 per annum; and the total cost of providing the High impact scenario is €7 021 358 per annum.[4]

Further, the welfare estimates reported in Table 11.6 for the weighted LCM are aggregated over the entire sampling frame to determine the total WTP (that is, total benefits) for the three scenarios described above. Based on the fraction of the sample agreeing to take part in the survey (58 per cent), the aggregate WTP to achieve the ecological and social conditions described in the Low impact scenario is €335 852 335; in the Medium impact scenario the aggregate WTP is €363 735 948; and for the High impact scenario, this amounts to €419 846 644. The aggregate benefits are therefore significantly higher than the total costs of each scenario. More specifically, the aggregate net benefits from the Low impact scenario is €335 351 463; €357 421 769 for the Medium impact scenario and €412 825 286 for the High impact scenario. Thus, the total net economic

Table 11.7 Cost estimates for improvement in wetland management

Management intervention	Cost in € (2005)[a]
Biodiversity:	
1. Improve water quantity by switching to water-saving irrigation technologies and construction of a dyke	4 000 000
2. Improve water quality with construction of waste water treatment plant	1 000 000
3. Protection, conservation and restoration of Priority Natural Habitats (92/43/EEC)	25 000
Increase OWSA:	
Open and maintain corridors in the reed bed	200 000
Research and education opportunities:	
1. Construction of a visitor centre	600 000
2. Monthly two-day researcher's bench (collect data/ samples, sort and browse)	84 000 /annum
Retraining farmers:	
1. Two seminars of 100 hrs for beginners, theory and practice	98 000
2. Cost (i.e., farmers' and profit and loss) of switching to non-irrigated crops[b]	1591.2 /ha/annum

Notes:
[a] These are one-time costs, unless otherwise indicated
[b] This is the difference between gross margin for non-irrigated crops (76.63 €/ha/annum), and gross margin for irrigated crops (1667.78 €/ha/annum).

Source: Miltos Seferlis, personal communication (EKBY, 2005)

benefits of wetland management increase with the impact of the management scenario. However, it should be noted that the benefit estimates are likely to be upwards biased due to the hypothetical nature of the payment commitment (that is, hypothetical bias). Therefore the net benefits generated by the alternative management scenarios should be considered as upper bound values.

POLICY IMPLICATIONS AND CONCLUSIONS

This chapter contributes to the limited literature on estimation of economic values of water resources, more specifically wetlands, using choice experiments to inform policies on efficient and effective management of water resources. As explained in the literature review presented in Chapter 2, the study presented in this chapter is one of the growing number of choice experiments carried out in the EU to value water resources, and currently the only wetland valuation choice experiment carried out in Greece. This chapter has demonstrated that the choice experiment method can be successfully employed to inform management of water resources, which have both public and private good values.

More specifically, the results indicate that there are positive and significant economic benefits associated with the ecological, economic and social attributes of the case study wetland in this chapter, that is, the Cheimaditida Wetland located in Greece. The impacts of social, economic and attitudinal characteristics of respondents on their valuation of wetland management attributes are significant and conform with economic theory. The application of the latent class model, which is generally employed to estimate preference heterogeneity for valuation of private goods, as presented in Chapter 7, revealed that there is considerable preference heterogeneity within the public for management of this water resource, which is a public good. This heterogeneity should be taken into consideration to ensure social equity, as well as the stakeholder participation and consultation requirements of the European Union's Water Framework Directive (WFD).

The total benefits derived from various wetland management scenarios are aggregated over the sampling frame, and compared to their costs. The net benefit estimates reveal that social welfare maximisation is achieved under the High impact scenario of wetland management, which provides higher levels of ecological, social and economic attributes. With the use of the benefits transfer method or the value inference method presented in Chapter 9 of this volume, this study can provide policy makers with useful information for management of other similar wetlands in Greece, as well as in Europe, given the current mandate under the EU's WFD, as well as the Habitats and Birds Directives.

ACKNOWLEDGEMENTS

We gratefully acknowledge the European Union's financial support through the Integrated Project to Evaluate the Impacts of Global Change on European Freshwater Ecosystems (Eurolimpacs), under the 6th Framework Programme. We would like to thank Darla Hatton-Macdonald, Andreas Kontoleon, David Maddison, Mark Morrison, Dimitris Papademas, Assimakis Psychoudakis, Athanasios Ragkos, Eric Ruto, Eric Van Dusen and Stuart Whitten for valuable comments, suggestions and fruitful discussions. We would also like to thank Argiro Christophi and Alexandros Theodoridis for their assistance in data collection. Finally, we are grateful to Miltiadis Seferlis for his assistance with the selection of the attributes and the cost estimates. All remaining errors are our own.

Some of the material in this chapter is reprinted from *Ecological Economics* – Birol *et al.* (2006a) – with permission from Elsevier.

NOTES

1. Katia Karousakis, Environment Directorate, Organisation for Economic Co-operation and Development. The views stated in the chapter do not necessarily represent the views of the OECD or its member countries.
2. For a detailed account of this choice experiment study, see Birol et al. (2006a).
3. The number of wetland management scenarios that can be generated from 5 attributes, 2 with 4 levels and the remaining 3 with 2 levels, is $4^2 * 2^3 = 128$.
4. To estimate the annual profit or loss per farmer, the following data was used: Total area of cultivated land, (*L*): 6250 ha; Total number of farmers, (*F*): 1470; Average land per farmer (*L*/*F*): 4.25 ha. Therefore, average annual profit or loss per farmer is 6762.39 (4.25 × 1591.15). Thus for example, the total cost of the high impact scenario is calculated as: [Biodiversity high (4 000 000 + 1 000 000 + 25 000) + OWSA high (200 000) + Research and Education Opportunities high (600 000 + 84 000) + Re-training 150 farmers (98 000 + (6762.39 × 150))] = €7 021 358 for the first year.

REFERENCES

Andrews, R.L., Currim, I.S. (2003), 'A Comparison of Segment Retention Criteria for Finite Mixture Logit Models', *Journal of Marketing Research*, 40(2): 235–243.

Angelakis, A., Diamandopoulos, E. (1995), 'Water Resources Management in Greece: Current Status and Prospective Outlook', *Water Science and Technology*, 32(9): 262–272.

Barbier, E.B., Acreman, M., Knowler, D. (1997), *Economic Valuation of Wetlands: A Guide for Policy Makers and Planners*, Ramsar Convention Bureau, Gland, Switzerland.

Bateman, I.J., Langford, I.H., Graham, A. (1995), *A Survey of Non-users' Willingness to Pay to Prevent Saline Flooding in the Norfolk Broads*, CSERGE Working Paper GEC 95-11. Centre for Social and Economic Research on the Global Environment, School of Environmental Sciences, University of East Anglia, Norwich, UK.

Bateman, I.J., Carson, R.T., Day, B., Hanemann, W.M., Hanley, N., Hett, T., Jones-Lee, M., Loomes, G., Mourato, S., Özdemiroğlu, E., Pearce, D.W., Sugden, R., Swanson, S. (2003), *Guidelines for the Use of Stated Preference Techniques for the Valuation of Preferences for Non-market Goods*, Edward Elgar, Cheltenham, UK and Northampton, MA, USA.

Bennett, J.J., Blamey, R.K. (2001), *The Choice of Modelling Approach to Environmental Valuation*. Edward Elgar, Cheltenham, UK and Northampton, MA, USA.

Bennett, J.J., Van Bueren, M., Whitten, S.M. (2004), 'Estimating Society's Willingness to Pay to Maintain Viable Rural Communities', *Australian Journal of Agricultural and Resource Economics*, 48(3): 487–512.

Bergmann, A., Hanley, N., Wright, R. (2006), 'Valuing the Attributes of Renewable Energy Investments', *Energy Policy*, 34(9): 1004–1014.

Birol, E., Cox, V. (2007), 'Using Choice Experiments to Design Wetland Management Programmes: The Case of Severn Estuary Wetland, UK', *Journal of Environmental Planning and Management*, 50(3): 363–380.

Birol, E., Karousakis, K., Koundouri, P. (2006a), 'Using a Choice Experiment to Account for Preference Heterogeneity in Wetland Attributes: The Case of Cheimaditida Wetland in Greece'. *Ecological Economics*, 60(1): 145–156.

Birol, E., Karousakis, K., Koundouri, P. (2006b), *Using Economic Methods to Inform Water Resource Management Policies: A Survey and Critical Appraisal of Available Methods and an application*, Science of the Total Environment, www.ayuquila.com/documentos/comparacion/metodos/devaloracion.pdf, accessed 27 September 2007.

Boxall, P.C., Adamowicz, W.L. (2002), 'Understanding Heterogeneous Preferences in Random Utility Models: A Latent Class Approach', *Environmental and Resource Economics*, 23: 421–446.

Brander, L.M., Florax, R.J.G.M., Vermaat, J.E. (2006), 'The Empirics of Wetland Valuation: A Comprehensive Summary and a Meta-Analysis of the Literature', *Environmental and Resource Economics*, 33(2): 223–250.

Brouwer, R., Langford, I., Bateman, I., Turner, R.K. (2003), 'A Meta-analysis of Wetland Ecosystem Valuation Studies', Chapter 5 in Turner, R.K., Jeroen, C., van den Bergh, J.M., Brouwer, R. (eds), *Managing Wetlands: An Ecological Economics Approach*. Edward Elgar, Cheltenham, UK and Northampton, MA, USA.

Carlsson, F., Frykblom, P., Liljenstolpe, C. (2003), 'Valuing Wetland Attributes: An Application of Choice Experiments', *Ecological Economics*, 47: 95–103.

Chave P. (2001), *The EU Water Framework Directive: An Introduction*, IWA Publishing, London.

Colombo, S., Hanley, N., Calatrava-Requena, J. (2005), 'Designing Policy for Reducing the Off-farm Effects of Soil Erosion using Choice Experiments', *Journal of Agricultural Economics*, 56(1): 81–95.

European Communities (2002), The *Water Framework Directive*, www.ec.europa.eu/environment/water/water-framework/pdf/waterislik_en.pdf.

FAO (2003), 'More Crop Per Drop', www.fao.org/english/newsroom/focus/2003/water.htm.

Greene, W.H. (1997), *Econometric Analysis*, Third Edition, Prentice Hall, New York.

Hu, W., Hunnemeyer, A., Veeman, M., Adamowicz, W., Srivastava, L. (2004), 'Trading Off Health, Environmental and Genetic Modification Attributes in Food', *European Review of Agricultural Economics*, 31: 389–408.

Kosz, M. (1996), 'Valuing Riverside Wetlands: The Case of the "Donau-Auen" National Park', *Ecological Economics*, 16: 109–127.

Krutilla, J.V. (1967), 'Conservation Reconsidered', *American Economic Review*, 57(4): 777–786.

Lancaster, K. (1966), 'A New Approach to Consumer Theory', *Journal of Political Economics*, 74: 217–231.

Louviere, J.J., Hensher, D.A., Swalt, J.D. and Adamowicz, W.L. (2000), *Stated Choice Methods: Analysis and Applications*, Cambridge, Cambridge University Press.

Luce, D. (1959), *Individual Choice Behaviour*, John Wiley, New York, NY.

McFadden, D. (1974), 'Conditional Logit Analysis of Qualitative Choice Behavior', in: Zarembka, P. (ed.) *Frontiers in Econometrics*, Academic Press, New York.

Morrison, M., Bennett, J., Blamey, R. (1999), 'Valuing Improved Wetlands Quality using Choice Modeling', *Water and Resource Research*, 35: 2805–2814.

OECD (2000), *Environmental Performance Reviews: Greece*, OECD, Paris.

Othman, J., Bennett, J., Blamey, R. (2004), 'Environmental Values and Resource Management Options: A Choice Modelling Experience in Malaysia', *Environment and Development Economics*, 9: 803–824.

Portney, P.R. (1994), 'The Contingent Valuation Debate: Why Economists Should Care', *Journal of Economic Perspectives*, 8: 3–17.

Psychoudakis, A., Ragkos, A., Seferlis, M. (2005), 'An Assessment of Wetland Management Scenarios: The Case of Zazari–Cheimaditida (Greece)', *Water Science and Technology: Water Supply Journal*, 5(6): 115–123.

United Nations Environment Program (UNEP) (2000), *Global Environmental Outlook*, Earthscan Publications, London.

US Water News (2006). www.uswaternews.com/archives/arcglobal/6towfarmiz.html.

Wedel, M., Kamakura, W. (2000), *Market Segmentation: Conceptual and Methodological Foundations*. Kluwer, Boston, MA.

Whitehead, J.C. (2006), 'A Practitioner's Primer on Contingent Valuation', in Alberini, A., Kahn, J. (eds), *Contingent Valuation Handbook*, Edward Elgar, Cheltenham, UK and Northampton, MA, USA.

Woodward, R.T., Wui, Y.S. (2001), 'The Economic Value of Wetland Services: A Meta-analysis', *Ecological Economics*, 37: 257–270.

WWF (2003), WWF's Water and Wetland Index: Critical Issues in Water Policy Across Europe, November. WWF Report. World Wide Fund for Nature, Madrid, Spain. WWF 2006. Drought in the Mediterranean: WWF Policy Proposals. July. WWF Report. World Wide Fund for Nature, Madrid, Spain.

12. Using the choice experiment method to inform river management in Poland: flood risk reduction versus habitat conservation in the Upper Silesia Region

Ekin Birol, Phoebe Koundouri and Yiannis Kountouris

INTRODUCTION

The Upper Silesia Region of Poland is susceptible to flooding as a result of centuries long mining activities in this area, which have significantly changed its landscape. The social, economic and environmental costs of imminent flooding in this region are expected to be very high. The economic costs of the floods of 1997 and 2001, for example, are estimated to be in the region of one billion USD (Brakenridge *et al.*, 1997; 2001). As a result of global climate change, the frequency and extent of floods and their corresponding economic costs are expected to increase in the near future, not just in Poland but also in the other EU countries (Nicholls *et al.*, 1999). Consequently, the EU has become more involved in flood risk reduction, aiming to direct funds to projects and policies to alleviate flooding risk in several flood prone areas of member countries, including the Upper Silesia Region of Poland, the case study in this chapter.

Land deformation caused by the mining industry and the subsequent floods has had another consequence. Unique ecological habitats have been formed in the flooded areas, harbouring important biodiversity riches, which should be conserved, according to the ecologists. In addition to the various economic values that these biodiversity-rich areas generate (see for example, Pearce and Moran, 1994; Bennett, 2003), they are also of high recreational value to the locals, and they have the potential to become an attractive tourism location in Poland. These habitats are, however, threatened by the current policies, which do not prohibit the mining industry from discharging its debris in the rivers, creating spoil heaps. According to the ecologists, if the current situation prevails, levels of biodiversity in this region, including the number of different species of plants and animals and their population levels, as well as the number of different habitats and their sizes, will drop significantly. As explained in the previous chapter, the EU is committed to conserving the ecological status, and especially biodiversity riches, in the wetlands and catchments, as stated in various EU regulations and directives. These include the Water Framework Directive (WFD, 2000/60/EC), Article 1(a) of which in particular calls for the prevention of further deterioration of European wetlands, their protection and the enhancement of their status, the EU Birds Directive (1979/409/EC) and the EU Habitats Directive (1992/43/EC).

A number of non-market valuation techniques have been employed to estimate the value of flood risk reduction in Europe. Brouwer and van Ek (2004) employed the integrated impact assessment method to estimate the benefits of flood risk reduction in the Netherlands. Ragkos *et al.* (2006) carried out a contingent valuation study to estimate the value of flood control in the Zazari-Cheimaditida Wetland in Greece. To our knowledge, no study has so far employed the choice experiment method to estimate the benefits of flood risk reduction. Various choice experiment studies implemented in Europe, however, have investigated the value of conserving biodiversity or one of its components (for example, a certain species) or conserving biodiversity as a part of a wider ecosystem (for example, wetland or forests) (see Carlsson *et al.*, 2003; Horne and Petäjistö, 2003; Birol *et al.*, 2006a; 2006b; Christie *et al.*, 2006; Birol and Cox, 2007). These studies are discussed in further detail in Chapter 2 of this volume. In addition, the choice experiment method has been applied to estimate recreational demand in Europe. Hanley *et al.* (2002), employ a choice experiment to model the demand for a recreational activity, rock climbing, in Scotland, and Horne *et al.* (2005) employ this method to inform forest management at recreational sites in Finland.

The study presented in this chapter is not only one of the first applications of the choice experiment method to value benefits from reduction in flood risk in Europe, but also aims to estimate the value of biodiversity, in addition to the local households' demand for recreational activities in this area. To this end, choice experiment and socio-economic data, as well as data on households' past recreational activities in the area and flood damage suffered in the past ten years, are collected from 192 households in the region. The results reveal that all households derive the highest benefits from reduction of flood risk to a low level, followed by recreational activities and biodiversity conservation in the area. These results have important repercussions for the design of efficient and effective river management projects and policies.

The rest of the chapter unfolds as follows: in the next section the case study area is described. The following section briefly presents the theoretical underpinnings of the choice experiment method and the econometric models employed in this chapter. The next sections describe the survey instrument, followed by the results of the choice experiment study and the value estimates derived. The final section concludes the chapter with policy implications for flood risk reduction, biodiversity conservation and recreation in the Upper Silesia Region of Poland, with implications for other EU countries.

THE CASE STUDY AREA

The choice experiment study reported in this chapter is implemented in the city of Sosnowiec, located in the Bobrek catchment, in the Upper Silesia Region of Poland. The region is an important industrial centre located within the Upper Silesian Coal Basin. Five rivers run through the wider area, the Biala, Brynica, Jaworznik, Wielonka and Rawa, making the region susceptible to flooding episodes (Figures 12.1 and 12.2).

The main economic activities in the area include heavy industry and mining, with some of the world's largest bituminous coal mines located in the region. The mines are concentrated close to the rivers, constantly changing and eroding riverbanks and their morphology. Mining activities have been taking place in this area for over two centuries. Scientific evidence from the Central Mining Institute, Silesian University, AGH University of Science and Technology, and Krakow University of Technology claim that the mining industry has significantly deformed the local landscape and the riverbed, thereby rendering the region extremely vulnerable to floods even after light rainfalls. Given the size of the local communities, it is estimated that approximately 50 000 individuals may suffer the effects of a flooding episode.

In 1992, the Polish government facilitated the construction of concrete barriers on the riverbanks in order to minimise the risk of flooding in the region. The mining industries were deemed responsible for protecting their mines by constructing spoil heaps on the riverbanks. This strategy, however, was not successful since it increased the speed of flowing water, thereby generating negative externalities for downstream communities. Moreover, recreational activities in the catchment became limited as a result of blocking the river access with concrete barriers. Furthermore this policy was not successful in providing flood control as the extensive floods of 1997 and 2001 can attest.

Source: Map of Hydrographic Division of Poland, Institute of Meteorology and Water Management (ImiGW), www.imgw.p 1/w1/internet/zz/zz_xpages/hydrografia/zasoby_ wodne.html.

Figure 12.1 Location of the study site in Poland

The high economic and social costs of flooding episodes are borne mainly by the local residents, but also by the overall national economy, as well as by the nearby countries. Despite these costs, floods have also brought about some benefits: unique ecological wetland habitats have been formed on those lands that have been flooded by the rivers. New species of both animals and plants live in these habitats. Ecologists from the Silesian University recognise these biodiversity riches and assert that they should be conserved. In addition, these habitats created by the rivers overflowing are now of high recreational value, with the potential to serve as an attractive tourism location. The continued existence of these habitats is currently under threat from pollution caused by the spoil heaps created by the mining industry.

THE CHOICE EXPERIMENT METHOD

As explained in the other chapters of this book, the choice experiment method has its theoretical grounding in Lancaster's model of consumer choice (Lancaster, 1966), and its econometric basis in random utility theory

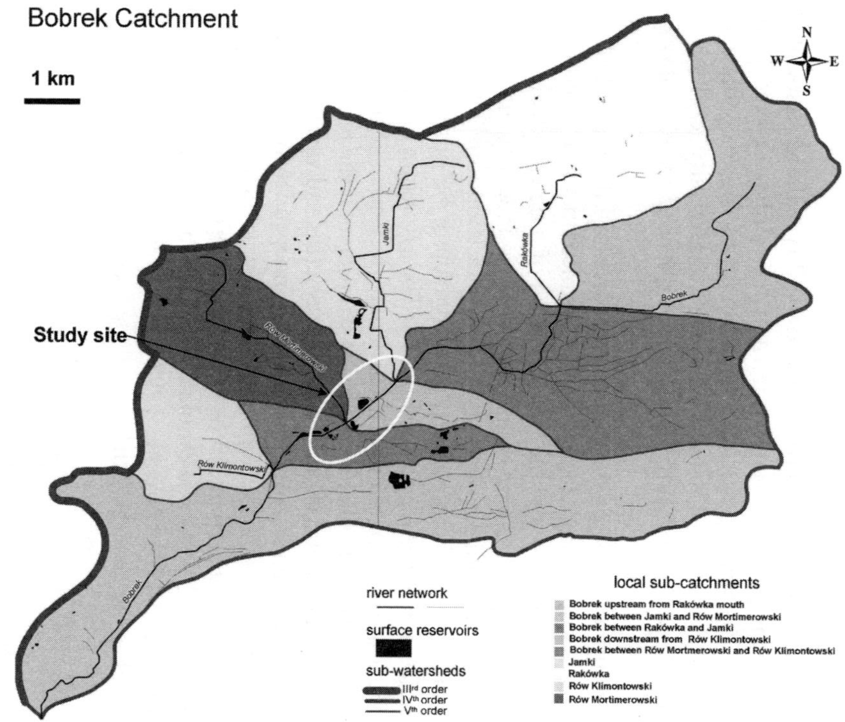

Source: Krakow University of Technology (Elzbieta Druzynska, personal communication, 2007): Map of Hydrographic Division of Poland, Institute of Meteorology and Water Management (ImiGW), www.imgw.p 1/w1/internet/zz/zz_xpages/hydrografia/zasoby_wodne.html.

Figure 12.2 Map of the Bobrek catchment

(Luce, 1959; McFadden, 1974). To illustrate the basic model behind the choice experiment presented here, consider a household's choice for a river management strategy and assume that utility depends on choices made from a set C, that is, a choice set which includes all the possible river management strategy alternatives. The household is assumed to have a utility function of the form:

$$U_{ij} = V(Z_{ij}) + e(Z_{ij}) \tag{12.1}$$

where for any household i, a given level of utility will be associated with any river management strategy alternative j. Utility derived from any of these alternatives depends on the attributes of the river management strategy (Z_j), such as the flood risk level, biodiversity level in the habitats and the level of difficulty of access to the river for recreational purposes.

The random utility theory is the theoretical basis for integrating behaviour with economic valuation in the choice experiment method. According to this theory, the utility of a choice is comprised of a deterministic component (V) and an error component (e), which is independent of the deterministic part and follows a predetermined distribution. This error component implies that the household's utility cannot be observed with certainty. Choices made between alternatives will be a function of the probability that the utility associated with a particular river management strategy j is higher than that of other strategies. Assuming that the relationship between utility and attributes is linear in the parameters and variables function, and that the error terms are identically and independently distributed with a Weibull distribution, the probability of any particular river management strategy j being chosen can be expressed in terms of a logistic distribution. Equation (12.1) can be estimated with a conditional logit model (CLM) (McFadden, 1974; Greene, 1997 pp. 913–914; Maddala, 1999, p. 42), which takes the general form:

$$P_{ij} = \frac{\exp(V(Z_{ij}))}{\sum_{h=1}^{C} \exp(V(Z_{ih}))} \tag{12.2}$$

where the conditional indirect utility function generally estimated is:

$$V_{ij} = \alpha + \beta_1 Z_1 + \beta_2 Z_2 + \ldots + \beta_n Z_n \tag{12.3}$$

where α is the alternative specific constant (ASC), which captures the systematic but unobserved information about households' choices, n is the number of river management strategy attributes considered, and the vectors of coefficients β_1 to β_n are attached to the vector of attributes (Z).

The assumptions about the distribution of error terms implicit in the use of the CLM impose a particular condition known as the independence of irrelevant alternatives (IIA) property, which states that the relative probabilities of two options being chosen are unaffected by the introduction or removal of other alternatives. If the IIA property is violated, the CLM results will be biased and hence a discrete choice model that does not require the IIA property, such as the random parameter logit model (RPLM), should be used. Another limitation of the CLM is that it assumes homogeneous preferences across households. Preferences are in fact heterogeneous however, as explained in other chapters of this book. Accounting for heterogeneity enables unbiased estimates of preferences, enhancing the accuracy and reliability of welfare estimates and enabling the prescription of policies that take equity concerns into account (Greene, 1997). As also discussed in other chapters, information on who will be affected by a policy change and the aggregate economic value associated with such changes is necessary for making efficient and equitable policies (Boxall and Adamowicz, 2002).

The RPLM can account for unobserved, unconditional heterogeneity in preferences across households. Formally:

$$U_{ij} = V(Z_j(\beta + \eta_i)) + e(Z_j). \qquad (12.4)$$

Similarly to the CLM, utility is decomposed into a deterministic component (V) and an error component stochastic term (e). Indirect utility is assumed to be a function of the choice attributes (Z_j), with parameters β, which due to preference heterogeneity may vary across households by a random component η_i. By specifying the distribution of the error terms e and η, the probability of choosing j in each of the choice sets can be derived (Train, 1998). By accounting for unobserved heterogeneity, equation (12.2) now becomes:

$$P_{ij} = \frac{\exp(V(Z_j(\beta + \eta_i)))}{\sum_{h=1}^{C} \exp(V(Z_h(\beta + \eta_i)))} \qquad (12.5)$$

Since this model is not restricted by the IIA assumption, the stochastic part of utility may be correlated among alternatives and across the sequence of choices via the common influence of η_i. Treating preference parameters as random variables requires estimation by simulated maximum likelihood. Procedurally, the maximum likelihood algorithm searches for a solution by simulating k draws from distributions with given means and standard deviations. Probabilities are calculated by integrating the joint simulated distribution.

Even if unobserved heterogeneity can be accounted for in the RPLM, however, this model fails to explain the sources of heterogeneity (Boxall and Adamowicz, 2002). One solution to detecting the sources of heterogeneity while accounting for unobserved heterogeneity is by including the interactions of individual characteristics with choice-specific attributes in the utility function. The RPLM with interactions can pick up preference variations in terms of both unconditional taste heterogeneity (random heterogeneity) and individual characteristics (conditional heterogeneity), and hence improve model fit. When the interaction terms with household characteristics are included, the indirect utility function estimated becomes:

$$V_{ij} = \alpha + \beta_1 Z_1 + \beta_2 Z_2 + \ldots + \beta_n Z_n + \delta_1 S_1 + \delta_2 S_2 + \ldots + \delta_l S_m \quad (12.6)$$

where as before, α is the ASC, n is the number of river management strategy attributes considered, and the vector of coefficients β_1 to β_n are attached to the vector of attributes (Z). In this specification, m is the number of household-specific characteristics employed to explain the choice of river management strategy, and the vector of coefficients δ_1 to δ_l are attached to the vector of interaction terms (S) that influence utility. Since household characteristics are constant across choice occasions for any given household, these only enter as interaction terms with the river management strategy attributes.

SURVEY DESIGN AND ADMINISTRATION

The first step in choice experiment design is to define the environmental good to be valued in terms of its attributes and their levels. It is essential to identify those attributes that the public considers important regarding the proposed policy change, as well as those levels that are achievable with and without the proposed policy change (Bateman *et al.*, 2003). The good to be valued in this choice experiment study is the river management strategy. Following discussions with scientists from the Central Mining Institute, the Silesian University, the AGH University of Science and Technology and the Krakow University of Technology, and drawing on the results of focus group discussions with the local population, three river management strategy attributes were chosen: surface and underground flooding risk, biodiversity found in the habitats and access to the river for recreational purposes. All three of these attributes were specified to have two levels.

The flood risk attribute refers to the risk of flooding in the area in the next 10 years. At the moment, measures such as building barriers are not undertaken, and hence the risk of flooding is high. If, however, both underground and surface barriers are built, the risk of flooding can be minimised. It is proposed that to avoid past mistakes, the surface barriers should be built of wood and the underground ones should be built of concrete. The river access attribute refers to the public's access to the riverbank for recreational purposes (for example, walking, cycling, fishing). At the moment access to the river is difficult, following the building of concrete walls a few years earlier. If however, concrete walls are demolished and the river is re-canalised similar to its natural state, it could easily be accessed for recreational purposes. Finally, the biodiversity attribute refers to the number of different species of plants and animals, their population levels, and the number of different habitats and their size in the river ecosystem in the next ten years. Even though as a result of flooding, biodiversity levels have increased to higher levels in the area, present regulations do not prohibit the mining companies from creating spoil heaps by discharging the waste products of their mining activities into the river. This malpractice poses a threat to the newly formed habitats, and is expected to decrease biodiversity levels significantly within the next ten years. If, however, mining companies are prohibited from creating spoil heaps and if reclamation activities such as afforestation take place, biodiversity levels can reach a higher level in ten years.

The payment vehicle was a percentage change in the local taxes paid by the households over the next ten years. A percentage change in the household's present level of tax was preferred to fixed changes in the tax level, since the former allows for a continuous monetary variable. Furthermore, allowing for higher and lower tax levels compared to the status quo enables understanding of whether the households are willing to pay to have higher/lower levels of these attributes or willing to accept compensation to relinquish higher/lower levels. Finally, taxation was preferred as a payment vehicle over voluntary donations since households may have the incentive to free-ride with the latter (Whitehead, 2006). Table 12.1 summarises the definitions of the attributes and their levels.

A large number of unique river management strategies can be constructed using these attributes and their levels. Using experimental design techniques (Louviere *et al.*, 2000) an orthogonalisation procedure was used that resulted in 32 pairwise comparisons of river management strategies. These were randomly blocked into four versions, each containing eight choice sets consisting of two river management strategies and an opt-out alternative, which represented the status quo, in which case no management actions would be undertaken. Inclusion of the status quo or another baseline scenario is important for the welfare interpretation of the estimates and

Table 12.1 Attributes, their definitions and levels

Attribute	Definition	Levels
Flood Risk	Risk of flooding in the area in the next 10 years	Low, *High*
River Access	Public's access to the river for recreational purposes in the next 10 years	Easy, *Difficult*
Biodiversity	Number of different species of plants and animals, their population levels, number of different habitats and their size in the river ecosystem in the next 10 years	*Low*, High
Local Tax	Percentage change in the monthly municipal tax paid by every household in the area in the next 10 years	−10%, −5%, 0, +5% +10%

Note: Status quo attribute levels are in italic.

Assuming that the following three river management strategies were the only choices you had, which one would you prefer?

Management strategy characteristics	Management strategy A	Management strategy B	Neither management strategy: status quo
Flood risk	Low	Low	High
Biodiversity	Low	High	Low
River access	Difficult	Easy	Difficult
Council tax	5% decrease	5% decrease	Same as now
I prefer (Please tick as appropriate)	Management strategy A □	Management strategy B□	Neither management strategy□

Figure 12.3 Example choice set

for their consistency with demand theory (Louviere *et al.*, 2000; Bennett and Blamey, 2001; Bateman *et al.*, 2003).

The choice experiment survey was implemented in March and April 2007 in the city of Sosnowiec, located in the Bobrek catchment, with in-house face-to-face interviews. Time and budget constraints allowed for a sample of 200 households from the local population. A quota sample was collected and the survey was administered to be representative of the local population in terms of income and geographical distribution (that is, distance from the river). Those household members who took part in the survey were by and large those who were the main household decision makers and/or heads of the households. In total, 96 per cent of those approached, that is, 192 households, were interviewed.

Table 12.2 Descriptive statistics of respondents and their households, sample size=192

Socioeconomic Variables	**Mean (std dev.)**
Age of the respondent (in years)	45.6 (16.2)
Household size	2.8 (1.1)
Monthly gross household income (in zloty)	2478.1 (1253)
Monthly household local tax (in zloty)	183.9 (11.8)
Household's distance from the river in metres	462 (249.8)
Number of flood episodes suffered in the last decade	2.52 (2.99)
Total damage to the household from floods in the last decade (in zloty)	7115.8 (6611)
Respondent with a university degree and above %	26
Household with at least one child %	70.8
Household visitor to the river for recreational purposes %	54.6
Household flooded %	13
Flooded household compensated %	28

The choice experiment survey started with the enumerators reading a statement identifying the current issues in the area regarding flood risk, biodiversity conservation and use of the river for recreational activities. Subsequently the respondents were presented with a description of the attributes used in the choice experiment and they were asked to state their preferred river management strategy among three such strategies in eight choice sets. Overall a total of 1536 choices were elicited from 192 households.

In addition to the choice experiment, the survey also collected social, demographic and economic data, including the respondents' age, gender, education, household income and local tax paid by the household, as well as information on whether the household used the river for recreational activities and flooding episodes that have affected the household in the past decade. Descriptive statistics for the key variables are presented in Table 12.2.

The sample households' average monthly income, average monthly local tax paid by the household and the demographic composition of the household, as well as the age and education levels of the respondents are representative of the population. Even though on average households are located almost half a kilometre (462 metres) away from the river, almost 13 per cent have been flooded an average of 2.5 times in the past decade. The total average damage suffered by flooded households in the past ten years is 7115.8 zloty (€1871), and for some this was as high as 25 000 zloty (€6574). Less than a third of these flooded households have been compensated, most of whom (49 per cent) by the mining industry, some (28 per cent) by the government and a minority (13 per cent) by an insurance company. Over half of the sample are regular visitors to the rivers. They stated that they use the river for a wide range of recreational activities, from walking and sailing to appreciating its aesthetic beauty and bird watching, as well as for educational purposes.

RESULTS

The data for econometric analysis were coded according to the levels of the attributes. Attributes with two levels (that is, flood risk, biodiversity level, river access) entered the utility function as binary variables that were effects coded as 1 to indicate low level of flood risk, high level of biodiversity and easy river access, and –1 to indicate high level of flood risk, low level of biodiversity and difficult river access (Adamowicz *et al.*, 1994; Louviere *et al.*, 2000; Hensher *et al.*, 2005). The attribute with five levels (percentage increase in local tax) was entered in cardinal-linear form, and then multiplied by the households' actual level of local tax, in order to calculate the level of this attribute for each household. Since this choice experiment involves generic instead of labelled options, the alternative specific constants (ASC) were set to 1 when either river management strategy A or B was chosen and to 0 when the households chose the status quo (Louviere *et al.*, 2000). A relatively more positive and significant ASC indicates a higher propensity for households to take no action to manage the river.

Retaining the assumption that observable utility function follows a strictly additive form, a CLM for the choice of river management strategy was estimated using LIMDEP 8.0 NLOGIT 3.0. The model was specified so that household choice was only affected by the ASC and the four attributes of the choice experiment. The results of the CLM for the pool of 192 households are reported in the first column of Table 12.3.

The results indicate that all attributes are highly significant determinants of management plan choice. Furthermore, the estimated coefficients have the expected signs. These indicate that individuals prefer low flood risk, high biodiversity and easy river access. Consistently with demand theory, the coefficient of the monetary attribute has a negative sign, indicating that individuals prefer alternatives with lower tax rates to those with higher tax rates. The positive and significant ASC captures other factors affecting choice that are not included in the model and can also be interpreted as an indication that the households prefer to move from the status quo to either river management strategy A or B.

Table 12.3 CLM, RPLM and RPLM with interactions

	CLM	RPLM		RPL with Interactions	
Variable	**Coefficient (s.e.)**	**Coefficient (s.e.)**	**Coeff. Std. (s.e.)**	**Coefficient (s.e.)**	**Coeff. Std (s.e.)**
ASC	0.381***	0.023		0.079	
	(0.105)	(0.161)		(0.148)	
Flood Risk	0.343***	0.777***	0.661**	0.289**	0.361
	(0.043)	(0.168)	(0.367)	(0.138)	(0.359)
Biodiversity	0.076**	0.183**	0.69**	−0.433***	0.456**
	(0.04)	(0.075)	(0.277)	(0.144)	(0.232)
River Access	0.137***	0.274***	0.303	−0.112	0.292
	(0.042)	(0.0748)	(0.444)	(0.15)	(0.408)
Tax Rate	−0.029***	−0.101***		−0.176***	
	(0.003)	(0.018)		(0.029)	
Flooded				0.849***	
• Flood Risk				(0.212)	
Flooded				−0.346**	
• River Access				(0.178)	
Flooded				0.056**	
• Tax Rate				(0.026)	
Visited				0.417***	
• Biodiversity				(0.117)	
Visited				0.257**	
• River Access				(0.121)	
Visited				0.043***	
• Tax Rate				(0.016)	
Income				0.00012***	
• Flood Risk				(0.529×10^{-4})	
Income				0.00017***	
• Biodiversity				(0.507×10^{-4})	
Income				0.00014***	
• River Access				(0.5549×10^{-4})	
Income				0.19×10^{-4}***	
• Tax Rate				(0.657×10^{-5})	
No. of observations	1536	1536		1536	
Log Likelihood Function	−1498.707	−1435.446		−1351.822	
ρ^2	0.11	0.15		0.2	

Note: *** Indicates significance at 1 per cent, ** Indicates significance at 5 per cent.

As explained above, the CLM imposes an assumption of IIA that can be unrealistic in many settings. If this assumption fails, the CLM is a misspecification. In order to test the assumption of IIA, the Hausman and McFadden (1984) test for the IIA property is carried out. This involves constructing a likelihood ratio test around the different versions of the model where the choice alternatives are excluded. If IIA holds then the model estimated on all choices should be the same as that estimated for a sub-set of alternatives (Hensher *et al.*, 2005, p. 519). The results of the test indicate that the IIA property is rejected at the 5 per cent level for two cases while it is inconclusive in the third case. Therefore the CLM may not be the appropriate specification for the estimation.

Consequently the data is estimated by using the RPLM, similarly to the case studies presented in Chapters 3 and 4 of this volume. In addition to circumventing the IIA assumption, the RPLM can take into account any unconditional unobserved heterogeneity among the households. In order to investigate whether or not the data exhibit unobserved unconditional heterogeneity, the RPL model is estimated using LIMDEP 8.0 NLOGIT 3.0. All choice attributes except the monetary payment were specified to be normally distributed (Train, 1998; Revelt and Train, 1998). The results of the RPLM are reported in the second column of Table 12.3.

The Swait-Louviere log likelihood ratio test rejects the null hypothesis that the regression parameters of CLM and RPLM are equal at the 0.5 per cent significance level. The use of the RPLM model therefore results in an improved fit, also suggested by the increase in ρ^2 from 0.11 in CLM to 0.15 in RPLM. This evidence supports our conclusion that the RPL model is the correct specification for the data.

The estimated standard deviations of the RPL are significant for flood risk and biodiversity. This implies that there is significant choice-specific unobserved unconditional heterogeneity for these attributes. Even though the standard deviation for the flood risk attribute is significant, it is not large enough to affect the overall sign of the coefficient, thus suggesting that the entire sample prefers lower flood risk to higher (Boxall and Adamowicz, 2002). However, the large and significant standard deviation for the biodiversity attribute implies that there are households that prefer lower levels of this attribute. Specifically 39.54 per cent of the respondents exhibit a negative coefficient for the biodiversity attribute, while for 18.29 per cent of the sample the estimated coefficient on river access is negative. In this specification the ASC becomes insignificant, implying that consideration of heterogeneity in this model eliminates the effect of households' unobserved information on their choice of a river management strategy.

Unobserved heterogeneity is often the result of differences in the socio-economic characteristics of the respondents (Boxall and Adamowicz, 2002).

In order to gain insight into the sources of unobserved heterogeneity and identify the socioeconomic characteristics that may provide its foundations, a RPLM with interactions was estimated. This method of interacting social and economic variables with choice attributes is also employed in Chapters 4, 5 and 13 of this volume. In this study, whether or not the households have been flooded in the last ten years, their income levels, as well as whether or not they visit the river for recreational purposes, were considered to be important determinants of choice. The results of the RPLM with interactions are reported in the third column of Table 12.3.

The Swait-Louviere log likelihood test suggests that the RPL model with interactions is an improvement over the RPLM. Furthermore, the explanatory power of the model increases relative to the RPL model without interactions, as indicated by the increase in ρ^2 to 0.2, which is considered to be an extremely good fit (Hensher *et al.*, 2005, p. 338).

The RPLM with interactions results in insignificant derived standard deviations for the river access and flood risk attributes, whereas the standard deviation for the biodiversity attribute is significant and large, revealing that some households prefer higher levels of biodiversity. More specifically, 17.12 per cent of the respondents prefer a higher level of biodiversity. Further, the results reveal that households that were flooded at least once in the past ten years are willing to pay higher taxes for river management strategies A and B and they prefer those river management strategies which generate lower flood risk and difficult river access. Households that visit the river for recreational purposes are more likely to choose those river management strategy alternatives with a high level of biodiversity and easy river access. They are also willing to pay higher taxes for river management. Finally, the higher the household income, the more likely it is that the household chooses a river management strategy with a low level of flood risk, a high level of biodiversity and easy river access, and these households are also willing to pay higher taxes for river management.

WILLINGNESS TO PAY ESTIMATES

The choice experiment method is consistent with utility maximisation and demand theory (Bateman *et al.*, 2003), so welfare measures can be calculated from the estimated parameters by using the following formula:

$$CS = \frac{\ln \sum_i \exp(V_{i1}) - \ln \sum_i \exp(V_{i0})}{\beta_{localtax}} \tag{12.7}$$

where CS is the compensating surplus welfare measure, $\beta_{localtax}$ is the marginal utility of income (represented by the coefficient of the monetary attribute in the choice experiment, which in this case is the local tax) and V_{i0} and V_{i1} represent indirect utility functions before and after the change under consideration. For the linear utility index, the marginal value of change in a single river management strategy attribute can be represented as a ratio of coefficients, reducing equation (12.7) to

$$WTP = -2\left(\frac{\beta_{attribute}}{\beta_{localtax}}\right) \qquad (12.8)$$

This part-worth (or implicit price) formula represents the marginal rate of substitution between payment and the river management strategy attribute in question, or the marginal welfare measure (that is, willingness to pay, WTP) for a change in any of the attributes. Since all three of the river management strategy attributes, that is, flood risk, river access and biodiversity, are binary, the WTP is multiplied by two (see Hu *et al.*, 2004).

The best fitting model in this study is the RPLM with interactions reported in the last column of Table 12.3. This function can be used to calculate the value assigned by the household to each river management strategy (Scarpa *et al.*, 2003), by modifying equation (12.8):

$$WTP = -2\left(\frac{\hat{\beta}_{attribute} + \delta_{attribute} \times S_1 + \ldots + \delta_{attribute} \times S_3}{\hat{\beta}_{localtax} + \delta_{localtax} \times S_1 + \ldots + \delta_{localtax} \times S_3}\right) \qquad (12.8')$$

Variables S_{1-3} are the three household-specific characteristics under consideration. Using the Wald Procedure (Delta method) in LIMDEP 8.0 NLOGIT 3.0, households' valuation of river management strategy attributes are calculated for the best fit RPLM with interactions and are reported in Table 12.4. The first column reports the WTP of the sample average, and the subsequent columns report the valuation of flooded households and visitor households, as well as those that are wealthy and poor.

The results indicate that the average household is WTP the highest level for low flood risk, followed by river access and biodiversity. This ranking of the attributes is the same for the four households types: flooded, visitor, wealthy and poor. When the four household types are compared, it can be seen that the flooded household is WTP the highest for low flood risk, whereas the wealthy household is WTP the most for biodiversity and river access attributes. In order to assess whether there are significant differences in the WTP values of these four household types, following Rolfe and Windle (2005), and Poe *et al.* (1994) a simple convolution process was

Table 12.4 Marginal WTP for river management strategy attributes for the RPLM with interactions for the average, flooded, visitor, wealthy and poor households (zloty[a]/household and 95% C.I.)

Attribute	Average Household	Flooded Household	Visitor Household	Wealthy Household	Poor Household
Flood Risk	14.5***	45.5**	21.5***	27.8***	11.2***
	(12.9–16.2)	(26.9–64.1)	(18.2–24.8)	(21.5–34)	(9.4–12.9)
Biodiversity	4.6***	4.6	12.5***	20.2***	−0.6
	(3.3–5.9)	(1.6–7.6)	(9.9–15.1)	(15.6–24.8)	(−2–0.9)
River Access	6.6***	−2.1	12.7***	21.7***	1.3
	(5.4–7.9)	(−3.6–7.7)	(10.4–15)	(17.1–26.3)	(−0.1–2.7)

Notes:
[a] 1 zloty= €0.257 (1 March 2007), at the time this choice experiment was carried out.
*** 1% significance level; ** 5% significance level with two-tailed tests.
Wealthy people are those whose average monthly gross income is greater than or equal to the value corresponding to the 75th percentile of the income distribution of the sample. Poor people are those whose average monthly gross income is less than or equal to the value corresponding to the 25th percentile of the income distribution.

Table 12.5 Proportion of WTP differences for river management strategy attributes falling below zero

	Flood risk	Biodiversity	River access
Flooded vs visitor	0.915	0.9993	0.9953
Flooded vs wealthy	0.8201	0.9985	0.9995
Flooded vs poor	0.97255	0.99035	0.74705
Visitor vs wealthy	0.88765	0.9775	0.9907
Visitor vs poor	0.99985	1	1
Wealthy vs poor	0.99335	1	0.99995

undertaken. After having calculated the WTP using the Wald Procedure (Delta method), differences between WTP values were calculated by taking one vector of WTP from another. The 95 per cent confidence interval is approximated by identifying the proportion of differences that fall below zero. The results are reported in Table 12.5.

The results of the Poe *et al.* test reported in Table 12.5 reveal that flooded, visitor and wealthy households' WTP for low flood risk is not significantly different from zero at the 5 per cent significance level. Therefore, poor households are WTP the least for reduction in flood risk, but this result might be due to these households' budgets (that is, their ability to pay) constraining their WTP. What percentage of these households have been flooded, whether or not and how much compensation they have received and their distance from the river should be investigated in greater detail in order to be able to recommend equitable flood risk reduction policies and projects. WTP for biodiversity differs across all household types at less than 5 per cent significance level. Wealthy households are WTP the most for conservation of biodiversity, followed by visitor households. For river access, flooded and poor households exhibit similar WTP values, and wealthy households are WTP the most for river access, followed by visitor households. For both the biodiversity and river access attributes, it is necessary to investigate further what fraction of wealthy households are visitors to the river for recreational purposes, as well as their answers to the follow-up questions aimed at differentiating between different sources of value, in order to differentiate between use and non-use values.

POLICY IMPLICATIONS

Capturing the welfare effects of flood risk reduction projects and policies is crucial for carrying out the appropriate cost-benefit analyses to inform those projects and policies that maximise economic efficiency while minimising flood risks. Even though the costs of flood control initiatives are relatively easy to calculate, estimation of the economic benefits of flood risk reduction is a challenging task. Similarly, for biodiversity conservation and recreational activities, estimation of the costs of biodiversity conservation or provision of recreational sites is generally easier than estimation of the benefits generated by these environmental goods and services. This is due to the public good nature of these environmental goods and services, as well as the use and non-use values attached to them, implying that there are no markets or market prices that could be used for the estimation of the economic benefits that would arise from projects or policy changes that affect them. Non-market valuation techniques, therefore, could be applied in order to estimate the total economic benefits generated by flood risk reduction, biodiversity conservation and provision of recreational services.

The study presented in this chapter employs the choice experiment method to investigate the local households' valuation of trade-offs between and ranking of the most important river management attributes in the Upper Silesia Region of Poland. This method is considered to be the most suitable non-market valuation method to study this environmental problem, since river management projects and policies affect multiple environmental services and goods. The river management attributes considered included flood risk reduction, conservation of biodiversity and facilitation of recreational activities in the area. The results reported in this chapter reveal that the average household values positively and significantly improvements in all of the river management attributes. They derive the highest benefits from reduction of flood risk, whereas their valuation of improvements in recreational facilities is half, and their valuation of biodiversity conservation at a high level is a third of their valuation of flood risk reduction. This ranking is similar across household types.

These results indicate that even though the main concern of these households is minimisation of flood risks, they also derive substantial benefits from recreational activities and biodiversity, that is, use and non-use values of the river. The river management strategies in this region should therefore be designed and implemented in such a way that the precautions taken to alleviate flooding (for example, building underground and surface barriers) also incorporate facilitation of recreational activities, for example by re-canalising the river similarly to its natural state, rather than building concrete surface barriers to minimise flooding risk. Further, the significant valuation of biodiversity by the locals necessitates the development and implementation of policies which prohibit the mining companies from creating spoil heaps by discharging the remnants of their mining activities into the river. Moreover, reclamation activities, such as afforestation, should be undertaken in order to conserve biodiversity riches in the area. These findings have implications for policies and projects for flood risk reduction in other EU countries, as the results estimated in this recent EU Member State reveal that conservation of the environment (for example, biodiversity according to EU directives and regulations) and minimisation of flood risks need not be conflicting objectives.

ACKNOWLEDGEMENTS

The authors acknowledge the financial support from the AQUASTRESS integrated project funded by the European Union Framework Programme 6. The authors would also like to thank Anna Adamus, Leszek Trzaski, Nickolaos Syrigos and Haris Giannakidis for their assistance in the development and implementation of the choice experiment survey.

REFERENCES

Adamowicz, W.L., Louviere, J., Williams, M. (1994), 'Combining Stated and Revealed Preference Methods for Valuing Environmental Amenites', *Journal of Environmental Economics and Management*, 26: 271–292.

Bateman, I.J., Carson, R.T., Day, B., Hanemann, W.M., Hanley, N., Hett, T., Jones-Lee, M., Loomes, G., Mourato, S., Özdemiroğlu, E., Pearce, D.W., Sugden, R., Swanson, S. (2003), *Guidelines for the Use of Stated Preference Techniques for the Valuation of Preferences for Non-market Goods*, Edward Elgar, Cheltenham, UK and Northampton, MA, USA.

Bennett, J.J. (2003), 'The Economic Value of Biodiversity: A Scoping Paper', presented to the National Workshop *The Economic Value of Biodiversity*, 22–23 October 2003. www.environment.gov.au/biodiversity/publications/scoping-paper/eco-bio.html, accessed 27 September 2007.

Bennett, J.J., Blamey, R.K. (2001), *The Choice of Modelling Approach to Environmental Valuation*, Edward Elgar, Cheltenham, UK and Northampton, MA, USA.

Birol, E., Cox, V. (2007), 'Using choice experiments to design wetland management programmes: the case of Severn Estuary Wetland, UK', *Journal of Environmental Planning and Management*, 50(3): 363–380.

Birol, E., Karousakis, K., Koundouri, P. (2006a), 'Using a choice experiment to account for preference heterogeneity in wetland attributes: the case of Cheimaditida wetland in Greece', *Ecological Economics*, 60: 145–156.

Birol, E., Smale, M., Gyovai, A. (2006b), 'Using a choice experiment to estimate farmers' valuation of agrobiodiversity on Hungarian small farms', *Environmental and Resource Economics*, 34(4): 439–469.

Boxall, P.C., Adamowicz, W.L. (2002), 'Understanding Heterogeneous Preferences in Random Utility Models: A Latent Class Approach', *Environmental and Resource Economics*, 23, 421–446.

Brakenridge, G.R., Anderson, E., Caquard, S. (1997), *Flood Archive Table 1997*, Dartmouth Flood Observatory, Hanover, USA. www.dartmouth.edu/~floods/Archives/1997sum.htm, accessed 27 September 2007.

Brakenridge, G.R., Anderson, E., Caquard, S. (2001), *Flood Archive Table 2001*, Dartmouth Flood Observatory, Hanover, USA. www.dartmouth.edu/~floods/Archives/2001sum.htm, accessed 27 September 2007.

Brouwer, R., Ek, R. van. (2004), 'Integrated Ecological, Economic and Social Impact Assessment of Alternative Flood Protection Measures in the Netherlands', *Ecological Economics*, 50(1–2), 1–21.

Carlsson, F., Frykblom, P., Liljenstolpe, C. (2003), 'Valuing Wetland Attributes: An Application of Choice Experiments', *Ecological Economics*, 47, 95–103.

Christie, M., N. Hanley, J. Warren, K. Murphy, R. Wright and T. Hyde (2006), 'Valuing the diversity of biodiversity', *Ecological Economics*, 58(2): 304–317.

Greene, W.H. (1997), *Econometric Analysis*, Fourth Edition, Prentice Hall, New York.

Hanley N., Wright R.E., Koop G. (2002), 'Modelling Recreation Demand Using Choice Experiments: Rock Climbing in Scotland', *Environmental and Resource Economics*, 22: 449–466.

Hausman, J., McFadden, D. (1984), 'Specification Tests for the Multinomial Logit Model', *Econometrica*, 52, 1219–1240.

Hensher, D., Rose, J., Greene, W. (2005), *Applied Choice Analysis: A Primer*, Cambridge University Press, Cambridge, UK.

Horne, P., Boxall, P.C., Adamowicz, W.L., (2005), 'Multiple-Use Management of Forest Recreation Sites: A Spatially Explicit Choice Experiment', *Forest Ecology and Management*, 207(1/2): 189–199.

Horne, P., Petäjistö, L. (2003), 'Preferences for Alternative Moose Management Regimes among Finnish Landowners: A Choice Experiment Approach', *Land Economics*, 79(4): 472–482.
Hu, W., Hunnemeyer, A., Veeman, M., Adamowicz, W., Srivastava, L. (2004), 'Trading Off Health, Environmental and Genetic Modification Attributes in Food', *European Review of Agricultural Economics*, 31, 389–408.
Lancaster, K. (1966), 'A New Approach to Consumer Theory', *Journal of Political Economics*, 74, 217–231.
Louviere, J.J., Hensher, D. Swait, J., Adamowicz, W. (2000), *Stated Choice Methods: Analysis and Application*, Cambridge University Press, Cambridge.
Luce, D. (1959), *Individual Choice Behaviour*, John Wiley, New York, NY.
Maddala, G.S. (1999), *Limited Dependent and Qualitative Variables in Econometrics*, Cambridge University Press, Cambridge.
McFadden, D. (1974), 'Conditional Logit Analysis of Qualitative Choice Behavior', in P. Zarembka, (ed.), *Frontiers in Econometrics*, Academic Press, New York.
Nicholls, R.J., Hoozemans F., Marchand, M. (1999), 'Increasing Flood Risks and Wetland Losses due to Global Sea-Level Rise: Regional and Global Analyses', *Global Environmental Change*, 9, S69–S87.
Pearce, D.W., Moran, D. (1994), *The Economic Value of Biodiversity*, Earthscan, London.
Poe, G.L., Severance-Lossin, E.K., Welsh, M.P. (1994), 'Measuring the Difference (X-Y) of Simulated Distributions: A Convolutions Approach', *American Journal of Agricultural Economics*, 76, 904–915.
Ragkos, A., Psychoudakis, A., Christofi, A., Theodoridis, A. (2006), 'Using a Functional Approach to Wetland Valuation: The Case of Zazari-Cheimaditida', *Regional Environmental Change*, 6, 193–200.
Revelt, D., Train, K. (1998), 'Mixed Logit with Repeated Choices: Households' Choice of Appliance Efficiency Level', *Review of Economics and Statistics*, 53, 647–657.
Rolfe, J., Windle, J. (2005), 'Valuing Options for Reserve Water in the Fitzroy Basin', *The Australian Journal of Agricultural and Resource Economics*, 49, 91–114.
Scarpa, R., Ruto, E., Kristjanson, P., Radeny, M., Drucker, A., Rege, J. (2003), 'Valuing Indigenous Cattle Breeds in Kenya: An Empirical Comparison of Stated and Revealed Preference Value Estimates', *Ecological Economic*, 45(3), 409–426.
Train, K.E. (1998), 'Recreation Demand Models with Taste Differences Over People', *Land Economics*, 74, 230–239.
Whitehead, J.C. (2006), 'A Practitioner's Primer on Contingent Valuation', in Alberini, A., Kahn, J. (eds), *Contingent Valuation Handbook*, Edward Elgar Publishing, Cheltenham, UK and Northampton, MA, USA.

13. Enjoy the silence: valuing rail noise abatement in Trento, Italy

Paulo A.L.D. Nunes and Chiara Maria Travisi

INTRODUCTION

The Italian overall noise regulation was set in 1995.[1] Since 1998, rail noise pollution has also been regulated by a law[2] that sets day-time and night-time limits on reception locations, depending on their vulnerability and distance from the railway. Residential areas or vulnerable receptors, such as schools and hospitals, therefore have lower limits than less vulnerable ones. Reception limits refer to a precise spatial area along the railway which includes receptors within 250 metres from it. This area is divided into two portions, named 'Zone A' and 'Zone B' respectively, 100 and 150 metres away from the railroad track, and characterised by different noise reception limits.

Almost one decade after the definition of the Italian national noise regulation, the implementation of the required noise abatement measures is still largely incomplete, and only very recently we have witnessed the rise of a national debate on how to proceed in order to abate rail noise below the current unacceptable limits. This chapter considers the case of the Brennero railway, located in the North-East of Italy, where for the first time in Italy local authorities are formally debating on the most preferable type of noise abatement strategy to be implemented (see Figure 13.1).

Recently the Italian Ministry of the Environment has indicated preference for noise abatement strategies based on substantial investments in renewing train vehicles and tracks rather than creating new noise barriers (for a discussion see Watkiss *et al.*, 2001). According to the Ministry, investments in train vehicles and/or tracks are technically expected to grant the required noise decrease at the lowest public cost.[3] However, there is no empirical valuation study that can confirm or reject such a technical statement for Italy. In addition, Italian local authorities can dispute this advice and consider the preferences of the affected population for alternative policy measures, that is, alternative noise abatement programmes. This flexibility, as introduced in the legislation, allows for the implementation of

Figure 13.1 Location of the Trento province

economic valuation studies of noise abatement programmes, such as the one presented in this chapter.

Challenging questions and new opportunities to assist policy makers with relevant insights into the best policy option against rail noise are therefore presented and discussed in this chapter. Important issues concern how to accelerate the implementation of the noise abatement regulation, as well as how to choose, among the range of possible noise reduction measures, those actions able to provide the highest welfare gain, that is, private benefits discounted from any externality values. Before discussing the Brennero case study, however, the next sections set the EU scene on rail noise mitigation and discuss relevant issues on the economic valuation of noise reduction.

SCOPING THE SCENE

Rail Noise Issues in the EU Political Context

Within the general political intention of reducing environmental transport externalities, rail transport is considered an important sector for policy intervention. When compared to road transportation, the railway generates lower air pollutant emissions, is associated with lower risks of fatalities and contributes to reducing traffic congestion. In some cases, however, railway lines (either old or new) are not accepted by the people living close to them due to concern about unacceptable noise levels, which are often over the current cut-off limits set by international and national legislation. The Green Paper *Future Noise Policy* of November 1996 by the European Commission[4] states that the 'public's main criticism of rail transport is the excessive noise level'. Sound evidences exist that in fact, excessive levels of noise can have important impacts on human welfare (for example, WHO, 2000; Wardman and Bristow, 2004) by producing psychological (for example, annoyance) and physiological (for example, hearing loss) consequences for people exposed. Moreover, despite the localised nature of rail noise, produced in well-defined areas around railroad tracks, estimates by the European Commission (CEC, 2003) indicate that 10 per cent of the European population is affected by rail noise levels higher than 55 L_{dn} dB(A),[5] which is the standard safety level indicated by the World Health Organization. In particular, according to the European Commission *Position Paper on the European Strategies and Priorities for Railways Noise Abatement* (CEC, 2003), in the coming years, a noise reduction of 10–15 dB(A) should be reached, on average, in order to protect the current population exposed to rail noise pollution.

While in the past railway noise has been reduced in Europe, in fact, the technological improvement was not primarily planned as a noise reduction measure, but was adopted because of other operational requirements (for more details, see CEC, 2003, p. 19). Disk brakes had to be used on modern coaches to allow speeds above 140 km/h. This was not, however, required for freight wagons, which is why noise generation from this type of stock is now the predominant railway noise issue in Europe, particularly concerning operations at night. The lack of technical progress in railroad tracks and train vehicles, therefore, still represents an impediment in tackling noise reduction.

In addition, current transport plans in Europe foresee high-speed trains running at speeds of up to 350 km/h to form a Trans-European high-speed railway network (CEC, 2004). Noise from high-speed lines, mostly operating during the day time, is the second main noise issue together with freight train noise. It often arises at the planning stage of new high-speed lines or services, when noise mitigation becomes a key requirement. Noise from high-speed trains has different characteristics from that of freight wagons. With increasing speed, aerodynamic noise from the upper part of the trains becomes dominant and most of the existing noise barriers are too low to shield this source. It follows that the height of noise barriers too will have to be accurately designed during the noise reduction planning stage.

The third main noise issue concerns urban rail transport. Trams and urban light systems mainly operate in densely populated areas where, as already discussed, rail noise annoyance has become a subject of social relevance. Here, noise reduction measures usually have a high profile in order to guarantee the highest level of protection. Nevertheless the benefits from noise annoyance reduction can be hampered by aesthetic or micro-climatic disutilities that are often associated with noise barriers. In this connection, the social acceptance of different noise abatement strategies should play a role too during the noise reduction decision making.

Finally, under the process of railway reform that started with the EU Directive 91/440, several changes in responsibilities or functions are currently taking place. Although there are different institutional settings in the various EU Member States,[6] it is nowadays commonplace to have a variety of different entities involved in the railway system, for example, operators, rolling stock owners, maintenance companies for rolling stock or infrastructure, infrastructure managers and the manufacturing industry. This splitting results in several formally separated parties responsible for railway noise abatement, which makes it even more important to create links for a common cost-effective strategy. In the Italian context, for instance, the recent splitting of responsibilities between rolling stock owners[7] and infrastructure managers[8] has created conflicts over the most preferred action to abate rail noise. Doubts have also arisen about which party should finance noise reduction measures, which is why there have been continual postponements of interventions against noise.

Thus the reduction of railway noise is acknowledged as an important priority in the European environmental policy agenda and there is a high potential for the abatement of railway noise in Europe thanks to the availability of sound technical rail noise reduction instruments (CEC, 2003). However, noise abatement measures can be very expensive and the challenge is how to identify the most economically viable implementation of such measures by selecting the most cost-effective noise reduction strategy among those available. To achieve this, it is necessary to balance the costs associated with a certain noise abatement strategy against its expected benefits, measured in monetary terms. In this respect, economists can offer a valuable contribution to the process of decision making, by providing monetary estimates of the benefits and costs of reduced noise, thus assisting policy makers in ranking alternative options on the basis of a complete cost-benefit analysis of alternative noise reduction strategies.

Measuring the External Costs of Rail Noise

Implementing a noise abatement strategy can produce both welfare losses and gains. The former involve financial and external costs. Financial costs are typically associated with an investment in new technologies on train vehicles and/or tracks, an investment in noise barriers, or a combination of both. External costs are, for instance, the aesthetic costs generated by high noise barriers, such as the disutility due to a loss of landscape view (for a taxonomy of noise welfare costs see Hunt, 2001). On the other hand, depending on the type of noise abatement instrument selected, a noise strategy will be able to achieve different levels of noise reduction, contributing to different extents to a minimisation of the negative impact that excessive noise levels can exert on human welfare (for example, see De Kluizenaar *et al.*, 2001). All such costs and benefits should be quantified to make possible a complete cost-benefit analysis.

While the financial costs of rail noise measures can easily be estimated on the basis of market prices, an accurate, complete and reliable monetary assessment of rail noise externalities requires the use of specific non-market valuation tools (for example, see Freeman, 2003), including both stated preference (SPM) and revealed preference (RPM) methods. So far the literature has been dominated by RPM studies. In particular, Hedonic Price (HP) models have been applied in order to infer the monetary value of noise externalities, by analysing the actual behaviour of individuals in the housing market. People react, *inter alia*, to the environmental characteristics of houses, including noise, and it is therefore possible to test whether property prices decrease as noise levels increase (for a review see Navrud, 2002). However, HP models are not able to capture non-use values, nor can they value the effects of a given noise reduction measure at the planning stage, before it has actually been adopted.

Alternatively, economists can rely on SPM valuation tools, including Contingent Valuation (CVM) and Choice Experiment (CE) methods.

Contingent valuation is a survey-based approach that directly estimates preferences for noise reductions. In CVM, respondents are asked to express their maximum willingness to pay (WTP) for one specific change in noise annoyance, as described in the survey. The Choice Experiment (CE) approach however, confronts respondents with a set of two or more policy alternatives, which differ in terms of attributes and attribute levels. The respondents are asked to choose their preferred option. One of the advantages of the stated choice methods is that multiple noise reduction policies, which are expressed in terms of different bundles of attributes, can be simultaneously evaluated even if they have not yet been implemented or lie outside the current institutional strategies (see Wardman and Bristow, 2004). A typical noise abatement policy involves various aspects that can have a significant impact on human welfare. What type of noise is targeted by the policy? What level of noise reduction does the policy grant? When and at what cost will the policy be implemented? CE can separately estimate the preferences of individuals for these aspects. On the other hand, CV mainly focuses on the valuation of one aspect or one fixed set of aspects. CE can therefore provide decision makers with substantially more information about the range of possible alternative noise policies.

So far, however, most Stated Preference Method (SPM) studies on transport noise have used CVM (for example, Soguel, 1994; Vainio, 1995, 2001; Pommerehne, 1998; Barreiro *et al.*, 2000; Navrud, 2000; Lambert *et al.*, 2001) with a focus on the road and aircraft sectors. We are aware of only one non-market valuation study that focuses on rail noise abatement (Weinberger *et al.*, 1991).[9] More recently, Clark (2006) studied the dynamics of residential property markets in three counties in Ohio, investigating the empirical magnitude of the impact of rail noise on the price of houses. According to the estimates of this hedonic price model, rail noise has a negative effect on property prices. This magnitude is statistically significant and ranges between 6.3 and 31.9 per cent. Other hedonic price studies report that rail noise reduces property prices by 2 to 4 per cent, according to Simons and El Jaouhari (2004), and by 10 per cent, according to Strand and Vågnes (2001). Finally Droste-Franke *et al.* (2006) estimate the costs of noise exposure due to road traffic, trains and aviation, using monetary values for noise impacts derived from their own calculations based on Metroeconomica (2001), Nellthorp *et al.* (2001) and Navrud (2003).

Against this background, this chapter presents a Choice Experiment approach to produce a monetary assessment of rail noise annoyance. The results discussed provide a twofold novelty. First, CE has not yet been used to value rail noise damages. Second, this is the first attempt to estimate the noise annoyance costs caused by railroad traffic in Italy.

THE SURVEY

Modelling Respondents' Behaviour with Respect to Noise Reduction

The statistical analysis of CE data is based on the Random Utility Model, which is assumed for the utility of the individual (McFadden, 1974). When the individual q chooses the noise alternative i, we assume that its utility can be modelled as follows:

$$U_{iq} = V_{iq}(\bar{x}_{iq}) + \varepsilon_{iq}$$

where U_{iq} is determined by two components: V_{iq} is the deterministic component, which is a function of the attribute vector x_{iq} of the noise management alternative I, and it can be interpreted as the indirect utility function; ε_{iq}, is the random part, which is unobservable directly by the researchers.

In our survey, we posit that in each of the choice sets, the respondent will select the noise management alternative with the highest indirect utility. The CE exercise implies a choice between two alternative noise management policies (to be provided by the local administration), each of which can imply different technical measures for noise abatement (for example, double glazed windows, barriers), and provide different levels of noise reduction expressed in decibels. But noise policies are costly to the local public administration, and the implementation of one of the possible noise programmes needs to be financed by contributions from citizens. Therefore, the noise policies vary with respect to level of noise reduction, type of technical measure and cost to the respondent, (see Table 13.1). We assume that the utility function of alternative i for respondent q is:

$$V_{iq} = \bar{x}_{iq}\beta + \bar{z}_{iq}\delta + \varepsilon_{hq}$$

where q denotes the respondent; i denotes the alternative noise policy; $\bar{x}$ is a vector comprised of the policy attributes; and $\bar{z}$ is a vector of interactions between the attributes and the individual characteristics of the respondent. β and δ are vectors of unknown coefficients. If the error terms ε are independent and identically distributed and follow the type I extreme value distribution, the probability that alternative i is selected out of S alternatives is:

$$P_{iq} = \frac{\exp(w_{iq}\gamma)}{\sum_{j=1}^{J}\exp(w_{jq}\gamma)} \quad \forall i,j \in S \text{ with } i \neq j,$$

Table 13.1 List of the attributes used in the choice experiment

Attributes	Levels
Noise reduction	9–11 decibel 12–14 decibel 14–15 decibel
Height of trackside barrier	4 to 6 metres 6 to 8 metres
Train and track technology	No investment New investments
Price of the programme (Euro/household/year$_{2006}$)	35 euro 37.5 euro 45 euro 55 euro 60 euro 65 euro 70 euro

where $\bar{w}$ is a vector containing $\bar{x}$ and $\bar{z}$, and $\gamma = [\beta' : \delta']$. Depending on the assumption about the distribution of the error term, the resulting statistical model is either a conditional logit, a multinomial probit or a related choice model (Green, 2002). The implicit marginal price of each attribute and the welfare changes associated with changes in the level of the attributes can then easily be derived. Assuming that the error terms ε_{iq} and ε_{jq} follow a Gumbel distribution with scale parameter λ (McFadden, 1974), usually standardised to 1, P_{iq} follows a conditional logit model.

We are now ready to apply this model to predict consumer choice behaviour regarding alternative options to reduce rail noise emission levels. First, however, we need to identify and measure other noise-abatement-related attributes that, together with the price, characterise the utility function of the respondent. This constitutes an important task in our empirical work, and it will be discussed in detail in the following sections.

Statement of the Noise Management Problem

Alternative well-established measures for reducing noise reception levels are available. It can be achieved through three types of measure: at the source (that is, maintenance of and new technologies for train vehicles and tracks); in the sound propagation path (that is, trackside barriers); or at the receptor (that is, sound insulation systems). In the past, the last type of measure was most common. As current practice in Europe, measures such as barriers (with high cost) or sound insulation windows (with limited effect) are mostly chosen instead of more cost-effective source-related measures. The reason for this is complex and includes several issues. Firstly the sound reduction measures were normally selected in relation to local noise reception limits, whereas vehicles often originated elsewhere and were beyond the influence of the local authorities. Secondly vehicle emission limits, which could enforce modification of the rolling stock, exist in only a few countries, whereas the application of traditional barriers and sound insulating windows does not need much innovation. In addition, the instruments to evaluate the best solutions from a cost-benefit point of view and to apportion the contributions of vehicles and tracks and the associated responsibilities have been applied only recently in this field.

In Italy, a decree of the Ministry of the Environment (DMA 29/11/2000), which is consistent with what is stated in the more recent *Position Paper on the European Strategies and Priorities for Railways Noise Abatement* (CEC, 2003), suggests that preference should be given to noise measures at the source (that is, either on vehicles or tracks) rather than to barriers and building insulation systems. However, the regulation recognises local conditions as a steering element in the noise reduction decision-making process and gives room to local authorities in charge of determining noise actions to operate discretionally. In this context, providing local authorities with sound advice in order to select the strategy that can guarantee highest benefits for local communities is pivotal. Therefore, more than with technical guidelines, which are already well-established, the evaluation of noise measures needs to be complemented by taking into account local conditions, including the preferences of the affected population for alternative policy solutions.

In the context of this study, located in the province of Trento, two radical positions are debated. On one side the local Environmental Protection Agency[10] is recommending intervening gradually along the railroad track, combining low-level noise barriers with some technological innovation in vehicles and railroad tracks, to be provided at a later stage. This would achieve, in two steps, the required level of noise reduction, also minimising the drawbacks of noise barriers for the people living or working in the vicinity of the railroad, in terms of aesthetic and micro-climate[11] changes. On the other hand, the Italian railway company (RFI), is strongly recommending actions that include high trackside barriers without any investment in technological innovation on train vehicles and tracks. This strategy would guarantee the immediate provision of the required level of noise reduction but at a higher collective cost in terms of aesthetic and environmental drawbacks.

To provide advice to the local authorities in Trento on the preferred noise abatement option to maximise social utility, a Choice Experiment approach was designed and a survey was distributed to a representative sample of the local affected population. Overall, noise interventions are planned on 31 sites (in 12 different municipalities) on a strip of 74 kilometres, for a total of 20 kilometres of noise barriers and an overall affected population estimated at about 2300 households (APPA, 2000). Our survey targets approximately 8.4 kilometres and 1400 households exposed to excessive noise levels within 'Zone A', living in five different municipalities along the Brennero railway. Of these, 511 households were randomly selected for the present study.

Instruments

The questionnaire consisted of three parts.[13] The first part focused on the respondents' noise perceptions; in this, we asked respondents their opinion on the current rail noise situation and asked them to talk about their own experience of noise, by means of a set of eleven questions. First we referred to noise in general terms and used six phrases relating to noise sensitivity to infer the respondents' noise profile. Using a six-point rating scale, respondents were asked to say whether they 'not at all' or 'totally' agreed with what was stated in each phrase. Second, we asked respondents how many hours they spent at home during working days and during weekends to infer additional information on their level of noise exposure. We then focused on rail noise and asked respondents to say whether it annoyed them, during the day or night. If they answered 'yes', the respondents were asked to indicate their own level of annoyance using a five-point scale (as recommended by ISO, 2003): 'not at all', 'slightly', 'moderately', 'very', 'extremely' annoyed. Those 'moderately', 'very' or 'extremely' annoyed were then asked to indicate which type of disturbance they suffered, during the day and night. A special question was used to understand whether the disturbance arose only from the rail noise emission, or whether it was also related to the track and train vibrations generated during the transit of trains. In fact, according to the results of the focus groups held in two of the seven sites surveyed, vibrations are also perceived as an important source of disturbance generated by closeness to the railway. We also asked whether the level of annoyance declared by the respondents (the householders) was either similar to that suffered by the other household members or higher or lower, and which type of disturbance they suffered. Finally we asked whether they had ever considered moving because of the rail noise, and whether they thought they lived in a noisy or quiet neighbourhood.

The second part of the survey introduced the policy choices and prepared the respondents for answering the CE questions. First we informed the respondents about the current level of noise pollution to which they were exposed, and the forecasts of the level of noise pollution due to the Brennero railway that would be reached by 2010 according to the local Environmental Protection Agency. For instance, the current noise exposure level is approximately 7 to 9 and 9 to 11 decibels over the limits during the day and night, respectively. We also showed the respondent a noise map of the area in which he/she lived showing the relation between noise level and distance from the railway. On this map the respondents could identify the actual site of their own home. Secondly we informed the respondent that the local administration was considering the provision of a noise abatement programme to reduce noise levels, and we described, using simple words, the main pros and cons of the two alternative types of noise reduction policy instruments that the local administration was considering. One policy instrument consisted of trackside noise barriers and the other involved some technological change either to the train or the railway lines, or to both. We explained that the maximum noise abatement capacity of noise barriers is approximately 15 decibels and that it increases as their height and sound-deadening power increase, although high and sound-absorbent barriers can inconvenience residential areas due to aesthetic and environmental drawbacks, such as reduced light and air circulation. On the other hand an improvement in technology, which is free from aesthetic impact, can also grant an additional reduction in vibrations, but it has a lower noise reduction capacity (up to 5 decibels). We then showed the respondents several visual simulations of barriers with different heights (see Table 13.1). The graphical simulation consisted of a succession of images showing a given site (corresponding to the respondent's site) either without or with the barrier (see Figure 13.2).

We also showed the respondents a graph, which we called the 'noise barometer', with examples of various noise levels that one can experience in daily life, and examples of noise reductions moving from one situation to another. Here noise reduction levels in decibels are also translated in terms of audible noise and explained in terms of increased distance from the noise source. The noise barometer was available to respondents during the whole CE exercise.

The third part of the survey gathered additional information in order to have a clear image of the respondents' profiles, attitudes, socio-economic conditions, exposure to noise, use values provided by the railway and so forth. Among other things, we asked the respondents: whether their home was provided with thermal and sound insulation systems; whether their home had a garden or a balcony, and, if yes, whether a noise barrier might spoil their recreational value; and the number of rooms and their exposure to the railway. Questionnaire debriefs closed the survey.

Figure 13.2 Example of visual aid showing a simulation of high trackside noise barriers

CE Questions

Prior to the CE questions, we clearly explained to the respondents that the implementation of a noise reduction policy which is able to reduce noise below the limits would be costly to the local administration (approximately €30–80 per household for the year 2006). We explained to respondents that the local administration was considering the possibility of introducing a new local tax for the year 2006. Two types of noise reduction measures were involved. We referred to barriers along the railway and technological investment in the trains and in the rail tracks. Barriers were described to the respondents in terms of height, ranging from 4 to 8 metres. Technological investment was described in terms of the current situation, and two investment programmes on train and railway technology, resulting in a reduction of rolling stock noise, traction noise and vibrations (see Table 13.1).

Following the above explanation, the respondents focused on the CE questions. They were instructed to choose between the two profiles (see Table 13.2). These corresponded to two alternative policies; they differed in

Table 13.2 Example of a stated choice question

Which of the two noise abatement options would you consider the most attractive for you?		
Attributes	**Option A**	**Option B**
Noise abatement	9–11 decibel (As if the distance between your place and the railway were increased 10 times)	14–15 decibel (As if the distance between your place and the railway were increased 30 times)
Noise barrier	4–6 metres	6–8 metres
Train and track technology	No investment	New investments
Cost of the programme	€35 household/ year 2006	€60 household/ year 2006
	☐ A	☐ B

Table 13.3 Noise abatement policies

Minus 9–11 decibel (Noise1) (As if the distance between your place and the railway were increased 10 times, for example, from 100 metres to 1 kilometre)
Minus 12–14 decibel (Noise2) (As if the distance between your place and the railway were increased 20 times, for example, from 100 metres to 2 kilometres)
Minus 14–15 decibel (Noise3) (As if the distance between your place and the railway were increased 30 times, for example, from 100 metres to 3 kilometres)

acoustic efficiency (noise reduction capacity), type, aesthetic (given by the height of the barrier) and the associated price.[14] The noise abatement policies are shown in Table 13.3.

As we can see, the acoustic efficiency of each policy is described by the level of noise reduction expressed in decibels. Three levels of noise reduction are used. The lower one (labelled Noise1) corresponds to the minimum level of noise reduction necessary to fulfil the limits set by the Italian noise regulation. It comes from the use of noise barriers with a height set at 4–6 metres and without any investment in trains and rail track technologies. The remaining ones refer to additional levels of acoustic protection. Noise2 refers to an acoustic reduction policy characterised by a noise barrier set at 4–6 metres, and an additional investment effort in technological innovation on trains. Noise3, alternatively, is the highest level of noise reduction that can be provided by the local administration. This is achieved by setting the noise barriers to 6–8 metres, with an investment in technological innovation on trains and tracks.

Price is the financial cost of purchasing the environmental quality by reducing the rail noise, expressed in terms of a new provincial tax for the year 2006 without any reduction of the provincial budget. The expected sign of this coefficient is negative, since the utility of individuals decreases as the financial burden increases.

We prepared all the combinations of the attributes levels, eliminating implausible or inconsistent ones. The choice sets consisted of two alternative profiles. The first one (the status quo option) is fixed and corresponds to a benchmark (that is, a minimum safety standard) policy that guarantees the minimum level of noise reduction able to fulfil the limits (that is, minus 9 to 11 decibels) using noise barriers (4 to 6 metres high) without any improvement in the railway and train technology. The second one varies from card to card and corresponds to a policy that provides additional noise reduction levels and a reduction in vibrations too, since it combines the use of noise barriers with improvements in train or railway line technology. Each respondent was presented with four CE questions. Before presenting the survey modelling and results we will briefly discuss some basic statistics of the questionnaire data.

MODELS AND RESULTS

Descriptive Statistics

The data were collected through in-person home interviews with 511 randomly sampled householders affected by rail noise pollution, which yielded 482 responses. A trained team of 23 experts from the Statistics Office of the Province of Trento were recruited and carefully instructed how to administer the survey. Prior to the survey, extensive focus groups were organised and a pre-test to check the validity of the survey instruments was carried out in February 2005 with another 50 households. The responses in the focus groups and the pre-test greatly helped to improve phrases in the questionnaire and develop a more understandable explanation of the good evaluated. In particular, information requirements, comprehension of noise reduction levels, visual aids, the payment vehicle and monetary bids were discussed during the focus groups.

Descriptive statistics on the socio-demographic characteristics of the respondents are summarised in Table 13.4. The sample significantly

Table 13.4 Descriptive statistics for socio-demographic characteristics

	Mean (s.d.) or percentage
Age	56.3 (16.95)
Over 65	31%
Female	49%
Household size	2.39 (1.26)
Has child below 12 years of age	16%
Years of schooling (>13)	51%
Years lived in the vicinity of the railway	23.00 (22.32)
Owns the place where she/he lives	72%
Has garden or terrace	84%
Cares about health issues	98%
Cares about environmental issues	94%
Fairly, very much or extremely informed on rail noise before the survey	77%
Uses the Brennero railway for work	7%
Uses the Brennero railway for tourism or other than work	38%
Household monthly income (€)	1742.5 (1007.66)

represents the population of households affected by rail noise in the province of Trento. We selected samples evenly from households living in buildings directly or indirectly exposed to the railway (that is, in the first or second row of buildings away from the railway). The average respondent is a 56-year-old householder who has been living in the vicinity of the railway for more than 20 years. Her/his household consists of about two persons, with one member younger than 12 in 16 per cent of the cases. The average household income (€1742 per month) is lower than that of Trento's population, which is estimated to be around €2400 per month. In 72 per cent of the cases, respondents own the place where they live, which usually has a garden or a terrace that is exposed to rail noise. Overall, the sample is highly sensitive to health and environmental issues and fairly well informed on the rail noise issue. In addition, the survey results indicate that respondents hardly use the Brennero railway, as they prefer to travel by car.

The survey also contained a set of questions designed to provide a better understanding of how sensitive respondents are to noise in general, and to rail noise in particular. Using a rating scale analysis ranging from 'strongly disagree' to 'strongly agree', which was coded from 1 to 6, the response results show that noise is highly perceived as an element of annoyance, with a sensitivity value up to a score of 5.48 (see Table 13.5).

Table 13.5 Noise sensitivity scores

	Mean (s.d.)
If I bought or rented a house, I would avoid proximity to busy streets, nightclubs or restaurants	5.48 (1.42)
Sometimes noise makes me nervous	4.12 (1.96)
If noisy while studying or working I shut the door or move to another room	4.70 (1.82)

Finally, the survey contained information regarding noise produced by railway infrastructures (see Table 13.6). According to the results, rail noise is perceived by the majority of the sample as an important environmental policy issue, when compared with other issues such as air and electromagnetic pollution, traffic noise and biodiversity depletion. Second, rail noise is identified by the respondents as a relevant factor in individual nuisance. In fact, this disturbance is identified by 85 and 74 per cent of the respondents as causing annoyance during the day and the night respectively. Third, vibrations in addition to noise are identified as an important element of rail nuisance. About 29 per cent of the respondents report that vibrations and noise are equally disturbing. Finally, the design of the sample is characterised by selecting an equally distributed number of respondents interviewed in two distinct spatial acoustic zones. The first area refers to households who live immediately alongside the railway, on average exposed to more than 70 decibels. The second area includes households living in an acoustic area somewhat further away with noise levels ranging from 60 to 70 decibels.

Indirect Utility Model Specifications

We work on two econometric model specifications (see Table 13.7). Model 1 refers to the economic analysis of the different policy attributes identified in the CE exercise in the respondent utility function. According to this model specification, Price refers to the cost of the policy to the respondents. Noise2 and Noise3 denote the variables for the level of noise reduction (see Table 13.1). The omitted variable, Noise1, corresponds to the minimum level of noise reduction able to fulfil regulation limits. The interaction between Noise2 and Height controls for the effect of the height of the barrier. We interpret this variable as an indicator of the aesthetic impact in achieving a Noise2 reduction exclusively based on noise barriers. In other words, Noise2 and Noise2*Height provide the same level of noise abatement, but the latter is reached by a policy instrument that relies on barriers set at 6–8 metres without any technological investments on trains and

Table 13.6 Descriptive statistics on rail noise perception, annoyance and exposure

	Mean (s.d.) or Percentage
Rail noise perception	
Compared to traffic noise, rail noise is 'more' or 'equally' important	72%
Compared to air pollution, rail noise is 'more' or 'equally' important	47%
Compared to biodiversity depletion, rail noise is 'more' or 'equally' important	71%
Compared to electromagnetic pollution, rail noise is 'more' or 'equally' important	65%
Rail noise annoyance	
Annoyed by noise during the day	85%
'Very much' or 'extremely' annoyed during the day	42%
Annoyed by noise during the night	74%
'Very much' or 'extremely' annoyed during the night	50%
Did think of moving because of rail noise	25%
Disturbed by rail noise when using garden or terrace	65%
Cannot rest quietly during the day	15%
Wake up easily during the night	39%
Get nervous	14%
Can't talk with relatives or listen to radio and TVs	56%
Noise and vibrations	
Only noise disturbs me	25%
Only vibrations disturb me	1%
Noise and vibrations disturb me equally	29%
Both noise and vibrations disturb me, but more noise than vibrations	31%
Both noise and vibrations disturb me, but more vibrations than noise	14%
Noise exposure	
Building with direct exposure to the railway	53%
Hours spent home during the week	6.7 (3.55)
Hours spent home during the weekend	8.2 (3.23)
Thermal or sound insulation systems installed	93%

tracks. *Ceteris paribus*, β_{PRICE}, β_{NOISE2} and β_{NOISE3} are parameters to be estimated and the respective magnitude refers to the marginal impact of Price, Noise2 and Noise3 on the respondent utility function. Finally, $\beta_{NOISE2*HEIGHT}$ provides the effect of a unit increment of the barrier's height on the probability of choosing a noise policy that reduces noise by

Table 13.7 Estimated coefficient

	Model 1	**Model 2**
Price	−0.016***	−0.135***
	(0.006)	(0.015)
Noise2	2.493***	1.432***
	(0.383)	(0.541)
Noise3	0.521***	0.655***
	(0.196)	(0.258)
Noise2*Height	−0.314***	−0.282***
	(0.057)	(0.066)
Price*Annoyance		0.020***
		(0.003)
Noise2*Income		0.0004***
		(0.738^{-04})
Price*Education		0.014***
		(0.002)
Sample	1905	1610
Pseudo-R^2	0.08	0.12
Log-likelihood ratio	−1273.304	−989.751
LR test of significance of all coefficients		27.86
		(p>0.001)

Note: Significance is indicated by *** for the per cent level, with standard error in parentheses.

12 to 14 decibel. β_{PRICE} can be interpreted as the coefficient of the cost of the noise policy instrument to the respondents.

Finally, as in Chapters 4, 5 and 12 of this volume, we investigate the effect of the population characteristics on the implicit price by adding interactions between attributes and socio-demographic and attitudinal variables. Formally, we estimate Model 2 (see Table 13.7). This model specification incorporates in the utility function the respondents' level of noise annoyance, income and education level.[15] It involves the interactions between Noise2, Price, Annoyance and Education. Annoyance is the level of noise annoyance during the day, based on a five-point Likert scale. We can therefore examine the differences in the valuation of one unit of rail noise reduction among different respondents' profiles according to their annoyance level. Income is a continuous variable and provides the household's monthly income. Education is a categorical variable ranging from zero to six (degree or PhD). This allows the examination of the effects of the characteristics of individual respondents on the valuation of the single attributes. From the coefficients of interactions we can investigate whether there is a difference in the marginal utility of price due to different annoyance or education levels, and whether there are differences in the marginal utility of Noise2 given the respondent's income.

EMPIRICAL FINDINGS

Valuation Results

Estimation results[16] are shown in Table 13.7. In Model 1 all variables are highly statistically significant. As expected, the sign of Price is negative and that of the level of noise reduction is positive. Significant coefficients of the level of Noise2 and Noise3 show that the valuation of noise reduction varies according to the relative level of provision. Respondents displayed the highest preferences for the measures that provide an additional level of noise reduction equal to Noise2 rather than Noise3, in respect to the minimum granted by the benchmark policy (that is, Noise1), confirming the decreasing marginal utility. As shown in Table 13.8, WTP for Noise2, a policy noise abatement strategy that relies on an investment both in trains or tracks together with a noise barrier set at a minimum level (at most 6 metres) is highly valued by the respondents. These show a WTP of about €156 per household for 2006.

However, if one portrays a maximum decibel abatement increasing barriers up to 8 metres, then the WTP decreases to around €32 per household. Confronting this estimate with the coefficient of the interaction between Noise2 and Height, which is negative and statistically significant, we can understand that respondents have a strong preference for a noise abatement policy targeted at investments in trains or rail technology rather than increasing the height of noise barriers. These results suggest that, as expected, the height of the barrier is perceived as a major drawback of the noise policy. This result, therefore, signals a strong disutility from the powerful negative aesthetic impact of such a construction.[17]

Table 13.8 Willingness to pay estimates

WTP	Model 1	Model 2
Noise2	156	70
Noise3	32	32
Noise2*Height	−20	−14

Note: Willingness-to-pay is expressed in € per household for the year 2006.

Table 13.9 Sensitivity analysis of the valuation results

Policy	Income level[1]	Average respondent[2]	Education +[3]	Annoyance +[3]
Noise2	≤ 2000	101	224	233
	> 2000	174	386	268
Noise3	≤ 2000	98	218	151
	> 2000	171	379	264

Note:
1. € per household per month.
2. Average respondent with respect to education and annoyance profile.
3. 'Education +' and 'Annoyance +' are measured at the third quartile of the distribution.

Results of log-likelihood ratio tests show that socio-demographic and attitudinal variables add significantly to Model 1. According to Model 2, which presented the highest goodness of fit when compared to alternative specifications, one can observe that the effect of the interactions with Income, Annoyance and Education are positive and highly statistically significant. This means that individual utility is sensitive to individual annoyance, which is subjectively measured by a five-point Likert attitudinal motivation scale, and to the income and education profiles of respondents, in the expected way.

In order to capture the empirical magnitude of the effect of these three socio-demographic factors, we provide a sensitive analysis to the valuation results in Table 13.9. The results refer to Noise2 and Noise3-type policies, whose values are estimated for a set of different income, education and annoyance profiles. These figures are computed by multiplying the related interaction estimate by individual profiles, measured at the sample mean and third quartile of the distribution. An average respondent (with respect to education and annoyance) with an income lower than €2000 per month, is associated with a marginal WTP for Noise2 and Noise3 levels of abatements equal to, respectively, €101 and €98. Similarly, we can see that an average respondent with an income higher than €2000 is associated with a marginal WTP for Noise2 and Noise3 levels of abatements equal to, respectively, €174 and €171. In a similar way, we can run the same valuation exercise, and thus estimate that the marginal WTP for Noise2 and Noise3, when considering changes in individual characteristics, namely the respondent's noise annoyance profile and education level.

Welfare Analysis and Policy Discussions

Standard economic theory suggests that WTP should be positively associated with the magnitude of noise reduction. Confirming this expectation, present valuation results show that individuals are on average willing to pay for noise reduction. In particular, both Noise2 and Noise3 are preferred to Noise1. In other words, respondents welcome additional noise reductions. Furthermore, we see that the WTP associated with Noise2 is higher than that associated with Noise3. This apparent counterintuitive result can be explained by the fact that the noise reduction associated with Noise3 is only possible with an additional increase in the height of the barrier. This is associated with a strong disutility even if the policy maker proposes providing ornamental vegetation to mask such a high barrier. A similar impact is embedded in the estimation of the Noise2*Height policy when the respective noise abatement level is compared to the Noise2 policy. Whereas the Noise2 policy is associated with a WTP of about €156, the Noise2*Height policy is associated with a negative WTP. This means that the respondents will not accept a reduction above the Noise1 level, which corresponds to the minimum level set by the law, if the proposed policy instrument relies exclusively on increasing the height of the barrier. The coefficient estimates for Price*Annoyance, Price*Education and Noise*Income in Model 2 suggest that individual noise perception and socio-economic profiles are likely to influence the WTP for noise abatement in a predictable way. In particular, respondents more annoyed by rail noise are more willing to pay to purchase noise abatement, as are respondents with a higher education or income profile (see Table 13.9). These results signal the importance of knowing as accurately as possible the respondents' socio-economic and attitudinal features, and of improving the methods for gathering such information.

Finally, and to conclude, estimation results for the twelve municipalities under consideration show that if no policy action is undertaken to make additional investments in the trains or railroad, and thus to reduce aerodynamic noise, traction noise and vibrations, a significant welfare loss may result. An aggregate estimate of the total welfare loss ranges from €358 800 to €887 800. This value is obtained by multiplying the sum of the noise abatement benefits, which is derived from the CE model and ranges from €156 to €386, by the total number of residents in that same strip line along the Brennero railway area, estimated at about 2300.

CONCLUSIONS

We developed a framework for the economic valuation of relevant features of rail noise policies using a CE approach. This allows us to understand the preferences of people exposed to rail noise for alternative noise abatement strategies, which are expected to differ according to a range of factors, including their acoustic efficiency, aesthetics and level of technical innovation. In this respect, our study confirms that CE can be a promising tool for improving noise abatement policies in the future, since it gives room for a highly informative, but quite complex survey design. A number of significant noise policy issues can be addressed simultaneously, thus providing an *ex ante* valuation of some important attributes of noise mitigation policies currently debated (for example, level of noise reduction, type of policy instrument).

The signs of the estimated coefficients are statistically significant and consistent with the theoretical predictions, including that respondents evaluate price increase negatively, while evaluating noise abatement positively. In particular, estimation results show that, *ceteris paribus*, respondents strongly prefer a noise policy that relies on an investment in technological innovation rather than an additional increase in the height of the barrier that might lead to unacceptable aesthetic and microclimatic costs to them. This outcome, therefore, confirms the EU and Italian recommendation that preference should be given to 'at the source' noise measures (based on technological investments) or at least, that investments in new technologies for train vehicles and tracks should be combined with more standard trackside barriers, not excessively high. According to our results, mixed noise measures might in fact provide the required level of noise abatement and ensure the public acceptance of the ultimate decision. Our estimations suggest that any additional noise protection programme is welcomed if, and only if, the cost associated with the investment in train technology does not exceed €887 800. This valuation should be considered, however, at best as a lower bound of the total benefit since the present study only considers the analysis of a single stakeholder, the residents, and furthermore, only the residents living within 'Zone A', where the acoustic level of noise is mapped at 70 dB(A) or more. Moreover, our study signals that an accurate analysis of the respondents' profiles is crucial to strengthen the robustness of the valuation results, which appear to be significantly sensitive to socio-economic and attitudinal features. Against this background, should the present valuation results be used on other policy sites, socio-economic and attitudinal features of respondents need to be accurately incorporated into the underlying benefit transfer exercise since the empirical evidence signals the importance of the valuation function of these explanatory variables.

ACKNOWLEDGMENTS

We are grateful to Roberto Camagni for helpful discussions. This research is supported by the Province of Trento. We would like also to thank the team of the Office of Statistics in Trento for their expert support in the survey design and execution. Finally, Trento Environmental Protection Agency has provided valuable data on noise, acoustic maps and elaborations.

NOTES

1. LGQ n. 447/1995.
2. DPR n. 459/1998 *Regolamento recante norme di esecuzione dell'articolo 11 della legge 26 ottobre 1995, in materia di inquinamento acustico ferroviario*).
3. In Italy, a decree of the Ministry of the Environment (DMA 29/11/2000), which is consistent with what is stated in the more recent *Position Paper on the European Strategies and Priorities for Railways Noise Abatement* (CEC, 2003), indicates that preference should be given to noise measures at the source (that is, either on the vehicles or on the tracks) rather than to barriers and building insulation systems.
4. Com(96)540.
5. Ldn = day/night level over the whole day with a 10 dB(A) penalty for night-time noise, from 22:00 hrs to 7:00 hrs.
6. These include integrated companies with a range of functions or separated companies.
7. Rete Ferroviaria Italiana (RFI) SpA.
8. Trenitalia SpA.
9. A CV survey by Navrud (2000) includes rail noise among noise annoyance and exposure questions but does not provide an estimation of WTP for rail noise abatement.
10. APPA (Agenzia Provinciale per la Protezione dell'Ambiente).
11. For instance, lower lighting in the case of opaque barriers, or greenhouse effects during summer in the case of transparent barriers.
12. Avio, Calliano, Rovereto, Trento, Zambana Nuova.
13. A full version of the questionnaire and visual aids is available upon request.
14. The questionnaire also explored the effect of the type of project financing. For further details see Nunes and Travisi (2006).
15. We also explored other model specifications. Those included here were chosen to show the highest goodness of fit.
16. Estimations provided using Limdep.
17. We also explored the statistical significance of an aesthetic improvement in the visual impact of the barrier by using ornamental vegetation. Several model specifications have rejected the econometric robustness of this effect. In short, respondents do not like increasing the barrier above the minimum level set by regulation, with or without ornamental vegetation.

REFERENCES

APPA, Agenzia Provinciale per la Protezione dell'Ambiente (2000), *Valutazione dell'Impatto Acustico e Dimensionamento degli Interventi di Mitigazione del Rumore Prodotto dalla Ferrovia del Brennero nel Tratto di Attraversamento della Provincia di Trento*, APPA – Provincia Autonoma di Trento.

Barreiro, J., Sānchez, M. and Vilardrich-Grau, M. (2000), 'How Much are People Willing to Pay for Silence? A One and One-half-bound DC CV Estimate', in *Proceedings of Internoise 2005*, 5, 3408–3412, Nice, France.

CEC, European Commission, CWG Railway Noise of the European Commission (2003), *Position Paper on the European Strategies and Priorities for Railway Noise Abatement*, European Communities, Luxembourg.

CEC, Commission of the European Communities, Directorate-General for Energy and Transport (2004), *The Trans-European High-Speed Rail System: Guide for the Application of the High-Speed TSIs of Council Directive 96/48/EC*, European Communities, Luxembourg.

Clark, D.E. (2006), 'Externality Effects on Residential Property Values: The Example of Noise Disamenities', *Growth and Change*, 37(3): 460–488.

De Kluizenaar, Y., Passchier-Vermeer, W. and Miedema, H. (2001), *Adverse Effects of Noise Exposure to Health. Report to the EC project UNITE*, TNO, Leiden, The Netherlands.

Droste-Franke, B., Schmid, S., Bickel, P. and Friedrich, R. (2006), *Urban Environmental Problem (Noise)*, Report to the GreenSense project, Research Project of the European Commission, co-ordinated by University of Bath, UK.

Freeman, A.M. (2003), *The Measurement of Environmental and Resource Values: Theory and Methods*, 2nd ed., Resources for the Future, Washington DC.

Greene, W.H. (2002), *Econometric Analysis*, 4th edition. Prentice Hall, Upper Saddle River, NY.

Hunt, J.D. (2001), 'A Stated Preference Analysis of Sensitivities to Elements of Transportation and Urban Form', in Proceedings of the 13th Annual Transportation Research Board Conference, 10–11 October, Washington.

ISO (2003), *Assessment of Noise Annoyance by Means of Social and Socio-acoustic Surveys*, ISO/TS 15666:2003, ISO, Jersey City, NJ.

Lambert, J., Poisson, F., Champlovier, P. (2001), 'Valuing Benefits of a Road Traffic Noise Abatement Programme: A Contingent Valuation Study', in *Proceedings of Internoise 2000, 29th International Congress and Exhibition on Noise Control Engineering*, 27–28 August, Nice.

McFadden, D. (1974), 'Conditional Logit Analysis of Qualitative Choice Behaviour', in Zarembka, P. (ed), *Frontiers in Econometrics*, Academic Press, New York.

Metroeconomica (2001), *Monetary Valuation of Noise Effects: Final Report to EC UNITE Project*, subcontracted to IER, Bath.

Navrud, S. (2000), 'Economic Benefits of a Program to Reduce Transportation and Community Noise: A Contingent Valuation Study', in *Proceedings of Internoise 2000, 29th International Congress and Exhibition on Noise Control Engineering*, 27–28 August, Nice.

Navrud, S. (2002), *The State-of-the-Art on Economic Valuation of Noise: Final Report to European Commission DG Environment, Department of Economics and Social Sciences*, Agricultural University of Norway, Ås.

Navrud, S. (2003), 'The State-of-the-Art on Economic Valuation of Noise', paper presented at the *ECE/WHO Pan European Program on Transport, Health and Environment, Workshop on Economic Valuation of Health Effects due to Transport*, 12–13 June 2003, Department of Economics and Social Science, Agricultural University of Norway, Stockholm.

Nellthorp, J., Sansom, T., Bickel, P., Doll, C. and Lindberg, G. (2001), *Valuation Convention for EC UNITE Project*, ITS, University of Leeds, Leeds, April 2001.

Nunes, P.A.L.D., Travisi, C.M. (2006), *Comparing Tax and Tax Reallocations Payments in Financing Rail Noise Abatement Programs: Results from a CE Valuation Study in Italy*, FEEM WP series 96-2006.

Pommerehne, W.W. (1998), 'Measuring the Environmental Benefits: A Comparison of Hedonic Technique and Contingent Valuation', in Bos, D., Rose, M. and Seidl, C. (eds), *Welfare and Efficiency in Public Economics*, Springer-Verlag, Berlin.

Simons, R.A. and El Jaouhari, A. (2004), 'The Effect of Freight Railroad Tracks and Train Activity on Residential Property Values in Cuyahoga County', Ohio, *The Appraisal Journal*, 72(3): 223–233.

Soguel, N. (1994), *Measuring Benefits from Traffic Noise Reduction using a Contingent Market*, CSERGE Working Paper GEG 94-03, University of East Anglia, Norwich.

Strand, J. and Vågnes, M. (2001), 'The Relationship between Property Values and Railroad Proximity: A Study Based on Hedonic Process and Real Estate Broker's Appraisals', *Transportation*, 28, 137–156.

Vainio, M. (1995), 'Traffic Noise and Air Pollution: Valuation of Externalities with Hedonic Price and Contingent Valuation Methods', Ph.D. thesis, Helsinki School of Economics and Business Administration.

Vainio, M. (2001), 'Comparison of Hedonic Prices and Contingent Valuation Methods in Urban Traffic Noise Context', paper presented at the 2001 *International Congress and Exhibition on Noise Control Engineering*, The Hague, The Netherlands, 27–30 August 2001.

Wardman, M. and Bristow, A.L. (2004), 'Traffic Related Noise and Air Quality Valuations: Evidence from Stated Preference Residential Choice Models', *Transportation Research Part D*, 9, 1–27.

Watkiss, P., Jones, R., Brand, C. and Forster, D. (2001), *Cost-effectiveness of Noise Reduction Measures*, Report to the UK Department for Environment, Transport and the Regions.

Weinberger, M., Thomassen, H.G. and Willeke, R. (1991), *Kosten des Lärms in der Bundesrepublik Deutschland*, Umwelt Bundesamt Berichte 9/91, Berlin.

WHO, World Health Organization, Regional Office Europe (2000), *Noise and Health*, World Health Organization, Copenhagen.

14. Concluding remarks and future directions

Ekin Birol and Phoebe Koundouri

SUMMARY OF THE CHAPTERS

This book has gathered the most recent state-of-the art choice experiment studies undertaken in various Europe Union (EU) countries, with the aim of revealing the wealth, diversity, quality and usefulness of choice experiment applications for informing environmental policy in Europe. To this end, case studies are presented covering a wide geographical area, from Greece to Ireland and from Finland to Spain, on a broad array of environmental, agricultural and natural resource issues, ranging from landscapes, biodiversity, cultural heritage, noise pollution, forests and water resources to food labelling. The values of several important attributes of these resources are captured as they accrue to various stakeholders, including local residents, the national public, tourists, visitors and food consumers. Furthermore, the implications of the value estimate results of these applications are discussed for informing the efficient, effective and equitable design, implementation and adaptation of various EU-level regulations, directives, schemes and plans related to environmental, agricultural and natural resources. Among the various EU policies that chapters of this volume inform are the EU Forest Action Plan, the Agri-Environmental Regulation, the Water Framework Directive, the Habitats Directive, the Food Labelling Directives and the Environmental Noise Directive, to name a few.

Chapter 2 presented a thorough review of choice experiment applications to the valuation of environmental, agricultural and natural resources in EU countries. This chapter, which has brought the reader up to date with the current status of the choice experiment method in Europe, was followed by four case studies on valuation of the various vital attributes of European landscapes. These case studies estimated the benefits generated by several attributes of landscape management throughout Ireland, in hilly and mountainous areas of England, in Brittany, France and in Galicia, Spain. The valuations of various stakeholders, including the general national public, the regional public and local residents as well as visitors to these landscapes were estimated. Overall, the results of these chapters disclosed valuable information about the different stakeholders' preferences for various attributes of the landscapes, whose production should be supported through EU Agri-Environmental Schemes.

Chapter 3 compared the benefits of landscape improvements with their costs to reveal that agri-environmental schemes contribute substantial benefits to rural landscapes. Chapter 4 estimated the values of benefits generated by landscape attributes to inform the revision of payments made to farmers. Chapter 5 found that the preferences of all stakeholders (local residents and visitors) for landscape attributes were the opposite of what the current policies are aiming to achieve. The final chapter on landscapes, Chapter 6, revealed that visitors value environmental attributes of landscapes more than cultural and historical ones, alluding to the use of market-based instruments (such as EU food labelling schemes of Protected Designation of Origin) in addition to agri-environmental payments for provision of efficient levels of all of these attributes.

Chapter 7 presented a case study investigating the UK food consumers' preferences for several food production methods, including genetically modified organisms (GMO). Consumers displayed considerable differences in their preferences, especially with respect to GM food. The findings of this study are not only informative for the development of EU-level GM food labelling and food security regulations, but also have implications for the EU's trade with other countries.

Chapters 8 through 10 reported case studies on forest resources management in Southern Finland, Catalonia, Spain and seven forests located in Great Britain, respectively. These chapters estimated the general public's and recreational visitors' valuations of several forest management attributes. The results of Chapter 8 indicated that in Finland, where forests are privately owned, the public exhibits considerable heterogeneity in their preferences for attributes of forest management. The Finnish public, however, are in agreement with regard to the choice of policy instruments which should be employed for conservation of forest resources. The findings of Chapters 9 and 10 revealed that the recreational benefits that forests generate are significant and large. Chapter 9 captured the values of important environmental functions of forests, such as erosion control and CO_2 sequestration, in addition to their recreational values. Chapter 10 provided value estimates for forest management attributes by recreational activity group (cyclists, horse riders, nature watchers and general visitors). These chapters provided evidence for the contribution of forests to welfare benefits, especially those associated with recreational uses of forests, thereby enhancing people's quality of life, in accordance with the EU Forest Action Plan.

Efficient management of water resources is investigated in Chapters 11 and 12. First, the Greek public's preferences for sustainable management of the Cheimaditida Wetland were explored. Trade-offs between quantitative and qualitative, ecological (for example, biodiversity and water area) and social and economic (education, research and employment) attributes of the wetland were analysed. The results showed that the use and non-use values the Greek public derive from the attributes of the wetland are substantial. A thorough cost-benefit analysis revealed that net total social benefits of sustainable management of the wetland are strictly positive and large. Following this, local residents' trade-offs between management of rivers for flood risk reduction versus biodiversity conservation and recreational activity provision were investigated in the Upper Silesia Region of Poland. It was found that the local residents who have suffered considerable damage from floods value river management plans that minimise flooding risk the most, whereas those who are wealthier are more concerned about the provision of recreational activities and biodiversity conservation in the catchment. These chapters aimed to inform several EU policies, most notably the Water Framework and Habitats Directives.

The final case study presented in this volume aimed to inform policies and projects for environmental noise reduction in accordance with the EU directive on the assessment and management of environmental noise. This chapter investigated Trento residents' preferences for different levels of noise and noise management strategies, namely investments in improving trains and track technology versus building high trackside barriers, and found that the residents preferred those noise abatement policies which focus on 'at the source' noise measures based on technological investments.

THEORETICAL ADVANCEMENTS

In addition to the wealth of information these case studies generated for informing European environmental, agricultural, natural resource management and food policy, they also presented several advances in the design, application and analysis of the choice experiment method.

Firstly and most importantly, possible sources of heterogeneity in the preferences of the populations studied were investigated in almost all of the case studies reported in this volume. As is well known, the standard workhouse model for choice experiment analysis, the conditional logit (CL) model, assumes homogenous preferences across respondents in a given population. Preferences, however, are heterogeneous and accounting for this heterogeneity enables unbiased estimates of individual preferences and enhances the accuracy and reliability of estimates of demand, participation, marginal and total welfare (Greene, 2000). Furthermore, accounting for heterogeneity enables the prescription of policies that take equity concerns into account. Information on who will be affected by a policy change and the aggregate economic value associated with such changes is necessary for efficient and equitable policy making (Boxall and Adamowicz, 2002).

Consequently, in this book various methods were employed to investigate preference heterogeneity. Chapters 3, 4 and 12 employed the random parameter logit (RPL) model (a specification of the mixed logit model), which accounts for unobserved taste heterogeneity by allowing model parameters to vary randomly over individuals (for example, Train, 1998). Even if unobserved heterogeneity can be accounted for in the RPL model, the model fails to explain the sources of heterogeneity (Boxall and Adamowicz, 2002). One solution to this, while accounting for unobserved heterogeneity, is by including the interactions of respondent-specific social, economic and attitudinal characteristics with choice-specific attributes and/or with the alternative specific constant in the utility function. Thus, in Chapters 4, 5, 12 and 13, the interactions of the choice attributes or the alternative specific constants with the social and economic characteristics of respondents (for example, age, gender, income, education, whether or not they have children, number of times the sites are visited) were included in RPL and CL models.

A recent model that investigates preference heterogeneity is the latent class model (LCM, another specification of the mixed logit model). In LCM, the population consists of a finite and identifiable number of groups of individuals (that is, segments), each characterised by relatively homogenous preferences, whereas each one of these segments differs substantially in its preference structure. This approach accommodates preference heterogeneity while allowing the number of segments to be determined endogenously by the data (Wedel and Kamakura, 2000). Chapters 7 and 11 employed the LCM to identify the different segments within consumers of GM food, and users and non-users of Cheimaditida Wetland, respectively.

Finally, heterogeneity in preferences can also be investigated by separating the respondents into various groups (segments or clusters), and by estimating the demand function for each group separately. Chapter 5, for example, divided the users of the landscape into main residents, second home residents and visitors, whereas Chapter 8 split the population into two groups according to their responses to attitudinal questions, and Chapter 10 divided the forest users into four groups according to the recreational activity they undertake in the forest. All these chapters estimated separate CL models for each of these groups and found that their preferences structures indeed differ.

Recently, choice experiment practitioners have been making use of psychometric data, that is, information on respondents' motivational, attitudinal and behavioural characteristics, in order to explain choice (see for example Boxall and Adamowicz, 2002). Psychometric data and factor analysis method were employed in Chapters 7 and 8. In Chapter 7, attitudinal indices were created from consumers' answers to several questions which revealed their attitudes, perceptions and behaviour towards GMOs in particular and food consumption in general. These indices were in turn used as explanatory variables in the LCM. In Chapter 8, factor analysis of the psychometric data on the respondents' attitudes towards conservation and management of forests enabled segmentation of the population into two groups, as explained above.

The main aim of the environmental valuation methods is to generate benefit or cost estimates to be used in cost-benefit analysis (or in other decision tools) relating to different policy options. In Chapters 4, 5 and 11, value estimates of attributes were taken a step further by either calculating the compensating surplus (CS) of various alternative policies or by carrying out a cost-benefit analysis after the calculation of the CS. In Chapters 4 and 5, CS values were calculated for various landscape management scenarios. While aggregating landscape improvement benefits across various stakeholders, Chapter 5 took equity concerns into account by weighting the value estimates of each stakeholder group according to their size and length of visit in the area. Moreover, Chapter 5 applied two social choice rules, namely Borda and Condorcet rules to determine the landscape management policy that maximises social welfare (Martin *et al.*, 1996). Chapter 11 demonstrated how the results of a choice experiment study could be used in a thorough cost-benefit analysis of policy changes. In that chapter, CS values of various wetland management scenarios were weighted against their corresponding costs. Finally, Chapter 3 contrasted individual-specific value estimates of improvements in landscape attributes with the average cost of the policy that produces these improvements.

The important role of experimental design in affecting parameter estimates and variances in error terms is well known (see Adamowicz and Deshazo, 2006). Chapter 3 took advantage of the recent advances in experimental design in the field of market research by implementing a sequential experimental design with an informative Bayesian update to improve the efficiency of estimates.

Although a crucial aspect of the policy design and appraisal process, the choice experiment method is a costly means of information generation, as are other environmental valuation methods (Pearce, 2005). To this end,

Chapter 9 proposed a novel and unique method of inferring values from existing ones, akin to the benefits transfer method. However, unlike benefits transfer, which transfers value between sites, the value inference method involves inference of values between goods and attributes at the same site. Chapter 9 demonstrated how the contingent valuation method can be employed to provide the value of a specific change in the management of the environmental good, and the choice experiment method can be employed to derive values of particular attributes of the good, in order to infer the values of a range of other alternative management outcomes.

FUTURE DIRECTIONS

Recent advances in the choice experiment method have highlighted the importance of investigating heteroskedasticity (Swait, 2007). Even though almost all of the published choice experiment studies carried out in the EU tackled the biases that might arise from taste heterogeneity, very few of them have investigated the consequences of heteroskedasticity in the error terms. It is expected that the forthcoming choice experiment studies carried out in the EU will be focusing on the treatment of heteroskedasticity along with taste heterogeneity.

As mentioned above, similarly to the other applied environmental valuation methods, the choice experiment method is a costly means of generating useful data for policy formulation. One way of minimising the costs of environmental valuation studies, while still generating valuable information for environmental policy, is the use of the benefits transfer method, which relies on information obtained in previous studies. As pointed out in Chapter 1, the choice experiment method is suitable for benefits transfer due to its ability to estimate the values of multiple attributes of an environmental good, which can allow for differences in improvements in the levels of environmental attributes between sites. The choice experiment method can also allow for differences in the social, economic and attitudinal characteristics of the populations when transferring value estimates. Even though there are only a few noteworthy studies in EU countries that employ choice experiment estimates to transfer values from a study site to a policy site (see for example, Hanley *et al.*, 2006; Colombo *et al.*, 2007), the cost-effectiveness and usefulness of the benefits transfer method for informing environmental policy and the advantages of the choice experiment method for this purpose call for further investigation of this issue.

Finally, for those environmental, agricultural and natural resource management issues that concern all or several EU countries at a time, there is a need to carry out pan-European choice experiment studies. Scarpa *et al.* (2005)

state that in the case of food labelling schemes (such as Protected Designation of Origin and Protected Geographical Indicator labels) pan-European studies may help explain the role of consumer preferences for certain products on the patterns of trade between Member States and inform future EU policies relevant to food and agriculture. This argument is also applicable to other food and agricultural issues, such as regulations pertaining to GMOs, which have implications for agriculture, food production and trade within the EU. Similarly, for resource management issues that concern several EU Member States at a time, choice experiment studies should be undertaken in all those countries. For example, the EU Water Framework Directive calls for water resources management at the river basin level. Several river basins in the EU are shared among multiple EU countries, so choice experiment studies should be implemented in all of those EU countries that share the river basin in order to inform their efficient management. Pan-European choice experiment studies could also help inform the meeting of certain EU level targets, such as the greenhouse gas emissions reduction targets of the Kyoto Protocol, in an efficient and equitable manner.

REFERENCES

Adamowicz, W.L. and J.R. Deshazo (2006), 'Frontiers in Stated Preferences Methods: An Introduction', *Environmental and Resource Economics*, 34(1): 1–6.

Boxall, P.C. and W.L. Adamowicz (2002), 'Understanding Heterogeneous Preferences in Random Utility Models: A Latent Class Approach', *Environmental and Resource Economics*, 23: 421–446.

Colombo S., J. Calatrava-Requena and N. Hanley (2007), 'Testing Choice Experiment for Benefit Transfer with Preference Heterogeneity', *American Journal of Agricultural Economics*, 89(1): 135–151.

Greene, W.H. (2000), *Econometric Analysis* (Fifth ed.), New York: Prentice Hall International.

Hanley, N., R.E. Wright and B. Alvarez-Farizo (2006), 'Estimating the Economic Value of Improvements in River Ecology using Choice Experiments: An Application to the Water Framework Directive', *Journal of Environmental Management*, 78: 183–193.

Martin, W.E., D.J. Shields, B. Tolwinski and B. Kent (1996), 'An Application of Social Choice Theory to U.S.D.A. Forest Service Decision Making', *Journal of Policy Modeling*, 18(6): 603–621.

Pearce, D.W. (2005), 'Does European Union Environmental Policy Pass a Cost-Benefit Test', *World Economics*, 5: 115–138.

Revelt, D. and K. Train (1998), 'Mixed Logit with Repeated Choices: Households' Choice of Appliance Efficiency Level', *Review of Economics and Statistics*, 53: 647–657.

Scarpa, R., G. Philippidis, and F. Spalatro (2005), 'Product-Country Images and Preference Heterogeneity for Mediterranean Food Products: A Discrete Choice Framework', *Agribusiness*, 21(3): 329–349.

Swait, J. (2007), 'Advanced Choice Models', in Kanninen, B.J. (ed.) *Valuing Environmental Amenities Using Stated Choice Studies*, Berlin: Springer.
Train, K.E. (1998), 'Recreation Demand Models with Taste Differences over People', *Land Economics*, 74: 230–239.
Wedel, M. and W. Kamakura (2000), *Market Segmentation: Conceptual and Methodological Foundations*, Boston: Kluwer Academic Publishers.

Index